MW01044549

The Rise of Discourse Markers

Discourse markers constitute an important part of linguistic communication, and research on this phenomenon has been a thriving field of study over the past three decades. However, a problem that has plagued this research is that these markers exhibit a number of structural characteristics that are hard to interpret based on existing methodologies, such as grammaticalization. This study argues that it is possible to explain such characteristics in a meaningful way. It presents a cross-linguistic survey of the development of discourse markers, their important role in communication, and their relation to the wider context of sociocultural behavior, with the goal of explaining their similarities and differences across a typologically wide range of languages. By giving a clear definition of discourse markers, it aims to provide a guide for future research, making it essential reading for students and researchers in linguistics, and anyone interested in exploring this fascinating linguistic phenomenon.

Bernd Heine is Emeritus Professor at the Institute of African Studies and Egyptology, University of Cologne. His main research areas are grammaticalization theory, endangered languages in Africa, and discourse grammar. His publications include more than 40 books and over 200 articles.

Gunther Kaltenböck is Professor of English Linguistics at the University of Graz in Austria. His main research interests are cognitive-functional grammar, corpus linguistics, language variation and change.

Tania Kuteva is Professor of English Linguistics at Heinrich Heine University Düsseldorf, and Professorial Research Associate of SOAS, University of London. Her main interests include grammaticalization, linguistic typology, language evolution, and discourse grammar.

Haiping Long is Professor at the English Department, School of Foreign Languages, Sun Yat-sen University. His research interests include grammaticalization, linguistic typology, historical linguistics, and discourse grammar.

The Rise of Discourse Markers

Bernd Heine
University of Cologne

Gunther Kaltenböck
University of Graz

Tania Kuteva
Heinrich Heine University Düsseldorf/SOAS, University of London

Haiping Long
Sun Yat-sen University

CAMBRIDGE
UNIVERSITY PRESS

CAMBRIDGE
UNIVERSITY PRESS

University Printing House, Cambridge CB2 8BS, United Kingdom

One Liberty Plaza, 20th Floor, New York, NY 10006, USA

477 Williamstown Road, Port Melbourne, VIC 3207, Australia

314–321, 3rd Floor, Plot 3, Splendor Forum, Jasola District Centre, New Delhi – 110025, India

79 Anson Road, #06–04/06, Singapore 079906

Cambridge University Press is part of the University of Cambridge.

It furthers the University's mission by disseminating knowledge in the pursuit of education, learning, and research at the highest international levels of excellence.

www.cambridge.org
Information on this title: www.cambridge.org/9781108833851
DOI: 10.1017/9781108982856

© Bernd Heine, Gunther Kaltenböck, Tania Kuteva, and Haiping Long 2021

First published 2021

A catalogue record for this publication is available from the British Library.

Library of Congress Cataloging-in-Publication Data
Names: Heine, Bernd, 1939– editor. | Kaltenböck, Gunther, – editor. | Kuteva, Tania, 1958– editor. | Long, Haiping, editor.
Title: The rise of discourse markers / [edited by] Bernd Heine, Gunther Kaltenböck, Tania Kuteva, Haiping Long.
Description: Cambridge, UK ; New York : Cambridge University Press, 2021. | Includes bibliographical references and indexes.
Identifiers: LCCN 2021011504 (print) | LCCN 2021011505 (ebook) | ISBN 9781108833851 (hardback) | ISBN 9781108987288 (paperback) | ISBN 9781108982856 (epub)
Subjects: LCSH: Discourse markers. | BISAC: LANGUAGE ARTS & DISCIPLINES / Linguistics / Semantics
Classification: LCC P302.35 .R57 2021 (print) | LCC P302.35 (ebook) | DDC 401/.41–dc23
LC record available at https://lccn.loc.gov/2021011504
LC ebook record available at https://lccn.loc.gov/2021011505

ISBN 978-1-108-83385-1 Hardback

For Helen Barton

Contents

List of Tables   *page* viii
Preface   ix
List of Abbreviations   x

1   The Development of Discourse Markers: An Introduction   1

2   Concepts of Analysis   56

3   English Discourse Markers   91

4   French Discourse Markers   144

5   Japanese Discourse Markers   167

6   Korean Discourse Markers   196

7   Discourse Markers in Language Contact   211

8   Discussion   236

9   Conclusions   267

References   273
Language Index   299
Author Index   300
Subject Index   304

Tables

2.1 The parameters and criteria of grammaticalization of
Lehmann ([1982] 2015: 132)   *page* 63

2.2 Contrasting changes typically observed in expressions
undergoing cooptation and grammaticalization   77

3.1 Hypothesized dates of cooptation of some English DMs   143

4.1 Hypothesized dates of cooptation of some French DMs   166

5.1 Contrasting changes typically observed in expressions
undergoing cooptation and grammaticalization   179

5.2 Century of first attestation of *na* elements in the history
of Japanese   185

5.3 Stages in the semantic development of Japanese *sate*   189

5.4 Hypothesized dates of cooptation of some Japanese DMs   195

6.1 Grammatical properties of twenty-five Korean DMs   197

6.2 Quantitative distribution of placement slots occupied by
twenty-five Korean DMs   199

6.3 Hypothesized dates of cooptation of some Korean DMs   209

7.1 Spanish *entonces* "then, therefore, thus" borrowed as a DM
in some Amerindian and Austronesian languages   217

7.2 Italian *allora* "then, at that time" borrowed as a DM in
some languages   218

8.1 Common source expressions of DMs   245

8.2 Deictic temporal adverbs as sources for DMs in some languages 248

8.3 Korean insubordinate DMs   249

8.4 Canonical imperatives of perception verbs as sources for DMs in
some languages   257

8.5 Variation in some Romance DMs derived from
"look" imperatives   258

9.1 Grammatical changes typically to be expected in
grammaticalization and cooptation   269

Preface

Discourse markers have been the subject of a wide range of studies over the course of the last decades. The data on which the present book rests are to a large extent taken from published and unpublished studies carried out by many researchers drawing on large text corpora and presenting detailed analyses on all aspects of the grammar and the history of discourse markers. We are grateful to these colleagues for not only sharing their research findings with us but also for guiding us in our attempts to arrive at viable interpretations of their findings.

Mentioning all the colleagues who have accompanied our study with comments, suggestions, and data would be near to impossible. Suffice it therefore to mention the following long list of colleagues who have contributed substantially to the present study in some way or other: Mikyung Ahn, Karin Aijmer, Mohammad Amouzadeh, Kate Beeching, Laurel Brinton, Claudia Claridge, Ulrike Claudi, Alexandra D'Arcy, Liesbeth Degand, Csilla Ilona Dér, Gaétane Dostie, Benjamin Fagard, Olga Fischer, Bálint Péter Furkó, Soleiman Ghaderi, Sylvie Hancil, Maj-Britt Mosegaard Hansen, Alexander Haselow, Christa König, Diana Lewis, Belén Méndez-Naya, Heiko Narrog, Azam Noora, Noriko Onodera, Sophie Prévost, Seongha Rhee, Anne-Marie Simon-Vandenbergen, Reijirou Shibasaki, Ryoko Suzuki, Elizabeth Traugott, and Richard Waltereit. The first and the third-named authors are deeply grateful also for the valuable support of the Alexander von Humbodt Foundation. We also wish to thank Elena Andonova, Isabella Greisinger, Sophia Lock, Danna Chandra Menendez, Janine Rehbehn, Lukas Mateusz Ostrowski and Anne Wolters, who have contributed to this work in various ways. Finally, we wish to express our gratitude to two anonymous readers for all their feedback on an earlier version of this book, and to Liz Steel for all the insightful work she did on editing this book.

The interpretations proffered in this study are not always entirely in accordance with the views expressed by some of the colleagues mentioned, and we apologize if there remain any misinterpretations in the present text. It goes without saying that none of these colleagues are to be held responsible for any views, shortcomings, or other deficiencies to be found in the book.

Abbreviations

1, 2, 3	first, second, third person
a.n.	note added by the present authors
ABL	ablative
ACC	accusative
ADD	additive
ADN	adnominal
ALL	allative
AUX	auxiliary
ATTR	attribute
BEN	benefactive
COMP	complementizer
CONN	connective
CONV	converb
COP	copulative verb
CRCM	circumstance
CU	coopted unit
DAT	dative
DEM	demonstrative
DET	determiner
DIM	diminutive
DM	discourse marker
DO	direct object
EMPH	emphasizer
END	sentence ender
EVID	evidential
EZ	*ezafe* marker
F	feminine
FP	final particle
FUT	future
GEN	genitive
GER	gerundive form
HESI	hesitation marker

HON	honorific
HOR	hortative
IMP	imperative
Lit.	literal meaning
LK	linker, linking form of verb
LOC	locative
NC1, 2, etc.	noun class 1, 2, etc.
NEG	negative marker
NF	non-finite marker
NML	nominalizer
NOM	nominative, nominalizer
O	object marker
PAS	passive
PAST	past tense
PE	polite ending
PL	plural
PM	pragmatic marker
POL	politeness
POSS	possessive
PREF	prefix
PRES	present tense
PROB	probability
PROG	progressive
PROM	prominence
PTC	particle
Q	interrogative marker
QP	question particle
QT	quotative marker
QUO	quotative
RESP	respectful
SB	subject marker
SFP	sentence final particle
SG	singular
SIM	simultaneous adnominal
SUBJ	subjunctive
SUF	suffix
T	transitivizing suffix
TMA	marker of tense, modality, or aspect
TOP	topic marker
V	verb
VOC	vocative

1   The Development of Discourse Markers
An Introduction

1.1   Discourse Markers

Discourse markers (henceforth: DMs) are widely believed to be more of a peripheral phenomenon of language use, and even more so of language structure.[1] Referred to in some earlier work as "disfluencies," "filled pauses," "fumbles," "pleonasms," "signals," "signs of poor elocution," "symptoms," and the like, they tend to be discussed in grammatical treatments only marginally, if at all. Oxford linguist Max Müller (1861: 346, 352) argued in the nineteenth century that DMs and the like "are playthings, not the tools of language," and this is a view that in some form or other is still found today. What tends to be ignored in many academic and non-academic discussions is that DMs play an important role in linguistic communication, especially but not only in spoken language use, belonging to the most frequently used linguistic expressions in many languages.

    The important role that discourse markers play in linguistic communication can also be seen in the fact that it may affect socio-cultural behavior beyond linguistic discourse. For example, in some parts of the world, specific DMs have assumed emblematic functions as signals of group identity. In contemporary Korean, the DM *makilay* and a few related forms are very popular among youngsters – to the extent that between 2011 and 2017 it was chosen as the name of a children's TV show, the *Makilay* Show (Rhee 2013).

    An example of a perhaps even more conspicuous role played by a DM as an emblem of social and cultural identity can be found in the East African country Kenya. The Kalenjin language is one of the major languages of this country, spoken by several million people. This language did not exist prior to World War II. There was a group of closely related "dialects," each with its own name and cultural identity but with no name in common. In the 1940s, there emerged an awareness of their linguistic and cultural unity among the speakers of these

---

[1] For a definition of "discourse marker," see (7) of Section 1.1.2. The term (linguistic) "discourse" refers generally to language in use and to how language is used in order to enact activities and identities (Bax 2011: 1).

dialects, and the term "Kalenjin" was proposed to refer to all these speakers and dialects, becoming the name of a monthly magazine in the 1950s and eventually the official name of both the language and its speakers. The name is derived from the form *kalenchiin* "I say to you," which is a DM of high frequency used in most though not in all of the dialects of the group.[2]

The sociolinguistic significance, and in particular the emblematic value that DMs may acquire is also reflected in situations of language contact, where DMs tend to be transferred easily from one language to another – more than most other kinds of linguistic expressions. But in spite of all the progress that has been made in the course of the last decades, the overall state of research on DMs is still far from satisfactory. Thus, the following observations, made at the end of the last century, still apply to a large extent up to the present:

The term DM typically refers to a more or less open class of syntactically optional, non-truth-conditional connective expressions. There is, however, wide disagreement about the nature of the connection DMs express, the nature and extent of the elements connected, and the grammatical status of the DM category. An inconvenient result of such disagreements is that the items (and uses of items) designated by the term DM on one definition sometimes overlap only minimally with those designated on another definition. Equally inconvenient is the fact that the referential overlap between the term DM and other similar terms, such as pragmatic marker and pragmatic particle, can in some cases be as great as that between variant definitions of the term DM itself. (Schourup 1999: 242)

Rather than with what DMs are, however, our concern in the present book is with how they came to be what they are – that is, with their historical development. To this end, a number of reconstructions of DMs will be presented. These reconstructions are in no way intended to do justice to the history of the relevant DMs, for which the reader is asked to consult the references cited. Rather, our interest is more narrowly with defining salient stages of grammatical development and with how this development accounts for why DMs are structured the way they are in their present-day usages.

1.1.1   Introduction

In a number of languages there are pairs of homophonous linguistic expressions that differ drastically from one another in their grammatical behavior. The following examples, taken from English (1), German (2), Spanish (3), Bulgarian (4), and Swahili (5), illustrate these differences (the relevant expressions are printed in bold).

---

[2] The morphological form of the expression is *k-a-len-chi-in* (*k*-1.SG-say-DAT-2.SG.O) "I say to you."

(1) English
    a *Jeff is **still** sick.*
    b ***Still**, Jeff is sick.*

(2) German
    a *Hier wohnen wir **sicher**.*
       here   live   we   safely
       "Here we live safely."

    b ***Sicher**, hier wohnen wir.*
       sure   here   live   we
       "Sure, here we live."

(3) Spanish (Arroyo 2011: 868)[3]
    a *Lo haré **bien**.*
       "I'll do it well."
    b ***Bien**, lo haré.*
       "Right, I'll do it."

(4) Bulgarian
    a *Tja raboti **dobre**.*
       she   works   well
       "She works well."

    b ***Dobre**, šte ti pomogna.*
       ok   will you help.1.SG.PRES
       "Ok, I'll help you."

(5) Swahili
    a *Hamisi yu-po   **sawa**.*
       Hamisi 3.SG-LOC.COP correct
       "Hamisi is fine."

    b ***Sawa**, Hamisi yu-po.*
       okay,   Hamisi 3.SG-LOC.COP
       "Right, Hamisi is here."

Considering that the expression concerned appears in final position in the (a)-sentences but in sentence-initial position in the (b)-sentences one may wonder if it is the position that is responsible for the difference in meaning. The answer is however in the negative. Take the German example: Instead of (2b) one could say something like (6), where the first expression, *sicher*, is the same as the expression *sicher* in (2b) but occurs in medial position of the sentence.[4] Thus, sentence-initial position does not seem to be a relevant factor to distinguish the two expressions.[5]

---

[3] The examples are constructed, the sources are Arroyo (2011: 868) for Spanish and Kibiki (2019) for Swahili. Otherwise, the sources are taken from our own data.

[4] The term "medial" position is used here more generally for placement slots other than the initial and the final one, or the left and the right periphery of a clause or sentence.

[5] Cf. Furkó's notion of the "quasi-initiality" of discourse markers (Furkó 2014: 293).

(6)   German
        Hier wohnen wir, **sicher,** *aber wir wohnen nicht* **sicher.**
        here live   we   sure but we live   not   safely
        "Here we live, sure, but we don't live safely."

The example in (6) also illustrates another property distinguishing the
(a)-expressions from the corresponding (b)-expressions: Their meanings may
be similar or related, but the fact that they can occur in the same sentence with
contrasting functions suggests that their meaning is not the same. But
these are not the only properties distinguishing the two, as the following
observations suggest.

First, the meaning of the (a)-expressions is part of the meaning of the
sentence (or clause), modifying or qualifying the meaning of the verb. That
of the (b)-expressions, by contrast, is not a semantic part of the sentence or
clause. Second, the function of the two is also different: Whereas the
(a)-expressions are adverbs qualifying the meaning of the verb, the function
of the (b)-expressions is commonly classified as "metatextual" (e.g., Traugott
2018: 27): Rather than to the content of the sentence, the meaning is "pragmatically conditioned" (Coulmas 1979: 240) – in other words, it relates
immediately to the situation of discourse, that is, the preceding discourse, the
attitudes of the speaker, and/or speaker–hearer interaction.[6]

Third, the syntax is also different: Whereas the (a)-expressions are constituents of the sentence – hence, belong to the sentence syntax, the (b)-expressions
are fairly independent of the syntactic structure of a sentence; as Arroyo (2011:
868) puts it with reference to example (3), they are characterized by "the
absence of a true syntactic function."

Fourth, the two also differ in their prosodic shape: Whereas the
(a)-expressions are firmly integrated in the intonation contour of the sentence,
the (b)-expressions tend to be set off from the rest of the sentence, often
occurring "in an independent breath unit carrying a special intonation and
stress pattern," as Traugott (1995: 7) puts it.

Fifth, there is a difference in semantic–pragmatic scope: The (a)-expressions
form one scope unit with the verb they modify. The scope range characterizing
the (b)-expressions, in contrast, is of a different nature. On the one hand, it is
not restricted to some part of the proposition but relates to the proposition as a
whole. On the other hand, it extends beyond the proposition to the context –
that is, to the situation of discourse where the sentence is produced.

And, sixth, there is also a difference in placement: Whereas the
(a)-expressions are restricted to positions reserved for adverbial constituents,
the (b)-expressions do not show such constraints; rather, they can –

---

[6] Concerning the "situation of discourse," see Section 1.1.2.

dependent on their particular function – also occur in other positions, even if the position at the left periphery of the sentence is the favorite position for many of them.[7]

These six properties seem to be of more general interest, for the following reasons. First, they are not restricted to the examples mentioned; rather, each of the five languages disposes of a whole set of expressions showing essentially the same properties. Second, they are not restricted to the five languages but can also be observed in other languages – thus, they seem to be of typological interest. And, third, the properties are not confined to one particular component of grammar; rather, they relate to grammar at large, extending from syntax to phonology (prosody) and from semantics to pragmatics.

The six properties will be the main concern of the chapters to follow, even if they do not conclude the list of contrasting properties distinguishing (a)- from (b)-expressions, as we will see in the next section (cf. (11) of Section 1.1.2). We will refer to the (a)-expressions summarily as "sentence grammar units" and to the (b)-expressions as discourse markers (DMs), following a widely used convention.

The main goal of the present book is to find out how to explain these differences. However, the account proposed is confined to historical reconstruction – that is, our interest is strictly with diachronic explanation. This means that we will not be able to deal with many of the questions that have been raised with reference to doublets like those in the examples of (1) through (5).

There is both massive evidence and wide agreement to the effect that DMs are as a rule historically derived from sentence grammar units – that is, the (b)-expressions illustrated in (2) through (5) can be traced back historically in some way to the corresponding (a)-expressions. The question then is: What is the mechanism that can be held responsible for this development? As we will see later in this chapter, this issue has been discussed controversially, and we will not only discuss the various views that have been voiced on this issue but also look for an answer to this question.

---

[7] Following a widespread convention we will be using here the terms "left periphery" and "right periphery" for linguistic expressions located, respectively, before or after a clause or sentence – that is, they are not part of a clause or sentence, typically being syntactically unintegrated (cf. Beeching and Detges 2014). These terms are useful within the framework used in this book, even if we are aware that there are a number of problems associated with the terms. First, they are not really fortunate considering that they impose a visual view of the linearization of language based on its written structure (Haselow 2016: 83). Second, in a number of languages having writing systems different from those found, e.g., in European languages, such as traditional Japanese, Hebrew, Urdu, or Persian, "left periphery" and "right periphery" are confusing in that they may have the opposite significance from the one they have in the former languages. And, third, the terms can refer to quite different concepts depending, for example, on which kind of adjacency pair is involved (see Traugott 2015). Concerning the term "periphery," see Cinque (1999).

1.1.2   A Definition

The term "discourse marker" (DM) is used in a wide range of senses and for quite a number of different phenomena. DMs are referred to with a variety of different terms, such as discourse particles (e.g., Schourup 1985; Abraham 1991; Aijmer 2002; Diewald 2006: 406), pragmatic markers (e.g., Brinton 1996; 2008; 2017; Fraser 1996; Aijmer and Simon-Vandenbergen 2009; Aijmer 2013; 2016; Beeching 2016; Traugott 2016), discourse connectives (Blakemore 1987: 105; Erman and Kotsinas 1993: 79), discourse operators (Redeker 1991: 1169; Gaines 2011), style disjuncts or conjuncts (Quirk et al. 1985: 631–45), speech act adverbials (cf. Aijmer 1997: 3), formulaic theticals (Heine, Kaltenböck, and Kuteva 2016: 56–58), discourse organizers (Pons Bordería 1998: 215), discourse signals (Lamiroy and Swiggers 1991: 123), "adverbials," or simply "conjunctions."

The above terms are by no means all identical in meaning, but refer to at least a set of the expressions that are classified here as "DMs." For example, for Lewis (2000: 15, 51) discourse connectives are a sub-set of DMs, and for Fraser (1999) DMs form a subset of pragmatic markers.

DMs serve to monitor the production and comprehension of texts and to provide processing instructions on how to interpret texts (cf. Carter and McCarthy 2006: 221). Having been the subject of many studies (see, e.g., Jucker and Ziv 1998; Aijmer 2002; Brinton 2008; Dér 2010, and especially Brinton 2017: 2–37 for overviews), they are defined here as in (7) (cf. Brinton 1995: 380; Schourup 1999; Andersen 2001: 81; 2014; González 2004; Furkó 2014).

(7)   Discourse markers are (a) invariable expressions which are (b) semantically and syntactically independent from their environment, (c) set off prosodically from the rest of the utterance in some way, and (d) their function is metatextual, being anchored in the situation of discourse and serving the organization of texts, the attitudes of the speaker, and/or speaker–hearer interaction.

The viability of the definition stipulated in (7) will be tested in Section 1.4 by means of findings that have been made in previous research on DMs. In accordance with this definition, DMs exhibit a set of grammatical properties that were already mentioned in Section 1.1.1; we will return to this set in (40) of Section 1.5.

We will say that in order for an expression to qualify as a DM it should conform to all four criteria in (7), even if in a few cases there may be reasons to hesitate if a given criterion is in fact fully met. For example, (7a) separates DMs from a number of other kinds of expressions but it is not always strictly observed, in that a number of DMs are not fully invariable. Thus, the Italian DM *guarda*, derived from the homophonous second person singular imperative *guarda!* "look!," can be said to be invariable; at the same time there are two variants in addition, namely the second person singular polite form *guardi* and the second person plural form *guardate* (Waltereit 2002: 984; see Section 8.4). Another kind of variability can be illustrated with Korean DMs. They are typically invariable but are often modulated with reference to politeness by means of the politeness suffix *-yo*. Thus, the DM *kuntey* "but," marking functions like topic shift, surprise, challenge, and discontent, changes to *kuntey-yo* to signal politeness (Seongha Rhee, personal communication of August 9, 2020; cf. Chapter 6.1).

(7b) relates to a widely made observation according to which both the meaning and the syntax of a sentence would essentially remain unaffected if a DM were omitted (see Section 1.4). (7c) is clearly the most vulnerable criterion: Prosodic separation is not an absolutely reliable criterion, being dependent on factors such as a relative speech rate, complexity of the expression, slot of placement within an utterance, emphasis, as well as other processing factors (see Section 1.4.4).[8]

The "situation of discourse" in (7d), relating to the concept of "discourse-deixis" as used by Weinreich ([1966] 1989: 69) or the extralinguistic context of Wilkins (1992: 129), provides the cognitive environment for interlocutors to design and interpret spoken or written texts.[9] "Being anchored in the situation of discourse" entails, for example, that information otherwise provided by the explicit coding structure of sentence participants is recoverable from that situation. The main components of the situation are (i) text organization, (ii) attitudes of the speaker, and/or (iii) speaker–hearer interaction.[10] The use of "and/or" in the preceding sentence draws attention to the fact that the three components are not neatly separated from one another, and typically more than one of the components are simultaneously involved, even if one of the components may be highlighted in a given context. For example, the English DM *actually* does not only serve (i), that is, the linking two units of discourse,

---

[8] An "utterance" is perhaps most commonly understood to be a piece of speech produced by a particular individual on a particular occasion. We follow many other authors, however, in extending the use of the term beyond speech to written text pieces. Utterances are said to contrast with sentences, in that the former tend to be taken to relate to "language-behavior" and the latter to the "language system" (cf. Lyons 1977: 239).

[9] Accordingly, DMs have been described as being related to the speech situation and not to the situation talked about (Jucker 1993: 436) or, as Waltereit (2006: 64) puts it with reference to pragmatic markers, they "situate their host unit with respect to the surrounding discourse and with respect to the speaker–hearer relationship."

[10] By using a DM, the speaker is assumed to take account of the hearer's likely subject knowledge and his or her topic interests and needs and purposes in listening. A larger set of components is distinguished in Kaltenböck, Heine, and Kuteva (2011: 861), where the situation of discourse was described in terms of the following network of components: Text organization, source of information, attitudes of the speaker, speaker–hearer interaction, discourse setting, and world knowledge.

but refers also to (ii), that is, to the expectations and thus to the cognitive state of the speaker (Taglicht 2001; Haselow 2017: 141).

Of the three components, text organization (i) is clearly the most salient one. It concerns general functions like commenting or elaborating on the preceding discourse, drawing attention to what follows, expressing a contrast between the preceding and the following discourse, highlighting specific points, etc. However, (i) need not be involved, or it may be backgrounded in specific contexts in favor of functions that focus on the role played by the speaker (ii), the hearer, or the relation between the two (iii).

The components (ii) and (iii) relate, respectively, to the terms "subjectivity" and "intersubjectivity" (cf. Traugott 1982; 1989; Traugott and Dasher 2002: 22), but the two terminologies must not be equated since, unlike the latter terms, (ii) and (iii) are used here strictly to refer only to *metatextual* functions, such as those expressed by DMs, as well as other expressions to be discussed in Section 2.4. On account of their metatextual functions, the use of DMs presupposes special inferential calculations of the kind described in Relevance Theory (see especially Schourup 1985; 1999; 2001; 2011; Blakemore 1987; 1988; 2002; 2007; Unger 1996).

The term "metatextual" was proposed in work on DMs by Traugott (1995: 6; see also Traugott 2018: 27).[11] It is used here for a level of discourse processing that serves to monitor the production of texts and to provide instructions on how to interpret the texts, such as also described by Stein 1985 and Stein (1990: 31–42). The term is similar to but must not be confused with that of "metadiscourse" (or "metadiscursive") as used in some research on text analysis, where the term stands broadly for discourse about discourse (e.g., Hyland 1998; 2005; 2017; Ädel 2006; 2012; Mauranen 2010; Zhang 2016). In this direction of research, DMs have played no noteworthy role, even if the linguistic expressions commonly classified as "metadiscourse units" serve functions similar to those of DMs, such as repairing, reformulating, commenting on linguistic form or meaning, clarifying, and managing terminology (Ädel 2012: 9). We will return to this issue in Section 8.1.

Attempts have been made to define DMs as a grammatical class,[12] but how to delimit such a class or category is an issue that is discussed controversially (cf. Furkó 2018), and many a student of DMs is inclined to treat them as an open class of units. However, to the extent that some linguistic expression conforms to the definition in (7) we will say here that it belongs to the category of DMs.

---

[11] In more general terms, a "metatextual unit" presents a statement whose topic is the text itself (Witosz 2017: 108; see also Genette 1982).

[12] As early as 1985, Zwicky (1985: 302–3) proposed to treat DMs as "a grammatically significant class of items, in English and other languages generally," based on their distribution, prosody, and meaning. The most detailed characterization of DMs that we are aware of is provided by Brinton (2017: 8–9, Table 1.1).

The definition in (7) would seem to take care of most of the expressions that have crosslinguistically been classified as DMs.[13] At the same time it differs from definitions proposed in the tradition of Schiffrin (1987), cf. (8), which state that DMs signal some kind of relationship between clauses, utterances, units of talk, or discourse segments. Examples of such definitions are provided in (9) and (10).[14]

(8)   [Discourse markers are] sequentially dependent expressions which bracket units of talk.

(Schiffrin 1987: 31)

(9)   [Discourse markers] impose a relationship between some aspects of the discourse segment they are a part of, call it S2, and some aspect of a prior discourse segment, call it S1. In other words they function like a two-place relation, one argument lying in the segment they introduce, the other lying in the prior discourse.

(Fraser 1999: 938)

(10)   By a DM I mean a metatextual marker that signals some kind of relationship between clauses/utterances.

(Traugott 2018: 27)

The reason for proposing the definition in (7) is that in a number of their uses, DMs do not necessarily signal a relationship as stipulated in (8), (9), or (10). For example, expressions such as *I think* and *you know* are commonly considered to be paradigm instances of English DMs. Yet, one may wonder if *I think* in an utterance like *Jeff lives **I think** in Greece* is fully in accordance with the definitions in (8) through (10), occurring within and having semantic–pragmatic scope over the phrase *in Greece*, not really bracketing units of talk or signaling a relationship between clauses or utterances (see also Section 8.3).[15] Similar observations can be made in languages other than English. For example, many discourse-initial DMs in Korean do not clearly refer to any discourse segments, simply expressing the speaker's attitude

---

[13] For a large list of English DMs, see Fraser (1990: 388). The definition in (7) is on the whole compatible with that by Crible (2017: 106), according to whom DMs "function on a metadiscursive level as procedural cues to situate the host unit in a co-built representation of on-going discourse."

[14] Haselow (2017: 141) distinguishes two kinds of views or perspectives on the nature and definition of DMs, namely a narrow and a broader one. Under the former, DMs are usually syntactically integrated and signal a propositional relationship between two neighboring textual units, where DMs are, e.g., conjunctions like "but," "because," "or," and "so." Under the latter, DMs are syntactically, semantically, and often prosodically independent. Whereas the definitions in (8–10) relate primarily to Haselow's narrow view, (7) is in accordance with his broader view.

[15] Elizabeth Traugott (personal communication of January 19, 2020) though points out that there *is* a relationship in at least some of the uses of *I think*. Nevertheless, according to the definitions

(Seongha Rhee, personal communication of August 9, 2020). In sum, by relying on the definition in (7) we are proposing a slightly broader concept of DMs than that implied in (8) through (10).

Text organization is certainly a paradigm function of DMs but, as has been pointed out in a number of studies, DMs cannot reasonably be reduced to it (cf. Schwenter 1996); signaling the speaker's attitude and/or engaging the hearer are also important parts of the functions of DMs. Thus, if DMs do signal a relationship between units of discourse, as they most commonly do, this is not their only function, as is argued in particular in Relevance Theory (e.g., Blakemore 1987; 2002; Schourup 1999; 2001; 2011). Accordingly, expressions as defined in (8) through (10) are therefore classified by some authors as discourse connectives. For Lewis (2000: 51), for example, discourse connectives are DMs "that signal a rhetorical relation between two or more discourse segments."

We will rather take the properties listed in (7) to be of help in deciding what is and what is not a DM, and will refer to linguistic expressions showing these properties as belonging to the category of DMs. In doing so we are aware that these properties are not the only ones that tend to be associated with DMs; a catalog of other features is listed in (11).

(11)   Features that have been suggested to characterize or define DMs
   a Their meaning is procedural rather than conceptual (e.g., Hansen 1997: 162; Fraser 1999: 944; Schourup 1999; Wilson 2011; Crible 2017: 106).[16]
   b They do not contribute to the truth conditions of the sentence (e.g., Blakemore 1988: 183; Fraser 1996: 167; Hansen 1997: 161; Schourup 1999: 232; Aijmer, Foolen, and Simon-Vandenbergen 2006: 101; Haselow 2017: 142).
   c They can normally be omitted without loss of grammaticality or propositional content, or their use is optional (e.g., Fraser 1988: 22; 1999: 944; Barth-Weingarten and Couper-Kuhlen 2002: 352; Jucker 2002: 212; but see also Dér 2010).
   d Their functions are restricted to the here and now of the situation of discourse in which they are used; accordingly, they have been classified as indexicals (Aijmer 2002; Aijmer, Foolen, and Simon-Vandenbergen 2006: 106; Furkó 2014: 292) or discourse deictics (Levinson 2006).
   e They cannot be negated.
   f They cannot become the focus of a cleft sentence.

---

in (8) through (10), *I think* in *Jeff lives **I think** in Greece* would not qualify as a DM – a procedure that is not adopted here.

[16] In some studies it is argued that DMs like *oh* or *well* do not contribute to the truth conditions of an utterance and are context-dependent expressions having no meaning of their own (cf. Schiffrin 1987: 127). We follow Schourup (1999: 243) in assuming that the issue is not "whether they lack meaning or not, but rather what kind of meaning they encode" – that is, their meaning is procedural rather than conceptual.

g They are unusually multifunctional (e.g., Jucker 2002: 213; Aijmer, Foolen, and Simon-Vandenbergen 2006: 103; Koo and Rhee 2018).

h They are highly frequent (e.g., Barth-Weingarten and Couper-Kuhlen 2002: 352; Traugott in press a: 6).

i They are characteristic of oral or speech-based discourse (Brinton 2008: 241).

j They are positionally variable (e.g., Hansen 1997; Barth-Weingarten and Couper-Kuhlen 2002: 352).

k They most commonly occur in clause-initial position or at the left periphery of an utterance.

l They are phonologically short (cf. Brinton 2017: 4; Traugott in press a: 6).

Most of the research that has been done on DMs is devoted to the functions expressed by them and, as this rich research has demonstrated, these functions constitute a serious challenge to existing theories of semantics. The definition in (7) does no more than hinting at these functions (cf. (7d)). Many detailed classifications have been proposed; suffice it to mention the succinct characterization proposed by Brinton (1996: 37–38; 2017), where the following kinds of general functions are distinguished: (a) to initiate or close discourse, (b) to aid floor management, (c) to fill a gap, (d) to mark boundaries, (e) to distinguish new and old information, (f) to mark sequential dependency, (g) to repair, (h) to express a response or attitude, and (i) to effect cooperation, sharing, or intimacy.

DMs have been classified, on the one hand, as a sub-type or metatextual subschema (Traugott 2018: 27) of pragmatic markers (Fraser 2009: 892–93) or of functional markers (Ghezzi and Molinelli 2014: 1–5) and, on the other hand, as a sub-type of parentheticals (Kaltenböck 2007: 31; Fischer 2007a; 2007b: 297ff.) or, as we will say here, of theticals (Kaltenböck, Heine, and Kuteva 2011; Heine 2013; 2018a; Heine et al. 2013: 165; 2017; see Section 2.4). What distinguishes them from many other theticals is that they are largely or entirely invariable and formulaic, that is, they typically do not allow internal morphological modification (cf. (7a)).

Not everybody might agree to call all the expressions discussed in this study DMs. But to the extent that they conform essentially to the definition in (7) they will be referred to here as "discourse markers" (DMs).[17] This means, for example, that one and the same form, like *still* in (1) of Section 1.1.1, can be a DM in some of its uses, like (1b) (*Still, Jeff is sick*) but not in other uses, like (1a) (*Jeff is **still** sick*). DMs have commonly been linked with grammatical or

---

[17] The term essentially corresponds to what Brinton (2017: 1) and some others call "pragmatic markers." This use of "pragmatic marker" is not the same as that of Fraser (2009) alluded to above. Note further that the terms "pragmatic marker," "discourse marker," and "modal particle" are defined differently by some authors (e.g., Fedriani and Sansò 2017: 2; Goria 2017: 440); we will return to these alternative definitions in Section 7.3.1.

functional categories, but also with lexical categories (e.g., Claridge 2013: 180; Fraser 2015: 48). However, on account of their particular properties, especially of (7b) and (7c), there are also reasons to argue that they are elusive to the distinction between lexical and grammatical expressions or categories.

The boundary separating DMs from other kinds of expressions, such as interjections (e.g., *oh*, *wow*), ideophones (e.g., *bang*, *plop*), formulae of social exchange (e.g., *please*, *bye-bye*), or modal particles is notoriously fuzzy (see, e.g., Aijmer and Simon-Vandenbergen 2009; Haselow 2011; Degand, Cornillie and Pietrandrea 2013: 1). Roughly speaking one may say that the first three do not typically show property (7d), while modal particles differ from DMs in not normally conforming to properties (7b) and (7c), but not everybody might agree with this characterization. However, in a number of their usages, some interjections (e.g., *oh*) and formulae of social exchange (e.g., *please*) conform to the definitional criteria in (7) and, hence, are treated here as DMs in such uses.

Furthermore, there is another type of expression whose status has been classified controversially yet which essentially conforms to the definition in (7) and, hence, is classified here as DMs, namely that of fillers, such as English *uh* and *um*, usually transcribed *er* and *erm*, respectively, in British English (e.g., Clark and Fox Tree 2002; O'Connell and Kowal 2004; 2005; Tottie 2011; 2014; 2015). Also called filled pauses, hesitation markers, hesitation fillers, or interjective hesitators, they constitute a crosslinguistically fairly common discourse-structuring device and will be the topic of Section 8.5.

Excluded from the category of DMs as defined in (7) are modal particles: "Uncontroversial" exponents of modal particles are syntactically and prosodically integrated in the sentence, their semantic–pragmatic scope is grammatically determined, and their placement is fixed close to the finite verb (Waltereit 2001; see also Detges and Waltereit 2007; 2016; Cuenca 2013). Modal particles are absent in English, being found especially in Germanic languages like German (*denn, doch, ja, wohl, schon*, etc.; e.g., Weydt 1969; Abraham 1991), Dutch (*ook*), or Norwegian (*nok*), but also in French (*bien, déja, donc, peut-être, quand-même, seulement*; see, e.g., Abraham 1991; Hansen 1998a; 1998c; 2008; Waltereit 2001; Fuschi 2013; Norde and Beijering 2014: 403; Detges and Waltereit 2016; Fedriani and Sansò 2017).

1.1.3 The Present Volume

The question of how DMs arise has generated quite some research activity. In 2011, Liesbeth Degand and Anne-Marie Simon-Vandenbergen edited a volume on the development of DMs, published as a special issue of the journal *Linguistics* (Volume 49, 2). Observing that there had been "an explosion of research on discourse markers" in the preceding two decades, the contributors to the volume, all known for their extensive record of research on DMs, were asked for their views on how to explain this development. More specifically, the contributors were asked which of the main hypotheses that had surfaced in previous work was best suited to account for this development: Grammaticalization, pragmaticalization, or perhaps "simple" semantic change?

The outcome of this project, which had a noteworthy impact on ensuing research, is commented on by Degand and Simon-Vandenbergen (2011) thus:

... we had not expected these contributions to be so unanimous in their rejection of pragmaticalization as a substitute term for the processes described. All authors plead for grammaticalization as the best possible explanation for the developments described, on condition that grammar is given a wider sense ... (p. 293)

The main goal of the present volume is to show that this outcome is in need of reconsideration. It is argued in particular that the rise and development of DMs cannot reasonably be reduced to one single mechanism of change, be that grammaticalization or pragmaticalization. DMs, as they are found in the languages of the world, are shaped, on the one hand, by the grammatical functions they fulfill and, on the other hand, by the role they play in processing linguistic discourse. Accordingly, it is argued that DMs are the joint product of two distinct mechanisms, namely grammaticalization, which accounts for example for the wealth of functions they express, and cooptation, a discourse strategy which accounts for most of their structural properties.

In accordance with this hypothesis, referred to in short as the "cooptation hypothesis," the present volume proposes an alternative account of the rise of DMs. To this end, an overview of earlier work is provided in the remainder of this chapter by summarizing the main concepts and hypotheses discussed there (Section 1.2) and pointing out problems (Sections 1.3 and 1.4), and Section 1.5 raises questions to be looked into in the chapters to follow.

Chapter 2 is devoted to the methodology employed in the book (see Section 2.1), which rests on the distinction between the two mechanisms of grammatical change mentioned, namely grammaticalization (Section 2.2) and cooptation (Section 2.3), the latter being a concept that has been proposed in the framework of discourse grammar (Section 2.4). Some issues relating to these mechanisms and their interaction are the topic of Section 2.5, and Section 2.6 describes how the cooptation hypothesis can be tested.

The hypothesis is then tested in Chapters 3–6, which are devoted to reconstructing the history of DMs back to their genesis, relying on existing publications and data. These four chapters are restricted to some languages for which appropriate written documents exist, namely English (Chapter 3), French (Chapter 4), Japanese (Chapter 5), and Korean (Chapter 6).

While these four chapters are concerned with some general lines of development characterizing the history of DMs, Chapter 7 draws attention to the fact that there is at least one other line leading to the introduction of DMs, namely via language contact. This chapter also differs from the preceding ones in looking at DMs from a crosslinguistic perspective, aiming at establishing regularities on how DMs are transferred from one language to another. Thus, whereas Chapters 3–6 adopt a language-internal perspective, Chapter 7 is based on a comparative perspective of DMs.

A comparative perspective is also adopted in Chapter 8, where some general features characterizing the development of DMs are pointed out (Section 8.2). But, in addition, the chapter discusses a range of topics that for some reason or other had to be ignored in earlier parts of the book. One topic concerns the status of the cooptation hypothesis within the general field of dual process models (Section 8.1), while Section 8.2 takes up issues relating to cooptation that could not be discussed in previous chapters.

Section 8.3 deals with the differential semantic–pragmatic scope of DMs, Section 8.4 deals with the special nature of DMs derived from imperative forms, and Section 8.5 is devoted to (hesitation) fillers, a class of linguistic expressions whose status as DMs has been discussed controversially in the earlier literature. In the final Chapter 9, the findings made in the book are briefly summarized and some conclusions are drawn.

Research on DMs over the last decades has contributed substantially to our knowledge of semantics, and in particular to the meanings and functions of linguistic discourse and its pragmatic foundations, both in synchrony and diachrony. But our interest is restricted to the overall grammatical development of DMs and we will therefore not be able to do justice to all the findings that have been made in the course of that research on the wealth of functions that DMs exhibit. The reader is referred to the sources cited to appreciate all those findings.

Another restriction is the following: DMs are of worldwide distribution and the perspective adopted in the book is a comparative and a typological one. For this reason, our main focus will be on features that DMs share across languages, and we will not be able to do justice to features that have been observed only in one or a few languages.

1.2   Previous Research

Take the following text example:

(12)   English (*The Guardian*, November 1, 2003; Bell 2009: 918, (11))
Such antics are nothing new. In January 1968, Jimi Hendrix unleashed his pent-up angst in Stockholm, smashing a hotel room to pieces. **Mind you**, during 1967, he'd found time to record two of the greatest albums ever made while being on tour.

The item *mind you* in (12) is called a "cancellative discourse marker" by the author (Bell 2009: 916), exactly like the DM *still* that we discussed in Section 1.1.1 and, in fact, it also shows the grammatical properties of DMs that we identified in Section 1.1.1 and corresponds to our definition of DMs in (7) of Section 1.1.2. The question to be looked into now is: How did *mind you*, or the many other DMs that there are in English, come to be what they are?

The rise and further development of DMs has been the subject of a wide range of studies and in the present section an overview of this research is provided. This overview is restricted in a number of ways. First, in accordance with the general theme of this book it takes account only of studies proffering diachronic explanations on the question of why DMs have the grammatical structure they do. Second, it is limited to what appear to be the main positions maintained in proposing explanatory accounts for the rise and development of DMs. And third, it is restricted to a brief characterization of these positions, and discussion of the evidence adduced in support of the positions had to be kept to a minimum for space reasons. (For more details, see in particular, Brinton and Traugott 2005: 136–40; Hansen 2008: 54–60; Degand and Evers-Vermeul 2015; Brinton 2017.)

1.2.1 Grammaticalization

By far the most frequently invoked line of explaining the development of DMs concerns grammaticalization. It is argued that regularities as they have been identified in grammatical change, including those to be observed in DMs, are best understood and described with reference to principles of grammaticalization. There are, however, different views on the nature and the relative contribution made by grammaticalization in this change, as we will see in the following survey.

1.2.1.1 The "All-Grammaticalization" Hypothesis

It is presumably Traugott (1995) who can be held responsible for most of the research relying on what we will refer to as the "all-grammaticalization" hypothesis, that is, for the claim that grammaticalization offers a tool for comprehensively describing and understanding the rise and development of DMs. Accordingly, she argues:

(13)   To treat it [the development of DMs; a.n.] as a case of something other than grammaticalization would be to obscure its similarities with the more canonical clines.

(Traugott 1995: 15)

On this view there is a distinction between "less canonical" and "more canonical clines" of grammaticalization, implying that DMs represent the former type of clines; we will return to this issue in Section 1.3.2.

The hypothesis was fleshed out in subsequent research (see the discussions, e.g., in Brinton 1996: 40–44; Waltereit 2002: 1004–7; Frank-Job 2006: 366). A particularly influential representative of this tradition is Brinton (e.g., Brinton 1996; 2008; 2017). Based on sound reconstruction work, using a wider array of criteria than other authors,[18] she deals with a substantial number of English DMs, called pragmatic markers by her, and related expressions such as comment clauses, insubordinate clauses, and epistemic parentheticals.[19] More generally, Brinton (1996; 2006; 2008; 2014; 2017) argues for an all-grammaticalization hypothesis to account for DMs: For her, like for Traugott (1995), processes of change leading to DMs "are understood as cases of grammaticalization" (Brinton 2017: 284).

The rise and development of DMs is in fact widely held to be the result of grammaticalization. The latter has been defined in this work as involving the development of new grammatical functions (Hopper and Traugott 2003: 18), and since "the development of new grammatical functions" also applies to DMs, grammaticalization is believed to also take care of DMs (e.g., Degand and Evers-Vermeul 2015: 60). We will return to this definition in Section 2.2.1.

In fact, work carried out over the last decades has been based most commonly on the assumption that grammaticalization is crucially involved in the rise and/or development of DMs and other discourse-specific constructions; the following is a representative selection of the studies concerned: Thompson and Mulac (1991); Traugott (1995); Auer (1996); Nakayama and Ichihashi-Nakayama (1997); Günthner (1999; 2000); Palander-Collin (1999); Traugott and Dasher (2002); Auer and Günthner (2003; 2005); Miyashita (2003); Günthner and Mutz (2004); Rhee (2004); Brinton and Traugott (2005); Brinton (2008; 2017); Diewald (2011a; 2011b); Van Bogaert (2011); Degand and Evers-Vermeul (2015: 60); see also López-Couso and Méndez-Naya (2014). Accordingly, Van Bogaert (2011: 296) concludes that "[m]ost studies of pragmatic markers consider grammaticalization as a central mechanism in the development of these kinds of expressions."

The criteria recruited in support of what is called here the all-grammaticalization hypothesis rest for the most part on the parameters of

---

[18] For a catalog of ten parameters of grammaticalization relevant to DMs, see Brinton (2010a: 61–62).

[19] "Epistemic parentheticals" (Thompson and Mulac 1991) belong within the larger class of "comment clauses" (Quirk et al. 1985: 1112ff.; cf. Brinton 2008), which are clausal parentheticals that function either as content disjuncts expressing "the speakers' comments on the content of the matrix clause" or as style disjuncts conveying "the speakers' views on the way they are speaking" (Brinton 2017: 171). Comment clauses "are parenthetical pragmatic markers [= DMs; a.n.]. What sets comment clauses apart from some other parentheticals and pragmatic markers is their clausal origin" (Brinton 2008: 241).

Lehmann ([1982] 2015) and the principles proposed by Hopper (1991).[20] For example, adopting this hypothesis, López-Couso and Méndez-Naya (2014) maintain that the development of the epistemic parentheticals *looks/seems/sounds/appears like* represents Hopper's (1991) principle of layering. Furthermore, there is said to have been decategorialization from a complement-taking predicate to a parenthetical clause.

The grammatical parameter of decategorialization (see Section 2.2.2) is in fact among the factors most frequently adduced in support of the all-grammaticalization hypothesis, and it is almost invariably *internal decategorialization* which is implied, that is, development within the expression concerned, rather than its relation to the surrounding text. For example, Brinton says:

(14)   In accordance with these studies, I believe that the diachronic evidence offers
        support for considering the development of epistemic parentheticals as a case
        of grammaticalization. They increase in morphological fixation (generally as
        first-person present-tense forms) and they undergo decategorialization from a
        subject-full verb construction to a particle-like parenthetical.

                                                              (Brinton 2017: 165)

Morphological fixation and changes from "subject-full verb construction to a particle-like parenthetical" concern the internal, rather than the external structure of a number of DMs such as *I think*, *if you will*, or *as it were* when they develop into unanalyzable expressions, a process described as functionalization (Bolly 2014: 33) or univerbation (Lehmann [1982] 2015: 89).[21]

In sum, work on the all-grammaticalization hypothesis has resulted in a number of findings that compellingly suggest that grammaticalization plays a role in the development of DMs. At the same time, this work has also revealed that there are problems with this hypothesis. For example, after presenting an impressive catalog of properties in support of the hypothesis, Brinton (2017: 29) concludes that "in some respects the development of pragmatic markers [= DMs; a.n.] diverges from what is thought to occur during grammaticalization." Problematic properties identified by her include the ones in (15).

(15)   Problematic properties of DMs identified by Brinton (2017: 29)
        a DMs do not commonly develop into clitics or inflections.
        b They do not typically reduce phonetically and fuse with the host form but
           remain independent items.

---

[20] See Section 2.1.2 for a discussion of these criteria.
[21] Univerbation obtains when a collocation of two or more words or morphemes loses its internal
     morphological boundaries and turns into a new, invariable word (cf. Lehmann [1982] 2015:
     161; see also Haspelmath 2011).

c They do not become an obligatory expression in a grammatical paradigm.[22]
d They do not become syntactically fixed.
e Their scope expands over larger segments of discourse.

Such observations appear to have induced some proponents of the all-grammaticalization hypothesis to propose a distinction between two perspectives of grammaticalization, namely between standard and nonstandard grammaticalization (Giacalone Ramat and Mauri 2011), or between a narrow or restricted and a wider or expanded view of grammaticalization (e.g., Traugott 1995; Hansen 1998b; Lenker 2000; Traugott and Dasher 2002; Brinton and Traugott 2005: 136–40; Brinton 2008; Degand & Simon-Vandenbergen 2011: 290; Diewald 2011a; 2011b; Prévost 2011; Van Bogaert 2011; Degand and Evers-Vermeul 2015: 77).

Most of the proposals of an expanded notion of grammaticalization can ultimately be traced back to Traugott (1995). There are two main arguments proposed to distinguish two different notions of grammaticalization, summarized by her thus:

The only two areas in which the development of DMs violates some recently-accepted criteria for grammaticalization are syntactic increase in scope and disjunction. (Traugott 1995: 14)

Following this line of diachronic account, Traugott and Trousdale (2013: 99–112) submit a more pronounced position on a new understanding of grammaticalization. Rejecting the term "pragmaticalization" (cf. Traugott 1995; 2007), Traugott and Trousdale (2013: 99–112) propose a distinction between two models of grammaticalization. In one model, referred to in short with the acronym "GR," grammaticalization is viewed as reduction and increase in dependency, while the second model, called "GE," views it as expansion.[23] As argued by the authors, this distinction is immediately relevant for understanding the development of DMs, which is said to involve "expansion" and, hence, is covered by the latter but not by the former model. We will look at this distinction in more detail in Section 1.3.2.2.

A wider view of grammaticalization can also be said to surface in the work of authors who propose that grammaticalization be analyzed as including pragmaticalization as a subclass (Prévost 2011: 391) – that is, who interpret phenomena commonly observed in studies of pragmaticalization to fall within the rubric of grammaticalization (see Section 1.2.2).

---

[22] But see also Haselow (2015: 180–81) on English *anyway*. Note further that Diewald (2011b) proposes to distinguish between language internal and communicative obligatoriness.

[23] For an appraisal of the distinction, see Heine (2018a). A critical review of Traugott and Trousdale (2013) is found in Börjars, Vincent, and Walkden (2015).

It would seem, however, that the "all-grammaticalization" hypothesis no longer quite receives the kind of support it once enjoyed; as Elizabeth Traugott (personal communication of March 28, 2020) informs us, she no longer thinks that the rise of DMs is a case of grammaticalization.

1.2.1.2 Specific Hypotheses

The question of how exactly grammaticalization leads from free lexical expressions to DMs has generated some research activity aimed at proposing plausible scenarios of development. Clearly the most widely discussed scenario is that by Thompson and Mulac (1991: 313–29), who suggest that epistemic parentheticals like *I guess*, *I think*, or *I suppose* are the result of a "type of grammaticalization in which a governing or head expression is reanalyzed as a governed or dependent expression." According to this hypothesis, called by Brinton (2006) 'the matrix clause hypothesis," such parentheticals arise as matrix clauses with dependent *that*-complement clauses. Deletion of the complementizer *that* then creates an indeterminate structure where the original matrix clause is reanalyzed as a parenthetical and moved to the medial or final position of a clause (see also Palander-Collin 1999). The constructed example in (17) illustrates the hypothesized development: (17a) presents the initial main clause–complement clause stage. In (17b), the complementizer *that* is deleted and the distinction between main clause and complement clause is "blurred." At the final stage in (17c) the erstwhile main clause (*I think*) is reanalyzed as an epistemic parenthetical and eventually a DM.

(17) Example illustrating the matrix clause hypothesis of Thompson and Mulac (1991; see Brinton 2017: 157)
  a Stage 1: *I think that the world is flat.*
  b Stage 2: *I think Ø the world is flat.*
  c Stage 3: *The world is flat, **I think**.*

This hypothesis has also been taken into account in a number of other studies. In a diachronic study of Middle and Early Modern English, Palander-Collin (1999) claims that the three degrees of grammaticalization proposed by Thompson and Mulac (1991) involve an increase in the use of *I think* with zero complementizer followed by a higher frequency of parenthetical uses, and suggests that the expression then be regarded as a pragmatic marker (see Van Bogaert 2011: 296).

The hypothesis, especially the claim of an intermediate stage of *that* deletion, has been subjected to critical analysis by a number of authors (Brinton 1996: 239–53; 2008: 44–46, 133–54; 2017: 155–62; Aijmer 1997: 6; Fischer 2007a: 105; Rissanen 2008). Aijmer (1997) does not find appropriate historical evidence to support the hypothesis (see also Brinton 2008: 191, 288–89). Accordingly, Dehé (2014: 66) concludes that with reference to comment clauses "there is no historically solid evidence for an unambiguous path from matrix clause to comment clause."

An alternative hypothesis of gradual development is proposed by Brinton (2008; see also Brinton 1996: 252). Analyzing English *I mean*, she presents a five-stage scenario. Unlike the matrix clause hypothesis, Brinton's scenario does not involve a "reversal" of syntactic hierarchy (main clause > parenthetical, subordinate clause > main clause). What her scenario involves is "deletion of an adverbial connective in cases where the logical connection of main and adverbial clause is contextually inferable" (Brinton 2017: 160); for a critical review, see Fischer (2007a).

Note, however, that Brinton does not discard the matrix clause hypothesis altogether, concluding that the latter accounts for some DMs or comment clauses, or parentheticals, but not for others. For example, she finds support for that hypothesis in the case of the rise of pragmatic parentheticals like *I/you* (modal) *admit* and *I'm just saying* (Brinton 2008; 2017: 289).[24]

These hypotheses are not the only ones that have been proposed to account for the change from a construction like (17a) to one like (17c); see Ross (1973), Hooper (1975), and Boye and Harder (2007) for detailed discussion of these hypotheses, see also Brinton (2017: 16–21).

1.2.2   Pragmaticalization

But there is also an alternative to grammaticalization. Observing that grammaticalization theory has problems with explaining features of DMs such as the ones in (15) of Section 1.2.1.1 induced some authors to argue for another distinct process, commonly referred to as pragmaticalization or, occasionally, as pragmaticization (Hayashi and Yoon 2006; 2010). On this view, grammaticalization describes the emergence of sentence-internal grammatical markers, while pragmaticalization describes that of text-structuring devices. Arguably the most succinct definition of it is that in (18).[25]

(18)   The term [pragmaticalization] refers to a process of linguistic change in which a full lexical item [. . .] or grammatical item [. . .] changes category and status and becomes a pragmatic item, that is, an item which is not fully integrated into the syntactic structure of the utterance and which has a textual or interpersonal meaning.

(Dostie 2009: 203)

---

[24] Brinton (2017: 18) furthermore notes that the following could also be covered by means of the matrix clause hypothesis: Parenthetical second-person forms (e.g., *you say/see/know*), impersonal constructions (e.g., *it seems/appears/is said/is rumored, that/it is to wit*), and third-person forms (e.g., *one hears, there's no doubt, God knows*).

[25] In a similar way, Frank-Job (2006: 361) proposes the following definition: "Pragmaticalization is regarded as the process by which a syntagma or word form, in a given context, changes its lexical meaning in favor of an essentially pragmatic, discourse interactional meaning."

Following Norde (2009: 21–24), one may define pragmaticalization in short as the development of DMs. On this view, then, the presence of DMs presupposes that of prior pragmaticalization. Erman and Kotsinas (1993: 79), who first proposed the term, argued that a lexical item develops "directly into a discourse marker without an intermediate stage of grammaticalization." The concept was subsequently developed further by Aijmer (1997), acquiring a number of adherents, presenting studies such as the following: Günthner (1999); Onodera (2000; 2004: 1); Dostie (2004); Frank-Job (2006); Ocampo (2006); Waltereit (2006); Hansen (2008: 58); Norde (2009: 21–23); Arroyo (2011); Defour et al. (2012); Beijering (2012: 56–59); Claridge (2013); Norde and Beijering (2014: 402); and Noora and Amouzadeh (2015).

Some authors avoid the term "pragmaticalization" but propose frameworks that can in a more general sense be related to this concept. The alternative terms used are reanalysis (Waltereit 2002: 988; 2006), discoursivization (Ocampo 2006: 307), and discursization (Claridge and Arnovick 2010: 183) – suggesting that the primary concern of these authors is with discourse at large rather than with sentence grammar.

On the pragmaticalization hypothesis, lexical or other expressions develop into DMs either without an intermediate stage of grammaticalization or via a kind of grammaticalization that differs from "canonical" grammaticalization in a remarkable way, the result being markers "mainly serving as textstructuring devices at [non-sentential] levels of discourse" (Erman and Kotsinas 1993: 79; see Brinton 2008: 61). It has also been suggested (e.g., Aijmer 1997; Dostie 2004; Günthner and Mutz 2004: 98; Claridge and Arnovick 2010: 167) that grammaticalization describes the emergence of sentence-internal grammatical markers while the notion of pragmaticalization would be more appropriate to describe the emergence of text structuring DMs.

As pointed out most clearly by Norde (2009: 21–24), the notion of pragmaticalization has been proposed essentially to account for the development of DMs and some related phenomena. This, however, is not the position taken by all students of DMs. For example, arguing that grammaticalization and pragmaticalization are independent of one another, Onodera (2000: 27; see also Onodera 2004: 203–5) observes that in Japanese there are, on the one hand, DMs whose development involved both grammaticalization and pragmaticalization. This applies, for example, to *demo* and related DMs. On the other hand, she also finds DMs in Japanese, such as *na* and related elements, that involved pragmaticalization but no grammaticalization; we will return to these markers in Chapter 5.

Some authors in fact argue that the main reason for distinguishing pragmaticalization as a distinct mechanism is semantic–pragmatic (e.g., Van Bogaert 2011: 316; see also Hansen 2008: 58–59; Kranich 2015: 184). For example, according to Hansen (2008; personal communication of January 24,

2020), pragmaticalization involves a shift in meaning from the content level to the context level.

The main point made in work on pragmaticalization is that the development of DMs is elusive to some of the criteria that have been proposed to define grammaticalization, in particular those of Lehmann ([1982] 2015; see Section 2.2.2).[26] It is most of all the properties listed in (19) that were adduced in favor of pragmaticalization.

(19)   The main properties commonly argued to distinguish pragmaticalization from grammaticalization
    a Syntactic detachability or isolation
    b Lack of fusion
    c Distinct prosody
    d Increase in semantic–pragmatic scope
    e Non-truth conditionality
    f Peculiar grammatical status
    g Optionality

With regard to (19a), grammaticalization is argued to involve syntactic integration, pragmaticalization, by contrast, leads from syntactically dependent to syntactically detached status (Aijmer 1997: 4); there is "an increase in syntactic freedom instead of syntactic fixation" (Norde 2009: 22; Beijering 2012). According to (19b), which is presumably related to (19a), items undergoing pragmaticalization do not fuse with other constituents, e.g., they do not normally become affixes (Norde 2009: 22). With reference to (19c), Aijmer (1997: 4) says that "speech-act adverbials," which include DMs, "occupy a separate tone unit after the main message."[27] Most authors converge on (19d), maintaining that, rather than to a reduction in scope, pragmaticalization leads to scope extension (e.g., Auer and Günthner 2005: 338; Brinton and Traugott 2005: 138; Norde 2009: 22) (see Section 1.3).

(19e) is captured in a number of different ways. Frank-Job (2006: 366) points out that "the content of an utterance is not altered if the DM is removed," and for Aijmer (1997: 3), truth conditionality "is of overriding importance for distinguishing grammatical(ized) and pragmatic(alized) expressions." (19f) refers to some unusual properties compared to "canonical" grammatical categories: Norde (2009: 22) in particular maintains that DMs do not belong to the categories traditionally considered "grammatical," that

---

[26] We are grateful to Maj-Britt Mosegaard Hansen (personal communication of January 24, 2020) for having reminded us of this.

[27] "Speech-act adverbials" include expletives and epithets (*you bastard*, *Oh God*) and adverbial expressions like *frankly speaking*, *to tell you the truth*, *you know*, *I think*, *if I may say so*, etc.) (Aijmer 1997: 4).

they do not become part of a paradigm,[28] and that "they do not become rule-governed" (i.e., there is no obligatorification). With reference to (19g), Frank-Job (2006: 366) points out that "the content of an utterance is not altered if the DM is removed" (see also Aijmer 1997: 3; Jucker 2002: 212; Waltereit 2002: 1005).[29] On account of such observations, Waltereit (2002) concludes with reference to Lehmann's ([1982] 2015) parameters of grammaticalization:

(20)   Hence, from an orthodox Lehmannian perspective, the rise of DMs cannot
         count as grammaticalization, because only two of its criterial properties (both
         of which belong to the paradigmatic axis) are fulfilled.
                                                                    (Waltereit 2002: 1005)

But there are also features pointed out in work on pragmaticalization that are compatible with a grammaticalization analysis (see e.g., Traugott 1995; 2007; Brinton 2017: 31–32 for discussion). According to Aijmer (1997: 5), this applies to the principles of specialization, divergence, layering, and renewal (see Hopper 1991: 22; Hopper and Traugott 1993: 113). Another one concerns high frequency of use (Frank-Job 2006: 364), which is widely held to be a paradigm feature of grammaticalized items, even if it is not uncontroversial. Furthermore, Frank-Job (2006: 366) observes that pragmaticalized items are characterized by "co-occurence in contiguity," that is, a DM can cooccur with the corresponding sentence grammar unit in the same utterance. Note, however, that the same can also be observed in grammaticalization, e.g., when the English future tense marker *be going to* co-occurs with its lexical source, the verb *to go*, in the same sentence (*He's going to go home soon*).

The concept of pragmaticalization, or "pragmaticization," has been used by Hayashi and Yoon (2006; 2010) to also account for what is commonly referred to as (hesitation) fillers, that is, markers corresponding to English *uh* and *um*; we will return to this issue in Section 8.5.

Pragmaticalization as an explanatory concept has been the subject of some debate in research on the rise of DMs. For example, Detges and Waltereit (2016) do not find it to be a useful concept since it is said to obscure the differences between DMs and modal particles. And, while acknowledging that pragmaticalization constitutes a relevant mechanism needed to understand the diachronic behavior of DMs, some authors propose to include it as a subclass of grammaticalization (Prévost 2011: 391). A change in view on the status of pragmaticalization can be observed in the work of Brinton: In her earlier work she observed that "[p]ragmaticalization, it seems to me, is just a subspecies of grammaticalization, not a distinct process" (Brinton 2010a: 64). Subsequently, however,

---

[28] But see also Haselow (2015: 180–81) on English *anyway*.
[29] As rightly pointed out in work on Relevance Theory (e.g., Schourup 1999: 231–32), however, the interpretation of an utterance would not be the same if a DM were removed.

she seems to have reconsidered the significance of pragmaticalization, as (21) indicates.

(21)   In this view, then, the development of pragmatic markers falls naturally under the rubric of grammaticalization, and pragmaticalization can be dispensed with altogether.

(Brinton 2017: 35)

A similar stance on pragmaticalization is found in Traugott (2007: 151), where she observes that "Occam's Razor suggests that 'pragmaticalization' is unnecessary as a separate type of change." And she furthermore notes that by adding that "some degree of pragmaticalization will be found in any change involving function as well as form, including the development of standard examples of grammaticalization such as auxiliaries" (Traugott 2007: 152). However, one may wonder whether the notion of grammaticalization is really comparable to that proposed in studies on pragmaticalization, and whether auxiliaries develop into "metatextual" markers, as DMs do.

In sum, proponents of pragmaticalization have identified a catalog of properties in DMs that are hard to reconcile with grammaticalization, and it seems that proponents of the all-grammaticalization hypothesis did not quite give these findings the kind of attention they deserve. It is the pragmaticalization hypothesis that revealed the main problems facing the all-grammaticalization view, and it encouraged us to look for alternative ways of solving these problems.

1.2.3   Lexicalization

In another line of explaining the peculiar behavior of DMs, attention is drawn to the end product of their development: Many DMs are transparently derived from morphologically complex phrasal or clausal expressions but end up as mono-morphemic, unanalyzable forms; in short, they move toward univerbation (Lehmann [1982] 2015: 89; Haspelmath 2011) or, as is suggested in that line of research, they undergo lexicalization.

Already alluded to in earlier work (e.g., Aijmer 1997), the lexicalization hypothesis is most strongly associated with the work of Wischer (2000) and Fischer (2007a; 2007b), but mention of it has also been made in other studies (e.g., Schiffrin 1987: 319). And it has not only been proposed for English and other European languages. As Rhee (2004: 419–20) demonstrates, lexicalization can also be observed in Korean, even if mainly found in the grammaticalization from interrogative pronouns and constructions to indefinite adverbs, or from clausal structures to invariable forms, as illustrated in (22).

(22)   Korean (Rhee 2019: 1)
        kuleha-n-tA-ey   >   *kuntey*
        be.so-SIM-place-at   "then; but"

Using the English DM *methinks* as an example, Wischer (2000) observes that an originally productive construction consisting of the combination of clause-initial recipient plus impersonal verb becomes fossilized and unproductive, stored as a whole in the lexicon as a "symbol," thereby enriching the lexicon. The process is interpreted by her as "the symbolification of a former free collocation" (Wischer 2000: 364): *Methinks*, she argues, is stored in the lexicon and classified as an "adverb" (see also Brinton 2017: 166).

At the same time, Wischer is also aware that the process cannot be reduced to lexicalization; rather, she adds that there is also grammaticalization since the latter may also involve coalescence and fossilization.

Arguing that DMs are the result of pragmaticalization, Claridge (2013: 180) concludes that English DMs like *as it were, so to speak/say*, and *if you like* can also be classified as lexicalized forms of the idiomatization subtype, having formal and semantic properties that are not completely derivable or predictable from the constituents of the construction or the word formation pattern (cf. Brinton and Traugott 2005: 96): Since they need to be learned as chunks, they are said to be part of the lexicon.

Another form of the lexicalization hypothesis is proposed by Fischer (2007b), who draws attention to the fact that phrases like *I think* do not follow the usual parameters of grammaticalization. Based on the observation that, in non-standardized languages, epistemic parentheticals are likely to form one lexical unit in the course of time, and that morphological bonding may occur, Fischer (2007a: 308–11; 2007b) argues that it is lexicalization rather than grammaticalization that can be held responsible for the growth of DMs and related parentheticals:

> Taking all of the above into account, I conclude that parenthetical phrases like *I think* etc. are best seen as formulaic tokens, undergoing lexicalization rather than grammaticalization. In this process, they lose some referential content, being narrowed down to a more epistemic, evaluative meaning. (Fischer 2007a: 117)

Reservations about the lexicalization hypothesis have been expressed most of all by proponents of the all-grammaticalization hypothesis. Thus, Brinton and Traugott (2005: 108) say:

> (23)   A major distinguishing feature between lexicalization and grammaticalization is the difference in output; lexicalized items move to the lexical pole on the lexical–grammatical continuum while grammaticalized items go the other way. In the former process, the item becomes more semantically contentful through "concretion," i.e., 'the addition of concrete meaning."

Another critical review of Fischer's lexicalization hypothesis, pointing in the same direction, can be found in Brinton (2017: 33–34, 166). Brinton (2017: 166) argues in particular that there is no appropriate evidence for treating epistemic parentheticals as "lexical units," as they do not constitute a major lexical category, and what appears to be involved is univerbation rather than lexicalization. And she adds that a "number of the central features that pragmatic markers share with the grammaticalization process are not found in the process of lexicalization" (Brinton 2017: 33). Furthermore, like Van Bogaert (2011: 317), she notes that there is an increase in productivity typical of grammaticalization but not of lexicalization.

In spite of all the problems that have been pointed out with reference to the lexicalization hypothesis, the boundary between grammaticalization and lexicalization in expressions developing into DMs and related discourse material such as rhetorical questions is at times hard to trace (see Rhee 2004). Furthermore, while it is widely assumed that DMs are grammatical rather than lexical units, this position is not entirely unproblematic. DMs differ from (other) grammatical units, for example, on account of their morphosyntactic independence, and are in fact treated by some as lexical units.[30]

1.2.4   Cooptation

Observing that studies on both grammaticalization and pragmaticalization have identified a number of properties characterizing the rise and development of DMs, Heine (2013, 2018a) argues that neither of the two on its own provides a comprehensive account to understand the nature of this process. On the basis of work on (paren)theticals (Kaltenböck, Heine, and Kuteva 2011; Heine et al. 2013), it is argued that one important force involved is provided by cooptation, a cognitive–communicative operation whereby a text segment such as a clause, a phrase, or a word is transferred from the domain or level of sentence grammar and deployed for use on the level of discourse organization (see Section 2.3).

For example, the sentence *Paris is, you probably know that, not the most attractive city in the world* contains the text segment *you probably know that*, which has been coopted and inserted in that sentence for purposes of discourse processing. Once such a text segment has been coopted, its meaning no longer relates to the propositional content of the sentence but rather is determined by the situation of discourse. It is no longer a syntactic constituent of its host sentence in the sense that it is not part of the argument structure of the verb or the syntactic hierarchy of the sentence. Furthermore, it tends to be set off prosodically, and to have wider semantic–pragmatic scope, becoming "a device of metatextual planning" (Heine 2013: 1239, 2018a: 39).

---

[30] Thus, Aijmer (2016: 30) concludes that "discourse markers are good examples of lexical items which are flexible and context-bound and therefore get their meaning only in the speaker–hearer negotiation."

Thus, coopted units exhibit grammatical properties that were pointed out in studies on pragmaticalization (see Section 1.2.2). Subsequent to cooptation, some of these units are used frequently and grammaticalize into DMs, thereby acquiring in addition also properties that are in accordance with parameters of grammaticalizaton. On the cooptation hypothesis, then, the rise and development of DMs is the result of the joint effect of two different mechanisms, as captured in (24).

(24)   Hypothesized development of discourse markers (Heine 2013: 1238–39)
         (Grammaticalization >) cooptation > grammaticalization

As is argued by Heine (2013: 1239), the development sketched in (24) is compatible with the pragmaticalization hypothesis that was discussed in Section 1.2.2 to the extent that pragmaticalization is interpreted not as a distinct process but rather as a combination of cooptation followed by grammaticalization.

The cooptation hypothesis has not gone unchallenged. Considering that the development of DMs is a long and gradual process, Degand and Evers-Vermeul (2015: 72) and Brinton (2017: 37) have problems with the character of cooptation as a "spontaneous" or "sudden" operation. As pointed out in Heine (2013; 2018a), however, cooptation constitutes only one step in the history of DMs, even if a dramatic one, while "the gradual rise of linguistic expressions as discourse markers" (Degand and Evers-Vermeul 2015: 72) is the result of grammaticalization, in accordance with the scenario in (24). Furthermore, in a strict sense cooptation is also a gradual process, extending from the first usage of a coopted expression to its eventual conventionalization (see the innovation model in (11) of Section 2.3).

1.2.5   Constructionalization

Instead of studying DMs in discourse at large or in isolation, they are analyzed in the model of construction grammar in terms of constructions having non-compositional meaning, that is, of stored pairings of form and function. Based on this model (Goldberg 1995; 2006; Croft 2001), a new way of looking at grammatical change is proposed in work that we will refer to summarily as diachronic construction grammar (see especially Hilpert 2008; 2013; Trousdale 2008; Traugott and Trousdale 2013; 2014). To this end, labels such as constructional change and constructionalization have been proposed to account for grammatical developments, which have traditionally been to some extent the concern of grammaticalization theory (see also Hilpert and Saavedra 2018).[31]

---

[31] Hilpert (2013: 16) defines "constructional change" thus: "Constructional change selectively seizes a conventionalized form-meaning pair of a language, altering it in terms of its form, its function,

Compared to other approaches, diachronic construction grammar provides a more global perspective of grammatical change. What the various constructionalist approaches to diachrony have in common is an understanding of grammatical change as "the sum of many individual metamorphoses of symbolic units," as Hilpert (2013: 3) puts it. Such a semantics-oriented view is in accordance with the micro-mechanism involved in producing grammatical change including grammaticalization such as described by Stein (2020).

Via constructionalization, or constructional change, it is argued in this framework, new symbolic associations of form and meaning are established. These associations may also include DMs, which are understood to be "atomic constructions" internal to larger constructions. In fact, many of the changes that have been identified in the development of DMs can also be described in terms of notions provided by the model of construction grammar, more specifically by using approaches such as constructional grammaticalization (e.g., Trousdale 2008; Van Bogaert 2011), constructional change (e.g., Hilpert 2013), or constructionalization (Traugott and Trousdale 2013).

Some forms of this general model have also been recruited to understand the development of DMs and related theticals. For example, van Bogaert (2011) approaches the study of complement-taking mental predicates (*I suppose, I believe, I reckon, I expect, I understand, I guess, I imagine,* and *I realize*) from the point of view of constructional grammaticalization, which, as she argues, "accommodates the grammatical peculiarities that disqualify them as canonical cases of grammaticalization" (van Bogaert 2011: 325). Traugott and Trousdale (2013: 110–12) show how the English adverb *beside(s)* developed into a DM ("discourse particle"), and Shibasaki (2018) observes that grammaticalization theory is unable to account for the structural changes of the Japanese DM *jijitsu* and decides to rely on diachronic construction grammar instead.

Findings made by students of construction grammar have provided a plethora of new insights into mechanisms leading to grammaticalization and, thus, provide an important tool for describing what happens in the development of grammatical structures. More than any other approach that we are aware of, diachronic construction grammar provides a fairly comprehensive understanding of changing grammatical markers in the context of constructional configurations.

---

any aspect of its frequency, its distribution in the linguistic community, or any combination of these." As this definition indicates, diachronic construction grammar is not restricted to linguistic phenomena but has also a strong "pragmatic" component. Traugott and Trousdale (2014: 257) make a distinction between "constructionalization" and "constructional change." The former is defined as the development of pairs of new forms with new meanings, irrespective of whether these are specific (i.e., substantive) signs or whether they are schemas. Constructional changes, by contrast, are restricted to "changes to features of extant constructions," that is, typically to only one component of a construction. As these definitions show, "constructional change" refers to different phenomena depending on which author is concerned. Unless stated otherwise, the term is used here in the more comprehensive sense of Hilpert (2013: 16).

In spite of all its merits, however, the framework is hard-pressed when it comes to answering the question that is the central concern of the present book, namely the following: How do DMs come to develop from expressions that are firmly integrated in the structure of a sentence to expressions that are neither semantically nor syntactically nor prosodically integrated – in other words, how do DMs acquire the set of properties they have, in particular the ones that we discussed in Section 1.1.1 (see also Section 1.5)?

We may illustrate this problem with the example of English *beside(s)*, discussed by Traugott and Trousdale (2013: 109–12) as a case of grammatical constructionalization (see Section 1.3.2.2 for more detailed discussion). Being historically derived from a Middle English adverb of sentence grammar, *beside(s)* developed into a clause-initial DM ("discourse particle"). Traugott and Trousdale (2013: 111) argue that this is an example of functionally induced "syntactic expansion." We assume that "syntactic expansion" means changing from syntactically less expanded to syntactically more expanded status, but not necessarily to syntactically unattached status, as it is characteristic of DMs. It remains in fact unclear how syntactic expansion could have led to a process whereby *beside(s)* acquired its grammatical properties as a DM, no longer being a syntactic constituent of the sentence, having metatextual function, and being apparently set off prosodically from the rest of the sentence.

To conclude, there still remain questions that need to be answered in order to turn diachronic construction grammar into a viable framework that is able to explain why DMs are structured the way they are.

1.2.6   Other Lines of Research

The explanatory concepts sketched in the preceding sections do not exhaust the range of approaches and terminologies that have been proposed to understand how DMs evolved and why they are structured the way they are.

Some of such alternative approaches recruited can in some way or other be linked to frameworks discussed earlier. For example, for Vincent, Votre, and LaForest (1993) the development of DMs can be described synchronically with the term "post-grammaticalization" (see Section 1.2.1). Simon-Vandenbergen and Willems (2011: 361) suggest that the development into more autonomous DMs with a clear pragmatic and discursive function is a case of "macrosyntactic grammaticalization," while Bolly and Degand (2013: 210) and Noora and Amouzadeh (2015: 94) propose the term "proceduralization" for the change from conceptual to procedural content. On the other hand, there are also approaches that can be related to work on pragmaticalization, such as the studies on reanalysis by Waltereit (2006), on discoursivization by Ocampo

(2006: 317), and on discursization by Claridge and Arnovick (2010: 183) (see Section 1.2.2).

Finally, the development of DMs has also been approached by means of alternative methodologies. Mention may be made in particular that, rather than having to decide between concepts like grammaticalization and pragmaticalization, Barth-Weingarten and Couper-Kuhlen (2002: 357) suggest viewing the development of DMs from the perspective of prototype theory and Taylor's notion of family resemblance (Taylor 1989: 108-21), looking at the status of DMs with reference to relative degrees of prototypicality.

1.3   Concepts and Questions

1.3.1   General Observations

As we saw in Section 1.2, there are a number of different mechanisms to account for DMs, but two main mechanisms stand out in the relevant literature, namely those of pragmaticalization and grammaticalization. With regard to the relationship between the two, a number of positions have been maintained. The most detailed analysis of the mechanisms and explanatory accounts is that by Degand and Evers-Vermeul (2015: 62), who propose the following list of hypotheses, building on Ocampo (2006):

(25)   Hypotheses on mechanisms responsible for the development of DMs according to Degand and Evers-Vermeul (2015: 62)
    a Grammaticalization
    b A special type of grammaticalization, namely pragmaticalization
    c Pragmaticalization
    d Sometimes grammaticalization, sometimes pragmaticalization
    e Neither grammaticalization nor pragmaticalization.

The relationship between grammaticalization and pragmaticalization is reduced by Heine (2013: 1219) to the following three positions: (i) The two are different mechanisms, (ii) pragmaticalization is a subtype of grammaticalization, and (iii) there is no pragmaticalization.

According to (i), pragmaticalization and grammaticalization are different phenomena and each should be understood and described in its own right (see Erman and Kotsinas 1993; Aijmer 1997; Günthner 1999; Günthner and Mutz 2004: 98; Onodera 2004: 14; Frank-Job 2006; Ocampo 2006; Norde 2009; Defour et al. 2010; Beijering 2012: 205). While not using the term, some notion related to pragmaticalization also surfaces in the work of Waltereit (2002: 1004–1006, 2006: 74), referred to as "reanalysis." Drawing on the parameters of Lehmann ([1982] 2015), he finds that DMs undergo neither paradigmaticization, obligatorification, condensation, coalescence, nor fixation. Accordingly, they should not be treated as instances of grammaticalization.[32]

According to (ii), pragmaticalization constitutes a subtype of grammaticalization (Wischer 2000; Barth-Weingarten and Couper-Kuhlen 2002: 357). Thus, Wischer (2000) argues that processes relating to pragmaticalization should be assigned to one subtype of grammaticalization that deals with text and discourse level phenomena (her "grammaticalization II"). Similarly, Barth-Weingarten and Couper-Kuhlen (2002: 357) treat the development of discourse functions of final *though* in English as an instance of pragmaticalization, suggesting that the latter ought to be subsumed as a specific subtype under the broad umbrella of grammaticalization. Another kind of position (ii) can be seen in the stance taken by Giacalone Ramat and Mauri (2011), who propose to distinguish between standard and nonstandard grammaticalization. Unlike the former, the latter concerns developments that pose problems to the parameters of Lehmann ([1982] 2015), such as that of Italian *tuttavia* "however" from temporal adverbial to textual connective.

According to (iii), that is, the "all-grammaticalization hypothesis," DMs are indubitably "part of the grammar" (Onodera 1995; Brinton 1996; Pinto de Lima 2002; Traugott and Dasher 2002: 158–59; Brinton and Traugott 2005: 139) – that is, there is no need to treat them separately from grammaticalization since the latter also involves "pragmatics." Consequently, grammaticalization theory is claimed to also take care of phenomena commonly subsumed under the term pragmaticalization, even if this position requires an extended notion of grammaticalization (Traugott 1995; Hansen 1998b; Lenker 2000; Traugott and Dasher 2002; Brinton and Traugott 2005: 136–40; Brinton 2008; Diewald 2011a; 2011b; Prévost 2011; Van Bogaert 2011).

1.3.2   On Re-defining Grammaticalization

For good reasons, students of DMs draw attention to the fact that these markers are hard to reconcile with the conventional machinery of devices commonly employed to describe and understand grammaticalization. Waltereit (2002: 1006), for example, observes that "there seems to be a very important difference between the rise of DMs and grammaticalization: The source constructions of DMs are very often syntactically independent by themselves." This observation has generated quite some research activity, resulting in a number of stimulating hypotheses, as we saw in our summary of this activity in Section 1.2. According to the predominant stance surfacing from this research, the

---

[32] At the same time, Waltereit (2002: 1006) also observes that "[p]aradigmaticization is a natural side-effect of the recruitment to a functional class, be this a category of grammar or the category of discourse markers."

most reasonable conclusion to be drawn from this situation is to expand the concept of grammaticalization to the extent that it also takes care of the rise and development of DMs.

This is the stance adopted by scholars adhering to what we dubbed in Section 1.2 the all-grammaticalization hypothesis. They make a distinction between two perspectives of grammaticalization, namely between a narrow or restricted and a wider or expanded view of grammaticalization, and it is the latter view that is needed to account for DMs (especially Traugott 1995; Traugott and Dasher 2002; Brinton and Traugott 2005: 136–40; Brinton 2008; Degand and Simon-Vandenbergen 2011: 290; Degand and Evers-Vermeul 2015: 77). A further elaboration of this view is presented by Traugott and Trousdale (2013: 99–112) with their distinction between grammaticalization viewed as reduction and increase in dependency and grammaticalization viewed as expansion.

The ultimate goal in much of this work appears to be to dispense with the traditional "narrow" view and re-define grammaticalization as expansion. The question then is: What is the evidence in support of such a re-definition? This is not a trivial issue since it is not restricted to the study of DMs but has implications for grammaticalization theory in general. We will look into this question in the remainder of the present section.

1.3.2.1 Problematic Features

The first seminal study proposing a wider perspective of grammaticalization is that by Traugott (1995: 14). The evidence in support of that proposal rests essentially on two arguments, already mentioned in Section 1.2.1.1, namely that the development of DMs violates two widely accepted criteria for grammaticalization, namely syntactic increase in scope and disjunction (Traugott 1995: 14). These arguments are now looked at in turn.

Scope

With "syntactic increase in scope," or "increase in syntactic scope," Traugott (1995: 4) refers most of all to the notion of "structural scope" as proposed by Lehmann ([1982] 2015: 152), who argues that grammaticalization is characterized by a decrease rather than an increase in scope.

The question of increase in scope, or scope expansion, generally constitutes a problematic issue in grammaticalization studies and is in need of a more detailed analysis (see also Unger 1996). For the purposes of the present study, suffice it to draw attention to the fact that there are different views on what "scope" exactly stands for. It would seem that there are at least three different notions that need to be distinguished, namely the ones in (26).

(26)   Notions of scope
         a Syntactic scope
         b Structural scope
         c Semantic–pragmatic scope

Syntactic scope is an important issue in some formal models of linguistics. Originally a logical–semantic term, relating to the application of operators, the term scope entered generative grammar at the beginning of the 1970s (see Narrog 2020). Thus, in some schools of generative grammar, grammaticalization is argued to entail a change from movement to a higher category to late merge and, hence, to scope expansion (van Gelderen 1993; 2004; Roberts and Roussou 2003). In the model of Role and Reference Grammar, grammaticalization-induced change corresponds to a shift from being an expression with scope over the nucleus of a clause to scope over the whole clause (Matasović 2008: 49; Nicolle 2012). And in the model of Functional Discourse Grammar (Hengeveld and Mackenzie 2008; 2011), phenomena falling under the rubric of grammaticalization also have been analyzed as necessarily leading to increase rather than reduction of scope. On the last view, grammaticalization involves unidirectional scope increase both on the representational and on the interpersonal level – as Hengeveld (2017: 13) puts it: Processes of grammaticalization entail "a stepwise and systematic increase in scope" on the content side.

A paradigm example of the application of generative syntax to grammaticalization can be found in Tabor and Traugott (1998). In the "C-command Scope Increase Hypothesis" of these authors, scope is equated with c-command: If node A asymmetrically c-commands node B, then node A has greater scope than node B (Tabor and Traugott 1998: 233). For example, the authors argue that the modern English modal verbs occupy an auxiliary position, which dominates the verb phrase in which main verbs are generated, while the Old English ancestors of these modals were like main verbs and were presumably generated in the verb phrase. Accordingly the authors conclude, for example, that the position of the Present-Day English auxiliary *will* has scope over its predecessor, that is, the position of the Old English lexical verb *wille* "want" (Tabor and Traugott 1998: 234).

Syntactic scope, thus, tends to be based on constructs of specific formal theories, such as assumptions on the relative position within a syntactic tree structure: The higher up a category is located in the hierarchical structure posited by the theory, the wider its scope is. And since grammatical expressions are claimed to be higher up in the hierarchy than the lexical expressions from which they are derived, grammaticalization predictably leads to an increase in syntactic scope. Thus, to the extent that she may have had a theory of this kind in mind we fully endorse Traugott's (1995: 15) suggestion that "syntactic scope increases must be allowed for in a theory of grammaticalization": Increase in syntactic scope is a predictable effect of grammaticalization.

Even if not based on a syntactic perspective, a similar conclusion is reached in two formalized models of functionalist grammar tradition, namely Role-and-Reference-Grammar (Van Valin and LaPolla 1997) and Functional Discourse Grammar (Hengeveld and Mackenzie 2008; 2011). For example, Hengeveld observes:

> ... processes of grammaticalization, seen as a combination of contentive and formal change, follow predictable paths: on the content side they entail a stepwise and systematic increase in scope, while on the formal side they entail a stepwise and systematic decrease in lexicality. (Hengeveld 2017: 13)

Scope in this sense contrasts sharply with Lehmann's ([1982] 2015: 152–53) notion of "structural scope," which is based on what he calls the "level of grammatical construction." Structural scope, as conceived by Lehmann, has little in common with earlier concepts of scope – be they syntactically or semantically defined, it relates to degrees of morphosyntactic inclusiveness, being concerned with the relative size of morphosyntactic constituents; as Narrog (2020) shows, it is ultimately a morphological rather than a semantic or a syntactic notion. For example, the structural scope of a Turkish case suffix extends over the preceding NP, but the structural scope of a Latin case suffix extends only over the noun; hence, Turkish case suffixes are claimed to have wider structural scope than Latin case suffixes. In a similar way, an auxiliary "functions at the VP level" whereas the verb from which it is derived via grammaticalization functions at the clause level. Accordingly, when the verb grammaticalizes into an auxiliary there is a decrease in structural scope from the clause level to the VP level.

In sum, syntactic scope of the kind sketched here predictably involves an increase in scope in grammaticalization. Cases of structural scope such as the ones adduced by Lehmann, by contrast, tend to have the opposite effect, leading to scope reduction from clause level to phrase level (NP or VP), and from phrase level to word level, as pointed out by Lehmann ([1982] 2015). This difference between syntactic and structural scope can be illustrated with the following example. One of the paradigm cases used by students of grammaticalization concerns the development from lexical verbs serving as main clausal predicates, as English *go (to)* does in (27a), into auxiliaries for functions of aspect, tense, or modality, like the future tense marker in (27b).

(27)   English
    a *Jane is **going to** Paris.*
    b *Jane is **going to** come soon.*

Relying on some notion of syntactic scope, Traugott (1995: 15) suggests that "developments of lexical verbs into auxiliaries can also be regarded as involving increase in syntactic scope (a shift from V > I, or reanalysis of a lexical as a functional head, see Roberts 1993)."

On the basis of structural scope, by contrast, the development of lexical verbs into auxiliaries is interpreted as involving a decrease from clause level to phrase level, rather than an increase in scope. Thus, when the lexical verb *go (to)* in (27a) is grammaticalized into a future tense auxiliary, as in (27b), its structural scope is said to have been reduced from the level of the clause to that of the verb phrase (Lehmann [1982] 2015: 152).

But the status of structural scope in grammaticalization is problematic. While Lehmann ([1982] 2015: 152–53) had claimed that it generally decreases, as it did in fact in example (27b), this is not always the case. A crosslinguistically fairly widespread kind of exception is provided by adverbs, adpositions, case markers, or markers of nominalization when they grammaticalize into markers of clause subordination (see Kuteva et al. 2019). Now, the former kinds of markers have structural scope over noun phrases or nouns while the latter markers have structural scope over (subordinate) clauses – hence, there is an increase in structural scope in the grammaticalization from phrases or words to clauses. For example, when the English preposition *like* (as in *She looks **like** her father*) was grammaticalized by the fourteenth century into a conjunction (*This is a pizza **like** I have never eaten before*), its structural scope increased from noun phrase to clause (see D'Arcy 2017: 60–61). For another kind of increase in structural scope, see Norde (2009: 126–29).

Furthermore, Norde (2009) demonstrates that there are also examples where structural scope remains stable, that is, where it does not change in grammaticalization. Accordingly, *pace* Lehmann ([1982] 2015: 152–53), structural scope does not really qualify as being a directional feature in grammaticalization, neither as a defining nor as a characterizing feature (see also Traugott and Trousdale 2013: 106): It may either decrease, remain unchanged, or increase.

But there is another, even more important observation. As we saw earlier in this section, syntactic scope operates over hierarchically organized syntactic tree structures, while structural scope operates over clauses and their constituents. The question now is: How do DMs relate to these two types of scope? There is an obvious, even if perhaps surprising answer: DMs have neither syntactic nor structural scope, for the following reason: DMs were defined in (7) of Section 1.1.2 as expressions that are syntactically independent, that is, they are not a syntactic part of the sentence or clause they are associated with (see also Section 1.4.3). This means that once a DM arises it loses its ability to signal syntactic or structural scope.

On this view then, the rise of DMs does not entail a change in the relative degree of scope features but rather experiences a change in kind, namely one from scope within some syntactic hierarchy or clause structure to loss of scope.

Instead of syntactic or structural scope, the notion proposed here is that of *semantic–pragmatic scope*, which defines the text segment that a DM functionally refers to, providing the semantic domain of operation of the DM (cf. Kaltenböck 2009: 56). Consider the example in (1), reprinted below as (28). The semantic–pragmatic scope of the sentence grammar unit *still* in example (28a) is limited by its function of an adverbial modifier (see also Swan 1982: 131), that is, the text segment *is still sick* forms a unit of semantic–pragmatic scope.[33] That of the DM *still* in (28b), by contrast, is wider: On the one hand, its scope refers to the proposition as a whole rather than a part of it. On the other hand, the domain of operation of scope extends beyond the proposition by referring to the situation of discourse, including the preceding and the following discourse piece, the attitudes of the speaker, and/or speaker–hearer interaction. That discourse piece may be implied rather than formally expressed, as seems to be the case in (28b), where the scope of *still* is likely to extend over the content of some unexpressed preceding piece of discourse.[34]

(28)   English (= (1))
    a *Jeff is **still** sick.*
    b ***Still**, Jeff is sick.*

Instead of the proposition as a whole, the semantic–pragmatic scope of a DM may also relate to some constituent of it – that is, it may be "subsentential" (Hansen 1998a: 73) or, as we will say here, constituent anchored. Thus, in example (29), the scope of the DM *well* is restricted to the following noun phrase *sex drive* (see Furkó 2014). Such cases of restricted scope are however ignored here, but we will return to them in Section 8.3, where the distinction between utterance anchored and constituent anchored DMs is discussed (see also Heine et al. 2017).

(29)   English (*Larry King Live*, March 14, 2004; Furkó 2014: 294)
    You're not going to have quality if you can't sleep and you itch and you bitch and you weep and you cry and you bloat and you can't remember anything and you don't have a, **well**, sex drive.

---

[33] According to some traditions of analysis, *still* in (28a) may be said to also have scope over the whole sentence. We are grateful to Heiko Narrog (personal communication of September 20, 2019) for having drawn our attention to this; see also Hansen (2008).

[34] In the following constructed example, the utterance *We should ask Jeff to take the kids to school* illustrates what the "preceding discourse" may consist of:

    A: *We should ask Jeff to take the kids to school.*
    B: *Still, Jeff is sick.*

Accordingly, when using the term "scope" in the present book this will, first, concern exclusively semantic–pragmatic scope. And, second, it will, on the one hand, be with reference to the behavior of scope relative to the host of a DM, which typically is the host proposition of the DM (that is, *Jeff is sick* in example (28b)), or a phrasal unit, as in (29). And, on the other hand, it will also concern the semantic–pragmatic scope of DMs beyond the proposition to larger parts of discourse. Thus, in (28b) it also concerns the content of the preceding discourse, which is essential for fully understanding the range of text to which the DM *still* refers.

Semantic–pragmatic scope thus has a double function, relating, on the one hand, to the host of a DM and, on the other hand, to its anchoring[35] (Heine et al. 2017). A similar understanding of scope has been proposed by Swan (1982) in his discussion of the thetical (extra-clausal) usage of the English adverb *sadly* (as in *Sadly, Alex lost the election*):

We may, perhaps, define the scope of an adverb as that which the adverb modifies, and expand the definition to cover not only linear modification (to the right and to the left) but also a great many relations (semantic and pragmatic) holding between an adverb and various other meta-linguistic and extra-linguistic elements. (Swan 1982: 131)

We will return to this issue in Section 1.4.5.

Disjunction

The second term invoked by Traugott (1995) is disjunction. It seems to stand mainly for syntactic detachment and freedom of an expression.[36] Disjunction is said "to occur in very specific syntactic and pragmatic domains – that of expressions the prime purpose of which is metatextual" (Traugott 1995: 14). Assuming that our interpretation is correct, then it stands exactly for the opposite of what is commonly observed in grammaticalization: It involves syntactic detachment rather than integration (cf. the definition of DMs in (7) of Section 1.1.2). At the same time, syntactic detachment is one of the paradigm features in the development of DMs, and the same applies to the rise of metatextual functions: As we will see in Section 1.4.3, both changes commonly take place when a linguistic expression is deployed for use as a DM. In short, "disjunction" in this case is incompatible with grammaticalization.

---

[35] The function of "anchoring" is described by Heine et al. (2017: 821) thus: "Via anchoring, the speaker establishes a semantic–pragmatic link either to a particular piece in the discourse or to a specific context."

[36] The term is not defined by Traugott (1995). For Quirk et al. (1985: 613), disjuncts "have a superior role as compared with the sentence expressions; they are syntactically more detached and in some respects 'superordinate,' in that they seem to have a scope that extends over the sentence as a whole." Tabor and Traugott (1998: 254) characterize DMs thus: "Typically they are disjunctive, requiring comma intonation, and they occur externally to SAdvs, [...]."

Scope expansion and disjunction, however, are not the only issues that the discussion by Traugott (1995) raises. Thus, when arguing that bonding and decrease in syntactic freedom should not be taken to be criterial for grammaticalization she presents cases of decliticization in Indo-European languages and Estonian as evidence (Traugott 1995: 3). For example, the Estonian free particles *ep* (emphatic) and *es* (interrogative) are known to be historically derived from clitics (Campbell 1991). Thus, they are instances of what Norde (2009: 201–4) calls debonding, that is, a change from bound morpheme to free morpheme. However, debonding is not a case of grammaticalization but rather of its opposite: It constitutes a subtype of *degrammaticalization* rather than grammaticalization (Norde 2009: 186).

In sum, some of the evidence provided by Traugott in arguing for a notion of grammaticalization that includes an increase in syntactic scope and disjunction must be taken with care. Most importantly, it would seem that in order to appreciate Traugott's argumentation it is important to distinguish changes that can be related to grammaticalization from changes that cannot. Take the following example:

(30)   Even though DMs become syntactically disjunct, and thereby may be used with special stress, they may be segmentally reduced (/ndid, nfækt, bsaidz/). This too is a process typical of grammaticalization (cf. reduction of <u>have to</u> > <u>hafta</u>).

(Traugott 1995: 14)

The two features addressed in (30) are (a) becoming "syntactically disjunct," on the one hand, and (b) becoming "segmentally reduced," on the other. Here (a) concerns the *external status* of an emerging DM, involving a shift from syntactic constituent of a sentence to syntactically unattached status, which contradicts what is commonly found in grammaticalization. By contrast, (b) relates to its *internal status*, which is in fact shaped by parameters of grammaticalization: When used recurrently, the internal form of an expression can be grammaticalized. In this way, an expression like *in fact* lost, for example, the internal morphological boundary between its two constituents *in* and *fact* (decategorialization) and was optionally reduced phonologically to /nfækt/ (erosion), turning into an invariable DM, as described by Traugott (1995).[37] Thus, (a) and (b) need to be separated, being the result of two contrasting mechanisms of discourse processing, as we will see in Chapter 2.

To conclude, it would seem that Traugott's (1995) treatment of grammaticalization is not without problems in that it does not always clearly distinguish phenomena that are related to grammaticalization from phenomena

---

[37] Concerning the grammaticalization parameters of decategorialization and erosion, see Section 2.2.2.

that are not. For example, she uses cases of decliticization from clitics to free forms, such as that of Indo-European relative, indefinite, and interrogative clitics, or that of Estonian *ep* and *es*, in order to establish that increase in syntactic scope belongs to grammaticalization. Ignoring the fact that grammaticalization generally leads to an increase in syntactic scope, as we saw earlier in this section, decliticization has been shown *not* to belong to grammaticalization, being an instance of degrammaticalization (Norde 2009: 201–4) – in short, a feature that has been shown to be the opposite of grammaticalization is adduced as evidence for grammaticalization.

Neither syntactic scope expansion nor increase in syntactic freedom ("disjunction") as they can be observed in DMs seem to be relevant criteria to argue for a wider perspective of grammaticalization. The former is not a discriminating feature since it does not apply to DMs, as we saw earlier in this section. And the latter does not apply because it is a characteristic of many types of degrammaticalization but not of grammaticalization. We will return to this issue in Section 1.4.

1.3.2.2 Reduction versus Expansion

We mentioned in Section 1.2.1.1 that Traugott and Trousdale (2013: 99–112) propose a distinction between two models, or approaches, or views of grammaticalization, summarized in (31).

(31)   Two views on grammaticalization (Traugott and Trousdale 2013: 99–112)
        a GR: grammaticalization is viewed as reduction and increase in
           dependency
        b GE: grammaticalization is viewed as expansion

In the model underlying (31a), referred to by the authors in short with the acronym "GR," grammaticalization is viewed as a reduction and increase in dependency, while the second model, called "GE," views it as expansion.[38] Examples cited for GR are claimed to include Givón (1979), Lehmann (2004, [1982] 2015), Heine and Reh (1984), Heine, Claudi and Hünnemeyer (1991), Bybee, Perkins, and Pagliuca (1994), Haspelmath (2004), and Boye and Harder (2012). GE is said to be the one used by Traugott after 1995, as well as a number of other authors (Elizabeth Traugott, personal communication).

It is most of all two kinds of evidence that the authors adduce in support of their distinction. On the one hand, they argue that there is a difference in the features of grammatical change highlighted; on the other hand, they suggest that GR and GE rely on different defining criteria.[39]

---

[38] For an appraisal of the distinction, see Heine (2018a). A critical review of Traugott and Trousdale (2013) is found in Börjars, Vincent, and Walkden (2015).

[39] In a personal communication of January 12, 2020, Elizabeth Traugott reminds us that the two models look at the same phenomenon from two different perspectives, where GR asks the

With regard to the former, Traugott and Trousdale (2013) propose a catalog of distinguishing features, in particular the ones now looked at in turn. As argued in Heine (2018a: 26–31), however, none of the features is entirely unproblematic. The following summarizes the main points made in Heine (2018a).

(a) Traugott and Trousdale (2013: 101) claim that the "concept of grammar adopted by many of the founders of the GR approach [...] until recently typically did not embrace such grammatical categories as topic and focus." This claim is questioned by Heine (2018a: 26), who draws attention to the fact that issues of information structure formed an important part in the work of these "founders" (in particular Givón 1975; 1979). Furthermore, Heine and Reh (1984) discuss not only the grammaticalization of both topic (theme) and focus categories but also the syntactic implications that these processes have for the languages concerned.

(b) Furthermore, Traugott and Trousdale (2013: 105–6) claim that the loss-and-gain model is a characteristic of GE rather than of GR. As pointed out by Heine (2018a: 28), however, both the term and the model were developed in the GR tradition by Heine, Claudi, and Hünnemeyer (1991: 110).[40] According to this model, grammaticalization cannot be reduced to losses of linguistic material but also tends to gain new meanings resulting from context-induced reinterpretation.

(c) Traugott and Trousdale (2013: 109) observe that, unlike GR, GE asks questions about how grammaticalization occurs in context. According to Heine (2018a: 28), however, such questions were asked already in the GR framework of Bybee, Perkins, and Pagliuca (1994), where it was argued in detail that context-induced reinterpretation accounts for much of what happens in grammaticalization, and in Heine, Claudi, and Hünnemeyer (1991) one chapter is devoted exactly to this issue. The significance of context in grammaticalization was expounded in the context model of Heine (2002) and surfaces in generalizations such as the following:

(32)   In the same way that linguistic items undergoing grammaticalization lose in semantic, morphosyntactic, and phonetic substance, they also gain in properties characteristic of their uses in new contexts.

(Heine and Kuteva 2002: 2)

---

question of what evidence there is for unidirectional reduction and GE what the effects of the reduction are.

[40] Elizabeth Traugott (personal communication of January 19, 2020) rightly observes, however, that the notion of such a model was already in the air in Traugott (1988) and Sweetser (1988).

(d) Traugott and Trousdale maintain that GE differs from GR in that it is able to deal with context expansion.[41] For example, "a form that is reduced semantically and has paradigmatic functions ... will also be available for a larger range of syntactic uses, and therefore its syntactic contexts may expand" (Traugott and Trousdale 2013: 109). According to Heine (2018a: 29), on the other hand, this was already a much discussed topic in grammaticalization studies of the 1970s, resulting in a range of publications by Givón, Li, and others (e.g., Givón 1971; 1975; Li and Thompson 1974; see also the contributions in Li 1975, and Givón 2015).

Context extension (or expansion) was in fact one of the central topics of GR research. Especially Heine, Claudi, and Hünnemeyer (1991) and Bybee, Perkins, and Pagliuca (1994) describe examples of a number of semantically reduced forms undergoing context extension. Such examples, which are not only found in Europe but also in other parts of the world, include but are not restricted to new syntactic contexts. As has been shown in Heine and Reh (1984: 183–212), for example, semantic reduction (desemanticization; see Section 2.2.2, (6b)) may even be responsible for the rise of new word order patterns. Crosslinguistically more widespread examples include verbs meaning "say" in direct speech constructions: Once these verbs are semantically reduced they may in fact develop a range of syntactic functions such as serving as quotatives, complementizers, purpose and cause markers, giving rise to new forms of complement clauses and adverbial clauses (e.g., Saxena 1988; Heine, Claudi and Hünnemeyer 1991: 158–59; Klamer 2000).

Furthermore, Heine (2018a: 29) points out that already in the GR tradition, grammaticalization was not reduced to expansion or extension; rather, the methodology employed "rests on the assumption that grammaticalization is based on the interaction of pragmatic, semantic, morphosyntactic, and phonetic factors" (Heine and Kuteva 2007: 33–34).

(e) Traugott and Trousdale (2013: 101) also note that the concept of grammar adopted by many of the "founders" of the GR approach does not include pragmatic markers such as *well* or *moreover*. In fact, DMs (or pragmatic markers) played a minor role in GR studies. But they were never excluded from the work in those studies. For example, in their discussion of discourse functions, Heine, Claudi, and Hünnemeyer (1991: 187) say that "wherever it is possible to trace the etymology of discourse markers, they are likely to originate from lexical material within the 'real world'."

[41] Elizabeth Traugott (personal communication of January 19, 2020) notes that this point does not specifically relate to work done in the GR tradition but rather to a number of earlier studies which pay no attention to context.

(f) Traugott and Trousdale (2013: 108) maintain that the difference in perspective between GR and GE also surfaces in the following definition adopted in the GE approach:

(33)   Grammaticalization is the change whereby in certain contexts speakers use parts of a construction with a grammatical function. Over time, the resulting grammatical item may become more grammatical by acquiring more grammatical functions and expanding its host-classes.

(Brinton and Traugott 2005: 99)

As observed by Heine (2018a: 30), however, this definition is not only compatible but is also in accordance with research carried out using GR: First, it assumes that use in context and context extension (or host-class expansion) are crucial for the rise of new grammatical functions (see (e)). And, second, both kinds of approaches use the notion "construction" and, in both, this notion is used in a pre-theoretical sense.[42]

To conclude, with regard to the features listed, it seems hard to establish that there is an intrinsic difference between the two models distinguished by Traugott and Trousdale (2013).

With regard to the defining criteria of the two models, Traugott and Trousdale (2013) argue that it is exactly the two criteria suggested by Traugott (1995) that distinguish the two models, namely scope expansion and increase in syntactic freedom (or "disjunction"): Both criteria are said to apply to GE but not to GR. As we saw in Section 1.3.2.1, however, scope expansion – of the type proposed by Traugott (1995) – can also be observed in cases of grammaticalization that have been identified within the GR tradition, like the development of modal verbs from deontic to epistemic meaning (e.g., Bybee, Perkins, and Pagliuca 1994). Thus, scope expansion does not seem to be helpful to distinguish the two models.

Increase in syntactic freedom is, as Traugott and Trousdale (2013: 107–12) claim, related to context expansion, which they say is taken care of in the GE model but not in the GR model. We observed in Section 1.3.2.1, however, that context expansion (or context extension) is a paradigm feature of grammaticalization of any kind, it can be viewed as the driving force for new grammatical forms and constructions to arise, as expounded in the context

---

[42] With reference to the definition of Brinton and Traugott (2005: 99), Traugott and Trousdale (2013: 108) say that "'construction' is here used in the pre-theoretical sense of string, constituent." Heine and Kuteva (2002: 2) proposed the following definition: "Grammaticalization is defined as the development from lexical to grammatical forms and from grammatical to even more grammatical forms. And since the development of grammatical forms is not independent of the constructions to which they belong, the study of grammaticalization is also concerned with constructions and with even larger discourse segments." For more details on this definition, see Section 2.2.1.

extension model of Heine (2002) and the host class expansion model of Himmelmann (2004).

There remains a problem not addressed by Traugott and Trousdale (2013), namely that "context extension" in grammaticalization and in DMs does not seem to be of the same kind. Suffice it here to illustrate the difference with two English examples adduced by Traugott and Trousdale (2013: 107–12) to distinguish GE from GR.

The first example concerns the English expression *as long as*: The examples in (34) represent three different stages of grammaticalization as a result of context extension: (34a) shows the first stage, where *as long as* has the function of introducing a comparative measure phrase. In (34b) it is extended to clausal complements, where it serves as a temporal connective, and in (34c) it appears in sentence-initial position in a context where it can be understood to function as a conjunction of conditional protasis.

(34)   English (Traugott and Trousdale 2013: 107)
        a *This plank is **as long as** that one.*
        b *Hold it in place as **long as** it is needed.*
        c ***As long as** you leave by noon you will get there in time.*

Context extension thus can lead to new grammatical functions and word order arrangements. But, as grammaticalization theory would predict, such changes take place *within* the sentence. This is different in the case of the second example presented by Traugott and Trousdale (2013: 107–12), involving the expression *beside(s)*, already mentioned in another context in Section 1.2.5. Originating in a body part noun, also denoting the long surface of an object, *side* was used in Old English with a number of prepositions, including *be*. The expression underwent several processes of grammaticalization, e.g., giving rise to the preposition and the adverb *beside(s)* in Middle English. But in Middle English there was also a different kind of "context extension," or "syntactic expansion." The Shakespeare example (35) illustrates this innovation.

(35)   English (1600 Shakespeare, *Merchant of Venice* II.i.15 [LION: Shakespeare];
        Traugott and Trousdale 2013: 111)
        In terms of choice I am not solely led
        By nice direction of a maiden's eyes;
        ***Besides,** the lottery of my destiny*
        Bars me the right of voluntary choosing.
        "In terms of choice (of a husband) I am not led solely by the dainty guidance
        of a maiden's eyes; in addition, the lottery of my destiny bars me the right to
        choose voluntarily."

As a result of this change, *beside(s)* became a clause-initial DM ("discourse particle"), acquiring properties which, unlike those of *as long as*, have little in common with the ones to be observed in grammaticalization. The description by Traugott and Trousdale (2013: 109–12) suggests that it is in particular the following properties that *beside(s)* acquired around 1600 or earlier: (a) Its meaning ("furthermore, in addition to what was said before, but not central to the argument") is no longer part of the sentence meaning. (b) Its function seems to be metatextual, relating the preceding discourse to what follows. (c) It is syntactically unattached: It is not a syntactic constituent of the sentence, being placed at its left periphery. (d) It seems to be set off prosodically from the rest of the sentence, as might be suggested by the fact that it is separated from its textual environment by punctuation marks (but see also Section 2.1). And (e) it has wider semantic-pragmatic scope over a larger piece of discourse.

These properties, in particular those in (b), (c), and (d), contradict generally accepted criteria of grammaticalization (see Section 2.2.2). Accounting for the development of *beside(s)* in terms of grammaticalization, or of any wider or extended view of it, therefore runs the risk of turning this term into a conceptually largely vacuous label. Barth-Weingarten and Couper-Kuhlen (2002: 357), for example, rightly point out that by relaxing Lehmann's [(1982) 2015] criteria of grammaticalization the danger is "that the term grammaticalization may itself bleach and ultimately no longer be meaningful in linguistic description."

To conclude, "context extension" involves changes of quite a different nature in the two examples presented and we will reserve this term for changes observed in expressions like *as long as*. Changes like that observed in *beside(s)*, by contrast, concern what will be referred to in ensuing chapters as cooptation (see Section 1.2.4, and especially Section 2.3) and – in fact – they constitute a major theme in the present book.

In sum, there does not appear to be entirely convincing evidence in Traugott and Trousdale (2013) in support of a distinction between two models or approaches to grammaticalization – neither the features of grammatical change proposed by the authors nor scope expansion and increase in syntactic freedom (or "disjunction") seem to be relevant criteria to argue for a new perspective of grammaticalization. Hence, we see no intrinsic reason to question the traditional definition of grammaticalization or the criteria used for defining it (see Section 2.2.2).

1.3.3   Do Discourse Markers Belong to Grammar?

The problem raised in the title of this section is phrased succinctly by Waltereit in the following question: "One might ask what kind of grammar allows grammatical items to be syntactically independent of sentence structure" (Waltereit 2002: 1008).

In the debate on the contribution of grammaticalization to the development of DMs, questions like those in (36) have been raised and discussed in some detail (e.g., Traugott 1995; Hansen 1998a; 1998b; Lenker 2000; Traugott and Dasher 2002; Brinton and Traugott 2005: 136–40; Brinton 2008; 2017: 34–35; Diewald 2011a; 2011b; Prévost 2011; Van Bogaert 2011), but most of all by Degand and Simon-Vandenbergen (2011: 287–88).

(36)   Questions
        a What is grammar?
        b Do DMs belong to grammar?
        c Are DMs part of the structure of a sentence?
        d What is the role of pragmatics in the development and use of DMs?

Question (36a) raises a theory-dependent issue that has remained as contro-versial as it used to be when the study of DMs developed into a new field of research in the 1980s. A couple of contrasting stances may illustrate the dilemma plaguing the distinction: For Traugott (1995: 4; 2003: 636), grammar encompasses linguistic pragmatics, and Traugott and Trousdale (2013: 95) go one step further in adopting a more comprehensive view of grammar, arguing that it "... includes not only morphosyntax, semantics, and phonology but also pragmatics, and discourse functions." Such a position, however, is not shared by all researchers. For Pons Bordería and Loureda Lamas (2018: 1), for example, grammaticalization is "one of the liveliest fields in pragmatics."

A broader conception of grammar of a different kind is proposed in the framework of discourse grammar, where two grammatical domains are distin-guished (Kaltenböck, Heine, and Kuteva 2011; Heine et al. 2013), namely one that relates to the level of sentence construction (sentence grammar) and another that is concerned with the metatextual level of discourse organization (thetical grammar), the latter serving to monitor the production of texts and to provide instructions on how to interpret the texts. On this view, DMs, jointly with an array of other linguistic material, belong to the latter level (see Section 2.4), and their rise is the result of a transfer from the former to the latter level (Heine 2013; see Sections 2.2 and 8.1).

With regard to (36b), some researchers are wondering whether DMs can unambiguously be classified as belonging to grammar. Waltereit (2002: 1004), for example, argues that "it is not even immediately obvious that DMs are part of the GRAMMAR of a language in the first place," and for Hansen (2008: 59) DMs "are, in an important sense, 'outside' the grammar (see also Dostie 2009: 202). Most authors, however, seem to converge on answering this question in the affirmative, classifying DMs as belonging to "grammar" (e.g., Fraser 1988: 32; Traugott and Dasher 2002: 11). This is also the position taken in most mainstream models of contemporary linguistics as well as in reference grammars of English, such as Quirk et al. (1985: 631–46), Biber et al. (1999: 1086–88), and Huddleston and Pullum (2002: 1356ff.), according to which DMs are treated in some way or other as parts of grammar, even if not necessarily belonging to the same grammatical category as the expressions from which they are historically derived (see Heine 2018a: 42–43).[43]

As for (36c), Brinton and Traugott (2005: 139) suggest that DMs "are part of the structure of the sentence."[44] It would seem that this suggestion is problematic if a sentence is defined, e.g., as the largest unit over which a rule of grammar can operate (Matthews 2007: 364). Such rules – however they are defined – operate over sentences but, as far as we are aware, not really over DMs, nor are DMs arguments or adjuncts of sentences. Similar observations have also been made by other students of DMs, as we will see in Section 1.4.3.

Underlying (36d) is the question whether DMs may not be "pragmatic" rather than "grammatical" phenomena. On the one hand, DMs are called "pragmatic" markers by a number of scholars (e.g., Brinton 1996; 2008; 2017; Defour 2007; Aijmer and Simon-Vandenbergen 2009; Aijmer 2013; 2016; Beeching 2016). On the other hand, one of the reasons to insist that the development of DMs can be described exhaustively as being the result of "grammaticalization" is that the alternative term "pragmaticalization" was claimed to be inadequate to capture the particular nature of this development (see, e.g., Diewald 2011a; 2011b; Prévost 2011: 408; Degand and Evers-Vermeul 2015).

As is argued in some studies, grammaticalization is part of and takes place within grammar, rather than somewhere else. However, being aware of the problems that this general issue raises, some authors opted for a more qualified position. Thus, for Fraser (1988: 32), DMs are part of the grammar of a language, but pragmatic in function. A somewhat different perspective is adopted by Degand and Evers-Vermeul (2015: 74–75). On the one hand, they assert that the development of DMs "falls within the scope of grammaticalization" and that DMs "are a part of the grammar." On the other hand, they suggest that two conceivable notions of grammar need to be distinguished:

(37)   Put simply, if grammar is restricted to semantics, phonology, morphology and syntax, DMs will not be viewed as the result of a grammaticalization process; if, in contrast, grammar is viewed as including discourse-pragmatic phenomena, then DMs will most probably find a satisfying account in terms of grammaticalization.

(Degand and Evers-Vermeul 2015: 61)

---

[43] The term "discourse marker" is used only in one of the three works mentioned, namely Biber et al. (1999: 1086–88), whereas in Quirk et al. (1985: 631–46) DMs are referred to as either conjuncts or style disjuncts, and in Huddleston and Pullum (2002: 1356ff.) as supplements.

[44] Elizabeth Traugott (personal communication of January 12, 2020) points out that "clause" is more appropriate for work on discourse markers than "sentence."

The crucial issue then is what exactly "discourse-pragmatic phenomena" are, the exact nature of which does not become entirely clear in that study. The question of which of the alternatives proposed in (37) is to be preferred had been answered by Traugott two decades earlier when she opted for a wider notion of both grammar and grammaticalization in her analysis of DMs:

(38)   The view of grammar adopted here is that it structures co[gn]itive *and* communicative aspects of language. It encompasses not only phonology, morphosyntax and semantics but also inferences that arise out of linguistic form, in other words, linguistic pragmatics such as topicalization, deixis.

(Traugott 1995: 5; original emphasis)

Such observations suggest that there is no general consensus on how question (36d) is best answered. Controversies on where grammar ends and pragmatics begins have strengthened our awareness of some of the features characterizing DMs. But whether, or to what extent, DMs qualify as "pragmatic" or "grammatical" entities is an issue that will not be of major concern here. Following a widespread convention we will refer to DMs as "grammatical markers" but have no problems with traditions calling and perceiving them as "pragmatic markers" instead. Considering that the boundary between the two is notoriously fuzzy one may wonder whether framing or phrasing discussions in terms of taxonomic distinctions like that between pragmatics and grammar is really helpful for understanding what DMs actually are about. In order to avoid the problems associated with the notion "pragmatics," the role of DMs is defined in the present study with reference to the "situation of discourse" (see Section 1.1.2).

1.4   Problems

There are a range of publications expressing dissatisfaction with existing accounts of DM genesis in some way or other, most of all with the all-grammaticalization hypothesis. For example, proponents of the hypothesis have been said to "give detailed descriptions of the diachronic development individual DMs go through ... but they fail to address the issue of delimiting the functional class of DMs" (Furkó 2014: 290). And Fischer (2007a: 280–97) draws attention to the fact that word order evidence suggests that there is no direct line from adjunct to disjunct adverbial, that is, from sentence grammar unit to (paren)thetical. Brinton (2017: 29) presents a list of features that are hard to reconcile with an all-grammaticalization hypothesis (see (15)), and Traugott and Trousdale (2013: 109–12) also point out that there are features found in DMs that were shown by students of pragmaticalization to be problematic for any analysis based on grammaticalization (see Furkó 2014: 293–95 for an insightful discussion).

Such features induce authors like Ocampo (2006: 317) and Norde (2009: 23) to argue that grammaticalization is movement toward syntax and morphology, whereas discourse markers move precisely to the opposite end, namely outside of syntax and toward discourse. Accordingy, Waltereit notes:

> With the rise of DMs, however, the communicative background is simply the sequential structure of the discourse (which is itself by definition not part of the grammar of a language), because the source constructions are grammatically independent. (Waltereit 2002: 1006)

A survey of studies on this issue suggests that it is most of all the following changes to be observed in the development of DMs that are hard to reconcile with observations commonly made in grammaticalization:

(39)   Properties to be observed in the development of DMs
        a From meaning as part of the sentence to meaning outside the sentence
        b From sentence grammar function to metatextual function
        c From syntactic constituent of the sentence to syntactically unattached status
        d From prosodically integrated to unintegrated or less integrated status
        e From more restricted semantic–pragmatic scope to wider scope
        f From positionally constrained to less constrained placement.

The catalog in (39) does not exhaust the number of changes that have been pointed out in the literature on DMs but they are presumably among the ones most frequently mentioned in some form or other. It goes without saying that there is great variation both within a given language and across languages with regard to how or whether the six changes are represented.

These six changes are now looked at in turn.

1.4.1   From Meaning As Part of the Sentence to Meaning outside the Sentence

When a DM evolves, it is no longer "semantically transparent" (cf. Van Bogaert 2011: 298–99), it is no longer a part of the meaning of the sentence, and no longer modifies the propositional content of a sentence or an utterance (Jucker 1993: 436; Fraser 1996; 1999: 936; Hansen 1997: 161; Lenk 1998: 52; Schourup 1999: 227). In other words, if the DM were omitted the meaning of that sentence would remain essentially unchanged – an observation that has been made in many studies (e.g., Espinal 1991: 730).[45]

---

[45] However, while omission of a DM does not normally modify the propositional content of an utterance, it does affect the kind of interpretation of the utterance intended by the speaker (see Schourup 1999: 231–32).

Meanings arising in grammaticalization, by contrast, shape the meaning of sentences, be that within a phrase or a clause, or between clauses, but not normally beyond the level of sentences. For example, in many languages, meaningful expressions used to structure noun phrases or adverbial phrases, such as demonstratives, nominalizing markers, adpositions, or case markers, were grammaticalized to markers of clause combining such as complementizers or relative clauses markers (see Kuteva et al. 2019 for examples). Such processes, however, were essentially restricted to the meaning content of sentences.

1.4.2   From Sentence Grammar Function to Metatextual Function

The term "metatextual" refers to the function of DMs as being anchored in and relating the meaning of a sentence to the situation of discourse, rather than being anchored in a sentence (Heine 2018a: 34). For example, Traugott (1995: 6–7) notes that the metatextual function of DMs can be seen more specifically in allowing speakers to display their evaluation not of the content of what is said, that is, the meaning content of sentences, but of the way that content is put together.

DMs have been described as signaling the commitment the speaker makes with regard to the text segment over which they have semantic–pragmatic scope (cf. Fraser 1988: 22; see Sections 1.3.2 and 1.4.5). They "function as instructions from the speaker to the hearer on how to integrate the host unit into a coherent mental representation of the discourse" (Hansen 1997: 161). Thus, they are related to the speech situation and not to the situation talked about (Jucker 1993: 436). As Waltereit (2006: 64) puts it, DMs (pragmatic markers) "situate their host unit with respect to the surrounding discourse and with respect to the speaker–hearer relationship" or, from another perspective, they constrain the interpretation of their host utterances by virtue of the inferential connections they express (Blakemore 1996: 332–33; Schourup 1999: 244).

The functions of DMs are commonly described as metatextual (Traugott 1995: 6, 2018: 27; Heine 2018a: 34). They are said to introduce higher-order speech acts (cf. Grice 1989: 362), as being extradiscursory (cf. Kac 1970: 627), metalingual (Maschler 1994: 334; Lenk 1998: 52), metalinguistic (Beeching 2016: 188), metadiscursive (Hansen 1998b: 236; Traugott 2014: 7), metacommunicative (Frank-Job 2006: 361),[46] nonrestrictive (Heine 2013: 1209), discourse-interactional (Frank-Job 2006: 361), as operating on the textual or

---

[46] According to Beeching (2016: 184, 188), DMs may be used for both metalinguistic and metacommunicative explanations, where the former have to do with the wording provided and the latter with the speech act or the intention involved.

discourse level (Wischer 2000: 64; Fagard 2010; Kaltenböck 2010), or "at the level of discourse rather than the clause or sentence" (Traugott 2007: 150), to serve as text structuring devices at different levels of discourse (Erman and Kotsinas 1993: 79), or as contributing to the interpretation of an utterance rather than to its propositional content (Fraser 1999: 946). And in relevance-theoretic studies, DMs are portrayed as serving to guide the hearer's linkage of an utterance to an appropriate context (Blass 1990: 77–79; Rouchota 1996; 1998; Blakemore 2002: 170; Schourup 2011).

Such features contrast sharply with those figuring in accounts that have been proposed for grammaticalization processes of any kind, in particular in cross-linguistic typological accounts (e.g., Kuteva et al. 2019). Expressions commonly providing the source for DMs serve functions of structuring sentences or parts of them, and they retain this property when undergoing grammaticalization, but not when giving rise to DMs (for an overview of such sources, see Section 8.2.2).

1.4.3   From Syntactic Constituent of the Sentence to Syntactically Unattached Status

DMs have been described as remaining external to the clause (Hansen 1997: 156), being generally not part of or only loosely attached to the syntactic structure (Jucker 2002: 212), being disjunctive (Tabor and Traugott 1998: 254) or syntactically disjunct (Traugott 1995: 14), syntactically isolated (Frank-Job 2006: 364), extrasyntactic (Brinton 2010a: 64), as occurring outside the syntactic structure or being only loosely attached to it (Brinton 1996: 33–35; Jucker and Ziv 1998: 3), being syntactic "orphans" (cf. Haegeman 1991) in that they do not interact with their host in terms of c-command-based relations, or else are independent of syntactic categorization (cf. Schourup 1999: 234). Furthermore, they cannot normally be questioned, they cannot become the focus of a cleft sentence, and they are not in the scope of a negated sentence (cf. Espinal 1991; Haegeman 1991).

For some authors, syntactic independence, detachment, or freedom is therefore one of the most conspicuous properties of DMs (Schiffrin 1987: 328; Traugott 1995: 1; Frank-Job 2006: 364; Furkó 2007; Brinton 2008: 241). Accordingly, the growth of DMs has been described as involving "an increase in syntactic freedom instead of syntactic fixation" (Norde 2009: 22; Beijering 2012). Being syntactically unattached, they tend to be positionally flexible, "they can occur in multiple positions in the clause" (Tabor and Traugott 1998: 254) (see Section 1.4.6).

Note, however, that there are some restrictions on what "syntactic independence" stands for, in particular the following: Even while being syntactically unattached, DMs may retain features of cohesive linkage with their host sentence, such as devices signaling coreference (Waltereit 2006: 65). And, furthermore, DMs are widely described as being optional expressions (see Section 1.2.2 (19g)), that is, a sentence may but need not host a DM. This might be taken to suggest that DMs require a host sentence but not the other way round – in other words, that DMs are not entirely syntactically independent (cf. Lewis 2011: 420). However, there is also evidence to show that some DMs can also occur as stand-alones, e.g., as distinct turns in conversations without there being any host sentence. English examples of such DMs include *okay*, *right*, *sure*, or *well*, a Korean example is provided by the DM *eti poca* "well, let's see" (Rhee 2020a; (1)).

Increases in syntactic freedom and movement outside of the sentence are features that are not compatible with any of the criteria that have been proposed for grammaticalization (e.g., Lehmann [1982] 2015; Heine and Kuteva 2002: 2–4): Grammaticalization usually leads in the opposite direction, toward decategorialization and bonding, almost invariably involving loss rather than gain of morphosyntactic independence (see Section 2.2.2).

1.4.4   From Prosodically Integrated to Unintegrated or Less Integrated Status

In a number of studies, it is pointed out that DMs tend to be prosodically set off from their host utterance (e.g., Zwicky 1985: 303; Schiffrin 1987: 328; Brinton 1996: 33; Hansen 1997: 156; 1998a: 66; Tabor and Traugott 1998: 254; Jucker and Ziv 1998: 3; Hancil 2013; Hancil and Hirst 2013; Traugott and Trousdale 2013: 110; Gonen, Livnat, and Amir 2015; Rhee 2019). They are described as forming a separate tone group (Brinton 1996: 33–35; Jucker 2002: 212) and as exhibiting a separate intonation contour (Onodera 2011: 620), requiring "comma intonation" (Hansen 1997: 156; Tabor and Traugott 1998: 254). They may become "intonationally disjunct" (Traugott 2014: 19–20), often occurring "in an independent breath unit carrying a special intonation and stress pattern" (Traugott 1995: 6). For example, in her analysis of English *anyway*, Ferrara (1997: 356) found that the pitch contour of the DM (her *anyway₃*) "is very distinct" from that of the other two uses of *anyway*. Similar observations were made by Matzen (2004) on the English DM *so*, where prosody in combination with context allows not only to determine that the DM is involved but also which of its functions is concerned.

The hedge "tend to be" added above indicates that distinct prosody is not consistently observed or even missing in specific DMs or contexts (Hirschberg and Litman 1993: 516; but see also Dér 2010: 15–16; Wichmann, Simon-Vandenbergen, and Aijmer 2010; Wichmann 2011: 335–36; Heine 2013: 1210 for discussion), and Dér and Marko (2010) show that DMs need not be preceded and/or followed by a pause. The ambiguous status of prosody in

DMs is characterized succinctly by Rhee (2019) with regard to a set of Korean DMs having *kule* as their base:

> An analysis of the *kule*-DMs shows that prosodic features, e.g., intonation contour, duration, subsequent pause, etc., indeed play an important role in determining DM functions, but they fail to uniquely characterize the DM functions in a robust way. (Rhee 2019: 6)

What is obvious, however, is that DMs are distinctly more likely to be separated prosodically from their environment than the expressions from which they are historically derived. Prosodic integration differs remarkably with regard to the position occupied by a DM in that it tends to be weak at the left periphery but strong at the right periphery of an utterance (e.g., Haselow 2015: 163).

In this respect, DMs differ from grammaticalizing items, which almost invariably lose features of prosodic distinctiveness on the way from lexical to grammatical expressions: They tend to be integrated in the prosodic structure of their host.[47] Loss of prosodic independence "leading to an item's inability to form a prosodic word of its own" has been pointed out to be one of the processes commonly associated with grammaticalization (Haspelmath 2011: 347). Thus, Wichmann concludes:

> [G]rammaticalization involves not only (and not always) the attrition of phonetic substance but more importantly the loss of prosodic prominence with concomitant loss of independence in intonational structure. (Wichmann 2011: 341)

1.4.5   From More Restricted Semantic–Pragmatic Scope to Variable Scope beyond the Sentence

As was observed in Section 1.3.2.1, the "structural scope" of Lehmann ([1982] 2015: 152–53) does not really qualify as a stable feature in grammaticalization: It can be reduced, expanded, or remain unchanged. And neither structural scope nor syntactic scope appear to be relevant to the rise of DMs, for the following reason: Once an expression gives rise to a DM it is syntactically unattached and, hence, loses its ability to signal syntactic or structural scope beyond syntactic units such as sentences.

But there is as a rule increase in semantic–pragmatic scope.[48] This increase leads, on the one hand, from scope over parts of a sentence to the whole sentence and, on the other hand, to content of discourse beyond the sentence

---

[47] As Wichmann (2011: 335–36) shows, this can also happen with frequently used DMs like English *of course* and *sorry*.

[48] With the hedge "as a rule" we wish to draw attention to the fact that there are a few exceptions. As observed by Hansen (1998a: 73–74; 2008: 57–58), DMs can have scope over larger pieces of text that include several sentences, or over parts of a sentence. The latter applies in particular to constituent anchored DMs, which will be discussed in Section 8.3.

(see Section 1.3.2.1). DMs are metatextual expressions (see Sections 1.1.2 and 1.4.2) and, hence, their scope is determined by the discourse structure (Detges and Waltereit 2016) rather than by grammatical structure, and they relate to the situation of discourse, that is, the attitudes of the speaker, the interaction between speaker and hearer, and the organization of texts (see Heine et al. 2017). Accordingly, their scope "is subject to discourse considerations" (Waltereit 2006: 65). What appears to distinguish the semantic–pragmatic scope of DMs from its equivalents in sentence grammar expressions is that it "makes reference to discourse, not to grammar," as Waltereit (2006: 65) puts it.

It would seem in fact that for many students of DMs it is fairly uncontroversial to assume that DMs "have larger scope than their etyma" (Waltereit 2002: 1005; Detges and Waltereit 2016), their scope "expands over larger segments of discourse" (Brinton 2017: 29), extending beyond the clause over the entire speech act (Hansen 1998b: 236), that they are the result of a process leading to a "wider interpretation" (Lewis 2011: 440) and an expansion in scope (Thompson and Mulac 1991; Traugott 1995: 1; Brinton 1996: 253, 2001: 194, 2008; Tabor and Traugott 1998: 254; Gohl and Günthner 1999: 59–63; Lewis 2011: 419; Traugott and Trousdale 2013: 109). Accordingly, the development of DMs is described as one of scope extension (e.g., Auer and Günthner 2005: 338; Brinton and Traugott 2005: 138; Norde 2009: 22), leading to "scope over discourse" (D'Arcy 2017: 59).

This is strikingly different in the case of grammaticalization. As was observed at the beginning of this section (see also Section 1.3.2.1), structural scope in the sense of Lehmann ([1982] 2015: 152–53) does not really qualify as a stable feature in grammaticalization. Syntactic scope, in contrast, generally increases but – unlike what happens in the rise of DMs – it does not essentially extend beyond the boundaries of syntactic constructions.

1.4.6 From Positionally Constrained to Less Constrained Placement

Being semantically and syntactically unattached, DMs are, ideally, unconstrained in their placement, that is, they may be found in various slots of a sentence. Accordingly, Hansen (2008: 58) notes that DMs (pragmatic markers) "frequently have great freedom of position within the host utterance, and are thus syntagmatically variable," and Tabor and Traugott (1998: 254) observe that DMs "occur in multiple positions in the clause."

Brinton and Traugott (2005: 138) conclude that Lehmann's ([1982] 2015: 158–60) notion of fixation or loss of syntactic variability is problematic for DMs since they are "often quite moveable" – a problem discussed by Van Bogaert (2011: 302–3) as the "decategorialization paradox" (see also Section

2.5.1). At the same time there are also constraints on placement, and these constraints are in accordance with the particular discourse functions expressed by DMs. The functionally preferred position is that at the left periphery of a sentence, followed by the right periphery, less commonly within the sentence.

To conclude, there is converging evidence to suggest that DMs are in general distinctly more flexible in their placement than the expressions from which they are etymologically derived, even if there are also DMs that are fixed at the left or right periphery. This observation is hard to reconcile with observations made in grammaticalization, according to which the development from lexical to grammatical expressions almost invariably entails reduction or loss in positional variability.

1.5   Conclusions

In the course of this chapter, a number of hypotheses were reviewed that have been proposed to account for the rise and development of DMs. The majority of these studies converge on arguing that it is the grammaticalization hypothesis, summarized in Section 1.2.1, that provides the most plausible account. But as we saw in Section 1.4, this hypothesis is problematic. For another problem see Section 2.2, but the most serious problem with the grammaticalization hypothesis can be seen in the features of DMs discussed in Section 1.4: These features are not only hard to reconcile with but even contradict what has commonly been observed crosslinguistically in grammaticalization (see Section 2.2.2 on defining criteria for grammaticalization). In accordance with our analysis in Section 1.4, these properties can be summarized as in (40).

(40)   Grammatical properties of discourse markers
    a Meaning: Their meaning is not part of the meaning of the sentence they are associated with.
    b Function: Their function is metatextual.
    c Syntax: They are not a syntactic constituent of the sentence in which they occur.
    d Prosody: They are likely to be set off prosodically from the rest of the sentence.
    e Semantic–pragmatic scope: They have scope over and beyond the sentence depending on their respective discourse function.
    f Placement: Depending on their discourse function they are flexible in their placement behavior, most commonly appearing in sentence-initial position.

The properties listed in (40) are based on findings made in previous research on DMs, and they are compatible with the definition of DMs stipulated in (7) of Section 1.1.2. This situation raises questions that are the central concern of the present book, in particular the following:

(41)   Questions
         a Are the properties in (40) only found in DMs?
         b How to account for the properties?

As we will see in Section 2.4, these properties are in fact not restricted to DMs. Accordingly, accounting for the properties require, on the one hand, a perspective that is not restricted to DMs. On the other hand, it also requires a diachronic perspective to understand how DMs come to acquire these properties, and this is the topic of the ensuing Chapters 3–6.

2   Concepts of Analysis

In Chapter 1, an overview was provided of what we know about the topic of the present book, that is, on how DMs arise. In the course of the discussion we observed that there remain problems that need to be looked into, and the present chapter proposes a framework of analysis to deal with these problems. The methodological tools on which this framework rests are outlined in Section 2.1.

A conclusion surfacing from the discussions in Chapter 1 is that grammaticalization forms an important component in the development of DMs but that cooptation plays an equally important role. These two mechanisms are therefore described in more detail in Sections 2.2 and 2.3, respectively, and a major concern in the remainder of the chapter will be with the respective contributions of the two and with how the two interact in shaping the structure of DMs. While grammaticalization is a well-established field of study, cooptation is a young field that evolved only recently (see especially Heine et al. 2017). For a better understanding of the latter, Section 2.4 looks at cooptation from a wider perspective, and Section 2.5 relates the two mechanisms to one another.

2.1   The Framework

The framework used in the chapters to follow is based on general principles of functional, usage-based linguistics, having both a diachronic and a typological perspective. The former perspective is the main concern of the book, to be discussed in more detail in Chapters 3–6. The data to be analyzed are mostly taken from previous work, relying on text corpora such as *The London–Lund Corpus of Spoken English* (see Svartvik 1990), the *British Component of the International Corpus of English* (see Nelson, Wallis, and Aarts 2002), or *The Corpus of Contemporary American English* (e.g., Davies 2008; 2010). These data on the whole provide a solid basis for our reconstruction of historical processes.

Selection of the languages analyzed was dictated mainly by the availability of appropriate historical text data. By far the largest amount of such data is

56

available for English, hence the number of English DMs, discussed in Chapter 3, by far outnumbers that of DMs in the other languages considered, namely French (Chapter 4), Japanese (Chapter 5), and Korean (Chapter 6).

The methodology employed is, on the one hand, that commonly used in work on the reconstruction of earlier language states by means of written records; a paradigm example of the application of the methodology can be found in the work of Brinton (1996; 2008; 2017). This is the methodology that was used extensively in previous reconstructions of the history of DMs to be discussed (see also Section 3.1). It is based on the assumption that an analysis of historical text documents allows for reconstructing features of both earlier states of language use and of the transition from one language state to another – that is, of language change. Some problems that we experienced in the course of our reconstruction work are discussed here (see also Section 2.3.2).

In addition, our framework is also based on findings that have been made in more recent work on discourse analysis (e.g., Kaltenböck, Heine, and Kuteva 2011; Heine 2013). These findings suggest that the development of DMs differs from that of many other kinds of linguistic material in that it cannot reasonably be reduced to gradual changes as they are commonly observed and described within the framework of grammaticalization theory (see Section 2.2). Rather, what is needed in addition is an understanding of the specific way in which linguistic expressions are deployed for new purposes of discourse organization, involving a mechanism called "cooptation," to be described in Section 2.3.

As observed in Section 2.2, grammaticalization is a gradual process that takes a long time, whereas cooptation is an instantaneous operation that may take place frequently in the history of a given information unit. In order to establish that grammaticalization has in fact taken place, the most reliable way is to demonstrate that there was a less grammaticalized expression at some earlier stage in the history of the language analyzed corresponding to a more strongly grammaticalized form of that earlier expression at some later stage, and that there was a development leading from the former to the latter.

A general observation, one that in fact incited us to embark on this book project, is that up to a certain stage in the history of a DM, development is in accordance with established parameters of grammaticalization. But at that stage there is a kind of 'quantum leap', to the extent that these parameters fail to clearly apply, and subsequently the grammatical structure of the expression, described in terms of the properties listed in (40) in Section 1.5, is no longer what it used to be, even if the ensuing history of the expression is again shaped by gradual evolution characterizing grammaticalization. This "quantum leap" is accounted for in this book, with reference to the notion of cooptation described in Section 2.3 (see also Heine 2013; Heine et al. 2017).

Such "quantum leaps" are not restricted to cooptation; rather, they can also be observed in other kinds of instantaneous cognitive–communicative operations like English word class conversion. But whereas the latter involves switches from one part of grammar to another, e.g., from nouns (*email*) to verbs (*to email*), in cooptation the switch is from one domain of discourse processing to another.

The reconstruction of DMs requires detailed historical analysis, and the problems associated with this analysis have been aptly discussed by Brinton (2017: 12–13) and Traugott (2018: 25–26). Since the rise of many DMs took place centuries ago, reconstruction work has to rely to a large extent on written historical documents. Such resources are not readily available for most languages of the world, and the selection of languages looked at in this book is therefore severely limited. European languages and languages from Eastern Asia will therefore figure prominently in the following discussions, where an enormous amount of reconstruction work has already been carried out.

But even in such languages, the analysis of the earliest phase in the rise of DMs is faced with a number of problems. First, while DMs also occur in written documents they are distinctly more common in speech (e.g., Jucker 2002: 210), and spoken language is for the most part not directly accessible to historical analysis via written documents. Accordingly, it may well happen that a given DM was in use for a long time but surfaced in written documents only decades or more later or, even worse, never appeared in writing and, hence, remains inaccessible to historical reconstruction. Furthermore, written documents, especially older ones, may not reflect the actual language use of the author but may be copies, or copies of copies, or replications of earlier texts, possibly modified in some way or other in the process of copying. And finally, one may also wish to mention that the written documents that are available reflect to quite some extent only the language use of a small, literate minority of the populations concerned, and that language use was possibly strongly influenced by translations from languages of "higher culture" such as Chinese, Greek, Latin, or French.

Second, a problem constantly arising in the analysis of historical documents concerns prosody. Essentially the only means of signaling prosodic discontinuities in written sources is via punctuation marks. And in fact, in many examples, the placement of commas and other orthographic conventions is of help in identifying features of prosodic distinctiveness. But, unfortunately, there are problems with punctuation marking: It neither necessarily serves the functions it does in modern publications, nor does it seem to have been consistent in early authors and, finally, it was frequently added only more recently. Note that current English punctuation practices developed only in the late eighteenth century, frequently imposed by editors on earlier texts (Jucker 2002: 212; Laurel Brinton, personal communication). Accordingly, our interpretation of prosodic features must be taken with care (see also Traugott 2015; 2016).

Given the problematic nature of punctuation marking for reconstructing prosody, the question is whether one might not be well advised to dispense with this issue altogether.[1] Prosody is an important part of speech behavior, and its reconstruction is therefore an important component of reconstruction work. Even if punctuation marks were added only by later editors, they would seem to provide a small piece of evidence of the following kind. Prosodic signals are normally intended by the speaker (or the writer) to provide the hearer (or reader) with cues on how to interpret a text. Now, if such signals are missing, an editor, in his or her capacity as a reader, may feel entitled to add appropriate signals to guide other readers in reconstructing the communicative intent of the writer. And to the extent that the editor's hypothesis on that communicative intent is of help in analyzing the relevant text we feel justified not to ignore it, as long as we make it clear to our readers how this hypothesis is to be evaluated. Note, however, that our reconstructions are not based solely on prosody; rather, prosody constitutes only one of the six criteria employed.

A third problem concerns "ambiguity." An inherent feature of grammaticalization is that in the transition of an expression from an earlier stage A to a later stage B there is an intermediate stage, the bridging stage AB, where an expression is indeterminate between a traditional usage A and an innovative usage B (Heine 1992) and, hence, is classified as being "ambiguous." The presence of "ambiguity" is commonly employed as evidence to classify a given process as having been due to grammaticalization. As we will see in Section 3.3, however, this procedure must be taken with care since in most of these cases it remains unclear what kind of conclusions can be drawn from such cases.

Problems associated with the cooptation hypothesis are mostly as follows: First, in some cases the hypothesis had to rely on very few historically attested examples. The question that arises in such cases is whether the examples concerned are in fact representative of a more general usage pattern or are the result of nonce formations that had no bearing on the general development of the expression concerned; note that cooptation is an operation that can take place and be repeated any time, and its result may fall into oblivion soon after its production (see Section 2.3). Second, a cooptation hypothesis must rest on grammatical evidence extending from syntax to phonology and from semantics to pragmatics, that is, it has to draw on a wide range of grammatical phenomena. Accordingly, even when there are several attested examples they may not contain sufficient grammatical information to construct a viable

---

[1] This question was put to us by an anonymous reader of an earlier version of this book.

hypothesis. Third, prosody constitutes an important parameter for reconstructing cooptation, yet written documents do not as a rule provide any solid information on prosodic features, as we noted earlier in this section.

Fourth, there are also problems with the dating of historical events. Time and again we had to use hedges like "around X," "at the latest," or "if not earlier" to establish the date of cooptation, and in the case of *well* ("between 1150 and 1250") and *no doubt* ("between 1350 and 1450") in Chapter 3 the closest we could get was by proposing a whole century as the timespan within which cooptation must have taken place. As Elizabeth Traugott (personal communication of January 19, 2020) reminds us, however, such problems are far from unexpected in the kind of reconstruction work concerned.

But perhaps the most serious problem that we were confronted with is the following: To what extent is it justified to reconstruct grammatical innovations on the basis of one or a handful of text examples? What information on historical events or states exactly can such examples provide? How do we distinguish between innovations as nonce creations and new but conventionalized use patterns (see the innovation model in (11) of Section 2.3)?[2] And what can an innovation that has been reconstructed on the basis of written records tell us about when and how that innovation first appeared in oral communication? As we will see in this and the following chapters, there is so far no entirely satisfying answer to such questions.

While the approach chosen in Chapters 3–6 is rooted essentially in language-internal reconstruction work, it also allows for some comparative interpretations, in particular for two kinds of comparisons, namely between two European languages (English and French), on the one hand, and between these European languages and two East Asian languages (Japanese and Korean), on the other. Attempts to extend our reconstruction work to languages in other parts of the world, especially to the unwritten languages of Africa, Australia, and the Americas, were unfortunately not successful, for the following reason: For none of these languages did we find appropriate diachronic resources to reconstruct in detail the history of DMs from their beginning to their present-day usage. Accordingly, we do not wish to claim that the findings discussed in the four chapters to follow represent a genuinely world-wide outlook of the rise of DMs.

Such an outlook, however, is attempted in Chapters 7 and 8, where our attention shifts from language-internal reconstruction to typological comparisons across languages, aimed at identifying regularities in the behavior of DMs across languages. As we will see in Chapter 7, the development of DMs is not necessarily restricted to language-internal processes but may as

---

[2] We are grateful to Elizabeth Traugott (personal communication of January 19, 2020) for having drawn our attention to such questions.

well be the result of language-external factors, and more specifically of language contact.

Our framework thus combines two different perspectives of analysis for a more comprehensive understanding of the study of DMs. Each of these perspectives highlights a different line of development but, as we will argue in Chapter 9, these lines are not incompatible with one another.

2.2   Grammaticalization

Since the appearance of early monographs on grammaticalization in the 1980s and 1990s (Lehmann 1982; Heine and Reh 1984; Heine, Claudi, and Hünnemeyer 1991; Hopper and Traugott 1993; Bybee, Perkins, and Pagliuca 1994), an abundance of works has appeared. The reasons for presenting a brief outline of it in the present section is, first, because grammaticalization constitutes one of the key notions of the present study. Second, while there is, overall, fairly wide agreement on what grammaticalization is about, there are also differences, as we saw in Section 1.3, and, third, there are also limits as to what an analysis in terms of grammaticalization can achieve. The following notes, thus, are meant to clarify how the term is used here. To this end, the outline is restricted to aspects of grammaticalization that are immediately relevant to the subject matter of the present study, namely the rise of DMs.

2.2.1   Definition

Grammaticalization is an essentially unidirectional process based on the context-induced manipulation of linguistic expressions in discourse (cf. the context extension model of Heine 2002). It is defined here as in (1).

(1)   Grammaticalization is defined as the development from lexical to grammat-
        ical forms and from grammatical to even more grammatical forms.[3] Since the
        development of grammatical forms is not independent of the constructions to
        which they belong, the study of grammaticalization is also concerned with
        constructions and with even larger discourse segments.

                                                        (Heine and Kuteva 2002: 2)

For example, the Old English lexical verb *willan* "want" developed into the future tense marker *will*, a grammatical form, and the latter developed further into a marker of epistemic modality (as in *Fred **will** be home by now*). In this definition, which is in some way or other in accordance with most of the over fifty definitions that there are, grammatical developments that do not conform

---

[3] The term "grammatical forms," or "grams," roughly corresponds to what is referred to in some other traditions as "functional categories."

to the definition are not strictly within the scope of grammaticalization theory (Kuteva et al. 2019).[4]

The definition is concerned with change in "forms," that is, form-meaning units, including the constructions of which they are a part, that is, with linguistic expressions having a pragmatic, a semantic, a morphosyntactic, and a phonological component. Thus, it differs from some other definitions which are restricted essentially to change in one component of grammar only, namely change in function, like that by Hopper and Traugott (2003) in (2), or in discourse prominence, like that of Boye and Harder (2012) in (3). Note that (2) covers essentially only one of the four main parameters that will be used in this book to describe grammaticalization, namely *context extension* (see Section 2.2.2 (6a)).

(2)   [Grammaticalization is] a term referring to the change whereby lexical items
       and constructions come in certain linguistic contexts to serve grammatical
       functions and, once grammaticalized, continue to develop new grammatical
       functions.

                                                    (Hopper and Traugott 2003: 18)

(3)   Grammaticalization is the diachronic change that gives rise to linguistic
       expressions that are by convention ancillary and as such discursively
       secondary.

                                                         (Boye and Harder 2012: 21)

Grammaticalization has been portrayed as ritualization (Haiman 1994) or routinization (Detges and Waltereit 2016), it can be said to have a number of effects on the linguistic material involved. One general effect is highlighted by Haspelmath (2004: 26) when he defines grammaticalization as a change "by which the parts of a constructional schema come to have stronger internal dependencies."

2.2.2   *Criteria*

Grammaticalization is most commonly described in terms of six criteria or parameters by Lehmann ([1982] 2015: 132), of four parameters by Heine and Kuteva (2007: 33–44), and/or of five principles by Hopper (1991: 25–29) (see also Dér 2013). The following survey is restricted to a general characterization of the analytic concepts distinguished by the authors concerned; for more detailed descriptions see the sources added in parentheses.

---

[4] Grammaticalization theory is neither a theory of language nor of language change; its goal is to describe grammaticalization, that is, the way grammatical forms arise and develop through space and time, and to explain why they are structured the way they are (Heine 2003: 575).

Table 2.1 *The parameters and criteria of grammaticalization of Lehmann ([1982] 2015: 132)*

	Axis	
Parameter	Paradigmatic	Syntagmatic
Weight	*Integrity*	*Structural scope*
Cohesion	*Paradigmaticity*	*Bondedness*
Variability	*Paradigmatic variability*	*Syntagmatic variability*

The most influential approach, taking structural synchronic notions as a basis for analyzing grammatical change, is that of Lehmann ([1982] 2015; see also Norde 2012).[5] He distinguishes three parameters and two axes, as shown in Table 2.1. Grammaticalization is described with reference to the relative degree to which a linguistic expression relates to the criteria concerned.

The six criteria distinguished are described in (4).

(4)   The criteria of Lehmann and their diachronic effects ([1982] 2015: 129–88])
   a *Integrity* (or paradigmatic weight): Desemanticization, phonological attrition, decategorialization (loss of semantic, phonological, and morphosyntactic features, respectively).
   b *Paradigmaticity* (or paradigmatic cohesion): Paradigmaticization (change from major to minor word class, and/or integration into a paradigm).
   c *Paradigmatic variability*: Obligatorification (becoming obligatory).
   d *Structural scope* (or syntagmatic weight of a grammatical form): Condensation (decrease in structural scope).
   e *Bondedness* (or syntagmatic cohesion): Univerbation, coalescence (leading to boundary loss and/or morphophonological integration).
   f *Syntagmatic variability*: Fixation (leading to a decrease in syntactic freedom).

Being concerned most of all with the incipient stages of grammaticalization and the more variable patterns of language use, Hopper (1991: 25–29) proposes five principles for identifying potential instances of grammaticalization, or "grammaticization" in his terminology. Note, however, that the principles in (5) are not understood to be definitional criteria, rather, they capture regularities of change and – importantly – these regularities "are not the exclusive domain of grammaticalization, but are common to change in general" (Hopper 1991: 32).

---

[5] This approach was already presented in Lehmann (1982) but, since it was slightly revised in later versions, we are referring here exclusively to the latest version available to us, namely that of 2015 (i.e., Lehmann [1982] 2015).

(5)   The principles of Hopper (1991: 22)
   a   *Layering*: New layers of structure arising via grammaticalization may coexist with older layers within a broad functional domain of a language, with the two or more kinds of layers interacting with one another.
   b   *Divergence*: It obtains when a lexical form undergoes grammaticalization but survives as an autonomous lexical expression, occurring side by side with its grammaticalized variant.
   c   *Specialization*: It refers "to the narrowing of choices that characterizes an emergent grammatical construction."
   d   *Persistence*: It "relates the meaning and function of a grammatical form to its history as a lexical morpheme."
   e   *Decategorialization*: It leads towards the loss of discourse autonomy of a form, where loss of autonomy also includes functional–semantic shift.

Rather than relying on synchronic notions and morphosyntactic categories, the parameters proposed by Heine and Kuteva (2007: 33–46; see also Heine and Kuteva 2002) capture salient features of forms undergoing grammatical change, based on the assumption that grammaticalization affects all major components shaping linguistic expressions. The four parameters distinguished are presented in (6).

(6)   The parameters of Heine and Kuteva (2007: 33–46)
   a   *Context extension*: The rise of new meanings when linguistic expressions are extended to new contexts, leading to context-induced reinterpretation.[6]
   b   *Desemanticization* ("semantic bleaching"): Loss or generalization of meaning content or functions in such contexts.
   c   *Decategorialization*: Loss of morphosyntactic properties characteristic of lexical or other less grammaticalized forms.[7]
   d   *Erosion* ("phonetic reduction"): Loss of phonetic substance, including prosodic features.

Furthermore, a distinction needs to be made between external and internal decategorialization (see Heine 2018a: 40, Table 3): The former concerns changes of a form in its relation to the surrounding text, for example, change in syntactic status, while the latter is concerned with changes within a form, for example, loss of internal morphological boundaries and the gradual coalescence into a word (Haspelmath 2011).

In our discussion of grammaticalization in the chapters to follow, we will draw on the parameters in (6) as our main, though not the only criteria of analysis. The reasons for this choice are the following: First, these parameters

---

[6] As observed in the Section 2.2.1, the parameter of context extension covers essentially the definition of grammaticalization as proposed by Hopper and Traugott (2003: 18).

[7] Note that the term "decategorialization" differs from that employed by Hopper (1991: 22) in that it is restricted to morphosyntactic properties, that is, unlike that of Hopper, it does not include meaning or function; see (5) above.

make it possible to look at each of the main components of grammar independently and in its own right, where (6a) involves the pragmatic, (6b) the semantic, (6c) the morphosyntactic, and (6d) the phonetic component. And second, the ordering of the four parameters reflects the diachronic sequence in which they typically apply: Grammaticalization tends to start out with context extension, which triggers desemanticization, subsequently decategorialization, and finally erosion. Erosion thus is the last parameter involved, and in many cases of grammaticalization it is not, or not yet, a relevant parameter.

We saw in Section 1.3.2 that there are some lines of research where a distinction is made between two perspectives of grammaticalization, namely between a narrow or restricted and a wider or expanded view of grammaticalization (e.g., Degand and Simon-Vandenbergen 2011: 290; Degand and Evers-Vermeul 2015: 77), or between grammaticalization viewed as reduction and increase in dependency versus grammaticalization viewed as expansion (Traugott and Trousdale 2013: 99–112). We will not deal with such distinctions further in the remainder of the present book for reasons that were given in Section 1.3.2.2 (see also Heine 2018a).

2.3   Cooptation

As we observed in Section 2.1, there is a second mechanism in addition to grammaticalization to be held responsible for the rise of DMs, namely cooptation. The present section provides a concise account of this mechanism to the extent that it is relevant to the analysis of DMs. For a more comprehensive account, the reader is referred to Heine et al. (2017).

2.3.1   Definition

Central to the present discussion is what was referred to in Section 1.1.3 as the "cooptation hypothesis" (see also Section 1.2.4). Cooptation can be illustrated with the examples in (7).

(7)   English (constructed examples)
    a *You **probably know already** that our chairman will resign next month.*
    b *Our chairman, **you probably know already**, will resign next month.*
    c *Our chairman, **you know**, will resign next month.*

The sentences in (7a) and (7b) both contain the text piece *you probably know already*, printed in bold, and the meanings of the two pieces are essentially the same. But the piece has quite a different grammatical status in the two examples. In (7a) it forms the main clause of the sentence, taking the clause *our chairman will resign next month* as its complement, the latter introduced by the complementizer *that* – in short, (7a) is a canonical example of English sentence grammar.

The grammatical properties of *you probably know already* in (7b), by contrast, are strikingly different, the piece is commonly described as a disjunct (see Espinal 1991 for a detailed description of such disjuncts), a parenthetical (Dehé and Kavalova 2007), or, in the framework of discourse grammar, a thetical (Kaltenböck, Heine, and Kuteva 2011), having the following grammatical properties: (a) Its meaning is not part of its host sentence, (b) its function can be said to be metatextual, relating its host utterance to the situation of discourse, more specifically to speaker–hearer interaction, (c) it is syntactically unattached, not being a syntactic constituent of the sentence or a syntactic hierarchy, (d) it is likely to be set off prosodically by means of intonation and/or pause features, frequently signaled in writing by punctuation marks, and (e) it can be moved to other positions of the sentence – in more general terms, it has essentially the properties that we proposed for DMs in (40) of Section 1.5.

And the observations made on (7b) also apply to the piece *you know* in (7c), which is usually classified as a comment clause, and more specifically as a DM: It also has the grammatical properties mentioned for (7b). What the pieces in (7b) and (7c) also have in common is that they are morphosyntactically somehow incomplete, or "elliptical" as some authors put it: They contain a subject and a verb, but lack a complement.

At the same time, there is also a difference between (7b) and (7c): *You probably know already* in (7b) appears to be compositionally transparent, morphologically analyzable, it may have been designed instantaneously and might never be repeated again, it is called an instantaneous thetical in the framework of discourse grammar (Heine, Kaltenböck, and Kuteva 2016: 188; Heine et al. 2017: 819–21). *You know* in (7c), by contrast, tends to be conceived as an unanalyzable expression used recurrently, much in accordance with our definition of DMs in (7) of Section 1.1.2, called a formulaic thetical in the framework of discourse grammar; we will return to this distinction in Section 2.4.

Thus, in spite of these differences between (7b) and (7c), the two differ dramatically from that in (7a) in their grammatical structure. The question then is how this difference can be explained. What is fairly uncontroversial is that (7b) and (7c) are historically derived from a construction like that in (7a) – that is, in the history of English there must have been a sentence grammar construction of the kind illustrated in (7a) that provided the source for the theticals in (7b) and (7c). But what is less obvious is how exactly that happened. As we saw in Section 1.2, this question has been discussed controversially, most of all in terms of grammaticalization.

But there are problems with the grammaticalization hypothesis, as pointed out in Section 1.4: It does not provide a plausible answer to this question and, more specifically, to how a DM like *you know* in (7c) acquired the grammatical properties mentioned. This is different in the case of the pragmaticalization hypothesis that was summarized in Section 1.2.2: It takes care of salient grammatical properties of DMs such as syntactic detachability, lack of fusion, distinct prosody, and increase in positional variability. However, we are not aware of any attempts by students of pragmaticalization to also account for the presence of theticals like *you probably know already* in (7b), in particular for the fact that such theticals exhibit essentially the same grammatical properties as DMs.

There is an alternative hypothesis, namely the one summarized in Section 1.2.4 and adopted here. On this hypothesis, the text piece printed in bold in (7b) can be derived from a construction like that in (7a) in a principled way, that is, there is an operation that makes it possible for speakers of English to coopt chunks of text like *you probably know already* in (7a) or *you know* in (7a) and insert them in another sentence. This operation is called cooptation.[8]

Cooptation is a cognitive–communicative operation which enables speakers to switch their perspective from the level of reasoning anchored in the meaning of sentences to a meta-level of reasoning immediately anchored in the situation of discourse (cf. Rhee 2013). By means of this operation, speakers transfer expressions available on the former level to express functions on the latter level for structuring their texts (cf. Heine et al. 2017). Cooptation is defined in the following way (see Kaltenböck, Heine, and Kuteva 2011: 874–75; Heine 2013: 1221; Heine et al. 2013: 204–5; Furkó 2014; Heine, Kaltenböck, and Kuteva 2016).

(8)   Cooptation is a fully productive operation whereby a chunk of sentence grammar, such as a word, a phrase, a reduced clause, a full clause, or some other piece of text, is deployed for use on the metatextual level of discourse processing, thereby turning into a thetical. Its functions are determined by the situation of discourse, serving (a) to overcome constraints imposed by linearization in structuring texts, (b) to provide the source of information, (c) to place a text in a wider perspective, e.g., by elaborating, proffering an explanation, a comment or supplementary information, (d) to describe the attitudes of the speaker, and/or (e) to interact with the hearer.

Coopted text chunks, that is, theticals like *you probably know already* in (7b) or *you know* in (7c), are – depending on their specific discourse function – placed at the left or right periphery of a sentence or within the sentence *without being grammatically integrated in the sentence.* When some segment of a text has been coopted this has in particular the grammatical effects listed in (9).

---

[8] The term "cooptation" must not be confused with its use by Lass (1990: 87; 1997), for whom cooptation is an alternative to referring to exaptation. Having adopted the term "exaptation" from evolutionary biology (Gould and Vrba 1982), Lass uses it in a more restricted sense for the redeployment of linguistic "junk" for novel purposes.

Note that these are exactly the changes that we observed in the rise of discourse markers (Section 1.5 (40)).

(9)   Common effects of cooptation (Heine et al. 2020)
    a Meaning: From meaning as part of the sentence to meaning outside the sentence.
    b Function: From sentence-structuring function to metatextual function.
    c Syntax: From syntactic constituent of the sentence to syntactically unattached status.
    d Prosody: From prosodically integrated to unintegrated or less integrated status.
    e Semantic–pragmatic scope: From more restricted to wider scope.
    f Placement: From positionally constrained to less constrained placement.

As stated in (8), cooptation is a "fully productive operation," that is, it can involve various kinds of text chunks. Coopted text chunks need not be and frequently are not fully-fledged clauses or phrases, for example, they can be "reduced clauses" like *you know* in (10a). Furthermore, they have their own illocution, not being restricted to declarative speech acts; rather, they may as well be interrogatives, as in (10b), imperatives (10c), or exclamatives (10d).

(10)   English (constructed examples)
    a *Our chairman, **you know**, will resign next month.* (= (7c))
    b *Our chairman, **can you believe it?**, will resign next month.*
    c *Our chairman, **don't tell anybody!**, will resign next month.*
    d *Our chairman, **what a pity!**, will resign next month.*

As the examples in (10) show, coopted text chunks tend to have the appearance of "elliptical" clauses or phrases. What matters is that any "missing" information be recoverable by the hearer from the situation of discourse (the "context"). Accordingly, Rhee (2015) notes with reference to "ellipsis" in Korean DMs like *kulem* "Right!" (see Section 6.1, Table 6.1):

> What has been ellipted is strategically withheld by the speaker to show that it is so obvious that it does not need to be explicitly expressed. The high degree of its being obvious warrants its ellipsis and at the same time serves as an endorsement of the truthfulness of what the previous speaker has just said. (Rhee 2015: 20)

Our reason for writing "elliptical" in quotation marks is that theticals, printed in bold in (10), are coopted as such and any additional information is recoverable from the knowledge that speakers and hearers are expected to share in the situation concerned.[9] While not necessarily honoring semantic and/or syntactic

---

[9] In some analyses, reduced clauses and other syntactically incomplete theticals have been described as having involved ellipsis. That such an analysis may be problematic is suggested by the fact that some "ellipted" text pieces turn out to be historically older than the corresponding

conventions of sentence grammar, cooptation is taken by interlocutors to result in well-formed utterances.

Which chunks of text qualify for cooptation is an issue that is in need of more research; for some generalizations, see Section 8.2.2.

The notion cooptation roughly corresponds largely to what Waltereit (2002: 988; 2006) calls "reanalysis," whereby a lexical or grammatical item is used at the discursive level, or to what Dostie (2009: 203) describes as category change, whereby a lexical or grammatical item "becomes a pragmatic item."

In some studies of DMs, effects of cooptation have been described in terms of metaphorical processes (see, e.g., Barth-Weingarten and Couper-Kuhlen 2002: 354, or Kim and Lee 2007: 46–47 on the Korean DM *icey*). Metaphorical transfer has been argued to form an important driving force in many grammaticalization processes (e.g., Claudi and Heine 1986; Sweetser 1987; 1988; Mkhatshwa 1991; Heine, Claudi, and Hünnemeyer 1991; Emanatian 1992). Whether metaphor can in fact be held responsible for the kind of transfer from one grammatical level of discourse to another as it can be observed in cooptation is a question that is in need of further research.

Cooptation is by no means the only cognitive–communicative operation enabling speakers to instantaneously switch their perspective from one part of grammar to another, or from one domain of discourse processing to another. An example of the former can be found in English word formation, especially in word class conversion, whereby a word is converted to another word class. Like cooptation, conversion is a productive operation which may lead instantaneously to the creation of new expressions. Such new expressions are theticals in the case of cooptation and new words belonging to another word class in the case of conversion. In the latter case, new verbs can be created from nouns (*net* > *to net*, *email* > *to email*), verbs from nouns (*to catch* > *the catch*, *to search* > *the search*), nouns from adjectives (*weekly* > *the weekly*, *red* > *the red*), etc. And like cooptation, conversion is an operation that is elusive to grammaticalization and, most importantly, it also can happen instantaneously: Speakers may propose new instances of conversion spontaneously, either to be replicated by other speakers or else to never being used again.

An example of the latter operation is provided by code-switching, whereby speakers alternate not between different parts of grammar but between two or more languages or language varieties in the context of a single conversation (e.g., Sankoff and Poplack 1981; Woolford 1983; Winford 2003). The two have in fact a number of features in common: Both are instantaneous operations, both appear to be more common in speech than in writing, and both can be said to involve an interaction of different coding conventions within a single

---

non-ellipted forms. For example, Brinton (2017: 202) observes that the English "reduced" forms *that/this said* predate the fuller forms *that/this being said/having been said*.

conversation, even if these conventions involve different languages or language varieties in the case of code-switching but different levels of the same language in the case of cooptation. As observed in Heine et al. (2017: 844–45), however, there are also differences between the two, and more research is needed on the relationship between them.

Cooptation may lead to "nonce'" formations, where the coopted expression is used once and never again. But once it has taken place the expression concerned may be used repeatedly and undergo the development sketched in a simplified format in the model of (11). With reference to this model, cooptation relates to X of Stage I.

(11)   Stages of development commonly observed in linguistic innovations
        I   Innovation: A speaker proposes a new form of language usage (X).
        II   Propagation: X is replicated by other language users, in some cases
             spreading to the speech community as a whole.
        III Conventionalization: X is used regularly, is entrenched, and becomes part
             of the established inventory of expressions and norms of the community
             concerned, thus resulting in language change.

The development in (11) can be arrested at any of the three stages, and presumably the vast majority of innovations that speakers propose do not proceed beyond Stage I. This could also apply to the thetical in (7b) (*you probably know already*), which may have been produced once and never again. But a few theticals develop further, going through all the three stages, and the mechanism responsible for new uses is invariably grammaticalization, eventually giving rise to DMs. Thus, the difference between (7b) and (7c) (*you know*) can be interpreted with reference to the model in (11) as one between Stage I and Stage III.

The innovation model applies in the same way to other kinds of cognitive–communicative operations, such as English word class conversion in the domain of word formation. Thus, as we observed earlier in this section, a speaker may propose some noun (e.g., *email*) to be converted to a new verb (Stage I). This new creation may or may not be taken up by other speakers. In the former case, a Stage II situation arises, and in the end, this can, but need not, lead to Stage III, where the new verb becomes part of the inventory of English verbs.

2.3.2   Reconstructing Cooptation

The innovation model sketched in (11) of Section 2.3.1 is by no means restricted to cooptation, noun-class conversion, and code-switching; rather, it applies as well to other kinds of change, such as lexicalization and – for the purposes of the present book most importantly – also to grammaticalization. As was observed in the Section 2.3.1, cooptation takes place at Stage I of the process. But much the same applies also to cases involving grammaticalization without cooptation, when speakers propose a new usage of existing material in specific contexts and, as in the case of cooptation, this usage may also consist of "nonce" formations. And the subsequent development to Stages II and III is also the same, being restricted in both cases to grammaticalization.

In sum, both kinds of processes are in accordance with the innovation model in (11), the crucial difference being the following: In one case, grammaticalization concerns material of sentence grammar, giving rise to "canonical" pathways of grammaticalization. In the other case, grammaticalization works on coopted material which emerges at Stage I, that is, on expressions showing the effects of cooptation listed in (9). These effects, that is, the emergence of a set of new grammatical properties, have the appearance of abrupt change, contrasting with the gradual step-by-step changes to be observed in grammaticalization. As was observed in Section 2.3.1, such effects can be observed daily when we form new theticals by transferring chunks of sentence grammar, like *you probably know already* in (7), for use on the metatextual level of discourse processing.

With its cooptation, an expression does not lose all of its semantic content; what happens, rather, is that instead of functioning on the sentence level, that content now relates to the level of discourse monitoring.[10]

Problems typically associated with the reconstruction of cooptation can be illustrated with the example of the Japanese DM *demo*. As the detailed reconstruction by Onodera (1995: 405–6; 2004; see also Section 5.2.2) suggests, *demo* has its origin in the unit-final segment [V-*te* + *mo*] (or [V + *de* + *mo*]), consisting of a verb (V), a copula marking the gerundive form of the verb (-*te* or *da/de*), and the clause-final adversative particle *mo* "but." Around the mid-sixteenth century, this segment appears to have been coopted, acquiring a metatextual function, shifting from clause-final to sentence-initial position, serving as a sentence connective, and changing from [V-*te* + *mo*] (or [V + *de* + *mo*]) to *demo*. The questions that are in need of further research are: When exactly in the sixteenth century did these grammatical changes occur? Did they appear already with the first instance of cooptation or did they evolve gradually in the development from Stage I to Stage III on the way to grammaticalizing into a DM? In particular, did the morphosyntactic change from the morphologically complex segment [V-*te* + *mo*] (or [V + *de* + *mo*]) to the unanalyzable marker *demo* coincide with cooptation or was it the result of subsequent grammaticalization? The data available do not allow for any conclusive answer to these questions.

---

[10] We are grateful to Laurel Brinton (personal communication of January 20, 2020) for having made us aware of this issue.

Similar questions arise time and again also in the diachronic analysis of other DMs. They are essential for understanding precisely what the nature and the contribution of cooptation is in the rise of DMs, and how the boundary between cooptation and grammaticalization is to be defined. To answer these questions, more historical information on the earliest phase in the development of DMs is needed.

As we will see in Section 3.3, however, much the same problem is also encountered in the reconstruction of grammaticalization, especially with reference to the identification of intermediate stages in the transition from earlier to later states of language use.

2.4   Discourse Grammar and the Role of Theticals

As observed in Section 2.3, the function of cooptation is to relate two levels or domains of discourse processing to one another. The distinction between these levels has been the subject of a number of studies (see Heine 2019 for an overview) and, as we will see in Section 8.1, this distinction exhibits significant neurolinguistic correlates (Heine, Kuteva, and Kaltenböck 2014; Heine et al. 2015; Haselow 2019; Heine 2019: 426–33). The present study relies on the framework of discourse grammar, where the distinction is described as one between sentence grammar and thetical grammar. Sentence grammar is organized in terms of propositional concepts and clauses and their combination – in the sense of Biber et al. (1999: 1069), it consists essentially of "clausal units," that is, clauses together with any dependent clauses embedded within them. It has been the only, or the main subject of mainstream theories of linguistics. The concern of thetical grammar is with theticals, that is, with linguistic discourse units which have metatextual functions and are immediately anchored in the situation of discourse.

DMs are not an isolated class of metatextual expressions; rather, they belong to the large class of theticals or, what in other research traditions is called parentheticals (e.g., Reinhart 1983; Dehé and Kavalova 2006; 2007; Blakemore 2007; Kaltenböck 2007; Schneider 2007a; 2007b; Dehé and Wichmann 2010; Dehé 2014). For example, Kaltenböck (2007: 31) treats DMs as one out of seventeen classes of parentheticals, other classes including comment clauses (e.g., *you know*), reporting clauses (e.g., *he replied*), question tags (e.g., *didn't he?*), etc. Theticals are defined as in (12).

(12)   Theticals are coopted units whose functions are determined by the situation of discourse, serving (a) to overcome constraints imposed by linearization in structuring texts, (b) to package text segments, (c) to provide the source of information, (d) to place a text in a wider perspective, e.g., by elaborating, providing an explanation, a comment or supplementary information, (e) to describe the attitudes of the speaker, and/or (f) to interact with the hearer.

The aim of the present section is to locate DMs within the domain of thetical categories.

Theticals are characterized by a set of grammatical properties, namely the ones in (13) (see Heine et al. 2020).[11] Examples illustrating these properties were provided in Section 2.3.1.

(13)   Grammatical properties characterizing theticals
        a Meaning: Their meaning is not part of the meaning of the sentence they are associated with.
        b Function: Their function is metatextual.
        c Syntax: They are not a syntactic constituent of the sentence in which they occur.
        d Prosody: They are likely to be set off prosodically from the rest of the sentence.
        e Semantic–pragmatic scope: They have scope beyond the sentence.
        f Placement: Depending on their discourse function they are flexible in their placement behavior.

The properties in (13) can also be expected to be found in the expressions that have been covered in the extensive literature on parentheticals. Nevertheless, there are reasons to distinguish the two terms, especially the following: First, theticals are defined with reference to the framework of discourse grammar (Kaltenböck, Heine, and Kuteva 2011; Heine et al. 2013). The term parenthetical, by contrast, is not normally defined in terms of some specific framework of linguistic analysis (but see, e.g., Dehé 2014). Second, while parentheticals tend to be described with reference to some or most of the properties listed in (13), the way they differ from other categories of grammar remains sometimes unclear. And third, whereas the term thetical relates to grammatical behavior in general, the term "parenthetical" is in many. of its uses restricted to semantic criteria (especially Urmson 1952; Hooper 1975) and may not correspond to the definition of theticals in (12), nor to the definition of the term parenthetical as it is used by other authors (e.g., Dehé and Kavalova 2007).

As was observed in Section 2.3, theticals are expressions that have been coopted for specific purposes of discourse processing. They serve a wide range of metatextual functions, especially the ones summarized in the definition of cooptation in (8) of Section 2.3. In general, these functions relate to the following areas of discourse processing or any combination thereof: Text organization, attitudes of the speaker, and speaker–hearer interaction.

---

[11] Most of the properties listed in (13) also figure in discussions of parentheticals. But there is a wide range of notions associated with the term "parenthetical," each highlighting specific manifestations of theticals. For example, Wiemer (2014: 450, fn. 23) defines parentheticals "as the output of a productive mechanism whereby lexical expressions (or whole syntagms) are downgraded to discursively secondary expressions."

The following examples may illustrate such functions. With the thetical *and I emphasise* <u>*could*</u> in (14) the speaker signals how the utterance is to be interpreted, highlighting the significance of one of the words used in the text segment (text organization). The thetical *I am sure* in (15), by contrast, adds information on the stance of the speaker vis-à-vis the utterance (attitudes of the speaker).

(14)   English (ICE-GB: s1b-059, #40; Kavalova 2007: 146; underlining in the original)[12]
        Madam will the Minister confirm that come the single uh Common Market that three hundred million EEC nationals <u>*could*</u> ***and I emphasise*** <u>***could***</u> *seek employment in this country without the need to obtain a work permit.*

(15)   English (ICE-GB: s2a-019-60)
        Just tell you who would like to ***I'm sure*** *know that the Queen is standing beside the Duke of Edinburgh.*

Theticals have been subclassified in a number of ways (Kaltenböck, Heine, and Kuteva 2011; Heine et al. 2013). For the purposes of the present study it is most of all two classifications that are of interest, namely one based on the constructional format and another based on the semantic anchoring of theticals.

With regard to their constructional format, three main types of theticals are distinguished (Heine, Kaltenböck, and Kuteva 2016: 188; Heine et al. 2017: 819–21), namely instantaneous, constructional, and formulaic theticals. *Instantaneous theticals* are fully compositional and can be designed spontaneously anytime and anywhere, and quite a few are uttered only once and never again. Thus, the following example of an instantaneous thetical, printed in bold, has the appearance of a freely composed clause – one that may never have been used before in this form and, conceivably, will never be produced again:

(16)   English (ICE-GB: s1b-075-68)
        We did feel uh ***union council was two or three weeks ago*** *when this was put to us that uh the increase from seven to sixteen uh was actually a very good idea.*

Constructional theticals are recurrent patterns or constructions of theticals having a schematic format and function. Accounts of a number of constructional theticals of spoken English are found in Kaltenböck (2007) and Dehé (2014: 3–6);[13] for another catalog see Kaltenböck, Heine, and Kuteva (2011:

---

[12] This example, as well as many other examples to follow, are taken from the *International Corpus of English* (ICE-GB).

[13] The constructional theticals treated by Dehé (2014: 44–46) in detail are non-restrictive (appositive) relative clauses, nominal appositions, comment clauses, reporting clauses, question tags, *and*-parentheticals, and *as*-parentheticals.

852–53, Table 1). In the terminology of Construction Grammar (Goldberg 1995; 2006; Croft 2001) they include both fully schematic and partially substantive constructions. Examples of fully schematic theticals are provided, for example, by comment clauses (see Brinton 2008), as in (17), reporting clauses, such as the one in (18), or phrasal appositions, as in (19).

(17) English (ICE-GB: s1b-048-124)
*The bulk of your your writing was done at a time when **I suppose** the who dunnit the sort of Agatha Christie novel was at its most popular.*

(18) English (Fforde 2003: 125)
*"My name is Hindley Earnshaw," **slurred the drunk**, "old Mr Earnshaw's eldest son."*

(19) English (Fforde 2003: 124)
*One of the men rose politely and inclined his head in greeting. This, I learned later, was Edgar Linton, **husband of Catherine Earnshaw**, who sat next to him on the wooden settle and glowered meditatively into the fire.*

An example of a partially substantive construction is found in (20), which is an *and*-thetical having the schematic format [*and* + clause] where *and* is the substantive part of the construction (see Kavalova 2007).

(20) English (ICE-GB: s1a-006 #325:1:B)
*By the time the luggage has come through **and planes are delayed anyway** you might as just might just as well say well come and meet us at eight or something and make it a bit decent for everyone.*

Formulaic theticals are unanalyzable, that is, their shape is largely or entirely invariable (see Kaltenböck, Heine, and Kuteva 2011: 870–72; Heine et al. 2013 for more details). They include formulae of social exchange (e.g., *Good morning!*, *hello!*, *please*) and interjections (e.g., *boy!*, *fuck!*, *hell!*). Another paradigm example of formulaic theticals is provided by DMs, such as *anyway*, *however*, *indeed*, *in fact*, *instead*, *I mean*, *now*, *okay*, *so*, *still*, *then*, *I think*, *well*, *what else*, or *you know*.

According to the second classification, theticals differ from one another also in their anchoring (Heine et al. 2017). Via anchoring, the speaker establishes a semantic–pragmatic link to the situation of discourse – that is, to the text, the attitudes of the speaker, and/or to speaker–hearer interaction. The following types of theticals are distinguished: (a) Constituent anchored theticals, (b) utterance anchored theticals, (c) context anchored theticals having a host, and (d) context anchored theticals without a host. DMs concern only types (a) and (b); hence, (c) and (d) are ignored here (see Heine et al. 2017: 821–28 for discussion).

Constituent anchored theticals have phrasal scope (Kaltenböck 2009: 52), that is, their semantic–pragmatic scope refers to one constituent of their host utterance, and they are placed either immediately before or after the anchor constituent. Many utterance anchored theticals also have uses as constituent anchored theticals, like the thetical *I think* in the following example, where its scope refers to the noun phrase *lecture three*.

(21)   English (ICE-GB: s1b-028-88)
         *Father McDade d'you remember in **I think** lecture three uh Rabbi Sacks said at one point faith is not measured by acts of worship alone.*

Utterance anchored theticals, which are the main topic of this book, select and have semantic–pragmatic scope over the content of the host utterance or even a larger piece of discourse. They do not show the kind of placement constraints that constituent anchored theticals do. Thus, the thetical *I would suggest* in (22a) could also be placed in some other slots of the utterance, as in (22b), including its right periphery, as in (22c).

(22)   English (ICE-GB: s2b-046-30)
         a *It's an issue which **I would suggest** will not go away.*
         b *It's an issue **I would suggest** which will not go away.*
         c *It's an issue which will not go away **I would suggest**.*

   To conclude, rather than forming an isolated category, DMs represent but one manifestation of the large pool of linguistic expressions defined as theticals in English or other languages that we are aware of: DMs are formulaic theticals being in most cases utterance anchored, but in some cases also constituent anchored (see Section 8.3).

2.5   Grammaticalization versus Cooptation

We saw in Sections 2.2–2.4 that there are two contrasting mechanisms that need to be distinguished for the reconstruction of DMs, and these mechanisms can be characterized thus: Grammaticalization enables speakers to develop new patterns and forms for constructing sentences, whereas cooptation makes it possible to transfer linguistic expressions to the metatextual level of discourse processing.

   In the present section we will deal with some of the effects that the two mechanisms have for reconstruction. The main differences between the two are highlighted in Section 2.5.1, while Section 2.5.2 makes a distinction between grammaticalization preceding and following cooptation. Section 2.5.3 briefly looks at some challenges facing the reconstruction of cooptation, and Section 2.5.4 finally turns to exceptional cases without cooptation.

2.5.1   *The "Decategorialization Paradox"*

Grammaticalization accompanies the lifespan of a DM from its beginning to its end. Cooptation, in contrast, occupies only a short, albeit intense phase in the

Table 2.2 *Contrasting changes typically observed in expressions undergoing cooptation and grammaticalization*

	Grammaticalization	Cooptation
Meaning	Change of meaning within the sentence	From meaning as part of the sentence to meaning outside the sentence
Function	Increasing functional dependence within the sentence	From function within the sentence to metatextual function
Syntax	Increasing syntactic integration within the sentence	From integrated to detached syntax
Prosody	Decrease in prosodic distinctiveness	Increase in prosodic distinctiveness
Semantic–pragmatic scope	Scope may change within the sentence	From scope within the sentence to scope over and beyond the sentence
Placement	Decrease in freedom of placement	Increase in freedom of placement

development of a DM, namely the phase when the expression concerned is transferred from the sentence level to the metatextual level of discourse. And the effects of the two mechanisms are equally different. Those of grammaticalization can be characterized with reference to the definition in Section 2.2.1 as gradually leading "from lexical to grammatical forms and from grammatical to even more grammatical forms" – in accordance with the parameters presented in Section 2.2.2. Thus, the expression concerned is gradually pressed into service for processing grammar, losing features that it had as a relatively free lexical or other form and increasingly becoming dependent on its grammatical environment.

The effects of cooptation are of a different kind. Being deployed for use on the level of discourse, the expression is freed from earlier constraints, no longer being dependent on its grammatical environment, and it acquires the properties listed in (9) of Section 2.3.1. Table 2.2 summarizes some general directions of change as they can be observed in many instances of grammaticalization as opposed to cooptation. Table 2.2 suggests that the two mechanisms have in fact contrasting effects, in the case of grammaticalization leading to a gradual loss of grammatical autonomy (Lehmann 2004: 155) or discourse autonomy (Hopper 1991: 30), or to stronger internal dependencies (Haspelmath 2004: 26), but to gains in grammatical and discourse autonomy or independence in the case of cooptation.

The different effects of the two mechanisms can be illustrated with the following example. English DMs like *if you will, as it were, I think*, etc. can be reconstructed back to semantically and morphosyntactically transparent lexical segments of sentence grammar. In accordance with Table 2.2, their development entailed two kinds of grammatical changes. In their external structure, their development was one of a gain of independence: As an effect of cooptation, they became syntactically detached, hence they lost their status as grammatical parts of the sentence. This affected their external status but not their internal one: In their internal structure, their development was one of increasing integration as a result of grammaticalization.

The observation that the development of such English DMs involves both decreasing external integration and increasing internal integration is referred to by Van Bogaert (2011: 302) from a different perspective as the "decategorialization paradox" facing grammaticalization studies:

> As a sign becomes more grammaticalized, it tends towards a fixed position in a given construction. This loss of syntagmatic variability is known as fixation. It can be seen that the evidence in favor of one grammaticalization criterion (decategorialization) flouts another (fixation). Thus, it would seem that the grammaticalization of CTMPs [complement taking mental predicates; a.n.] is plagued by a "decategorialization paradox. (Van Bogaert 2011: 302)

On the analysis proposed here, summarized in Table 2.2, the development of DMs is in fact fairly predictable rather than paradox, in that the two mechanisms involved have somehow contrasting effects: In their *internal* structure, DMs are integrated via decategorialization and bonding (see Section 2.2.2) – hence there is "fixation." Accordingly, *if you will*, *as it were*, and *I think* developed into more or less invariable expressions, having essentially no more internal morphological boundaries. In their *external* structure, by contrast, the opposite can be observed as a result of cooptation: Rather than integration or "fixation" there is an increase in syntactic freedom. Accordingly, rather than losing "syntagmatic variability," *if you will*, *as it were*, and *I think* gained variability vis-à-vis their host sentence.

2.5.2   Kinds and Degrees of Grammaticalization

2.5.2.1 Early versus Late Grammaticalization

Grammaticalization is best defined as a gradual process, and DMs differ greatly from one another in the extent to which they have been grammaticalized; thus, they can be arranged along a chain of relative degrees of grammaticalization. This development is cut across by cooptation, and the grammaticalization of DMs can be divided into two phases, namely one preceding and one following cooptation, and we will refer to the former as "early grammaticalization" and the latter as "late grammaticalization." While both conform to the definition and the principles of Section 2.2, they highlight different aspects of grammatical change.

Early grammaticalization tends to involve but is not restricted to what is commonly known as "primary grammaticalization," that is, the development from lexical to grammatical expressions (Givón 1991; Breban 2015; Breban and Kranich 2015; Kranich 2015).

While grammaticalization is important for the development of DMs, early grammaticalization need not be involved. For example, English adverbs like *now, still, then,* or *well* were coopted to serve as theticals apparently without there having been any pronounced effects of early grammaticalization. And much the same applies to a number of other languages having DMs that can be traced back to temporal or evaluative adverbs, as will be shown in the chapters to follow.

There are, however, also languages where such adverbs bear witness to a phase of early grammaticalization. For example, Korean DMs like *kuntey* and *kulem* can be reconstructed back to complex structures having the appearance of insubordinate clauses (see Evans 2007; Kaltenböck 2016) before they were grammaticalized into adverbials, as shown in (23).

(23)   Examples of internal decategorialization and erosion in two Korean DMs
        (Rhee 2019: 1)

	Source form		DM
a	*kuleha-n-tA-ey*	>	*kuntey*
	be.so-SIM-place-at		"then; but"
	"where it is so; whereas"		
b	*kuleha-myen*	>	*kulem*
	be.so-if		"right"
	"if it is so"		

Frequent examples of early grammaticalization are provided by adverbial phrases developing into adverbs and adpositions before being coopted. For example, French *à la rigueur* "at the rigor" was an adverbial phrase in the fifteenth century, subsequently grammaticalizing into the adverbial *à la rigueur* "harshly, strictly, rigorously," and it is only in the eighteenth century that the adverbial seems to have been coopted, turning into the DM *à la rigueur* (Prévost and Fagard 2018). In a similar way, Latin *in fine* "in the end," gave rise to the prepositional phrase *en (la) fin* in early French before it was grammaticalized into the temporal adverb *enfin* "in the end" and thereafter coopted into a DM (Hansen 2005a: 45). A third French example can be seen in *alors* "then, now," a grammaticalized form of Latin *ad illam horam* (or possibly *illa hora* "at that hour"; Hansen 1997: 163). It underwent further grammaticalization at the end of the thirteenth century, being extended to contexts where causal meanings evolved and, from the fourteenth century on, also occasionally conditional meanings. Cooptation of *alors* as a DM must have taken place in the fifteenth or sixteenth century, if not earlier (Degand and Fagard 2011; Degand and Evers-Vermeul 2015: 75–77).

English also provides examples of early grammaticalization leading to univerbation. For example, the expression *in fact* became frozen as a bare adverbial phrase in the mid-eighteenth century. But as a DM it is documented only at the beginning of the nineteenth century (Traugott 1995: 10). And the adverbial phrase *in dede* "in action" of Middle English had been grammaticalized into an epistemic adverbial by the mid-fifteenth century before it was coopted and turned into a DM around the end of the sixteenth century (Traugott and Dasher 2002: 159–64).

However, such processes leading to univerbation are not restricted to early grammaticalization, they also occur occasionally after cooptation, that is, in late grammaticalization.

Early grammaticalization also involves meaning. For example, a crosslinguistically widespread source for DMs is provided by temporal adverbs for "now" and "then," which may in specific contexts acquire consecutive, concessive, causal, or some other functions prior to their cooptation and development into DMs, as the case of French *alors* "then, now" shows (Degand and Fagard 2011; Degand and Evers-Vermeul 2015: 75–77).

Late grammaticalization follows cooptation, that is, it works on theticals:[14] The expression is no longer a constituent of the sentence, having the properties of theticals listed in (13) of Section 2.4, and it now develops gradually into a DM. It is typically associated with "secondary grammaticalization" (Givón 1991; Breban 2015; Breban and Kranich 2015; Kranich 2015). In terms of the parameters in (6) of Section 2.2.2, this development can be described as follows:

(a) *Context extension.* This is possibly the most conspicuous parameter involved in the development after cooptation: No longer being subject to syntactic constraints, the expression now tends to be exposed to a wider range of contexts, with the result that there can be a virtual "explosion" of new discourse functions arising in new contexts, as aptly described in the many studies on DMs that there are. Note also that, based on a pragmaticalization framework, Maj-Britt Mosegaard Hansen (2008; personal communication of January 24, 2020) argues that pragmaticalization involves a shift in meaning from the content level to the context level. Grammaticalization typically entails restrictions in positional flexibility.

---

[14] Maj-Britt Mosegaard Hansen (personal communication of January 24, 2020) suggests that "late grammaticalization" relates to what some scholars classify as pragmaticalization, and Laurel Brinton (personal communication of January 20, 2020) wonders "how theticals can be subject to (primary or secondary) grammaticalization (after cooptation) since presumably they aren't grammatical at all (they aren't part of sentence grammar)." In the present view, both thetical grammar and sentence grammar are part of grammar and grammaticalization applies to both domains of grammar. The difference is that thetical grammar works on the level of discourse processing and sentence grammar on the level of sentences. As expounded in Section 2.2.2, we argue that late grammaticalization can be described exhaustively in terms of the parameters proposed for grammaticalization.

However, the opposite can be observed in late grammaticalization, for the following reason: Context extension may have the effect that the thetical is placed in new slots within a sentence, thereby gaining positional flexibility. For example, with its cooptation presumably between 1150 and 1250, English *well* was placed preferably in the utterance-initial position. But after 1500 its use underwent massive context extension and *well* increasingly appeared in other positions of the sentence (cf. Jucker 1997: 104; Defour and Simon-Vandenbergen 2010: 669; see Section 3.2.11). Similarly, the English expression *no doubt* was coopted presumably in the period between 1350 and 1450, placed clause-initially in its first attestations. But later instances of it between 1570 and 1640 are not only found initially but also medially and finally (Simon-Vandenbergen 2007: 26–27).

Context extension in late grammaticalization thus is one of the factors contributing to the remarkable positional flexibility that DMs exhibit. For example, out of the twenty-five Korean DMs that will be presented in Table 6.2 of Section 6.1, three quarters (nineteen, 76%) can be placed in all three placement slots, that is, at the left or right periphery or in medial position.

(b) *Desemanticization.* A general semantic effect on theticals grammaticalizing into DMs is that they will lose some or all of their lexical content in specific contexts in favor of procedural discourse functions,[15] and there will increasingly be loss of sensibility to truth conditions. For example, presumably the most common source of DMs in the languages across the world is provided by temporal adverbials meaning "now" and "then," including English *now* (Aijmer 2002) and *then* (Haselow 2011) (cf. Section 8.2.2, Table 8.2). With their cooptation, the expressions concerned lose semantic features relating to referentiality and truth conditionality, and they also gradually lose their temporal meaning.

Desemanticization typically precedes erosion (see later in this section; see also Heine 2018b), but it seems that the two can also coincide in time in the development of DMs. For example, loss of the erstwhile predicative formative *da* in the Japanese DM *wake da* from the 1880s onwards (= erosion) was apparently accompanied by a slight change in the function of the DM, in that the loss of *da* correlates with desemanticization, namely a weakening or even loss of the speaker's evaluative judgment towards the content of the utterance, at the same time leading to a stronger involvement of the hearer (Suzuki 2006: 47–49; see Section 5.2.8).

---

[15] In contradistinction to conceptual expressions, the main function of procedural expressions is "to help the hearer *understand* an utterance by finding the intended combination of context, explicit content and cognitive effects" (Wilson 2011: 12).

(c) *Decategorialization.* Once an expression has been coopted, it may still exhibit internal compositionality, that is, there still can be morphological variability in its form. For example, after its cooptation between 1350 and 1450, the English expression *no doubt* had a number of variants, including *out of doubt* and *without doubt*, before it gradually developed into a largely invariable DM (Davidse, De Wolf, and Van Linden 2015). But, subsequently, the thetical may lose its internal morphosyntactic distinctiveness, and morphological components of the expression will gradually fuse into an unanalyzable form – a process commonly known as univerbation (Lehmann [1982] 2015: 89).[16]

Note, however, that the development leading to univerbation is restricted to *internal* decategorialization: In its external status, the expression does *not* undergo decategorialization, that is, the relation of the expression to the surrounding text usually remains unaffected in late grammaticalization.

(d) *Erosion.* On the whole, erosion has no strong impact on the grammaticalization of theticals into DMs, especially when mono-morphemic expressions are concerned. This tends to be different with poly-morphemic theticals. While some theticals remain largely unchanged on their way to becoming DMs (cf. *as it were, if you will*), others are phonetically reduced: With their fusion into unanalyzable forms, their phonetic substance is likely to be reduced. Erosion may, on the other hand, affect the segmental substance of the form. Segmental erosion is not a parameter that is widely used in the development of DMs – DMs "do not typically reduce phonetically," as Brinton (2017: 29) observes. Nevertheless, it does occur. For example, the French DM *enfin* "finally, in the end" (< *en* "in" + *fin* "end") can be reduced to *'fin*, being frequently denasalized and realized as [(a)fɛ] (Hansen 2005b: 168), and French *écoute donc* "so listen!" was reduced to *coudon* in the Quebequian French DM derived from it (Dostie 2004; Bolly 2014: 30).

In the English examples of (24) there are, in addition to decategorialization (univerbation), also occasional losses of phonetic substance (see also Van Bogaert 2011: 301). Examples in (24a–c) concern phonetic erosion, that is, phonetic segments, while those in (24d–h) show morphological erosion, that is, loss of morphological elements (Heine and Kuteva 2007: 42–44). The Korean examples that were presented in (23), by contrast, seem to involve only phonetic erosion.

---

[16] As a rule, this process takes place already in early grammaticalization (see earlier in this section).

(24)   Examples of erosion in English DMs (cf. Jucker 2002: 211–12;
         Brinton 2017: 30)

	Source form		DM
a	*I dare say*	>	*I dessey*
b	*look ye/thee*	>	*lookee*
c	*you know*	>	*y'know*
d	*as you say*	>	*you say*
e	*I guess*	>	*guess*
f	*I pray you*	>	*(I) pray*
g	*look you*	>	*look*
h	*say to me/us*	>	*say*

On the other hand, there can also be suprasegmental erosion in late
grammaticalization, involving the loss of prosodic features of the expression
concerned. Especially theticals developing into sentence-final DMs may, as a
result of frequent use, lose part or all of their prosodic distinctiveness and be
gradually integrated in the intonation group of the preceding text segment.

2.5.2.2 Weakly Grammaticalized Discourse Markers and "Conjuncts"

The gradual nature of grammaticalization has been described by means of a
variety of terms, such as "scale" (Lehmann [1982] 2015: 22; Heine and Claudi
1986), "continuum" (Heine and Reh 1984: 15), "chain" (Claudi and Heine
1986; Craig 1991: 455–56; Heine, Claudi, and Hünnemeyer 1991: 220–28;
Heine 1992), or "cline" (Hopper and Traugott 2003: 6–7). Considering that
"chain" is the only one of the terms that accounts for the interlocking structure
generally characterizing grammaticalization, this term is preferred here.[17]

Late grammaticalization can be described as such a chain, extending from
least to most strongly grammaticalized expression – that is, from free thetical
to fully-fledged DM. DMs differ greatly from one another with regard to where
they are located along this chain. But, in spite of all the rich information that
there is on the meanings and functions of DMs, the information on their
grammatical structure that exists is for the most part too scant to precisely
locate them along this chain.

In addition to the diachronic distinction proposed in Section 2.5.2.1 there is
also a synchronic one that is relevant for understanding the behavior of DMs.
According to the latter, two prototypical kinds of DMs can be distinguished,
namely strongly and weakly grammaticalized ones. *Strongly grammaticalized*
DMs correspond to the prototypical notion of "formulaic theticals" (Section
2.4), and of DMs, as they were defined in (7) of Section 1.1.2: They (a) have

---

[17] The term "interlocking structure" refers to the fact that, rather than leading directly from A to B,
grammaticalization processes commonly involve an intermediate stage AB, resulting in overlapping change of the kind A > AB > B (Heine 1992).

little, if any lexical meaning content, (b) they are multi-functional, expressing a wider range of discourse functions, (c) they exhibit marked features of desemanticization and decategorialization and in some cases also of erosion, and (d) they are restricted to one invariable form. The majority of DMs to be discussed in this book belong to this type.

Weakly grammaticalized DMs are located along the early stages making up a chain of grammaticalization: (a) They have retained part of the lexical meaning content they had prior to cooptation, (b) they tend to be monofunctional, expressing only one or a very limited range of discourse functions, (c) they show no or only little desemanticization and decategorialization and no erosion and, rather than being restricted to one invariable form, (d) they may exhibit pronounced morphosyntactic variation.

English examples of weak grammaticalization appear to be *I admit*, *in addition*, or *instead*. The marker *I admit* may be used as an example: As the description by Brinton (2017: 169–90) suggests, *I admit* (a) has retained much of its lexical meaning, (b) the range of discourse functions expressed by it is highly limited, (c) it shows little in terms of grammaticalization, and (d) rather than having one invariable form it includes a number of variants, described by Brinton (2017: 168) with the formula [*I/you* (modal) *admit*], namely *I admit*, *I will admit*, *I must admit*, *I have to admit*, *you admit*, *you will admit*, *you must admit*, and *you have to admit*.

Note that the notion "weakly grammaticalized DMs" also includes DMs which exhibit hardly any traces of grammaticalization. This applies most of all to young markers, in particular to DMs that evolved only recently. For example, the Japanese DM *jijitsu*, coopted from the noun *jijitsu* "fact," arose only towards the end of the nineteenth century or at the beginning of the twentieth century, hence there conceivably was not enough time to undergo any noticeable grammaticalization (Shibasaki 2018; see Section 5.2.5).

At the same time, there are also a few examples suggesting that grammaticalization can take place within the fairly short timespan of less than two centuries. For example, turning into a DM by the late eighteenth century, Korean *maliya* subsequently underwent several rounds of grammaticalization. Its functions were extended to include that of a pragmatic hedge in the early twentieth century, and more recently it assumed a counter-expectation function and a negative emotion marking function (Ahn and Yap 2013: 47–48; see Section 6.2.3).

One may wonder whether weakly grammaticalized DMs in fact qualify as DMs, especially since (d) raises a problem with regard to our definition in (7) of Section 1.1.2. To the extent that they have been treated as such by authors on whose analyses we rely, however, we will include such markers in our discussions, being aware that this position may not be shared by everyone.

Like strongly grammaticalized DMs, weakly grammaticalized ones are coopted expressions and, hence, are by definition theticals (see Section 2.4).

A substantial subgroup though not all of the latter have been described in the grammar tradition of English as conjuncts, conjunct adverbials (Quirk et al. 1985: 631–47), linking adverbials (Biber et al. 1999: 133, 875–92), supplements, connective adjuncts, or indicators (Huddleston and Pullum 2002: 775, 1354–55, 1740–41). Such terms are not used here because they are not fully in accordance with the definitional criteria adopted here. For one thing, not all expressions that have been subsumed under these terms are in accordance with our definition of theticals in (13) of Section 2.4. And for another thing, terms such as "adverbial" and "adjunct" are suggestive of notions of sentence grammar, used typically for a specific word class or kind of participants in the syntactic hierarchy of a sentence and/or for elements modifying the meaning of a clause, a verb, an adjective or an adverb.

Theticals, by contrast, are not part of syntactic hierarchies nor do they modify the meaning of their host sentence (see (13) of Section 2.4), and much the same applies typically also to conjuncts. Conjuncts, such as *however, in addition,* or final *though* (as in . . . *but he looks pretty fit, though*; Quirk et al. 1985: 632), can be said to have metatextual function, expressing how the speaker views the connection between two units of discourse, they have a relatively detached and "superordinate" role and are "markers of peripherality," characterized by separation from the rest of the clause by intonation boundaries in speech or by commas in writing, and they cannot be the focus of a cleft sentence, nor can they be the basis of contrast in alternative interrogation or negation (Quirk et al. 1985: 52, 631–32).

Weakly and strongly grammaticalized DMs occupy different spaces along a chain of grammaticalization but there is frequently no clear boundary separating the two. Furthermore, one and the same DM can be associated with different context-dependent usages, being weakly grammaticalized in some contexts but strongly grammaticalized in other contexts. For example, English *I think* has been found to serve, on the one hand, as a fairly variable thetical ("reduced parenthetical clause"), being suggestive of a weak degree of grammaticalization. On the one hand, it also shows usages as a strongly grammaticalized, invariable expression, allowing no variation in subject and tense marking – in short, showing the characteristics of a paradigm instance of a DM (see Biber et al. 1999: 197; Kaltenböck 2007: 47).

2.5.3   Some Effects of Cooptation on the Grammatical Status of DMs

For a student of grammaticalization, DMs exhibit a range of somewhat puzzling features. In the course of Chapter 1 we identified a number of such puzzling features – that is, features that set DMs apart from grammaticalizing expressions having no history of cooptation. These features are in particular the ones listed in (25).

(25)   Some features distinguishing DMs from non-coopted grammaticalized
          expressions (see Section 1.1.2, (11); Section 1.2.1.1, (15); see also Brinton
          2017: 29)
          a They do not commonly develop into clitics or affixes.
          b They do not fuse with the host form but rather remain independent units.
          c They do not become syntactically fixed.
          d They are positionally variable.
          e They are unusually multifunctional.

It would seem that these features can be accounted for with reference to the
effects of cooptation. A comprehensive account would be in need of a separate
study; suffice it here by way of illustration to draw attention to one of these
effects, namely that of syntax.

As was observed in (9c) of Section 2.3.1, a linguistic expression undergoing
cooptation will change from syntactic constituent of the sentence to syntactically unattached status. This change has two major implications. On the one
hand, it concerns the relation of the expression to its immediate text environment: Being syntactically unattached, the expression is distinctly less likely
than an expression not having undergone cooptation to enter into contact with
its semantic, morphosyntactic, and phonetic environment, that is, with its host
sentence. It may therefore not be surprising that the expression will neither
cliticize on nor fuse with some adjacent part of its host (cf. (25a–b)).[18]
Furthermore, being syntactically unattached, the expression is also unlikely
to enter into any fixed syntactic relation with its host (cf. (25c)).

On the other hand, being syntactically unattached also entails that coopted
expressions are fairly unconstrained with regard to their placement, and many
can occur in almost any position within or at the periphery of their host (cf.
(25d)). And this observation can also be held responsible for (25e), that is, for
the fact that DMs exhibit a high amount of multifunctional (or polyfunctional)
uses: Being parts of sentence grammar, grammaticalizing expressions without
a history of cooptation are syntactically constrained in the way they can be
extended to new contexts. Such constraints do not exist in coopted expressions: Being syntactically unattached, they can be, and in fact are frequently
extended to a range of different contexts. And since new contexts tend to
trigger the rise of new functions, DMs are likely to develop distinctly larger
sets of grammatical functions than other grammaticalizing expressions.

To conclude, the observations made in this section make it possible to
understand why DMs exhibit specific grammatical features such as those in
(25). Note, however, that these observations are not based on appropriate

---

[18] As was noted in Section 1.4.4, however, prosody provides a partial exception to this generalization: Prosodic integration differs remarkably with regard to the position occupied by a DM in
that it tends to be weak at the left periphery but strong at the right periphery of an utterance.

empirical evidence and it is hoped that such evidence will become available in future research.

2.5.4   *Grammaticalization without Cooptation*

It was observed in Section 2.5.2 that DMs are typically characterized by a development where grammaticalization is cut across by the operation of cooptation. However, there are a few exceptions, most notably those involving the following paths of development, which are crosslinguistically fairly common:

(a) Imperative > DM
(b) Interjection > DM

There is an obvious explanation for these exceptions: Both interjections and imperatives are theticals, usually conforming to the properties listed in (13) of Section 2.4. Accordingly, in their further development into DMs there is no cooptation; their development is restricted to grammaticalization, and more precisely to late grammaticalization in accordance with the patterns described in Section 2.5.2. The pathway in (a) will be dealt with in more detail in Section 8.4. (b) is in need of further research; it can be illustrated with the following example. The English expression *oh* used to be an interjection having an exclamatory function in Early Modern English – a function it has retained up to today. But, as the description by Jucker (2002: 229) suggests, *oh* was in some of its uses also grammaticalized in Present-Day English, turning into a fully-fledged DM for a change of state of information.

As we will see in Section 3.2.6, the Japanese sentence final particle *na* also provides an example of a DM whose history was confined to grammaticalization, yet involving neither imperatives nor interjections. And much the same applies to the DMs to be discussed in Chapter 7, which are the result of borrowing: Having been borrowed as DMs from their donor language, they do not undergo cooptation in the receiver language.

2.6   Conclusions

The position taken in this book to some extent echoes that taken of Waltereit, when he argues:

It seems that there are certain properties of "classical" grammaticalization that are shared by the rise of DMs, and that there are other properties of "classical" grammaticalization that are not shared by the rise of DMs. Instead of minimizing these differences, I would like to suggest that linguists should be grateful for them and analyze them in more detail, because they might tell us important things about the nature of both discourse markers and grammaticalization. (Waltereit 2002: 1004)

What Waltereit calls "classical grammaticalization" is in fact the notion that was described in Section 2.2 and that we will rely on in the chapters to follow. It is this notion that accounts for the principle of unidirectionality, which constitutes the backbone of grammaticalization theory and is highlighted in most definitions of grammaticalization, including the one presented in Section 2.2.1. For example, lexical items tend to lose part or all of their semantic, syntactic, and prosodic autonomy when developing into grammatical markers. Accordingly, when we encounter grammatical changes in the opposite direction, as they can be observed in the development of DMs, then this would seem to be in need of an explanation other than in terms of grammaticalization.

Alternative explanations are proposed, on the one hand, in work on pragmaticalization (Section 1.2.2). It was in fact students of pragmaticalization who first demonstrated that DMs exhibit a range of grammatical properties, in particular the ones that were listed in (19) of Section 1.2.2, which are hard to reconcile with grammaticalization. Hence, those properties are in need of a separate explanation to understand why DMs undergo a shift in meaning from the content level to the context level (Hansen 2008), or turn into "pragmatic items" (Dostie 2009: 203). The account proposed in this chapter is largely compatible with the pragmaticalization hypothesis but differs from the latter in two important aspects: First, rather than one unitary mechanism, the present account assumes that there are two distinct mechanisms involved, namely cooptation followed by grammaticalization. And second, unlike pragmaticalization, the cooptation hypothesis is based on a wider perspective of discourse structuring – one that accounts not only for DMs but also for other kinds of grammatical categories such as comment clauses, reporting clauses, non-restrictive relative clauses, as well as formulaic categories like interjections, formulae of social exchange, question tags, expletives, exclamatives, etc. (see Section 2.4).

On the other hand, an alternative account is also proposed in studies on degrammaticalization (e.g., Ramat 1992; Heine 2003; Andersen 2006; Norde 2009). But none of these studies are able to explain the properties characterizing the development of DMs (see (9) of Section 2.3). At the same time, it is exactly these properties that arise when speakers coopt text material for structuring their discourses, and – as we saw in Section 2.4 – DMs constitute only a small part of this text material.

The aim of the present study is to test the cooptation hypothesis by means of diachronic data in an attempt to trace the history of DMs back to its beginnings. The hypothesis entails a number of generalizations on grammatical change, most of all the ones in (26).

(26)   Grammatical changes to be expected in the genesis of a DM
         a Cooptation marks a distinct stage in the development of a DM.

b With its cooptation, an expression normally acquires the set of new grammatical properties listed in (40) of Chapter 1.5, namely usually the following:

(i)   Its meaning is not part of the meaning of the sentence it is associated with.

(ii) Its function is metatextual.

(iii) It is not a syntactic constituent of its host sentence.

(iv) It is likely to be set off prosodically from the rest of the sentence.

(v)   It has variable semantic–pragmatic scope over and beyond the sentence depending on its discourse function.

(vi) In accordance with the functions it fulfills it is placed preferably at the left periphery, less commonly at the right periphery, or within the sentence.

c These properties seem to appear all at once, rather than evolving gradually one after the other.

d While subsequently being exposed to grammaticalization, these properties remain largely unchanged in the ensuing history of the DM.

The effects of grammaticalization are of a different nature. It is most of all two interrelated effects that modern DMs tend to exhibit, involving the parameters of desemanticization and context extension (see Section 2.2.2). With regard to the former, DMs, first, lose all or part of their earlier lexical meaning. Second, they are no longer affected by the truth conditions of their host sentence (e.g., Jucker 1993: 436; Aijmer 1997: 2; Asher 2000). And third, they change from conceptual to procedural meaning (e.g., Hansen 1997: 162; Fraser 1999: 944; Schourup 1999; Wilson 2011; Crible 2017: 106).[19]

Context extension is arguably the most conspicuous effect of grammaticalization: In much the same way as DMs are desemanticized, their use is extended to new contexts inviting new discourse functions, frequently resulting in a plethora of new, pragmatically complex usages of DMs.

As we saw in Section 2.3, theticals arise instantaneously but, like other linguistic innovations (see (11) of Section 2.3), those developing into DMs need some time to be conventionalized (Section 2.5.2). A given DM may have evolved five or more centuries ago but, perhaps surprisingly, the properties listed in (26b) that it had acquired then are likely to survive up to the present.

---

[19] Laurel Brinton (personal communication of January 20, 2020) is wondering how change from conceptual to procedural meaning differs from change from lexical to metatextual meaning (i.e., cooptation). As the work by students of Relevance Theory suggests (especially Blakemore 1987; 1988; 2002; 2007), the former change may take place either within sentence grammar or within thetical grammar, whereas the latter invariably leads from sentence grammar to thetical grammar via cooptation. While change from conceptual to procedural meaning has been argued by a number of researchers to be a characteristic of DMs (see (11a) of Section 1.1.2), it is not restricted to the development of DMs and, hence, is not included in our definition of DMs in (7) of Section 1.1.2.

There are two partial exceptions though, and both concern grammaticalization. One concerns prosody: Due to frequent use, the DM may gradually adapt to the adjacent text and as a result lose some or all of its prosodic distinctiveness, especially when used at the right periphery of an utterance.

The second possible exception concerns placement. With its cooptation, the DM is likely to be strongly associated with one specific slot of an utterance, most commonly with its left periphery. But subsequently the DM is likely to be extended to new contexts and new placement slots (see the grammaticalization parameter of context extension in (6a) of Section 2.2.2) – with the effect that at later stages of its development the DM is likely to show greater positional variability than it had at its initial stage.

It is the hypotheses in (26) that will be tested in the chapters to follow, with a view to verifying or falsifying the cooptation hypothesis. To this end, more than twenty DMs are looked at in more detail, where Chapter 3 is devoted to English DMs, and Chapters 4, 5, and 6 to French, Japanese, and Korean DMs, respectively.

3 English Discourse Markers

3.1 Introduction

The question raised in this and the following chapters is the following: How do DMs arise, and how does this process account for the somewhat peculiar properties characterizing DMs, such as the ones listed in (26) of Section 2.6? To answer this question, we will be looking at a number of historically documented cases of DMs. The data and methodology on which the following chapters rely have been provided in the course of the last decades by many researchers, drawing on large text corpora and presenting detailed analyses on all aspects of the grammar and the history of DMs, most of all on their meanings and discourse functions (see Section 2.1). But, in addition, our analysis will also draw on the theoretical concepts presented in Sections 2.2 and 2.3. Our methodology will therefore be based on findings made both in grammaticalization studies and in discourse analysis.

In the following treatment, each DM is looked at in its own right without reference to alternative markers with which it may share close structural and/or diachronic relationships. For example, the English DMs *if you like* and *if you will* are similar in form and function (see Claridge 2013; Brinton 2014) but, as we will see later in this chapter, they differ remarkably in their historical development. And much the same applies to French *en fait* and *au fait* (Defour et al. 2010; Simon-Vandenbergen and Willems 2011). In this respect we do not always follow the authors on whose data we rely. For example, the English DM *if you like* is discussed by Claridge (2013) for good reasons jointly with *so to speak*, *so to say*, and *as it were*, but for equally good reasons jointly with *if you choose*, *if you prefer*, and *if you want* by Brinton (2014).

The drawbacks that our procedure may entail are characterized by Pons Bordería in the following way:

Papers studying "The grammaticalization of the DM X" were the norm, as if the evolution of any DM were a one-place single journey along the history of a language, overlooking the fact that any DM has grouped, clashed, shifted and moved among groups of related DMs. (Pons Bordería 2018: 8)

A structural characteristic of a number of DMs is in fact that they tend to cluster into what we will refer to loosely as "families" of DMs, or "meso-constructional schemas" (Traugott 2008), or "networks of overlapping grammatical patterns" (Fried and Östman 2005: 1775; see also Diessel 2019) – that is, groups of markers sharing features of close semantic, morphological, and/or etymological relationship. The English DMs *if you like* and *if you will*, or French *en fait* and *au fait* can be said to form or be part of such families but, even more commonly, such families are found in some other languages. In Korean there is a family of what Rhee (2019) calls *kule*-DMs, expressing consensus or agreement on what the previous speaker has said (Rhee 2015: 10, 15). Derived from *kule* '"be so," the markers include *kulay, kulssey, kuntey, ku (le)n(i)kka*, and *kulem*. The markers are not only similar in function but most of them arose in the same period between 1894 and 1917 when pre-modern novels were written in Korean (see Chapter 6). Similarly, in Japanese there is a family of particles having a range of similar discourse functions and being associated with three main usage patterns corresponding to differences in placement. Onodera (2004: 157) refers to this family as the *na* group, it consists of the particles *na, naa, ne, nee, no, nono*, and *noo*. Their general function is characterized by Onodera (2007: 241) as expressive, but they also play an important role as "involvement markers" (see Chapter 5).

It would therefore seem reasonable to discuss such families in toto, as some of the authors cited in fact do. But the main goal of this book is to identify regularities of grammatical change as they are attested in individual DMs as a basis for comparative analysis, reserving the analysis of "families" of DMs for a separate study.

3.2   Case Studies

It is the following English DMs that are discussed in the present section:

3.2.1 *After all*
3.2.2 *Anyway*
3.2.3 *I mean*
3.2.4 *If you like*
3.2.5 *If you will*
3.2.6 *Instead*
3.2.7 *Like*
3.2.8 *No doubt*
3.2.9 *Right*
3.2.10 *So to say/so to speak*
3.2.11 *Well*
3.2.12 *What else*

Considering that the goal of this book is to look at DMs from a comparative and a worldwide perspective, we will have to ignore many features of English DMs that are suspected to be of a more language-specific nature.

3.2.1   *English* After all[1]

The expression *after all* is commonly, though not always, found among the elements that are classified as English DMs, even if its use is fairly infrequent in corpora of spoken texts. For example, Beeching (2016: 34, Table 2.1) found only five tokens of it in her text corpora, compared for instance to 1,172 tokens of *I mean*, 1,914 of *you know*, or 4,226 of *well*. Among the functions of the DM, two clearly stand out, namely a justifying (or justificative) and a concessive (or counter-expectation) one, where the former is strongly associated with use in initial or medial position and the latter with the final position of a clause (Traugott 2018: 29–31; see also Lewis 2000: 31).[2] Example (1a) illustrates the justifying use of the DM in initial position and example (1b) the concessive use in final position.

(1)　　a　English (Sp, Bridgeman; Lewis 2000: 131, Table 5.2)
　　　　　*Firms will often see merger as an "easy way out"; **after all**, nobody in*
　　　　　business prefers to face competitive pressure.

　　　　b　English (2005 *Washington Post* [COCA]; Traugott 2018: 31, (6c))
　　　　　. . . it makes me think that perhaps this reading thing might catch on
　　　　　***after all**.*

After all typically establishes a link between two discourse segments, creating a justifying, concessive, or other relation between the two. However, there is not necessarily a first segment as long as the relevant information is recoverable from the situation of discourse, as in the following example of justifying *after all*.

(2)　　　English (Blakemore 1996: 338; Lewis 2000: 133, (11))
　　　　[The speaker takes an extremely large slice of cake]
　　　　***After all**, it is my birthday.*

---

[1] We wish to express our gratitude to Diana Lewis (personal communication of February 19, 2020) for critical comments on the present section.

[2] Rather than "justifying" and "concessive," Lewis (2000: 129) uses the terms justificative and counter-expectational *after all*. Based on the Rhetorical Structure Theory of Mann and Thompson (1987), Lewis (2000) proposes to distinguish counter-expectation from concession in that, unlike the latter, the former is non-relational (Diana Lewis, personal communication of February 19, 2020).

The present section provides a concise account of the rise of the DM *after all*. The account is confined to some salient grammatical characteristics of the process; for more detailed discussions, especially of the meaning and meaning changes of *after all*, the reader is referred to the diachronic analyses by Lewis (2000: 122–35; 2007) and Traugott (2018: 26–43).

From at least the mid-sixteenth century up until the early seventeenth century, *after all* appears to have been restricted to uses as a temporal adverbial phrase of sentence grammar, referring to the end of a temporal succession of immediately preceding speech events ("after some unspecified events that can be inferred from the context," "at the end"; Lewis 2007: 94; Traugott 2018: 41). It consisted of the preposition *after* and a noun phrase (e.g., *after all this fooling*) or the pronoun *all*, as in the following example, where the meaning of *after all* can be paraphrased "then, at the conclusion of the speech events" (Traugott 2018: 34).

(3)   English (1559, Helsinki, Machyn, Diary; Lewis 2000: 125, (3a); see also Traugott 2018: 35, (12))
        *... and doctur Whyt bysshope of Lynkolne dyd pryche at the sam masse; and **after all** they whent to his plasse to dener.*

Cooptation for purposes of discourse structuring must have taken place in the seventeenth century, with *after all* now typically occurring clause-initially but frequently preceded by contrastive conjunctions like *but* or *yet*:

(4)   English (1663, Hist, Pepys, Diary; Lewis 2000: 126, (4a))
        *... my Lord avoided speaking with him, and made him and many others stay expecting him, while I walked up and down [with my Lord] above an hour ... And yet, **after all**, there has been so little ground for his jealousy of me, that I am sometimes afraid that he do this only in policy to bring me to his side by scaring me.*

In such uses, the temporal sense of *after all* is still there but clearly weakened in favor of a contrastive or antithetical sense, already expressed by *yet* in (4), it "becomes a signal of counter-expectation," also denoting "in the end" (Lewis 2000: 126). *After all* does not seem to be part of the meaning of the sentence, it no longer needs to refer to immediately preceding events, it seems to be prosodically set off from its environment, and it is no longer a syntactic constituent of the sentence. Over the seventeenth and eighteenth centuries, the contexts of *after all* tend to be compatible with both a counter-expectation reading and an "in the end" reading (Lewis 2007: 96).

Which text piece of sentence grammar may have served as the source for cooptation cannot be established on the basis of the data presented by Lewis (2000: 122–35) and Traugott (2018: 26–43). Conceivably, such a text piece was provided by prepositional phrases as in *after all this*, which Traugott (2018: 38) finds to be attested very frequently from the 1650s on.

In the late seventeenth century, *after all* with pragmatically inferred concessive meaning was emerging in final position, even if justifying (justificative) readings were also available in initial position (Traugott 2018: 38). By around 1700 then, *after all*, as in (5), had acquired grammatical properties that allow classifying it as a DM.

(5)   English (1700 Congreve, *Way of the World* v; Traugott 2018: 36, (12a))
       *Why, if she should be innocent, if she should be wronged **after all**? I don't know what to think.*

Traugott describes this situation thus:

In examples like those in [(5); a.n.] *after* is not temporal, and *all* does not refer to "everything." Instead, *after all* signals concessive stance, e.g. "despite what I/others have said/thought." This is a DM use with contrastive meaning. Temporal finality has been backgrounded while the implicature of unexpected conclusion has been foregrounded. (Traugott 2018: 36)

While earlier *after all* occurred predominantly clause-initially it subsequently "moves down the clause," as Lewis (2000: 124, 130) puts it, and in final position it turned into a non-compositional DM, whose grammatical structure can be sketched as in (6).

(6)   Grammatical properties characterizing *after all* as a DM around 1700
       a Meaning: Its meaning was not part of the meaning of the sentence it was associated with, being non-referential and expressing concessivity, signaling that a tactical/strategic move involving the speaker's attitude is being made.
       b Function: Its function was metatextual, cueing "the speaker's metatextual stance toward the relationship between two segments" (Traugott 2018: 37).
       c Syntax: It is no longer a syntactic constituent of the sentence.
       d Prosody: There is no information on the prosodic shape of the DM but occasional use of punctuation marks before and after it (e.g., Traugott 2018: 36, (12b)) might suggest that it was or could be set off prosodically from the rest of the sentence.
       e Semantic–pragmatic scope: Its scope extended over the discourse segments that it relates to one another.
       f Placement: Its main position was now clause-final, but it also occurred in initial position, with the meaning "in the end" (Traugott 2018: 37).

The structure in (6) has largely been retained up until Present-Day English. Changes involved, first, the function of *after all*: The concessive meaning of *after all* on its own was firmly established in the eighteenth century, and changes now concerned most of all the development of *after all* as a justificative marker (Lewis 2007). Up to well into the nineteenth century, *after all* had overlapping counter-expectation and "conclusive" readings ("in sum" or "after considering everything"), and the latter then developing into justificative *after all* (Lewis 2007: 96). By around 1900, there was a clear correlation between function and placement: The justificational function was strongly associated with the left periphery, and the concessive function with the right periphery of a sentence, being unintegrated syntactically.

Second, there was a change in the placement of *after all* (cf. (6f)). Being extended to a wider range of contexts, *after all* had acquired common usages in all three major positions at the left and the right periphery and sentence-medially by the mid-nineteenth century. The DM is found in Present-Day English clearly most frequently in initial position, followed by final and medial placement (see Traugott 2018: 33, Tables 2.1A and 2.1B). And third, change also involved prosody (i.e., (6d)): As observed by Lewis (2000: 131), *after all* in final position no longer forms an intonation group of its own. Note that, unlike DMs in initial position of a sentence or clause, in final position they easily lose features of their prosodic distinctiveness, to the extent that they tend to be integrated within the intonation contour of the preceding clause (on similar observations in Korean DMs, see Section 6.1).

The role played by grammaticalization in the development of *after all* was most of all of two kinds. On the one hand, it involved a gradual process from free, fully compositional prepositional phrase (*after* + NP) to the non-compositional particle *after all*, mainly via internal decategorialization of an earlier lexical phrase. When exactly this process of univerbation into an unanalyzable expression set in is not entirely clear on the basis of the data available. Presumably, it started out prior to cooptation when *after all* was still used as a temporal adverbial (Lewis 2007: 94) and was largely concluded when *after all* had been established as a DM.

On the other hand, grammaticalization involved context extension and desemanticization, whereby in specific contexts *after all* gradually lost its temporal meaning in favor of discourse structuring functions such as signaling contrasts between two pieces of discourse. This process also set in before cooptation, when the use of *after all* was extended to contexts "implicating causal reasoning" ("in the end"; Traugott 2018: 41). But as the descriptions by Lewis (2000; 2007) and Traugott (2018) show, the process was most pronounced following the cooptation of *after all*, shaping much of the semantic history of the DM after 1700. By the mid-nineteenth century, it was found primarily with justificational meaning in initial position ("my reason for saying x is"; Lewis 2007; Traugott 2018: 41).

To conclude, the DM *after all* can be understood to be the joint result of grammaticalization and cooptation. Grammaticalization can be held responsible for the emergence of an invariable particle, over time changing from contentful to procedural meaning and acquiring a range of context-induced new functions. With its cooptation and establishment as a DM around 1700 or slightly earlier, by contrast, *after all* acquired a new set of grammatical properties characteristic of theticals (see Section 2.4), or "extra-clausal" expressions (Dik 1997), and these properties have largely survived its ensuing history, determining its grammatical status in Present-Day English.

3.2.2 *English* Anyway[3]

According to Ferrara (1997: 347) there are three main usages of *anyway*, namely an additive ("besides"; cf. (7a)), a dismissive ("nonetheless"; cf. (7b)), and a resumptive one ("reconnecting segments of discourse").

(7)   English (Ferrara 1997: 347, (3b), (3a))
        a *They didn't marry because he was of a different faith and too old **anyway***
          (= besides).
        b *He was a fickle man but she loved him **anyway*** (= nonetheless).

Only the second usage is that of a DM, classified by Fraser (2009) as a topic orientation marker. The DM is associated with two main usages, namely at the left periphery of an utterance, illustrated in (8), and at its right periphery, cf. (9); see Haselow (2015: 183, Table 2) for a comparison of the two contrasting uses of the DM. The former has to do with upcoming discourse (Aijmer 2016: 53), indicating a specific conception of what will be going on in emerging discourse relative to the prior discourse while in the latter usage, *anyway* is described by Aijmer (2016: 53) as modal and intersubjective, linking two units that have already been produced, expressing a conceptual–conditional relation (see Haselow 2015 for detailed discussion of various treatments of *anyway*; see also Aijmer 2016). Prosodic integration with the surrounding text tends to be weak at the left periphery but strong at the right periphery of an utterance, but right-periphery *anyway* can be intonationally stressed or unstressed (Haselow 2015: 163, 169). The two usages are different to the extent that they can occur in one and the same utterance, as for example in *Anyway – I wanted to go anyway.*

(8)   English (ICE-GB s1a-051, 4-5; Haselow 2015: 163, (1a))
        B: *I seem to get slower and uh (.) I don't walk well nowadays (.)*
        ***Anyway** what can one expect (.)*

(9)   English (ICE-GB s1a-100, 132-3; Haselow 2015: 163, (1b))
        A: *right well she can get in for a quid then can't she*
        B: *oh she said she could get in **anyway***

In addition, *anyway* is also found as a stand-alone, (e.g., *Anyway.*) with the function of closing an unresolved topic (Aijmer 2016: 53).

The DM can be traced back to the Old English noun phrase *ænig weg* "any way, path, route," changing to Middle English *any wei/way*, which was

---

[3] We wish to thank Alexander Haselow for all his assistance in working on this section.

grammaticalized to an adverbial meaning "in any way or manner, by any means," already attested in Late Middle English (1350–1500) (Haselow 2015: 172). The expression *any way* continued to occur as an infrequently used clause-internal adverbial of sentence grammar in Early Modern English (1500–1710).

The earliest attested example of *anyway* (or *any way*) in a construction possibly related to its later development into a DM is found in the following text piece, where *any way* might have been ambiguous between a sentence grammar adverbial and a discourse-grammatical marker:

(10)   English (CLMETEV: Goldsmith, *The vicar of Wakefield*, Ch. 21 [1766]; Haselow 2015: 174, (13))
        *"I suppose, my dear," cried he, "we shall have it all in a, lump." – "In a lump!" cried the other, "I hope we may get it **any way**; and that I am resolved we will this very night, or out she tramps, bag and baggage."*

Haselow (2015: 174) provides a rich analysis of this example, suggesting that both interpretations seem possible. However, whether in fact cooptation had already taken place at this stage cannot be established beyond any reasonable doubt. In the absence of unambiguous grammatical evidence it remains unclear in particular whether an interpretation in terms of a discourse-structuring marker, that is a thetical, is really that of the speaker who uttered (10) or that of the analyzing linguist. As we observed in Section 2.1, ambiguous cases of this kind are generally ignored in the present work. Note that such possibly "ambiguous" uses continued to occur right into Late Modern English (1710–1920). Nevertheless, it is possible that use of *any way* in this kind of final-position construction provided a model for cooptation, paving the way for the rise of the DM *anyway* almost a century later; more text data are needed to decide on this issue.

The text data available suggest that around the mid-nineteenth century, roughly between 1840 and 1865, if not earlier, *anyway* clearly had acquired the main hallmarks of a coopted unit and of a DM. Example (11) illustrates this usage at the right periphery (RP) and (12) at the left periphery (LP). As the datings suggest, the former conceivably occurred slightly earlier than the latter.

(11)   English (CLMETEV: Thakeray, *Vanity Fair*, Ch. XXXI [1847/48]; Haselow 2015: 175, (15))
        *... "My service to ye, me fine Madam, and I am glad to see ye so cheerful," thought Peggy. "It's not YOU that will cry your eyes out with grief, **anyway**."*

(12)   English (CLMETEV: Collins, *The woman in white*, Ch. VI [1859/60]; Haselow 2015: 177, (17a))
        *Laura's face and manner suggested to me that this last consideration had occurred to her as well as to myself. **Anyway**, it is only a trifling matter, and I am almost ashamed to put it down here in writing ...*

The main evidence showing that *anyway* had turned into a thetical by the middle of the nineteenth century or earlier is summarized in (13).

(13) Evidence for cooptation of *anyway* around the mid-nineteenth century (see Haselow 2015)

   a Meaning: The meaning of *anyway* is no longer part of the meaning of its host sentence, its validity is not bound to or inferentially linked to the propositional content of its host.

   b Function: *Anyway* now seems to function as a metatextual unit, it establishes a sequential relation between discourse units rather than relations within the sentence (Haselow 2015: 180), marking the unit it accompanies as contextually linked to prior discourse.

   c Syntax: Changing from sentence-internal to sentence-external expression it now lacks constituent status, it "neither governs any of the constituents of the structural units it refers to, nor is itself governed by any other constituent" (Haselow 2015: 176, 180).

   d Prosody: It is likely to be set off prosodically, forming an intonation unit of its own (Haselow 2015: 178).

   e Semantic–pragmatic scope: It has wider scope, extending over a sequence of discourse units. At the left periphery, it has scope over larger chunks of discourse while at the right periphery it has scope over two adjacent units of talk (Haselow 2015: 180, 183).

   f Placement: It changed from clause-internal adverbial to DM placed at the right or the left periphery of its host.

Thus, the grammatical structure of coopted *anyway* differs dramatically from that of the sentence-internal adverbial *anyway*. We did not find any convincing evidence to suggest that the changes in (13) took place gradually, one after the other; rather, the properties listed in (13) all appear to have been in place around the mid-nineteenth century, surviving the subsequent history of the DM largely unchanged into Present-Day English.

At the left periphery, *anyway* is used to dismiss prior talk as secondary, exhibiting "a discourse-structuring function in that the speaker prepares a particular type of contribution in on-going discourse,"[4] "It has no effect on any of the discourse units it links on the illocutionary level" (Haselow 2015: 176, 178).

A further observation suggesting that *anyway* has detached itself from the sentence grammar unit *any way* is the following. It is now used with a

---

[4] Left periphery *anyway* was ambiguous between a sentence grammar (adverbial) and a DM interpretation. In fact, it quite commonly happens that coopted units can occur in the same context as the expression from which they are historically derived. As Haselow's (2015: 176) discussion clearly shows, the meaning and function of the two are very different. Another difference typically to be expected is that the two are or can be prosodically separated. This might also apply to left periphery *anyway*, which is separated by a comma from the following utterance in example (12).

procedural rather than a conceptual function. Univerbation leading from *any way* to *anyway* roughly appears to coincide with cooptation, occurring almost exclusively in dialogic contexts (cf. Haselow 2015: 175, 178). The first attested example of right periphery *anyway* written as a single word dates back to 1847–48 (Haselow 2015, (14)) and of left periphery *anyway* to 1859–60 (Haselow 2015, (17a)).

Univerbation into an unanalyzable item, however, is not a diagnostic for cooptation: As we saw in Section 2.5, it may precede, coincide with, or follow cooptation in the development of DMs. Note further that the present instance is also of limited value as a diagnostic because it reflects a new orthographic convention, first appearing in dialogic contexts, rather than actual language use.

In a similar way as in other languages (see Chapters 4–6), cooptation marked a dramatic change in the history of *anyway*, one effect being that the expression is now fully established in the right periphery (RP) and the left periphery (LP) of its host utterance. Haselow concludes:

> To sum up, *anyway* became established as a discourse-grammatical marker with procedural functions in the LP and RP in the middle of the nineteenth century, but ambiguous uses in the RP occurred already toward the end of the eighteenth century. The original adverbial function survived with the noun phrase *any way* in medial position ... (Haselow 2015: 178)

Grammaticalization took place, on the one hand, preceding cooptation, when *anyway* gradually changed from noun phrase into more abstract adverbial, losing its concrete lexical content via desemanticization and its internal word boundary via internal decategorialization (see Section 2.2.2). On the other hand, there also appears to have been late grammaticalization following cooptation whereby *anyway* gradually developed some kind of paradigmatic relationship with other DMs, namely *then*, *though*, *but*, and *actually* in the case of right periphery *anyway* (Thompson and Suzuki 2011; Haselow 2013), and *actually*, *well*, and *so* in the case of left periphery *anyway* (Haselow 2015: 180–81). Haselow describes this development thus:

> As a grammaticalized element, *anyway* became integrated into a paradigm of peripheral markers, i.e. it became a member of a set with elements with the same positional restrictions and a common function or categorical value, thus contrasting with other members of the paradigm. (Haselow 2015: 180)

3.2.3   *English* I mean

Also called a "filler," a "hesitation marker," a "fumble," a discourse marker, or a lexicalized clause (Schiffrin 1987: 319), *I mean* is commonly though not always (cf. Fraser 1990: 392) classified as a DM. Brinton (2008: 111, 113) calls it a comment clause that contrasts, e.g., with *you know* in that it denotes less expected or predictable repairs (see Brinton 2008: 111, 113 for discussion). Beeching (2016: 183) divides the functions into non-pragmatic marking or canonical usages (e.g., *do you mean meaningful?*), emphatic and tag forms (e.g., *if you know what I mean*), and fully fledged pragmatic marking usages, that is, what we call here the DM uses. As elsewhere in this study, our interest here is with the distinction between Beeching's first-named usage, where *I mean* is a lexical verb and a sentence grammar constituent, illustrated in (14), and as a DM, cf. (15), and we will refer to the former as *I mean$_1$*. The latter, called parenthetical *I mean* by Brinton (2008: 125) and a pragmatic marker by Beeching (2016), will be referred to as *I mean$_2$*, a multifunctional DM which "is used to establish and negotiate meaning with the hearer" (Beeching 2016: 185). Its main functions are listed in (16), where (16c) accounts for the overwhelming majority of usages.

(14) English (2018 Traugott 2018: 27)
      *By a DM **I mean** a metatextual marker that signals some kind of relationship between clauses/utterances.*

(15) English (1986 *The Herald* 1 [ACE]; Brinton 2008: 116, (8c))
      *Do we need the one-cent coin? **I mean**, how long has it been since one could buy something for a cent ...?*

(16) The main functions of *I mean$_2$* (Beeching 2016: 185–90)
      a Self-repair
      b Hesitation
      c Clarification, exemplification, elaboration, reformulation
      d Concession and nuancing ("... **I mean** ... *but*")
      e Hedging

While there are a few occurrences of *I mean* with a metatextual sense in Old English (*ic mæne*), the rise of the DM *I mean$_2$* appears to be located in Middle English. Semantically, a metatextual function, namely to express a reformulation, appears in Chaucer's *The Canterbury Tales* (1392–1400), but this function is expressed by *I mean$_1$* rather than *I mean$_2$* (see Brinton 2008: 121, (17)). However, already at that time there are uses of *I mean$_2$* in Middle English. Early attestations of *I mean* that Brinton (2008: 119–20) provides date back to the end of the fourteenth century, and they concern both *I mean$_1$*, as in (17), and *I mean$_2$* as a "reduced parenthetical" in (18). In its thetical use, *I mean$_2$* (*I mene*) occurs either on its own, as in (18), or with an adverbial, clausal, or nominal complement, as in (19), where its complement is *charitee* "charity."

(17) English (1390 Gower, *Confessio Amantis* 1.15 [*MED*]; Brinton 2008: 119, (13a))
      *That is love, of which **I mene** To trete.*
      ["that is love of which I intend to treat"]

(18)   English (1392–1400 Chaucer, *The Canterbury Tales*; Brinton 2008: 127, (28c))
*Medleth namoore with that art, **I mene**, / For if ye doon, youre thrift is goon ful clene.*
["meddle no more with that art, I mean, for if you do, your success will be gone completely"].

(19)   English (1415 Hoccleve, *Address to Sir John Oldcastle* [Hnt HM 111] 1 [*MED*]; Brinton 2008: 121–22, (19b))
*The ladre of heuene, **I meene charitee**, Comandith vs, if our brothir be falle In to errour, to haue of him pitee.*
["the ladder of heaven, **I mean** charity, command us, if our brother is fallen into error to have pity with him"]

That (17) represents *I mean₁* is suggested by the fact that it is syntactically integrated both externally, being the main verb of a relative clause, and internally, taking an infinitival complement. In (18) and (19), by contrast, it appears to be syntactically independent, being syntactically licenced neither by the preceding nor the following clause, and prosodically set off, as might be suggested by the use of commas (see Section 2.1).

In addition, there are a number of what Brinton (2008: 125) calls "indeterminate structures." For example, in (20) it remains unclear whether initial *I mean* acts as a main clause without object complement or without complementizer, or else as a thetical (or parenthetical) at the left periphery of the utterance.

(20)   English (1477–84 Caxton, *The Prologues and Epilogues* 37 [HC]; Brinton 2008: 125, (25b))
I mene / *Maister Geffrey Chaucer hath translated this sayd werke oute of latyn in to oure vsual and moder tonge.*
["I mean Master Geoffrey Chaucer has translated this said work into our usual mother tongue"]

The question here is: Can indeterminate structures like that in (20) be taken to present an intermediate stage of ambiguity characteristic of grammaticalization? As we will argue in more detail in Section 3.3, the answer is in the negative, for the following reason: Ambiguity such as that in (20) can be due to a number of different factors, in particular either (a) being intended the writer, (b) being due to the particular interpretation volunteered by the researcher, or simply (c) being due to lack of appropriate contextual and/or grammatical information. For example, with regard to (c) it is quite possible that the two different interpretations proposed by Brinton were distinguished by means of prosodic features but that these features were not marked in the written text – hence, that there actually was no ambiguity or indeterminacy involved at the time when (20) was produced in the fifteenth century. In short, more information, especially prosodic information, would be needed to decide how (20) is to be analyzed. Until such information becomes available we will assume that the question just raised must in fact be answered in the negative: There is so far no compelling evidence to claim with confidence that (20) represents a case of intermediate structure as it is characteristic of grammaticalization.

Brinton (2008: 120) notes that unequivocal examples of "parenthetical *I mean* used in the first appositional sense – the self-repair or mistake editing sense – do not occur until the Early Modern English period" in the seventeenth century, giving examples such as (21).

(21)   English (1625 Fletcher, *The Humorous Lieutenant* iii.i [*OED*]; Brinton 2008: 120, (16b))
        *Set 'em off Lady **I mean** sell 'em.*

Example (21) is in fact an instance of *I mean₂* but, as we argue, it reflects a later use of *I mean₂*. Cooptation must have taken place more than two centuries earlier – that is, *I mean₂* was already in place around 1400, as the example in (18) suggests.

To conclude, by the end of the fourteenth century, *I mean₂* must have been available, that is, cooptation of *I mean₂* from *I mean₁* appears to have taken place at some stage in the late fourteenth century, if not earlier. There are no unambiguous clues to suggest that the expression had undergone a noteworthy amount of grammaticalization at that stage. *I mean₂* in Middle English and Early Modern English primarily served the organization of texts, denoting mostly "namely, that is" (Brinton 2008: 127).

Grammaticalization took place subsequently, as is suggested by the following observation. Appositional *I mean₂* ("parenthetical *I mean*") in the self-repair or mistake editing sense and the reformulation sense (e.g., "in other words") occurs for the first time in Modern English (Brinton 2008: 121) and might reflect the first major wave of grammaticalization.

We concur with Brinton in observing that there is little support for the matrix clause hypothesis proposed by Thompson and Mulac (1991), according to which the thetical originates in a main clause grammaticalized to a parenthetical (see also Beeching 2016: 204). Brinton proposes an alternative scenario of gradual evolution: "The predominant structure – *I mean* followed by a phrasal category [NP, VP, AP, PP, AdvP; a.n.] – is the most likely source of this parenthetical structure" (Brinton 2008: 127). The stages she proposes are listed in (22).[5]

---

[5] For a related proposal based on a synchronic, generative framework see Emonds (1973).

(22)   Stages in the development of the DM *I mean* according to Brinton (2008: 127)
  a *I mean* governs a phrasal expression and has scope within the sentence.
  b The bonds between *I mean* and the phrasal expression are weakened or loosened.
  c *I mean* can begin to be postposed to the phrasal expression.
  d The phrasal expression is then reanalyzed as an independent clause.
  e *I mean* is reanalyzed as a syntactically free parenthetical with scope over the sentence and over discourse, and it can be pre- or postposed to clausal expressions.

Stages (22a) and (22e) are well attested both in earlier periods of English and in Present-Day English, while we do not find fully concrete evidence for the remaining stages (22b–d), that is, for a gradual transition from *I mean$_1$* to *I mean$_2$*: Note that both (22a) and (22e) appear roughly at the same time around the end of the fourteenth century and it seems hard to establish not only how but also when such a process could have taken place.

Nevertheless, Brinton's reconstruction is compatible with ours if one assumes that (22b–e) reflect effects of cooptation, which seems to be responsible for the following changes that must have taken place toward the end of the fourteenth century:

(23)   Effects of cooptation in the shift from *I mean$_1$* to *I mean$_2$*
  a Meaning: From meaning as part of the sentence to meaning outside of the sentence.
  b Function: From sentence-internal to metatextual function.
  c Syntax: From sentence-internal reduced clause to syntactically independent expression.
  d Prosody: From prosodically integrated constituent to an expression that tends to be, or may be prosodically set off.
  e Semantic–pragmatic scope: From scope within the sentence to scope over the situation of discourse: "It increases its scope from relating to phrasal or clausal complements to functioning on a global level" (Brinton 2008: 131).
  f Placement: From positionally constrained expression to DM that can be placed within the sentence or at its left or right periphery (cf. Brinton 2017, Table 6.2).

Beeching (2016: 204) observes that examples of *I mean* between the fourteenth and the seventeenth centuries tended to be syntactically integrated and to have a signifying sense. This might suggest that after the split into *I mean$_1$* and *I mean$_2$*, the former continued to constitute the main option used by speakers or writers to structure their texts.

There is reason to assume that subsequent to its cooptation *I mean$_2$* underwent a number of processes of grammaticalization, as aptly pointed out by Brinton (2008: 130–31), namely the following (see Section 2.2.2, (6)). First, there was context extension: "By a process of invited inferencing, *I mean* acquires non-referential (pragmatic or procedural) meanings such as mistake editing, clarification, precision, and exemplification" (Brinton 2008: 131). Second, there was desemanticization whereby *I mean* lost its lexical meaning, changing from lexical verb to DM, acquiring a number of procedural functions, such as mistake editing, clarification, precision, and exemplification (see Brinton 2008: 130–31 for discussion). We found no evidence to the effect that desemanticization had taken place already prior to 1400.[6] After 1400, *I mean* was well established as a thetical: It was fairly free in its placement, had wide scope rather than being restricted in its scope to phrasal or clausal complements, and it was typically associated with a text organizing function ("namely, that is"; Brinton 2008: 127), even if a lexical reading was presumably still available.

Brinton (2008: 132) remarks that *I mean* acquired subjective and intersubjective meanings and concludes that this was due to grammaticalization. Note, however, that this is not a process that is restricted to grammaticalization, it could as well have been the result of cooptation, whereby the expression was transferred to the metatextual level anchored in the situation of discourse, in particular to the attitudes of the speaker ("subjectification") and speaker–hearer interaction ("intersubjectification").[7] And it is exactly these components that appear to have been centrally involved in the development of the DM *I mean₂*.

In addition to desematicization, *I mean₂* also experienced internal decategorialization leading to univerbation, becoming largely frozen in its first person singular, present tense form, and having lost "the ability to be modified by adverbials or to take phrasal or clausal complements" (Brinton 2008: 130–31).[8] And there are also traces of erosion (or phonological attrition): Brinton (2008: 131) observes that *I mean₂* tends to be reduced to [əmi:n] or [mi:n].

To conclude, the fact that *I mean₂* gained, rather than lost syntactic independence, assumed the metatextual functions mentioned, and experienced an increase in semantic–pragmatic scope cannot reasonably be attributed to grammaticalization but is a predictable outcome of cooptation (Section 2.3). As we just saw, there are also features of grammaticalization characterizing the use of *I mean₂*. But on the basis of the data available it would seem that the main grammatical properties of *I mean₂* in Present-Day English, such as the ones listed in (23), can be traced back to the late fourteenth century, or earlier,

---

[6] It is quite possible that there was a prior phase of grammaticalization of *I mean*. But if there was, it does not relate to the cooptation hypothesis proposed here.

[7] As shown in Kaltenböck, Heine, and Kuteva (2011), the meaning of theticals is determined by the situation of discourse, whose components include text organization, speaker attitudes, and speaker–hearer interaction (see Section 2.3).

[8] Maj-Brit Mosegaard Hansen (personal communication) doubts whether *I mean* is in fact a "frozen" unit.

when the expression was transferred from the level of sentence grammar to the level of discourse monitoring.

3.2.4   *English* If you like

The DMs of Present-Day English include the items *so to speak* or *so to say*, *as it were*, and *if you like*. As Claridge (2013: 161) shows, all are formulaic expressions that, depending on their discourse function, can appear in various slots of a sentence, and fufill a basic hedging function. Our interest in this section is restricted to *if you like* (Claridge 2013; Brinton 2014), illustrated in (24). Brinton (2014) analyzes a "family" of related DMs, namely *if you choose, if you like, if you prefer, if you want*, and *if you wish*, referring to them as indirect conditional *if*-elliptical clauses (*if*-ECs):

> Indirect conditional *if*-ECs have the characteristics of what Kaltenböck, Heine, and Kuteva (2011) call "conceptual theticals": that is, the features of being syntactically independent, prosodically set off from the rest of the utterance, positionally mobile, and internally built upon the principles of sentence grammar, but elliptical (2011: 853). Borrowing a concept from Huddleston and Pullum (2002: 1350–1362), Kaltenböck et al. describe the semantics of theticals as "non-restrictive," by which they mean that they are not semantically part of the host clause but concern the "situation of discourse" (2011: 856). (Brinton 2014: 275)

These indirect conditionals are included in the class of style disjuncts of Quirk et al. (1985: 1095), of disjunct adverbial clauses of Espinal (1991: 726–27), of supplements of Huddleston and Pullum (2002: 1350ff.), or the "adverbial clauses/clausal adjuncts" of Kaltenböck (2007: 30). On the present analysis, they are formulaic theticals (or parentheticals in other terminologies, as that of Dehé and Kavalova 2007) belonging to the class of formulaic insubordinate clauses (Heine, Kaltenböck, and Kuteva 2016: 57). According to the data analyzed by Claridge (2013: 181, fn. 5), the DMs *as it were, if you like*, and *so to speak* are used clearly more frequently by male than by female speakers. A modern example of the thetical *if you like* is presented in (24).

(24)   English (2011 COCA: ACAD; Brinton 2014: 271, (1b))
         *As an exercise, try taking your series' main characters and standing them at the edge of the abyss, face to face with the ultimate power of evil, the devil, **if you like**.*

An eighteenth century usage of *if you like* as an expression of sentence grammar is found in (25), where *if you like* forms a conditional protasis clause postposed to the preceding main clause *Go with me*, having lexical meaning and being semantically and syntactically integrated.

(25)   English (1723 Johnson, *Love in a Forest*; ED; Brinton 2014: 281, (16b))
         *Assuredly the Thing is to be sold, Go with me, **if you like**, ...*

Earliest instances of coopted, metalinguistic *if you like*, being detached from the host clause, are found in the first half of the nineteenth century (Brinton 2014: 272), presumably first in the 1820s (see Claridge 2013: 178), attested somewhat earlier in North America, cf. (26), than in Great Britain, cf. (27): *if you like* no longer contributes to the meaning of the sentence and has metatextual function (Claridge 2013: 174).

(26)   English (1823 COHA, *North American Review*, 1823; Claridge 2013: 174, (23a))
        *The humbleness, meanness **if you like**, of the subject, together with the homely mode of treating it, brought upon me a world of ridicule by the small critics, ...*

(27)   English (1875 T. E. Bridgett, *Our Lady's Dowry* II.xi.336; OED; Claridge 2013: 163, (2c); Brinton 2014: 272, (2))
        *They were placed in churches by simple faith, or credulity **if you like**, but not by wilful fraud.*

They seem to have involved constituent anchored rather than utterance anchored units (see Section 8.3) because the scope of *if you like* is restricted to the noun phrase *meanness* in (26) and to *or credulity* in (27). While *if you like* follows its host in both examples there are also a few early examples where it precedes (e.g., Claridge 2013, (22b)).

Compared to its sentence grammar source, the coopted unit *if you like* has the appearance of a doubly elliptical text piece, lacking both its verbal complement and its apodosis main clause. But there are also examples where the protasis clause appears to have been coopted *in toto*, that is, together with its complement; cf. (28), where the protasis clause is *if you like it better*. However, the exact nature of the cooptation history does not become entirely clear on the basis of the data available. An interesting hypothesis is suggested by Brinton (2017: 285–87) according to which insubordinate *if you like* can be traced back to a construction involving an apodosis clause, frequently an imperative clause ("Call it X"), that refers to an explicit speech act of naming, as in (29).

(28)   English (1769 Sterne, *Tristram Shandy*; ECF; Brinton 2014: 284, (23b))
        *so edging herself a little more towards him, and raising up her eyes, sub-blushing, as she did it – she took up the gauntlet – or the discourse (**if you like it better**) and communed with my uncle Toby, thus.*

(29)   English (1865 Carroll, *Alice in Wonderland*; CLMETEV; Brinton 2014: 287, (28c))
        *The Red Queen shook her head, "You may **call it** 'nonsense' **if you like**," she said, ...*

Irrespective of which construction exactly served as a model, with its cooptation in the nineteenth century, *if you like* appears to have acquired the properties in (30). But conceivably, elliptical uses of *if you like* with its literal uses, as in (29), might represent an intermediate stage prior to cooptation (on the significance of "intermediate stages," see Section 3.3). In the rise of *if you will* as a thetical, however, there apparently was no intermediate stage of the kind commonly observed in grammaticalization (see Claridge 2013: 176).

(30)   Effects of cooptation in the rise of *if you like* (cf. Claridge 2013: 179–80; Brinton 2014: 275–76)

   a   Meaning: Its meaning is now non-referential, no longer part of the sentence meaning; note that the pronoun *you* does not truly function in a referential manner (Claridge 2013: 162).

   b   Function: It has a metatextual function, or metacommunicative meaning (Claridge 2013: 179), e.g., that of explicitly or implicitly calling for the hearer's agreement (Brinton 2014: 276).

   c   Syntax: It is "extra-sentential" and syntactically non-integrated. Occasionally it constitutes a separate utterance.

   d   Prosody: It is presumably prosodically independent, usually set off by commas.[9]

   e   Placement: It has limited mobility, following, or less commonly, preceding the constitutent it refers to. This restriction is due to its use as a constituent anchored DM from its beginning (see Section 8.3).

3.2.5   *English* If you will

The English expression *if you will* is called a comment clause (Brinton 2008: 162–83), a discourse marker, a disjunct expressing meta-linguistic comments (Quirk et al. 1985: 618), a disjunct adverbial clause (Espinal 1991: 726–27), an *if*-elliptical clause (Brinton 2014: 273), or a formulaic insubordinate clause (Heine, Kaltenböck, and Kuteva 2016: 56–58; Kaltenböck 2016). (31) is an example showing its present-day use.

(31)   English (2012 COCA: SPOK; Brinton 2014: 271, (1f))
       *And it's at that moment when HIV becomes a human epidemic, starts moving down the rivers and into the birthplace of the epidemic, **if you will**, in Central Africa.*

Brinton (2008: 163–67) notes that *if you will* occurs in many of the same contexts as *as it were* and serves the same metalinguistic function, and she describes the main function of *if you will* thus:

(32)   It is used metalinguistically with metaphors or figures of speech, with foreign words, and with words which are inappropriate stylistically (and thus

---

[9] We did not find sufficient information on whether or how cooptation affected the prosodic behavior of *if you like* (cf. Section 2.1).

enclosed in quotation marks); it may occur when the speaker is searching for the correct formulation, is uneasy with the characterization (but may think the hearer prefers it), or is unsure whether the hearer will accept the characterization; and finally it may serve as a more general hedge ("if you wish to call it that" > "if I may be allowed to call it that").

(Brinton 2014: 271)

The earliest attestations of *if you will* presented by Brinton (2008: 169–70) date back to the tenth and eleventh centuries, containing both sentence grammar and thetical (parenthetical) expressions, although the latter are still relatively infrequent.[10] In example (33) the two co-occur, where the former (*Gif þu wille*) appears sentence-initially, taking a complement clause introduced by *þæt* "that." The latter (*gif þu wilt*) is placed sentence-finally, but it may also appear in initial or medial position, as in (34), where it is inserted within the sentence.

(33)   English (10th c. *Leechdoms, Wortcunning and Starcraft of Early England,* Book II 214; Brinton 2008: 169, (8c))
       Gif þu wille *þæt þin wamb sie simle gesund þonne scealt þu hire þus tilian* **gif þu wilt**.
       "If you wish that your womb be continually healthy then you should attend it thus if you will."

(34)   English (c. 1000 *The Old English Life of St. Giles* 218 [DOEC]; Brinton 2008: 169, (8a))
       ealswa þu miht nu, **gif þu wilt,** *æt God gebiddon þæt þes man gehæled wurðe*
       "also you might now, if you will, entreat of God that this man be healed"

The expression, like *gif þu wilt* in (34), still had referential or propositional meaning in Old English but, as we argue, it was already a thetical in usages such as (34). The description by Brinton (2017: 168–71) suggests in fact that it already exhibited the grammatical properties of a coopted unit, namely the ones in (35). We are not aware of any evidence suggesting that the rise of *gif þu wilt* was the result of a gradual process characteristic of grammaticalization, although there is no information on developments prior to the tenth century.

(35)   Effects of cooptation in the rise of *if you will* (cf. Brinton 2014; 2017)
       a   Its meaning was no longer part of the sentence meaning.
       b   It appears to have had a metatextual function.
       c   It was no longer a syntactic constituent of the sentence of (34).
       d   It seems to have been prosodically separated from the rest of the sentence, as the commas to its left and its right suggest (but see Section 2.1).
       e   It was no longer positionally constrained, occurring in initial, medial, or final position of the sentence (Brinton 2017: 168).

[10] The following account, though not the interpretation proffered, is based entirely on Brinton (2008: 168–80).

Once an expression has been coopted, this affects its external and its internal structure in different ways: Its external status changes from sentence constituent to sentence-external thetical. Depending on its specific discourse function it may now be placed at the left or the right periphery of the sentence or else be inserted somewhere within the sentence. In its internal status, both the form and the meaning of the expression are still largely what they used to be prior to cooptation. But when used recurrently, the expression may grammaticalize in accordance with the parameters discussed in Section 2.2.2 (see Section 2.5.2 on late grammaticalization):

(36)   Grammaticalization following cooptation (Heine and Kuteva 2007: 33–44)
        a Context extension: The expression is extended to new contexts inviting new meanings.
        b Desemanticization: It loses semantic features in favor of the new functions evoked or supported by new contexts.
        c Internal decategorialization: The morphological components of the expression lose their morphosyntactic identity and coalesce into an invariable, particle-like unit.

The existing evidence suggests that grammaticalization neither preceded nor coincided with cooptation; rather, it must have set in subsequently – that is, after *if you will* had turned into a thetical in the tenth century. The way this happened is described in detail by Brinton (2008: 177–80); the following is a short summary in accordance with the parameters in (36):

> *Context extension.* By the modern period, *if you will* was extended from directive contexts, where its meaning was "if you are willing [to do so]," to non-directive contexts inviting the meaning "if you are willing [to say so]," and eventually to contexts where it assumed the function of a general hedge on the speaker's claim.
>
> *Desemantization. If you will* gradually lost its propositional meaning in favor of new meanings evoked or supported by the new contexts, such as expressing what Brinton (2017: 179) calls negative politeness. And it also seems to have lost its significance as an expression that is sensitive to referentiality and truth conditions.
>
> *Internal decategorialization.* The three components of *if you will* of the expression gradually lost their morphological distinctiveness and coalesced into an invariable DM, "undergoing internal, morphological fixation into a single, unalterable form" (Van Bogaert 2011: 308) – a process commonly referred to in grammaticalization theory as univerbation.

To conclude, the internal structure of *if you will* exhibits the main hallmarks of grammaticalization, as described by Brinton (2008: 162–83). The expression turns from morphologically transparent conditional protasis clause into a fixed, invariable DM. At the same time we saw earlier that in its *external* structure *if you will* has features that are incompatible with grammaticalization, being the result of earlier cooptation: Rather than becoming morphosyntactically fixed, it gained morphosyntactic freedom by becoming syntactically independent from its host sentence (see (35c)) – with the effect that, like other theticals, *if you will* in Present-Day English is neither part of the syntax nor of the meaning of the sentence in which it occurs. This seemingly peculiar phenomenon, to be observed in a number of English DMs, is characterized by Van Bogaert (2011: 302) as the "decategorialization paradox." As we already saw in Section 2.5.1, however, this is far from a paradox phenomenon since it is to be predicted on account of the fact that cooptation and grammaticalization have in some sense opposite effects on grammatical development.

Among the grammatical changes typically associated with cooptation as listed in (9) of Section 2.3 there are two that are in need of qualification, namely that cooptation leads from restricted semantic–pragmatic scope to variable scope over and beyond the sentence and from positionally constrained to largely unconstrained placement ((9e) and (9f)). It would seem in fact that this generalization is in need of qualification. In Heine et al. (2017: 823), a distinction is made between utterance anchored and constituent anchored coopted units (theticals).[11] Our interest in this book is mainly with the former: They constitute the majority of theticals and the generalizations in (9) of Section 2.3 apply exclusively to them.

Constituent anchored theticals have one particular constituent of the utterance as their host rather than the utterance as a whole, and this constituent is typically a noun phrase or an adverbial phrase. Unlike utterance anchored theticals, they have semantic–pragmatic scope over that constituent and are placed immediately before or after that constituent.

Some utterance anchored theticals can also be used as constituent anchored theticals, with the effect that in such uses, both their semantic–pragmatic scope and their placement are restricted to the constituent concerned. This also applies to *if you will*. The data provided by Brinton (2017: 168–71, (8), (9)) suggest that *if you will* might have been essentially an utterance anchored thetical in Old and Middle English, cf. the Old English example (34). But in the modern period from the mid-sixteenth century onward there are also instances of constituent anchored *if you will*. Thus, the example (37) of a seventeenth century text suggests that *if you will* is anchored in and has scope over the noun *Quatrumvirate* rather than the whole sentence, in that the

---

[11] In addition, there are two further types which need not concern us here, namely context anchored coopted units having a host, and context anchored coopted units without a host (Heine et al. 2017: 823).

"landing site" of the thetical seems to be provided not by a sentence but rather by a noun phrase.

(37)   *The whole Triumvirate, or **if you will**, Quatrumvirate are included*
         (1684 Goddard, *Plato's Demon; or the State-physician Unmaskt* 53 [*OED*];
         Brinton 2017: 171)

This situation might suggest that constituent anchored *if you will* was a later innovation. In fact, this would not seem to be an isolated development. As the reconstruction by Davidse, De Wolf, and Van Linden (2015) shows, the DM *no doubt* arose in Middle English also as an utterance anchored thetical with scope over the sentence as a whole. But in Late Modern English (1710–1920), the use of *no doubt* was extended to contexts where its semantic–pragmatic scope was restricted to one constituent of the sentence – that is, where it turned into a constituent anchored DM.

Both cases are best interpreted as instances of grammaticalization following cooptation, taking place in specific contexts and leading to a reduction in semantic–pragmatic scope from sentence to phrasal constituent – having the effect that the DM concerned is also restricted to placement immediately before or after that constituent.

We will return to this subject in Section 8.3.

3.2.6   *English* Instead[12]

Use of English *instead* includes in particular two distinct but etymologically related expressions, illustrated with the examples in (38).[13] The expression *instead of* in (38a) is a complex replacive preposition. *Instead* in (38b), by contrast, is a thetical, being both syntactically and prosodically independent, typically separated in writing by a period or colon from the preceding and a comma from the following clause. It is called by Lewis (2011: 416) a DM expressing "the coherence relation of Antithesis, a type of contrastive relation involving mutually exclusive states of affairs."

(38)   English (cf. Lewis 2011: 434, (19))
         a ***Instead of** paying by the piece, I paid by the day.*
         b *I didn't pay by the piece. **Instead**, I paid by the day.*

The complex preposition *instead of* derives from a combination of the preposition *in*, the Old English noun *stede* "place, spot, locality" and the

---

[12] We are grateful to Diana Lewis (personal communication of June 16, 2019) for critical comments on an earlier version of this section.

[13] The following sketch is based on Lewis (2011). She discusses *instead* together with *rather* and, in fact, the two have much in common both in their functions and their development. For space reasons we are restricted here to the former, for which she presents a more detailed analysis.

possessive marker *of* (see Schwenter and Traugott 1995), having a replacive function ("B in place of A") in Late Old English. It goes back to a nominal possessive construction, illustrated in (39). Up to the late sixteenth century, the vast majority of occurrences of *stede* "place" refer to a physical place (Lewis 2011: 424). As a preposition *in stede of* was used at the latest in the fifteenth century, cf. (40).

(39)   English (c1567, Skelton Tales; Lewis 2011: 425, (7))
         *Therfore, I wyll not goe to Warre: my wyfe shall goe **in my steade**.*

(40)   English (c1460, *Towneley Plays*; Lewis 2011: 427, (9))
         ***In stede of** drynk thay gaf me gall.*

Since the eighteenth century, "*instead* alone as an adverbial again can be seen as information compression: the replaced item is now ellipted, to be recovered from the context" (Lewis 2011: 427).[14] On the basis of the data presented by Lewis (2011: 428), *instead* appears to have turned into a thetical and an incipient DM by around 1800 or earlier, with (41) being the earliest example provided.

(41)   English (1799, Jane Austen, *Letters*; Lewis 2011: 428, (11))
         *I am not to wear my white satin cap to-night, after all; I am to wear a mamalone cap **instead**.*

The reasons for this hypothesis are the following: *Instead* in (41) is no longer part of a noun phrase as *instead of* is, nor is it a constituent of the sentence, it has semantic–pragmatic scope over both clauses of the sentence, and its function has also changed. Thus, Lewis observes: "There is thus a functional split, in terms of their role in the information structure of utterances, between *instead of* and *instead*" (Lewis 2011: 428). Note, however, that there is no information on the prosody of *instead* in (41).

In spite of the split, *instead* retained a number of features of earlier *instead of*. First, both involve a coherence relation between two mutually exclusive situations, S1 and S2 (Lewis 2011: 416). And second, one of these situations expresses an informationally salient idea and the other a backgrounded idea (Lewis 2011: 438–39). But the split between *instead of* of sentence grammar and thetical *instead* led to some noteworthy changes, which can be summarized as follows:

---

[14] In accordance with general findings made on cooptation (Heine, Kaltenböck, and Kuteva 2016; Heine et al. 2017), we argue that the coopted unit was *instead*, that is, there is no need to invoke "ellipsis" as an explanation. Note that according to Tabor and Traugott (1998: 250), *instead* is an ellipted form of *instead of this*. Lewis (2011: 433), however, observes that *instead of this/that* is relatively rare in the corpus data.

(a) Meaning: Cooptation resulted in what Lewis (2011: 439) calls "a split between a pattern in which the expression occurs with an informationally salient idea and one in which it occurs with a backgrounded idea." Prior to cooptation, *instead of* served as a preposition (or conjunction) introducing the backgrounded idea. As a result of cooptation, *instead* turned into a thetical expressing an alternative between two incompatible states of affairs, it shifted from a preposition introducing the backgrounded idea to a marker presenting the informationally salient idea in the second sentence.

Since both expressions have been retained up to Present-Day English, the difference in information structure can be shown with the following example, where (42a) represents non-coopted prepositional *instead of* and (42b) coopted *instead*: Whereas *instead of* in (42a) introduces the backgrounded idea, *instead* in (42b) introduces the clause presenting the informationally salient idea.

(42)   English (cf. Lewis 2011: 434, (19)) (= (38))
         a ***Instead of*** *paying by the piece, I paid by the day.*
         b *I didn't pay by the piece.* ***Instead***, *I paid by the day.*

(b) Function: *Instead* acquired a metatextual function, introducing the discourse schema in (43), where *instead* assumed the function of a connective linking two situations, S1 and S2. In this schema, S1 and S2 are typically represented by full clauses or sentences, but S1 may as well stand for a larger discourse segment consisting of a series of sentences.

(43)   S1 [backgrounded] – S2 [informationally salient], *instead*

(c) Syntax: *Instead of* was syntactically integrated, both internally and externally: Internally, in that it required a noun phrase or a non-finite clause as its complement, and externally in that it had the status of a sentence participant. In contrast, *instead* no longer seems to have been syntactically integrated: It no longer is a participant of the sentence.
(d) Prosody: There is also reason to assume that *instead of* was part of the intonation unit of the clause in which it occurred, whereas *instead* was prosodically set off. While there is no direct information on its early use in speech, use of a comma in some of the early text examples, like (44), suggests that there was some kind of prosodic break between *instead* and the following text piece (but see also Section 2.1).

(44)   English (1866, Lucie Duff Gordon, letter; Lewis 2011: 428, (13))
         *He would not work on a Sunday, but **instead**, came mounted on a splendid tall black donkey.*

(e) Semantic–pragmatic scope: There was also a change from scope over the complement of *instead of* to wider scope extending over or beyond the clause or the sentence as a whole (Lewis 2011: 427).[15]

(f) Placement: Prior to cooptation, *instead of* was restricted to the position immediately preceding its complement. After cooptation, *instead* was initially placed at the right periphery, as in (41), but it could also occur in other positions, including the pre-verbal position, as in (45), repeated from (44). Placement of *instead* in initial position followed its scope extension (Diana Lewis, personal communication of June 16, 2019).

(45)   English (1866, Lucie Duff Gordon, letter; Lewis 2011: 428, (13))
         *He would not work on a Sunday, but **instead**, came mounted on a splendid tall black donkey.*

With the emergence of thetical *instead*, its predecessor *instead of* did not disappear. In (46) there is an early example of the two co-occurring, and both have been retained up until Present-Day English.

(46)   English (1817, Jane Austen, letter; Lewis 2011: 433, (17))
         *The consequence is, that **instead of** going to town to put myself into the hands of some physician as I shd otherwise have done, I am going to Winchester **instead**.*

In sum, the DM *instead* owes most of its grammatical properties to cooptation, like those just listed, and these properties have been retained in Present-Day English. But its history following cooptation appears to have been one of grammaticalization. *Instead* does not refer back to any specific item in the previous clause but primarily marks the selection of an alternative between two incompatible states of affairs. By the twentieth century, *instead* came to be commonly used in sentence-initial position, as in (47) (Lewis 2011: 428–29), presumably due to context extension requiring a negated form of the preceding clause (Lewis 2011: 432, 434).

(47)   English (1921, D. H. Lawrence, "Rex"; Lewis 2011: 428, (14))
         *... it was bed-time, but we would not go to bed. **Instead** we sat in a row in our night-dresses.*

To conclude, the development of *instead* appears to have been in accordance with the general line of evolution of DMs sketched in (48): The first stage was

---

[15] Lewis (2011: 428) argues that there was "underspecification or scopal vagueness" in the scope of *instead* between event and participant orientation. Be that as it may, what seems to be uncontroversial is that after its cooptation, semantic–pragmatic scope over the whole clause was at least one possible function of *instead*. Diana Lewis (personal communication of June 16, 2019) notes that there is evidence that *instead* acquired its wide scope before occurring in initial position. This suggests that change of *instead* to the initial position cannot be held responsible for the change in scope of *instead*.

one of early grammaticalization whereby a prepositional phrase (something like *in stede of*) gave rise to a composite preposition (*instead of*), turning via loss of morpheme boundary into an invariable function word. Subsequently there was cooptation of *instead*, finally followed by a second round of grammaticalization in the direction of a DM.

(48)   Hypothesized development of discourse markers (repeated from
        Chapter 1.2.4; Heine 2013: 1238–39)
        (Grammaticalization >) cooptation > grammaticalization > discourse marker

3.2.7   *English* Like

There are few English items disposing of as many different uses as the item *like* does – as D'Arcy (2017: 3) says, its various uses "contribute to the panoply of functions that make it appear as though *like* can do all things and appear in all places." These uses include, for example, that of a verb (*She likes me*), a noun (*and the like*), a preposition (*He looks like his mother*), a conjunction (*That was a pumpkin like I have never seen before*), a suffix (*The sculpture looked quite human-like*), a quotative marker (*And he's like, That's not my suitcase*), or an extender (*and stuff like that*), but these examples do not conclude the range of uses associated with *like* (see, e.g., Underhill 1988; Meehan 1991; Romaine and Lange 1991: 244; Beeching 2016: 126–55; D'Arcy 2017: 24–44 for details).

In addition, *like* occurs also as a DM and our interest here is primarily with this item, exemplified in (49).

(49)   English (Romaine and Lange 1991: 244, (25))
        *And there were **like** people blocking, you know?*

One of the reasons for including the DM *like* in this chapter was that we had assumed that this DM arose only recently in English discourse and therefore might allow reconstructing some of the dynamics underlying the emergence of DMs in speech without having to rely only on written resources. For example, Streeck wrote in 2002: "The oldest source in which I have encountered the discourse marker *like* is Jack Kerouac's (1958) novel, *The Subterraneans* ..." (Streeck 2002: 588; see also Underhill 1988; Meehan 1991). Subsequently it turned out, however, that our assumption was wrong: As the seminal analysis by D'Arcy (2017) reveals, and as we will see in the following paragraphs, *like* is actually not one of the youngest English DMs.

Beeching (2016: 127–28) distinguishes the following main functions of the DM (referred to by her as pragmatic marker): (a) Exemplifying, (b) approximative, (c) focuser, and (d) hedging,[16] and she adds:

---

[16] As a fifth function, Beeching (2016: 128) presents that of quotative *be like*, which is ignored here.

The ability of *like* to flag approximation makes it eminently recruitable as a means of hedging discourse. As a pragmatic marker, *like* has an overarching core function, which is to flag approximation and hedge discourse … (Beeching 2016: 127)

In earlier research, one distinct DM *like* was identified (e.g., Romaine and Lange 1991; Streeck 2002). The work by D'Arcy (2017) shows, however, that there are actually three pragmatic or metatextual uses that need to be distinguished. The first use, illustrated in (50), is called that of a "sentence adverb," described by D'Arcy (2017: 61) as a clause-final parenthetical disjunct, we will refer to it here as *like₁*. It is functionally similar to some other DMs in that it can be glossed as "as it were" or "so to speak" (cf. Section 3.2.10). This function signals to the hearer that the proposition only resembles or approximates reported events.

(50)   English (COHA/Uncle Tom's Cabin/1852; D'Arcy 2017: 15, (14d))
         *He was quite gentle and quiet **like**.*

The second use is what she calls the (discourse) marker use, referred to here as *like₂* and illustrated in (51). It expresses textual relations by linking the current utterance to prior discourse and signals exemplification, illustration, elaboration, or clarification, typically occurring on the left periphery of the sentence (D'Arcy 2017: 14, 62). It is widely attested in speech materials across varieties of English.

(51)   English (MU/73m/1875; D'Arcy 2017: 14, (16a))
         *You'd never believe Pig Route. **Like,** you'd need to see the road to believe it.*

The third is called the (discourse) particle, referred to here as *like₃*, cf. (52). Prosodically integrated, it expresses a wide range of discourse functions, including hedging, mitigating, highlighting the following information, establishing common ground, solidarity, or intimacy between interlocutors, and it also may serve as a filler (cf. Section 8.5). *Like₃* appears to frequently function as a constituent anchored DM (see Section 8.3).

(52)   English (AYR/75m/1925; D'Arcy 2017: 15, (51b))
         *They were just **like** sitting, waiting to die.*

Both *like₂* and *like₃* were exported by British emigrants to other parts of the world, like North America and Australia (D'Arcy 2017: 56).

All three variants are in accordance with our definition of DMs in (7) of Section 1.1.2:[17] As the description by D'Arcy (2017) suggests, they are invariable

---

[17] Note that our definition differs from the convention proposed by D'Arcy (2017: 57), for whom "discourse markers" are, in the sense of Schiffrin (1987), discourse deictics that bracket units of discourse, are clause-initial, and are fundamentally subjective pragmatic devices, whereas discourse particles occur at multiple sites within an utterance and their functions are primarily interpersonal and intersubjective.

expressions, their meanings are not part of the meaning of their host utterance, they are syntactically detached, not being arguments of the sentence, and their function is metatextual, relating a text in some way or other to other parts of the text, the attitudes of the speaker, and/or to speaker–hearer interaction. Their prosodic status, though, is overall unclear on the basis of the information available, although we observed earlier that *like₃* is prosodically integrated.

In our discussion we are ignoring the quotative marker *(be) like*, that is, the use of *be like* to introduce reported speech – despite all the scholarly attention that it has received (e.g., Romaine and Lange 1991; Streeck 2002; Beeching 2016: 131–32; D'Arcy 2017: 37–44), as well as the fact that Romaine and Lange (1991: 245) also classify it also as a "discourse marker." Note that quotative *be like* entered British English only very recently (Beeching 2016: 152). The reason for this omission is, on the one hand, that the quotative marker is structurally and functionally different from the DM and, on the other hand, that its status as a discourse-pragmatic device is complex and would need separate treatment. For example, Beeching notes:

> Strictly speaking, the use of *be like* to introduce direct speech cannot be considered to be a pragmatic marking usage, on the criterion that *be like* cannot be omitted – it is essential for the syntactic well-formedness of the utterance. (Beeching 2016: 131)

How then did the DM *like* arise? To answer this question we draw on the rich resources provided by D'Arcy (2017) but propose a slightly different interpretation of them in accordance with the framework sketched in Section 2.1.

All evidence available suggests that the DM *like* is etymologically unrelated to the verb *like*, the latter going back to Old English *lician* "to please/be sufficient." Rather, the DM can ultimately be traced back to the Proto-Germanic root **galīkaz* of which the Old English adjective *gelic* "similar, same" is a later reflex, cognate with Proto-Germanic **līk*, Old English *lic* "body, corpse, form" (Meehan 1991: 39; Romaine and Lange 1991: 271).

As a preposition, taking nominal or pronominal complements, *like* is attested from circa 1200 in Early Middle English. Subsequently, the use of the preposition was extended and grammaticalized into a conjunction, alternating with *as*, to link the main clause with a subordinate clause, and in this capacity it has been found since the fourteenth century. From the fifteenth century on, a second use of the conjunction arose (as in *They look at me **like** I'm dirt*), where *like* alternates with *as if* and *as though*, but this usage remained stylistically somewhat restricted (Romaine and Lange 1991: 261, 271, fn. 6; D'Arcy 2017: 60–61).

We follow Romaine and Lange (1991: 261) and D'Arcy (2017) in hypothesizing that it was the conjunction that provided the model for coopting *like* as a discourse-pragmatic device, that is, as a thetical initially placed at the right periphery of the clause.

The variant *like₁* ("sentence adverb") of the DM has been documented since roughly the mid-eighteenth century, occurring clause-finally. (53) provides the earliest occurrence of *like₁* in D'Arcy's data base.

(53)   English (1753 OBP/Trial of William Peers/1753; D'Arcy 2017: 201, (1))
         *I cannot, they were quarrelling **like***; *I went out of the room and left them quarrelling.*

Clause-final *like* appears to have had a particularly strong impact on British English, where its use continues to be salient up to the present (Beeching 2016: 155).

It took only a fairly short time for *like₂* (the "discourse marker") to evolve, attested since the 1780s and occurring clause-initially, as in (54). On the way from *like₁* to *like₂*, the use of the DM was in fact extended from clause-final to clause-initial placement, or from the right to the left periphery of the sentence.

(54)   English (1789 OBP/Trial of William Ward/1789; D'Arcy 2017: 202, (2))
         *They were down both together, and the young man that is along with me now, he parted them, **like** one parted on one side the cart, and one on the other.*

In the 1840s, the DM is described as representative of the speech of uneducated, older, rural males in Westmoreland, and some of the negative valuations associated with the DM have persisted up to the present (cf. D'Arcy 2017: 49). And before the mid-nineteenth century, *like₂* "developed meanings of elaboration or clarification of discourse intent. In other words, it took on the full discourse marking function," "its scope broadened from over the proposition to over the discourse, marking relations between sequentially dependent units" (D'Arcy 2017: 62). The frequency of the DM (*like₂*) increased over the second half of the twentieth century (D'Arcy 2017: 14). At present, *like₂* is found most frequently clause-initially or before a noun phrase or a verb, and more recently the DM also appears to be acquiring the function of signaling that the speaker is taking the floor (cf. D'Arcy 2017: 65).

In a final step then, *like₂* developed into the particle *like₃* in the second half of the nineteenth century,[18] found in northern England, Australia, the USA, and Canada. It led to the following changes: (1) It underwent desemanticization, losing referential and semantic content, like the core semantics of approximation, comparison, and similarity, in favor of functions relating to speaker–hearer interaction ("interpersonal and intersubjective pragmatic meanings"), and (2) its scope expanded, extending from the textual to the interpersonal level (D'Arcy 2017: 63, 65). Occurring clause-internally, *like₃* was initially restricted to placement before noun phrases, prepositional phrases,

---

[18] But D'Arcy (2017: 52) also notes that the first unambiguous uses of *like* as a discourse particle (*like₃*) are attested from the start of the twentiethth century.

verb phrases, and adverbial phrases. The following is an early example of *like₃* use, where it can be glossed "for example" and seems to function as a constituent anchored DM (see Section 8.3):

(55)   English (1887 BLV/88m/1887; D'Arcy 2017: 63, (40a))
         That's right, as well as doing our retail business he did quite a wholesale
         business on laundry soaps, patent medicines, toilet soaps, ah, teas, coffee,
         *and all **like** uh heavy work clothes, overalls, horse blankets, ah, hammocks,*
         sealers.

The above three-stage reconstruction of the DM is in accordance with that of D'Arcy (2017: 65):

In short, the "traditional" use of *like* as a sentence adverb [= *like₁*; a.n.], where it occurs in final position and has backward scope, represents an older layer in which this form functioned meta-textually. From there, it developed a marker function [= *like₂*; a.n.] and it subsequently emerged as a particle [= *like₃*; a.n.] as well. In short, these are not separate, variety-specific, developments. They represent different stages of development in the evolution of a discourse feature.

The evidence available suggests that with its cooptation in the second half of the eighteenth century, *like₁* and *like₂* came to contrast sharply in their grammatical structure with their predecessors of sentence grammar, namely the preposition and the conjunction *like*, no longer taking nominal, clausal, or any other complements. By turning into a DM, *like* must have acquired the properties listed in (56).

(56)   Grammatical properties hypothesized to have characterized *like* in its rise as a
         DM in the late eighteenth century
         a Meaning: It was no longer part of the meaning of its host sentence.
         b Function: It acquired metatextual functions, expressing textual relations by
            relating the current utterance to prior discourse and signaling functions like
            exemplification, illustration, elaboration, or clarification.
         c Syntax: It was now syntactically detached, no longer being an argument of
            the verb.
         d Prosody: There is no conclusive evidence.
         e Semantic–pragmatic scope: Its scope broadened from within to over the
            proposition to over the discourse, marking "relations between sequentially
            dependent units" (D'Arcy 2017: 62).
         f Placement: It first moved to the right periphery of the clause, slightly later
            also to the left periphery, and finally also to other positions – hence, it is
            overall positionally variable in accordance with its respective functions.

None of the properties listed in (56) can reasonably be reconciled with criteria of grammaticalization as they are described in Section 2.2.2. In particular, changes suggestive of an increase, rather than a decrease, of syntactic and functional autonomy are not only incompatible with but even contradict what is normally observed in grammaticalization.

Based on the description by Romaine and Lange (1991) and D'Arcy (2017), the overall development of the DM *like* can be depicted as in (57). In accordance with a number of other DMs surveyed in Chapters 3–6, it involved early grammaticalization leading from preposition to conjunction, followed by cooptation in the eighteenth century, and finally late grammaticalization within the DM (cf. Section 2.5.2).

(57)   From conjunction to DM *like* (where > = grammaticalization, >> = cooptation)
        Preposition > Conjunction >> DM *like₁* > DM *like₂* > DM *like₃*

It is possible that there were two factors that favored the cooptation from conjunction to DM. According to Romaine and Lange (1991: 261) it may have been the variable use of the item *like*, occurring as a preposition, a conjunction, a suffix, etc. that made it eligible for reanalysis as a syntactically detached and positionally mobile DM. On the other hand, D'Arcy (2017: 61) observes that on the way from preposition to conjunction and to DM, *like* experienced both extension of its scope and its increasing role in expressing speaker attitude, and that these changes may have provided favorable conditions for its selection as an epistemic stance marking thetical and DM. Conceivably, both factors played a role but more research is needed on this issue.

To conclude, most of the grammatical properties that the present-day DM *like* exhibits appear to be due to its cooptation, presumably in the second half of the eighteenth century, if not earlier. But grammaticalization also contributed substantially to this development. The most pronounced process was early grammaticalization from preposition to conjunction – a paradigm change that is crosslinguistically widely attested (see Kuteva et al. 2019). Late grammaticalization followed common lines of development involving most of all context extension from the right periphery (*like₁*) to the left periphery (*like₂*), and eventually to other positions, accompanied by desemanticization leading to a gradual loss of the lexical content of comparison and/or similarity accompanied by gains in discourse structuring functions. Desemanticization was also involved in the transition from marker to particle, that is, from *like₂* to *like₃*, when the DM was apparently reduced in some contexts to the role of a filler akin to *um, em, er* and the like (cf. D'Arcy 2017: 65). And there was conceivably also loss of phonetic substance (erosion) or, in this case, prosodic substance on the way from *like₂* to *like₃* in that the latter is said to no longer be prosodically distinct, having been integrated in the intonation unit of its host clause (cf. D'Arcy 2017: 16).

3.2.8   *English* No doubt

The English discourse segment *no doubt* has a variety of different uses. The analysis by Davidse, De Wolf, and Van Linden (2015), on which the following discussion rests, shows that the two kinds of uses in (58) in particular can be singled out. In both, *no doubt* forms an argument of the verb, which is a possessive verb in (58a) but an existential verb in (58b). And *no doubt* itself also has an argument, namely a clausal one introduced by the complementizer *that* in (58b) but with no complementizer in (58a).

(58)   English (Wordbanks *Online*; Davidse, De Wolf, and Van Linden 2015: 26, (3), (5))
        a ... *"I've no doubt I'll see you at dinner soon ..."*
        b *Brown stands accused of not promoting enough young players, Vogts of over-promoting them. Whatever happens to be the worst crime is open to debate, but* **there is no doubt** *that what transpired in the Faroe Islands was the punishment.*

But there is also a different kind of usage where *no doubt* neither forms an argument nor takes an argument – that is, where it is essentially "syntactically invisible." This usage is illustrated in (59).

(59)   English (Wordbanks *Online*; Davidse, De Wolf, and Van Linden 2015: 53, (71))
        "... Hablet has his own plans." "To invade Hythria, **no doubt** *..."*

The difference between the uses of *no doubt* in (58) and in (59) is fairly conspicuous, and our interest in this section is with accounting for this difference. In doing so, we will refer to the usages in (58) as *no doubt$_1$* and to the ones in (59) as *no doubt$_2$*. Whereas *no doubt$_1$* can be classified as a constituent of sentence grammar, *no doubt$_2$* is a formulaic thetical, classified by Simon-Vandenbergen (2007) as a DM. As such, it exhibits the entire gammut of positional variability: It occurs initially, as in (60), medially (61), and finally (62), and it is also found as an utterance of its own (63). Simon-Vandenbergen summarizes the usage of *no doubt$_2$* thus:

Summing up, the syntactic positions that *no doubt* takes point to its development into a parenthetical marker. It is an epistemic expression which can be thrown into the clause at almost every point where the speaker thinks fit. (Simon-Vandenbergen 2007: 17)

(60)   English (NC, G3H, 1005; *Weekly Hansard*, Simon-Vandenbergen 2007: 15, (11))
        *"***No doubt,*** *Mr. Deputy-Speaker, you will wonder how rail transport could relate to the Scottish bus passengers' consultative committee (...)"*

(61)   English (BNC, CGB, 796; Simon-Vandenbergen 2007: 15, (10))
        The reign of the ultra-model will, **no doubt,** *continue for a time.*

(62)   English (BNC, FSP, 1462; Simon-Vandenbergen 2007: 14, (8))
        What had he come out with? The unfaced truth, **no doubt.**

(63)   English (BNC, JYD, 1327; Simon-Vandenbergen 2007: 14, (9))
        "Got your husband picked out already?"
        "Not yet. But I can assure you I'll give it my full attention."
        *"***No doubt.***" His smile was hard.*

In Present-Day English, *no doubt₁* and *no doubt₂* exhibit nearly the same degree of frequency of use.[19]

As elsewhere in this book, our account is restricted to historical reconstruction. The early development of expressions having *no doubt* as their nucleus is summarized by Davidse et al. thus: *There/it + be + no doubt* clauses emerge in multi-clausal contexts with negative polarity and modal grammatical meaning. They are also associated with parenthetical uses from the start. Thus, from their early history on, clausal *no doubt* expressions are associated with parenthetical uses (Davidse, De Wolf, and Van Linden 2015).

There are a number of early uses of forms with *no doubt₁* as their nucleus and having epistemic meaning. The earliest clear occurrences suggestive of *no doubt₂* are found in the period between 1350 and 1450. Their function was to express either certainty or less than full certainty as in the following example (**ne doute**), whose original stems from around 1387 but is attested in a manuscript of circa 1450:

(64)   English (PPCME, a1450 (a1387) Purvey *CGosp.Prol.Mat.* (Hrl 6333) I, 58; Davidse, De Wolf, and Van Linden 2015: 36, (23))
*And where I haue translatid as opinli or opinliere in English as in Latyn, late wise men deme, that knowen wel bothe langagis, and knowen wel the sentence of holi scripture. And wher I haue do thus, or nay, **ne doute**, thei that kunne wel the sentence of holi writ and English togidere, . . . moun make the bible as trewe ans as opin, ӡea, and opinliere in English than it is in Latyn.*
"And where I have translated as clearly or more clearly in English than in Latin, let wise men judge, who know both languages well, and know the contents of the holy scripture well. And where I have done thus, or no, no doubt, they who know well the contents of the holy scripture and English also, . . . can make the holy bible as true and as clear, yea, and more clear in English than it is in Latin."

No doubt₂ was part of a family of similar expressions, or a network of overlapping grammatical patterns (Fried and Östman 2005: 1775), such as *out of doubt* and *without doubt*, suggesting that it had not yet crystalized into an invariable DM. The following is another early example of the schema (**with-owtten dowte**), attested in a manuscript of circa 1440, the original being from around 1349:

(65)   English (PPCME, c1440 (a1349) Rolle (Thrn) 44; Davidse, De Wolf, and Van Linden 2015: 37, (24))
*Cry mercy, and aske anely saluacyon by þe vertu of his percyouse passion meekly and tristely, and **with-owtten dowte** þou sall haf it, ...*
"Cry out mercy, and humbly and faithfully ask only salvation by the virtue of his revered passion, and without doubt, you will have it, . . .)."

---

[19] According to Davidse, De Wolf, and Van Linden (2015: 50), *no doubt₂* ("adverbial" *no doubt*) accounts for 47.6 percent and *no doubt₁* (existential and possessive *no doubt*) for 52.4 percent of the uses.

The expressions are presumably the result of contact-induced replication ("loan translation") of the French borrowing *saunz doute* "without doubt," the latter first occurring in English between 1250 and 1350 (Simon-Vandenbergen (2007: 25–30).[20] There are three instances of *saunz doute* as a loan from French which are attested in the romance *Kyng Alisaunder*. That this loan is a thetical is suggested, first, by the fact that its use is not licenced by the grammar and, second, that it is set apart from its host clause by a comma. Furthermore, *saunz doute* is strikingly similar in form and meaning to the later thetical *no doubt*, and Simon-Vandenbergen (2007: 28) suggests that the French expression may have influenced the development of the probability meaning of *no doubt*.[21] Note that the Present-Day French adverb *sans doute* expresses probability, like English *no doubt*. In any case, interpolated *no doubt* (i.e., *no doute*) is clearly attested as a thetical by 1350–1420, as the following example shows:

(66)   English (1350–1420, Purvey, *The Prologue to the Bible: Religious treatises*; Simon-Vandenbergen 2007: 26 (52))
..., *but loke that he examyne truli his Latyn bible, for* **no doute** *he shal fynde ful*
manye biblis in Latyn ful false, if he loke manie, nameli newe; ...[22]

The information available suggests that *no doubt* was coopted as such, rather than as a clausal unit that later on was truncated:[23] We do not find convincing evidence to suggest that the thetical *no doubt* may have developed out of something like *there is no doubt* via grammaticalization (see Simon-Vandenbergen 2007: 23 for discussion); according to Laurel Brinton (personal communication of January 20, 2020), *there is no doubt* could be an expansion of *no doubt*.

Classified as a disjunct, i.e., an "adverbial" that is not part of sentence grammar but whose meaning typically has scope over the whole clause (Quirk et al 1985: 618–28, Brinton 2008: 131), *no doubt$_2$* exhibits most of the properties to be predicted for cooptation (see (9) of Section 2.3). These properties can be described as in (67); for more details, see Davidse, De Wolf, and Van Linden (2015):

---

[20] The noun *doubt* itself is a Middle English borrowing from Old French, first attested around 1225 (Davidse, De Wolf, and Van Linden 2015: 29).

[21] The noun *doubt (doute)* was borrowed in Middle English from French, where it meant "fear," "hesitation," or "doubt" (Simon-Vandenbergen (2007: 31).

[22] Shortened quotation; for full text, see Simon-Vandenbergen (2007: 26).

[23] Similar views are expressed by Elizabeth Traugott (personal communication of January 19, 2020) and Laurel Brinton (personal communication of January 20, 2020), even if they do not phrase their analyses in terms of cooptation.

(67)   Grammatical effects of cooptation as observed in *no doubt₂*[24]
          a Meaning: While not dramatically different from its meaning prior to
             cooptation, *no doubt₂* is no longer part of the sentence meaning.
          b Function: Losing its function as a constituent of a sentence, *no doubt₂*
             acquired a discourse-oriented functionality.
          c Syntax: Having turned into a "disjunct," *no doubt₂* lost its status as a
             sentence constituent.
          d Prosody: While there is no information on the prosodic structure in the
             early text examples that are available, the use of commas in some of the
             examples, such as (64), might suggest that *no doubt₂* was not, or not fully
             integrated in the prosodic structure of the sentence (see Section 2.1).
          e Semantic–pragmatic scope: *no doubt₂* now has scope over the whole
             sentence.
          f Placement: With its cooptation, *no doubt₂* acquired more positional
             flexibility. As a result of subsequent context extension, it could now
             appear not only utterance initially but also utterance finally, with the
             medial position coming to predominate since Early Modern English.

In sum, *no doubt₂* exhibits all the main hallmarks to be expected from an expression moving out of the sentence onto the level of discourse monitoring. There is no convincing information to argue that the changes in (67) were the result of grammaticalization; on the contrary, the changes listed in (67) essentially contradict what is commonly to be observed crosslinguistically in processes of grammaticalization (see Section 2.5.1).

But subsequent developments were shaped by a gradual grammaticalization of *no doubt₂*. First, it came to be increasingly used in contexts that suggest the meaning "less than full certainty," as in (68) where the modal *may* hints at a possibility.

(68)   English (PPCEME, 1570-1640; Davidse, De Wolf, and Van Linden 2015:
          41, (32))
          *And **no doubt** there may infinit examples be brought.*

A second change concerns the extension of *no doubt₂* to concessive discourse contexts, which have persisted until the present day. In this usage, the proposition associated with *no doubt₂* is first posited as being true, only to be backgrounded straight away by a second, conflicting argument which is perceived as more important in the speaker's argumentation. The clause containing *no doubt₂* has a rhetorically concessive function, in that it "preempts" a possible objection.

Third, *no doubt₂* occurred clause-initially in its first attestations. But later instances of it between 1570 and 1640 are not only found initially, but also

---

[24] We are grateful to Laurel Brinton (personal communication of January 20, 2020) for having suggested the phrasing of this sentence in (67).

medially and finally, typically though not consistently set off by punctuation marks (Simon-Vandenbergen (2007: 26–27). This effect of context extension presumably accounts for the situation in Present-Day English where *no doubt₂* can occupy the initial and final, but frequently also a medial position in the sentence.

And finally there was also another noteworthy change in Late Modern English whereby *no doubt₂* acquired new uses as a constituent anchored DM, no longer relating only to the entire proposition but rather to a very precise part of it. This reduction of semantic–pragmatic scope meant a shift of the DM away from the level of propositional segments to that of smaller units of discourse, such the adverbial *in part* in (69); we will return to this issue in Section 8.3.

(69)   English (CLMETEV, 1847 Cottle, *Reminiscences of Samuel Taylor Coleridge and Robert Southey*; Davidse, De Wolf, and Van Linden 2015: 49, (53))
        *She [Mrs. Hannah More] is, indisputably, the first literary female I ever met with. In part, **no doubt**, because she is a Christian.*

3.2.9   *English* Right

With regard to the many usages of the English expression *right*, Méndez-Naya (2006) deals with the adverb *right* and Méndez-Naya (2019) with the emergence of the intensifying function of the adjective *right*. She highlights three main kinds of structures, namely *right* as an adjunct, a modifier, and a DM.[25] As an "adjunct" it is a modifier at the VP or the clause level, as in (70), where *right* serves as a manner adjunct meaning "according to right, correctly, well." As a "modifier" it has scope over an adjective or an adverb, frequently glossed "very," or "most," and functioning at the phrasal rather than the clausal level, as *right* does in *right snippy* of (71).

(70)   English (FLOB K05: 41; Méndez-Naya 2006: 143, (1))
        *Not a power, or a force, but simply a people who do things **right**, who have faith in themselves.*

(71)   English (Brown P03: 108; Méndez-Naya 2006: 144, (9))
        *Miss Kizzie had been **right** snippy ever since they were married, though you'd have thought a namesake would have brought her round.*

As a DM, *right* serves mainly to signal an interactive relationship between speaker, hearer, and discourse. Its functions include that of an attention

---

[25] We are grateful to Belén Méndez-Naya for valuable comments on an earlier version of the present section. For a detailed synchronic and diachronic analysis, see Méndez-Naya (2006; see also Méndez-Naya 2019).

catcher, as in (72), of a sort of question tag, as in (73a), or as a response form, indicating understanding or agreement, as in (73b).

(72)   English (FLOB L13: 96; Méndez-Naya 2006: 145, (11))
         *"**Right**," he said briskly, "I'm going now. I'm sorry we've had this unfortunate scene but –."*

(73)   English (Frown L05: 35; Méndez-Naya 2006: 146, (13))
         a *"Just a small point to be verified. No reading glasses were found, **right?**"*
         b *"**Right**. Just sunglasses."*

The grammatical structures of *right* in (70) and (71) are both suggestive of units of sentence grammar, contributing to the meaning of the sentence, being syntactically and presumably also prosodically integrated as adjuncts or modifiers; we will refer to them, respectively, as *right$_1$* and *right$_2$*. In (72) and (73), by contrast, we follow Méndez-Naya (2006) in classifying *right* as a DM, referred to here as *right$_3$*: It seems to exhibit the properties of DMs listed in (40) of Section 1.5, being detachable from the sentence, having a characteristic intonational contour, and typically occurring either in initial position, as in (72), or in final position, as in (73a) – positions that tend to be associated with DMs. Furthermore, like a number of other English DMs, it can be used as a stand-alone, that is, it may form a complete utterance on its own, as in (73b).

All the uses of *right* illustrated here can be traced back to the Old English adjective *riht* "straight, not bent" or the adverb *riht-e* "straight; in a direct course or line," appearing first as an adjunct and subsequently as a focusing modifier meaning "exactly, just" (Méndez-Naya 2006: 147). Early uses of the adverb involved *right* as an adjunct (*right$_1$*), later on giving rise to modifier uses (*right$_2$*) via grammaticalization. This change, which began already in Old English, had some implications for the structure of the expression, leading to a restriction of semantic–pragmatic scope from adjunct having the whole predication in its scope to phrasal modifier, and from relatively unconstrained placement to a position immediately before or after the modified expression. And it also entailed decategorialization (see Section 2.2.2): Unlike *right$_1$*, *right$_2$* no longer could be modified by an adverb. At the close of the Middle English period, however, *right$_2$* became positionally fixed before a focused modifier (Méndez-Naya 2006: 152).

Middle English was characterized by the function of *right$_2$* as an intensifier (e.g., *right good*), but by the second half of the fifteenth century it can no longer be regarded to be a productive intensifier. It was retained only in fossilized forms, associated for example with honorifics, as in *right honorable father, right singular lady,* and in fixed expression, such as *right glad* (Méndez-Naya 2006: 157).

The rise of the DM *right$_3$* falls within the period 1640–1710; it is summarized by Méndez-Naya thus:

The Early Modern English period, however, witnesses the emergence of a new, more grammatical function of *right*, that of discourse marker. Two possible sources were proposed for this use, the adverb *right* in adjunct function in expressions like *You say/ think/deem right*, and the adjective *right* in structures like *you are right* or *that's right*. It is argued here that the second source is the most likely one. (Méndez-Naya 2006: 165)

One of the five early examples of *right₃* that Méndez-Naya (2006: 157–58) found is reproduced in (74), where there is a repeated instance of *right₃*, and in (75) a slightly later example is presented. In both examples, the DM expresses speaker–hearer interaction, where the speaker signals agreement with a preceding statement. The author argues that the DM *right* is more likely to have developed from the corresponding adjective than from the adverb *right₁*, even if clauses like *you say right*, *you guess right*, or *you think right* are also conceivable sources of the DM. Méndez-Naya (2006: 161) observes, however, that the latter clauses "do not seem to be frequent enough to be the input for the development."

(74)   English (1707 HC, E3, 1707, Farquhar, *The Beaux Stratagem*, 63; Méndez-Naya 2006: 157, (34))
         Mrs. (Sull.) *The Devil's in this Fellow; he fights, loves, and banters, all in a Breath. – Here's a Cord that the Rogues brought with'em, I suppose.*
         (Arch.) **Right, right**, *the Rogue's Destiny, a Rope to hang himself.*

(75)   English (1765 ECF, 1765, Brooke, *The Fool of Quality*, Vol. 5, 256; Méndez-Naya 2006: 163, (40))
         Don't be alarmed, my Lord, says she, Women of my Condition know always where to stop. **Right**, *Madam, said I, but possibly you might not be quite so successful in teaching me where to be stopped.*

With its rise as a DM between 1640 and 1710, *right₃* appears to have acquired all the main properties suggestive of cooptation, as summarized in (76).

(76)   Grammatical changes associated with cooptation as observed in *right₃* (cf. Méndez-Naya 2006)
         a Meaning: While retaining the lexical meaning of its adverbial source *right* ("correct(ly)"), *right₃* was no longer part of the meaning of its host sentence.
         b Function: Rather than modifying a clause or a phrase, its function was now to relate two pieces of discourse to one another and to the interaction between speaker and hearer, e.g., as an attention getter.
         c Syntax: It lost its status as a sentence constituent, now being an extra-sentential marker, most obviously when used as a syntactic stand-alone.
         d Prosody: Both the use of punctuation marks before and after it and the fact that it was now used as a stand-alone suggest that it must have been prosodically set off from the rest of the text (but see also Section 2.1).
         e Semantic–pragmatic scope: It acquired scope beyond the sentence and over the situation of discourse.
         f Placement: With its cooptation, *right₃* became strongly associated with the initial position, but at some stage also with the final position as a kind of question tag or response form.

There is no convincing information to argue that the changes in (76) were the result of grammaticalization, or more generally of a gradual process. For example, "the linguistic data do not provide evidence for an intermediate stage as a sentence adverbial" (Méndez-Naya 2006: 161) – that is, for a stage suggestive of a process of gradual transition. Méndez-Naya furthermore draws attention to the fact that concomitants of grammaticalization like condensation and fixation are not only not met but rather are reversed.

After its cooptation between 1640 and 1710, *right₃* underwent further grammaticalization, e.g., losing its ability to be modified by adverbs, and turning into a fully-fledged DM. And the main thetical properties of *right₃* listed in (76) appear to have been retained largely unchanged in the Present-Day English DM *right₃*, co-existing side by side with its sentence grammar predecessors *right₁* and *right₂*.

3.2.10   *English* So to speak/So to say

The DMs of Present-Day English also include the items *so to speak* or *so to say*, *as it were*, and *if you like*. As Claridge (2013: 161) shows, all are formulaic expressions that, depending on their discourse function, can appear in various slots of a sentence, and fulfill a basic hedging function. Our interest in this section is restricted to *so to speak* and *so to say*, treated by Claridge (2013: 161) as one unit. This DM is illustrated in (77), where it "comments on *savior to the world* as not the choice of the speaker, but as something attributed to Wilson and cast into doubt by the speaker." Thus, it serves basically as a constituent anchored DM, having the preceding phrase *as a savior to the world* in its scope (see Section 8.3).

(77)   English (BNC F88: 45; Claridge 2013: 161, (1b))
        Wilson thought that he would er emerge from the war as a savior to the world, **so to speak**.

In Present-Day English, the DM *so to say/so to speak* does not have a corresponding sentence grammar counterpart, but this was different in the past. Early occurrences of it, as in (78), represent sentence grammar uses, being clausally fully integrated constructions with meanings paraphrasable as *than to say that* and functioning as a complementation of the verb (Claridge 2013: 170).

(78)   English (1554 in Foxe *A. & M.* (1563) 910/2, OED; Claridge 2013: 170, (13))
        Nothing can bee sayde more vncerteyne, or more parabolical and vnsensiblie than **so to say**.

Claridge (2013: 170) points out, however, that there are already fully integrated early sentence grammar uses of *so to speak* that carry a meaning which is very similar to the distancing and hedging nature of the DM *so to speak/so to say* in Present-Day English, as in (79).

(79)   English (a1640, J. Ball Answ. to Can. I (1642) 101, OED); Claridge (2013: 170, (14a))
         The Conformists (I use that Word because you are pleed **so to speake.***)*

Most likely, cooptation took place in the mid-seventeenth century (see Claridge 2013: 178). The earliest attestations provided by Claridge (2013) are found in the middle of the seventeenth and early eighteenth century, cf. (80): *So to speak* is inserted within the sentence, no longer being a semantic or syntactic part of the sentence.

(80)   English (a1658 J. Durham *Expos. Rev.* i. (1680) 15, OED; Claridge 2013: 170, (14b))
         There is most sensible footing and, **so to speak,** *gripping to be gotten by looking to the Mediator.*

Conceivably, the rise of the DM *so to say/so to speak*, like that of French *pour ainsi dire* (lit. "in order to so say") and German *sozusagen* (lit. "so to say"), was influenced by the Latin model of *ut ita dicam* (lit. "as so I should say") but there is no conclusive evidence to strengthen a loan translation hypothesis (Claridge 2013: 173).

The description by Claridge (2013) suggests that attestations like that in (80) exhibit most of the properties to be expected from coopted units. The properties are summarized in (81).

(81)   Grammatical effects of cooptation as observed in *so to say* and *so to speak* (cf. Claridge 2013: 170, 179–80)
         a   Meaning: They are not part of the sentence meaning, and *speak* and *say* do not refer to an act of oral communication any more.
         b   Function: Their function is metacommunicative, roughly paraphrasable as "the word or expression referred to might be a less than usual or perfect choice or have some interesting peculiarities that need highlighting." They can be classified as interpersonal in the sense that the choice of expression (and the labeling) is attributable to the speaker and/or left to the hearer for ratification.
         c   Syntax: They are extra-sentential and structurally non-integrated. Rather than by rules, their use is governed by conversational goals and principles.
         d   Prosody: The punctuation marks may be indicative of prosodic boundaries (cf. (80); but see also Section 2.1).
         e   Placement: Their position is extra-sentential and they represent positional mobility, being found in various positions of the sentence in accordance with their respective discourse function.

There are no indications that the emergence of these properties was the result of a longer gradual process; all properties seem to have appeared in the same general time period around the mid-seventeenth century. There were a few early examples, though, which can be interpreted as being ambiguous between a sentence grammar and thetical meaning. Thus, *soo to saye* in (82) could either be understood as being grammatically fully integrated, being a complement of the clause *they have commission of God*, or else it could be a metatextual comment by the speaker – hence, being a thetical (i.e., parenthetical in the terminology of Claridge 2013: 171, (18)). It remains unclear whether this ambiguity is the result of the communicative intents of the speaker or writer or whether the text available is not sufficiently discriminative to establish which of the two interpretations was intended; we will return to this issue in Section 3.3.

(82)   English (1545 CEEC, Gardin, 1545; Claridge 2013: 171, (18))
        They note the Kinges Majestie not to see the truth. They condempne al the
        Parlament of ignoraunce, and saye to the people they have commission of
        *God **soo to saye**.*

In addition to cooptation, the development of *so to say*/*so to speak* also involved grammaticalization, but its role was apparently not highly pronounced, as observed by Claridge in (83) on the three DMs covered by her.

(83)   The processes that the three constructions have gone through on their way to
        becoming idiomatic pragmatic items are sometimes or partly shared with
        those grammaticalized items undergo. Semantic bleaching, persistence, sub-
        jectification, decategorialization, divergence, ossification of form and
        specialization are cases in point . . .
                                                                (Claridge 2013: 180)

Corpus data suggest that such uses as theticals were not very common in the seventeenth and eighteenth centuries. It is only from 1820 onwards that there was a remarkable increase in their frequency. And there were a number of similar theticals surfacing in the nineteenth century, such as *so to call it* (1797) *so to express it* (1833), or *so to speak it* (1874), cf. (84).

(84)   English (1833 J. H. Newman *Arians* II. iii. (1876) 163, OED; Claridge 2013:
        172, (19b))
        *That there is (, **so to express it**,) a reiteration of the One Infinite Nature of God.*

Their relationship to *so to say*/*so to speak* is not entirely clear (Claridge 2013: 172). Conceivably, they were new thetical formations but their creation may have been influenced by the presence of the earlier DMs *so to say* and *so to speak*.

3.2.11   *English* Well

Like most of the other items discussed in this chapter, the item *well* shows two contrasting uses, illustrated in the constructed example (85) that we had used already in the introductory Section 1.1.1.

(85)   English
    a *Jeff writes* **well**.
    b **Well**, *Jeff writes*.

The expression *well* in (85a) is an adverb while that in (85b) is a DM, the two differing from one another in a number of properties, and we know that the latter is historically derived from the former. The objective of the following remarks is to look into the development leading from the former to the latter in order to account for these properties.

The DM *well* differs from a number of other English DMs in that there appears to be little social stigmatization associated with its use (Beeching 2016: 70). Defour and Simon-Vandenbergen (2010) argue that its core meaning is "positive appraisal," and Aijmer (2013: 47) calls it a "friendly" pragmatic marker, serving to cement social relationships and creating solidarity within the group. According to Jucker (1993: 438, 440), the DM *well* "is some kind of signpost, directing the way in which the following utterance should be processed by the addressee," while for Beeching the main function of the DM in ordinary conversation can be summed up as "flagging a demurral" (Beeching 2016: 52).

Its functions are however complex, having been the subject of a number of analyses (e.g., Schiffrin 1987: 102–27; Jucker 1997; Aijmer and Simon-Vandenbergen 2003; Furkó 2007; Cuenca 2008; Beeching 2016: 51–75). Jucker (1993; 1997) found four distinct uses in Modern English, namely (a) as a frame for introducing a new topic or prefacing direct reported speech; (b) as a qualifier prefacing a reply which is only a partial answer to a question, (c) as a face-threat mitigator prefacing disagreement; and (d) as a pause filler bridging interactional silence. In a more recent study, Beeching (2016) distinguishes nine functions of the DM *well*, namely the ones in (86).

(86)   Functions subserved by the DM *well* (Beeching 2016: 53–56)
    a Hesitation
    b Transitional *well*
    c Changing the topic
    d Raising an objection
    e Prefacing a dispreferred response
    f Taking a turn/polite interruptions
    g Other-correction
    h Self-correction
    i Quotative *well*

Beeching concludes:

Schourup's summary (2001: 1056) of a gestural, interjective *well* which shows that "the speaker is engaged in on-the-spot, pointedly epistemic consideration prefatory to continuation" is the most satisfactory unifying account of *well*. (Beeching 2016: 74)

Cooptation is a ubiquitous operation which may take place repeatedly in the history of a linguistic expression, and in the history of *well* it possibly happened repeatedly. The first instance can be traced back to Old English. Derived from Indo-European *wel- "to will, wish," the earliest uses of *well* as a DM are found in Old English, where *wella* (or *wel la*) was used on an interpersonal level as an emphatic attention getting device, apparently in an attempt to imitate spoken language (Jucker 1997: 96–97). Serving as an attention signal, its meaning can be paraphrased as "listen to what I have to tell you" (Jucker 2002: 221). *Wella* was placed at the beginning of a speech or at the beginning of a conclusion after an exposition. It collocates in all cases with a vocative, like *min drihten* "my Lord" in (87).

(87)   Old English (Boethius 40, 4; Homilies 1.23.574-6; Jucker 1997: 97, (10))
         *. . . and cwæð Þa on his geðance; **Wella** min drihten. hwæt ic her nu*
         hreowlice hæbbe gefaren.
         (and said then in his thought, "Alas, my Lord, what! how pitiably have I now
         fared here!")

There is no information on the circumstances giving rise to the growth of this interjection-like use of Old English *wella* (or *wel la*), in particular on whether it appeared suddenly or evolved gradually. What is obvious, however, is that with its appearance it showed the main hallmarks of a DM, serving speaker–hearer interaction, having a metatextual function rather than lexical meaning, and occurring outside the sentence it was associated with (cf. Brinton 1995: 380; Jucker 1997: 97).

With its disappearance, the attention-getting interjective usage also disappeared, and Jucker (1997: 96) does not see any direct development leading from Old English *wella* to the DM *well* found in Middle English.[26] In none of the examples from the Old English period does *well* show its modern usage of qualified acceptance.

The second instance of what we assume to be a case of cooptation of *well* must have appeared at some point between 1150 and 1250. Defour and Simon-Vandenbergen (2010: 653–654) mention example (88) as its first attestation, where *well* occurs at the left boundary of the utterance, apparently having a text structuring function that introduces a new section in ongoing discourse. With its use, *well* connects a first part of the text (*he com bi þis forwundede mon*) to a newly introduced continuation, and it is apparently not a semantic or syntactic constituent of the utterance. Still, Brinton (personal communication of January 20, 2020) observes that *well* in (88) could be an adverbial rather

---

[26] Note, however, that the Old English examples already tend to occur together with a reporting clause and can therefore be seen as direct precursors of the Middle English DM *well*, even if the latter now functions on the textual level to introduce direct reported speech (Jucker 1997: 105).

than a DM, and *well* had not yet undergone desemanticization, that is, in examples like (88) it still has retained its semantic content (Defour and Simon-Vandenbergen 2010: 654).

(88)   English (1150–1250 HC, Lambeth Homilies: 1150–1250; Defour and Simon-Vandenbergen 2010: 653–54; (7))
        *... he com bi þis forwundede mon. **Wel** he com bi him; þa he bicom alswich alse he; wiþute sunne ane. He wes iwunde mid wine and smirede mid oli.*
        "... He passed by this wounded man. Well, he went up to him; then he became exactly just as he (was); only without sin. He was bedaubed with wine and anointed with oil."

The first Middle English text segments suggestive of cooptation that Jucker (1997: 98–100) provides are dated 1470, showing uses of *well* like in (89), where *well* occurs both as an adverb (*Ye sey well*) and as a DM (*"Well," seyde thys lady*):

(89)   Middle English (1470 HC CMMALORY 1470; Jucker 1997: 99, (17))
        *"Ye sey well," seyde the kynge. "Aske what ye woll and ye shall have hit and hit lye in my power to gyff hit." "**Well**," seyde thys lady, "than I aske the hede of thys knyght that hath wonne the swerde, ..."*

Text segments like (89) are described by Jucker thus:

At this period in the history of English *well* is used in a very rigid frame. It occurs at the beginning of direct reported speech and is followed immediately by a parenthesis consisting of a verb of speaking and an indication of the speaker (e.g., *"Well," seyde sir Launcelot, "take this lady and the hede,"* HC CMMALORY 1470). Only two verbs occur in this position: "say" and "quethe" in the forms *sayd* or *seyde* and *quoth*. In these contexts *well* can be described as a frame marker. In some sense it can be viewed as a paragraph marker. All of them are closely related to spoken language, and all of them occur utterance-initially. (Jucker 1997: 99)

In addition to its textual function, the meaning of *well* already has an interpersonal component, signaling to the hearer acknowledgment or reception of information (Defour and Simon-Vandenbergen 2010: 656, 658). As in the case of Old English *wella*, there is no plausible evidence suggestive of a gradual grammaticalization leading to the rise of the DM *well* in Middle English. But the main properties suggestive of cooptation appear to already have been in place by 1500 or earlier, cf. (90).

(90)   Hypothesized effects of cooptation in Middle English *well*
        a Meaning: From meaning as part of the sentence to meaning outside of the sentence.
        b Function: From sentence-internal adverbial function to function on the discourse level marking textual and interpersonal functions (Jucker 1997: 91, 97).
        c Syntax: From sentence-internal adverb to syntactically independent DM.

d Prosody: Punctuation marking (cf. (89)) suggests that *well* changed from prosodically integrated constituent to prosodically marked expression (but see also Section 2.1).

e Semantic–pragmatic scope: From scope within the sentence to scope over the situation of discourse

f Placement: From position defined by its adverbial status to placement preferably in utterance-initial position.

Jucker (1997: 100) suggests that in all of the text segments quoted from Middle English *well* can be paraphrased by "if this is so" or "ok then." In addition to introducing reported speech and an "if this is so" meaning, Beeching (2016: 71) observes already the beginning of a "demurring" or qualifying response-marking function.

The ensuing history of *well* after 1500 can be described mainly as one of grammaticalization. Until then, *well* had mainly been followed by expressions of agreement or elaboration, but now the DM increasingly introduces a sense of modification, disagreement, or concession (Defour and Simon-Vandenbergen 2010: 669). The utterance-initial position is retained in Early Modern English but the DM is extended to new contexts beyond its Middle English use in reported speech, and it loses its association with spoken language, now occurring also in diaries, handbooks, and in fiction. Furthermore, it is increasingly extended to contexts not involving direct speech, and in addition to indicating the speaker's acknowledgement of a preceding speaker turn, it serves as a basis for the speaker to develop his or her personal argument (Defour and Simon-Vandenbergen 2010: 659–60, Table 6). In the seventeenth century *well* acquired the function of a face-threat mitigator, and quotative and continuative uses are also documented in the eighteenth century (Beeching 2016: 73).

And *well* was no longer restricted to the utterance-initial position (cf. Jucker 1997: 104, (36)). In addition to new functions arising there was also loss of earlier functions. In particular, most utterance-prefatory uses of *well* in Shakespeare's plays express agreement, but this usage later on declined, being obsolete in Present-Day English (Schourup 2001: 1049; Beeching 2016: 71).

To conclude, the history of the DM *well* is one of both continuity and discontinuity. Continuity can be seen in its gradual functional diversification from its earliest uses in the ninth century to the present. For example, already in the Old English examples, the DM expressed an acceptance of a situation, and this function appears to have accompanied its history across the centuries.

Discontinuity must have come in already in Old English when *well* (that is, *wella, wel la*) arose as a DM. There probably was no continuous development from Old English to Middle English (Jucker 1997: 105). Conceivably therefore, *well* experienced two separate waves of cooptation, one in Old English and the other in Middle English, but this hypothesis is in need of further support. With its rise as a DM in the fifteenth century, if not earlier, however, *well* acquired its main grammatical properties that were listed in (90), and these properties survived largely unchanged in the ensuing centuries up to Present-Day English. Compared to the dramatic shift from adverb to DM in Middle English, subsequent changes were distinctly less dramatic, their main effects being that *well* acquired an array of new functions via grammaticalization. Thus, Jucker observes:

> From Middle English onwards the development is more continuous. All the Middle English and Early Modern English functions appear to survive into Modern English. In this sense it is not so much a continuous development as a continuous diversification, with new functions developing alongside the old functions that continue to exist. (Jucker 1997: 105)

To conclude, the history of *well* is characterized by massive context extensions and functional changes, as described by Jucker (1997), Schourup (2001), and in particular by Defour (2007) and Defour and Simon-Vandenbergen (2010). With regard to its overall grammatical development, it is most of all the properties listed in (90) that distinguish the DM from its etymological source, the adverb *well*. These properties were acquired in Middle English before 1500, and they have been retained largely unchanged up until Present-Day English.

3.2.12   *English* What else

The uses of the English information unit *what else* include two main variants, which we will refer to as *what else$_1$* and *what else$_2$*. (91) illustrates *what else$_1$*, having propositional meaning, being an argument of an object clause. It corresponds in every respect to what we call a sentence grammar unit: It is a functional part of sentence organization, being syntactically and prosodically integrated, having restrictive meaning in the sense that its meaning is shaped by its function as a clausal argument, and its position is fixed: *what else$_1$* occurs in the position prescribed by its syntactic function as the subject of the complement clause *what else is available in the pub*.

(91)   English (*What's brewing*, BNC, 1991; Brinton 2008: 213, (10b))
        *The price reflects **what else** is available in the pub* ...

What else$_2$ in (92), by contrast, is classified by Brinton (2008: 218) as an elliptical interrogative clause and a comment clause, and it has the function of a DM, or pragmatic marker (Lenk 1998: 189–202; Brinton 2008: 212). Whereas *what else$_1$* in (91) expresses an "indirect inquiry for some undetermined additional or different thing," the DM in (92a) can be paraphrased as "would you expect anything other"; it is used when speakers "have lost the train of thought they were following and are retracing it, or when they want to recall an additional aspect they consider worth mentioning, in order to add something important to what they had said before" (Lenk 1998: 192). Salient functions of *what else₂* are (a) to call on the hearer to agree with the speaker's beliefs concerning the expectedness of the action described, (b) to emphasize information which follows, or (c) to present affirmative replies ("certainly") (Brinton 2008: 212–14).

(92)   English (Saturday Evening Post, 1992; Brinton 2008: 213, (11a))
       a *Of course, on Monday nights they settle down to watch*
          – what else – *"Murphy Brown."*
       b *Of course, on Monday nights they settle down to watch "Murphy Brown"*
          – what else.

Instead of being conceptual–propositional, the meaning of *what else₂* is described as procedural, and *what else₂* is not an argument of any kind. Rather, it corresponds to our definition of DMs in (7) in Section 1.1.2: It is an invariable expression, semantically and syntactically independent from its environment and set off prosodically from the rest of the utterance, and it is positionally fairly free. Thus, instead of (92a) it is possible to say (92b), that is, it can be placed utterance-finally, or it can occur as a stand-alone, that is, as an utterance of its own, as in the text example of (93).

(93)   English (1992 Harding, *The Nightingale Gallery* [BNC]; Brinton 2008: 214, (12a))
       "So you think that Allingham's death was by natural causes?" "Oh, of course! **What else?** *There's no mark of violence. No sign of poison," Sir Richard answered.*

Furthermore, *what else₂* has a metatextual function in that it relates to recurrent experiences and expectations characterizing the situation of discourse (see Brinton 2008: 214). And unlike *what else₁*, *what else₂* in (93) has semantic–pragmatic scope over the discourse rather than over some constituent of the utterance (Brinton 2008: 217).

The earliest attestations of *what else* provided by Brinton (2008) date back to Early Modern English in the sixteenth century, and they concern both *what else₁*, as in (94), and *what else₂* in (95) and (96). This reconstruction is based on the following observations: *what else₁* (i.e., *what els*) in (94) has the sense "whatever else" and occurs as the final expression of a listing of noun phrases, that is, it is syntactically integrated. In (95) and (96), by contrast, it is syntactically independent, forming an utterance of its own; hence it has the appearance of a thetical stand-alone, having the sense of "certainly" in an emphatic reply in (95) and "the function of retrieval of information by the speaker" in (96) (Brinton 2008: 215–16).

(94)   English (1579 *Expos. Termes Law s.v. Reservation* [*OED*]; Brinton 2008: 215, (14a))
         *Theyr reseruations were as wel ... in vittailis, whether flesh, fishe, corne, bread, drinke, or **what els**, as in money.*

(95)   English (1540 Palsgrave, *The Comedye of Acolastus* V, v [ED]; Brinton 2008: 216, (18a))
         But I se my father, but what now may I do? may I go to hym? **what els**, *Father I haue synned into the heuen and before the, nor here after I am not worthy to be called thy sonne.*

(96)   English (1573 Gascoigne and Kinwelmersh (trans.), Euripides' *Iocasta: A Tragedie* II, ii [ED]; Brinton 2008: 215, (16a))
         Eteocles: *And wilt thou then I vse some other reade?*
         Creon: ***What else?*** *be still awhile, for haste makes wast.*

The fact that both *what else$_1$* and *what else$_2$* first appeared around the same time in the sixteenth century raises the question of whether the former was immediately followed by the latter. In the absence of more detailed historical information, there is no reasonable answer to this question.

While *what else$_2$* was coopted at the latest by 1573 there is no clear evidence whether grammaticalization played any role in its rise. That its early uses illustrated in (95) and (96) represent incipient stages of grammaticalization is a possibility that cannot be ruled out. But, irrespective of this possibility, the structure and meaning of *what else$_2$* in (95) and (96), clearly differs from *what else$_1$* in (94) in the following features: (a) Its meaning is not part of the utterance meaning; rather, it is described by Brinton (2008: 217) as metacommunicative, subjective and interpersonal. (b) It is not part of the sentence syntax; rather it is syntactically independent. (c) It has (semantic–pragmatic) scope over the utterance as a whole rather than over some constituent of it.

Brinton (2008: 217–18) describes the earliest attested uses of *what else$_2$* in (95) and (96) as an affirmative reply meaning "certainly," and as subjective. Such uses are characteristic of theticals: Information units of sentence grammar express conceptual–propositional meaning but when coopted as theticals they tend to replace that meaning with functions shaped by the situation of discourse, and speaker attitudes and speaker–hearer interaction are central components of the conceptual–pragmatic universe of the situation of discourse (Kaltenböck, Heine and Kuteva 2011: 861–64). In sum, there does not appear to be any reasonable argument to assume that grammaticalization played a significant role in the rise of the "certainly"-thetical *what else$_2$* in the sixteenth century.

And much the same appears to have happened when *what else* experienced a second development as a comment clause (or DM), let us call it the "what else would you expect"-thetical *what else$_3$*. This development took place much later, in Late Modern English, when the expression acquired a new schematic function, namely the "metacommunicative" sense "what else would you expect," as in (97). We follow Brinton (2008: 217) in assuming that the "what else would you expect"-thetical *what else₃* derives from the interrogative use of *what else* in full questions. Like *what else₂* of Early Modern English in the sixteenth century, the new DM had all the formal properties of a thetical, as we pointed out at the beginning of this section with reference to (92a).

(97)   English (1915 Dixon, *The Foolish Virgin* p. 350 [UofV]; Brinton 2008:
         216, (17b))
         *"What on earth possessed him to undertake such a task?" "The love of a
         beautiful woman – **what else?**"*

In Present-Day English, *what else₁* is used fairly infrequently compared to the thetical uses of *what else₂* and *what else₃*: The last two account for 86.6 percent in the British and 77.7 percent in the American data of Brinton (2008: 212).

To conclude, there is evidence to suggest that *what else* served as a thetical from the earliest stage of its documentation in the sixteenth century, and that all its main features are due to this development, resulting in the rise of two constructional theticals, namely the DMs *what else₂* and *what else₃*. These features of *what else* are summarized in (98).

(98)   Grammatical effects of cooptation: English *what else₂* (Brinton 2008:
         217–18)
         a Meaning: It developed a variety of pragmatic uses as a comment clause,
            not being part of the meaning of the sentence.
         b Function: Its functions are metatextual, mainly relating to speaker–hearer
            interaction.
         c Syntax: No longer having argument status, it is not a constituent of the
            sentence.
         d Prosody: It is prosodically set off from its textual environment, signaled,
            e.g., by a question mark.
         e Semantic–pragmatic scope: Its scope extends over the discourse rather
            than over some constituent of the utterance.
         f Placement: It may occupy different syntactic positions. In addition, it can
            occur on its own as a stand-alone.

Evidence suggestive of grammaticalization concerns most of all the change of *what else* from interrogative clause to fixed expression with particle-like status, that is, a formulaic thetical and a DM. This change seems to be due to decategorialization, whereby the morphemes *what* and *else* lost their morphological distinctiveness and merged into an invariable marker, as has happened also with a number of other English DMs like *as it were*, *if you will*, *for example*. Whether this univerbation of *what else* occurred prior to or after cooptation cannot be established on the basis of the data available.

Thus, *what else₂* appears to be another straightforward product of cooptation followed by grammaticalization. The development of *what else₃* remains unclear, conceivably it represents a grammaticalized form of *what else₂*, but it may as well have been a separate case of cooptation also having *what else₁* as a source.

3.3   Problems of Reconstruction: Gradual Change and Intermediate Stages

It is well-known to students of historical linguistics that there are especially two assumptions that guide the reconstruction of earlier stages of grammaticalization, namely (a) that change is gradual and (b) that it involves intermediate stages in the transition from one stage to another. These assumptions have in fact been employed extensively in the research summarized in the course of this chapter. At the same time, we also saw that there are problems with these assumptions when it comes to reconstructing the development of DMs. These problems are investigated in the present section.

The main problem with (a), surfacing in many publications on the rise of DMs, concerns gradualness of grammatical change: It constitutes one of the cornerstones of grammaticalization theory and of the procedures used in historical reconstruction. Accordingly, if it is possible to establish that the development of a given DM involved gradualness then this is taken to prove that that development involved grammaticalization rather than any other mechanism. And in fact, we saw in Section 2.5 that gradualness is an inherent feature both in the early and in the late development of DMs. At the same time, we also saw that gradualness is highly constrained: It concerns for the most part only the *internal structure* of evolving DMs rather than their external structure: Neither in this chapter nor in the chapters to follow do we find appropriate evidence to show that the effects of cooptation on the external structure of the expressions concerned, such as loss of syntactic and prosodic integration, are due to gradual grammaticalization.

Thus, we observed in the preceding sections that the development of DMs like *after all, I mean, if you like*, etc. involved internal grammaticalization, gradually leading to loss of internal morphological compositionality and lexical meaning and to the gradual emergence of invariable markers having procedural functions. In their *external* structure, however, these markers changed fairly abruptly at some specific stage in their development once they were coopted. For example, we saw in Section 3.2.9 that the expression *right* has a long history, to be traced back to Old English. And this history was shaped by grammaticalization, gradually leading, e.g., from adjunct (*do things right*) to modifier (*right snippy*). But during the period between 1640 and 1710, *right* must have been coopted (*Right, Madam, said I*), and this shift must have been fairly dramatic. As the description by Méndez-Naya (2006) suggests, the shift had the effect that *right* changed from adjunct and modifier to syntactic stand-alone, from meaning as part of the sentence to meaning outside the sentence, from function within the sentence to metatextual function, and from prosodically integrated to uninte-grated status, etc. (see (76) of Section 3.2.9).

In sum, rather than being a problem for reconstruction, lack of gradualness in the external structure of an evolving DM is to be expected and, hence, would seem to provide evidence in favor of the cooptation hypothesis.

The problem with (b) concerns intermediate stages in the development of DMs. When discussing the methodology used in this book in Section 2.1 we drew attention to the problem of "ambiguity" in linguistic reconstruction. As observed earlier in the present section, one important procedure in historical reconstruction consists of searching for intermediate stages of change in order to establish that there was a transition from one historical state to another. An inherent feature of grammaticalization can be seen in the fact that in the transition of an expression from an earlier state A to a later state B there is an intermediate stage of "ambiguity," called the bridging stage AB, where an expression is indeterminate between a traditional and an innovative usage – hence, where there is ambiguity in accordance with the chain model of Heine (1992).[27] The presence of "ambiguity" is therefore commonly employed as evidence to classify a given process as having been due to gradual gramma-ticalization rather than to something else, such as pragmaticalization or cooptation (see for example Erman and Kotsinas 1993: 79).

In fact, in a number of studies on the rise of DMs, including some of those surveyed in this chapter as well as in the following chapters, this procedure was adopted for reconstruction. It would seem, however, that this procedure is not without problems, for the following reason: In many cases it remains unclear what "ambiguity" or "intermediate stage" exactly stand for. We may illustrate the problem with the example of *anyway*, which was discussed in Section 3.2.2.

On its way from adverbial of sentence grammar to DM in the nineteenth century, *anyway* (or *any way*) exhibited the usage shown in (99) where its function appears to be ambiguous between that of a sentence grammar adver-bial (A) and a syntactically detached discourse-grammatical marker (B), that is, a thetical:

(99)   English (CLMETEV: Goldsmith, *The Vicar of Wakefield*, Ch. 21 [1766]; Haselow 2015: 174, (13)) (= (10) of Section 3.2.2)
         *"I suppose, my dear," cried he, "we shall have it all in a, lump." – "In a lump!" cried the other, "I hope we may get it **any way**; and that I am resolved we will this very night, or out she tramps, bag and baggage."*

---

[27] The notion of "ambiguity" is not the same in all those cases; see Traugott and Trousdale (2013: 199) on different types of ambiguity.

Haselow (2015: 174) in fact observes that (99) allows both interpretations, and the possibility cannot be ruled out that we are dealing with an intermediate structure, where *anyway* signals the stage of transition between an earlier A and a later B. However, this is only one possibility of interpretation: Conceivably, the author of (99) had intended to convey only A rather than B or AB, or only B – in other words, without any further contextual, semantic, syntactic, and/or prosodic cues it does not seem possible to establish beyond any reasonable doubt which of the various interpretations is in accordance with the communicative intents of the speaker or writer concerned.

Cases such as (99) are unfortunately fairly common (see for example Section 3.2.3 on *I mean*) and we will encounter more of them in the chapters to follow. What they suggest is that in such cases it is not possible to formulate a credible hypothesis on the presence or absence of an intermediate stage – that is, on whether "ambiguity" is due to (a) the communicative intent of the speaker or writer, (b) the particular interpretation by the researcher, or else (c) to lack of appropriate contextual or grammatical information. In view of this problem, using such cases of ambiguity as a basis for formulating a hypothesis on some "intermediate stage" of grammaticalization would seem to be empirically questionable and we do not include such cases as relevant pieces of evidence in our reconstruction work.

To conclude, generalizations on gradualness and intermediate stages provide powerful tools for reconstructing grammaticalization. As was argued in the present section, however, both must be taken with care when reconstructing the rise and development of DMs.

3.4   Discussion

For space reasons we were restricted in this chapter to a dozen cases studies; similar observations can be made with other English DMs. The analyses presented in this chapter were, however, faced with a number of problems, including the ones discussed in Section 3.3. But in spite of such problems, relating to the data that we were able to access, the evidence available was overall sufficient to formulate viable hypotheses on the rise of English DMs. As Table 3.1 shows, the dates reconstructed cover a large timespan in the history of the language, extending from around 1000 AD or earlier in the case of *if you will* to the nineteenth century in the case of *if you like* and *anyway*.

The reconstructions sketched in this chapter were meant to test the generalizations that were proposed in (26) of Section 2.6 and, in fact, the reconstructions seem to be on the whole in support of those generalizations. First, even if the corpus data on which our reconstruction work rests was generally not entirely satisfactory for our purposes, it turned out that it is overall possible for all the DMs surveyed to identify some specific period of time when the

Table 3.1 *Hypothesized dates of cooptation of some English DMs*

Discourse marker	Approximate date of cooptation
if you will	Tenth century
well	Between 1150 and 1250
no doubt	Between 1350 and 1450
I mean	Late fourteenth century
what else	1573 or earlier
so to say/so to speak	Mid-seventeenth century
right	Between 1640 and 1710
after all	1700 or slightly earlier
like	Second half of eighteenth century
instead	Around 1800 or earlier
if you like	First half of nineteenth century
anyway	Roughly between 1840 and 1865, if not earlier

relevant chunks of sentence grammar can be assumed to have been transferred to the level of discourse processing.

Second, our reconstructions suggest that with their transfer, the expressions concerned acquired essentially the whole range of grammatical properties of theticals listed in (26b) of Section 2.6. Third, unlike what would be expected if that change had been the result of grammaticalization, these properties did not evolve gradually one after the other but rather seem to have appeared jointly following cooptation. And finally, in spite of all the grammaticalization processes that the theticals subsequently underwent on the way to turning into DMs, these properties survived largely unchanged right into Present-Day English.

But the history of English DMs was also shaped substantially by grammaticalization, as demonstrated in great detail by the authors cited in this chapter. For example, in accordance with the grammaticalization parameters of context extension and desemanticization (see Section 2.2.2), most DMs lost their sensitivity to truth conditions and part or all of their earlier lexical meaning while at the same time gaining a wealth of new discourse functions.

4 French Discourse Markers

4.1 Introduction

The observations made in Chapter 3 suggest that the cooptation hypothesis proposed to account for the development of DMs entails that a number of previous analyses of DMs and other theticals be looked at from a slightly different perspective. This perspective does not question the reconstructions proposed by the authors concerned but proposes an additional view to understand how DMs evolve.

As the present chapter may show, this perspective is not only supported by the development of English DMs. French DMs have been analyzed in a wide range of studies (e.g., Hansen 1998a; 1998b; 2005a; 2005b; 2008; Dostie 2004; 2009; Schneider 2007a; 2007b; Defour et al. 2010; 2012; Degand and Fagard 2011; Prévost 2011; Bolly 2014; Degand and Evers-Vermeul 2015; Detges and Gévaudan 2018; Prévost and Fagard 2018). These studies were not restricted to French spoken in European countries but include also analyses of French as spoken in Canada (e.g., Dostie 2004; Vincent 2005) or in the Democratic Republic of Congo (de Rooij 2000).

4.2 Case Studies

The present chapter looks at a number of French DMs for which there is an appropriate database for reconstructing how they came into being. For more details on the nature and the history of the DMs concerned the reader may wish to consult the references cited.

4.2.1 *À la rigueur*
4.2.2 *À propos* and *À ce propos*
4.2.3 *Alors*
4.2.4 *En fait* and *Au fait*
4.2.5 *Enfin*

As elsewhere we made an effort to look at each DM in its own right rather than treating related markers together (see Section 3.1 for a justification of this procedure). In the present chapter, however, there are two exceptions to this procedure because the development of the DMs concerned seems to have been interrelated to a great extent. These markers are *à propos* and *à ce propos* in Section 4.2.2 and *en fait* and *au fait* in Section 4.2.4.

4.2.1   French À la rigueur[1]

In their corpus-based analysis of the expression *à la rigueur* (lit. "to the rigor"), Prévost and Fagard (2018) distinguish three main types, called use types 1, 2, and 3; we will refer to them, respectively, as *à la rigueur₁* (usually glossed "harshly, strictly, rigorously"), *à la rigueur₂* ("exactly, accurately"), and *à la rigueur₃* ("at a pinch," "if necessary," "if need be," "maybe," having concessive overtones). *À la rigueur₁* and *à la rigueur₂* are described by Prévost and Fagard (2018) as verbal adverbials and sentence adverbials, respectively. As their description suggests, they are constituents of sentence grammar. *À la rigueur₃*, by contrast, is called a "hedging discourse marker."

The detailed reconstruction work carried out by these authors suggests the following general development (see especially Prévost and Fagard 2018: 226, Table 2):[2] Both *à la rigueur₁* and *à la rigueur₂* were already in use in the sixteenth century, but the former was clearly more common. This situation changed in the eighteenth and nineteenth centuries, when *à la rigueur₂* became the more common one. The use of both increased in the seventeenth century, but from the eighteenth century onward, the use of both gradually declined; the last occurrence of *à la rigueur₂* that Prévost and Fagard (2018: 218) identify is dated 1967. There are no more attestations of the two in the twenty-first century.

The DM *à la rigueur₃* is not attested in the sixteenth and seventeenth centuries, the first instance of it is found in the eighteenth century. Subsequently its use increased dramatically, with the result that in the twenty-first century it is the only one surviving.

Example (1) illustrates the lexical use of the expression in Medieval French of the fifteenth century, where *à la rigueur* has its nominal meaning "at the rigor," functioning as the head of a construction of nominal possession.

---

[1] We are grateful to Sophie Prévost for valuable comments on an earlier version of this section.

[2] Prévost and Fagard (2018: 226) distinguish a separate category of ambiguous uses. As Sophie Prévost (personal communication of September, 26, 2019) informs us, ambiguity relates to the information that is available to the authors rather than necessarily to the communicative intents of interlocutors or the actual structure of the expressions concerned; we have discussed this issue in Section 3.3.

(1)   French (1485 J. Juvenal des Ursins, *Exortation faicte au roy*; Prévost and
        Fagard 2018: 221, (1))
        ... aussi semble il, tout consideré, que si est il que luy devez faire
        misericorde, et la preferer **à la rigueur** *de justice.*
        "... and it seems, all things considered, that you ought to be merciful, and
        prefer mercy rather than the rigors of Justice."

Around that time, instances of *à la rigueur₁* are already found, translated as
"(to treat) harshly," cf. (2). It is a verbal argument, a syntactically dependent
adverbial mostly placed post-verbally (Prévost and Fagard 2018: 224).

(2)   French (1508 N. de La Chesnaye, *La Condamnation de Banquet*; Prévost and
        Fagard 2018: 223, (14))
        Or avez vous plaine science, Puissance, auctorité, vigueur: Pour tant, ma
        dame Experience, Pugnissez les **à la rigueur**.
        "Now you have full science, power, authority and vigor: Therefore, my lady
        Experience, punish them [*à la rigueur*: severely]."

The second use type, *à la rigueur₂* "exactly, accurately," is also a syntactically integrated adverbial, but it is not a true argument of the verb. Like *à la*
rigueur₁ it is a sentence grammar adverbial dependent on the verb, also most
often placed postverbally. It can be traced back to Classical French, but there
are no early text examples of it and we therefore have not much to say about it
in our diachronic interpretation. A modern example of it is found in (3).

(3)   French (1961 M. Foucault, *Folie et déraison: Histoire de la folie à l'âge*
        classique; Prévost and Fagard 2018: 224, (16))
        ... Au XVIIIe siècle, on redéecouvre cette distinction, et on la prend **à la**
        rigueur *...*
        "... In the 18th century, the distinction was rediscovered, and taken [*à la*
        rigueur: in a strict sense, *severely] ...*"

According to the data available, the first use of the expression as a thetical,
suggestive of *à la rigueur₃* and translated as "strictly speaking," dates back to
1713, cf. (4). In this usage, it is set off by punctuation marks, it has much wider
semantic–pragmatic scope than *à la rigueur₁* and *à la rigueur₂*, and it does not
appear to be a constituent of the clause, occurring either in medial position or
at the left periphery, later on also at the right-periphery.

(4)   French (1713 F. de Fénelon, *Traité de l'existence et des attributs de Dieu*;
        Prévost and Fagard 2018: 222, (7))
        Ces paroles tendent à signifier quelque vérité; mais elles sont, **à la rigueur**,
        indignes et impropres. Ce qu'elles ont de vrai, c'est que l'infini surpasse
        infiniment le fini.
        "These words tend to convey some truth: but they are, [*à la rigueur*: strictly
        speaking], neither dignified nor fair. What truth they have, is that the infinite
        infinitely surpasses the finite."

In addition to being an utterance anchored DM, *à la rigueur₃* also occurs as a constituent anchored DM, as in (5), where it is anchored in the noun phrase *une Lorraine* "a (a woman from) Lorraine" rather than in the sentence as a whole.

(5)   French (2009 S. Weil, *Chez les Weil: André et Simone*; Prévost and Fagard
       2018: 225, (22))
       *Les soeurs de Bernard regrettèrent qu'au lieu d'épouser une Alsacienne ou à
       la rigueur une Lorraine, leur frère ait choisi une Galitzianerin.*
       "Bernard's sisters regretted that, instead of marrying a woman from Alsace or
       [*à la rigueur*: possibly, at a pinch] Lorraine, their brother would choose a
       Galitzianerin."

To conclude, *à la rigueur₃* appears to have turned into a thetical in the early eighteenth century, if not earlier, and it became a full-fledged DM, acquiring the properties listed in (6). There is no grammatical evidence to suggest that the properties in (6) emerged in a gradual way one after the other in the history of *à la rigueur₃*.

(6)   Properties suggestive of cooptation in the development of French *à la
       rigueur₃* (see Prévost and Fagard 2018)
       a Meaning: It is semantically disjunct, it is no longer integrated in the
          meaning of the sentence it is associated with. It "has no bearing on the
          predicate or the utterance, but only on a discourse level" (Prévost and
          Fagard 2018: 230).
       b Function: It has a metatextual function.
       c Syntax: It turned from a syntactically integrated clause-internal adverbial
          into a largely or entirely non-integrated DM.
       d Prosody: It appears to be set off prosodically, as is suggested by the
          frequent use of commas and other punctuation marks (but see Section 2.1).
       e Semantic–pragmatic scope: It acquired a distinctly wider scope.
       f Placement: It acquired positional flexibility, turning from a sentence-
          internal expression placed mainly post-verbally to one that can appear in
          virtually any syntactic position (Prévost and Fagard 2018: 226).

In addition to cooptation in the early eighteenth century, the history of *à la rigueur₃* was also shaped by grammaticalization. The first wave of grammaticalization took place prior to its emergence as a DM, hence involving early grammaticalization: Already in the sixteenth or seventeenth century it seems to have undergone internal decategorialization leading to univerbation by gradually changing from the morphologically compositional adverbial phrase *à la rigueur* "to the rigor," illustrated in (1) above, into the invariable, monomorphemic adverbial *à la rigueur₁* "harshly, strictly, rigorously."

The second wave was mainly semantic, starting out with *à la rigueur₁* as an adverbial to *à la rigueur₃* as a DM and involving the meaning changes found in (7). As would be expected in grammaticalization, with the change from one meaning to the other, the earlier meaning was not replaced by the new meaning; rather, it continued side by side with the latter (cf. Hopper's 1991: 22 principle of persistence).

(7)   Semantic change of *à la rigueur* from the seventeenth century to the twenty-first century (Prévost and Fagard 2018: 227, figure 2)
(a) "harshly" > (b) "strictly" > (c) "exactly" > (d) "at a pinch" > (e) "if necessary" > (f) "maybe"

Grammaticalization involved simultaneously context extension, desemanticization, and the emergence of new meanings in novel contexts (see Section 2.2.2). One important change, leading from *à la rigueur₁* to *à la rigueur₂* uses was conceivably triggered by the extension of the adverbial to a large spectrum of verb types (Prévost and Fagard 2018: 230).

4.2.2   *French* À propos *and* À ce propos

The expression *à propos* has a number of different uses (see Prévost 2011). More specifically, it occurs, on the one hand, in postverbal position, where its function is described as a manner adverb meaning "(in an) appropriate (way)," cf. (8).

(8)   French (Prévost 2011: 401, (19))
*Il est arrivé **à propos** pour réveiller la soirée.*
"He arrived **at the right moment** to wake up the party."

On the other hand, it is found in preverbal position, syntactically separated from the rest of the sentence, often by a pause, signaled by a punctuation mark, as in (9). It indicates a smooth or a more abrupt discourse shift, glossed as "by the way," and serves to reinforce, or even create, discourse coherence. In (9), for example, it indicates a smooth discourse shift, a digression:

(9)   French (V. Larbaud, *Beauté, mon beau souci* . . . 1923; Prévost 2011: 392, (1))
*Nous irons dîner à l'Ange Bleu d'Abergavenny. **A propos**, ma chère, ce n'est plus que dans le Pays de Galles qu'on trouve la vraie petite auberge anglaise du bon vieux temps.*
"We'll have dinner in the Blue Angel in Abergavenny. **By the way**, my dear, only in Wales can we find a true typical English inn as in earlier times."

While placed at the beginning of a sentence, *à propos* can be preceded by some other DM, like *tiens* "there" in (10).

(10)   French (Prévost 2011: 395, (7))
*Tiens, **à propos**, j'ai croisé Paul ce matin: il veut récupérer son échelle.*
"There, **by the way**, I met Paul this morning, he wants to get his ladder back."

In accordance with the convention adopted in previous chapters we will refer to the former uses of *à propos* as *à propos₁* and the latter as *à propos₂*.

For good reasons, Prévost (2011: 393) is hesitant to include *à propos₂* in the large class of French discourse markers (e.g., Hansen 1997; 1998a; 1998b; Dostie 2004; Vincent 2005; Rossari 2006). For the purposes of the present discussion, however, we will refer to it as a DM, considering that it corresponds essentially to the criteria proposed in (7) of Section 1.1.2.

As argued by Prévost (2011), there are two possible sentence grammar expressions that may have contributed to the emergence of the DM *à propos₂*, namely the erstwhile adverbial phrases *à propos de* (lit. "at subject of") and *à ce propos* (lit. "at this subject").[3]

In Middle French, *à propos de* formed a prepositional phrase having the grammatical status of a verbal complement, as in (11) (Prévost 2011: 397).

(11)   French (C. de Pizan, *Le livre de la paix*, 1412; Prévost 2011: 398, (11); bold print in the original)
        Et se puet entendre en figure cest exemple, c'est assavoir que quant peuple voult monter plus hault qu'il ne doit, Dieu envoye entre eulx confusion qui les fait cheoir. Et pour ce, **à propos de telz gens dit trop bien Orace** *que ilz sont aucuns qui se cuident avoir les yeulx plus fors que le spere du souleil, mais en eulx efforçant d'y regarder s'avuglent eulx mesmes.*
        "And his illustration may be understood as an exemplum, that is to say that when a people tries to raise itself higher than it should, God sends them confusion and makes them fall. This is why **Orace says**, with reason, **about such persons** that they think themselves capable of looking at the sun, but blind themselves in so doing."

Cooptation must have taken place in the sixteenth century or earlier when *à propos de* + NP was placed in preverbal position, being syntactically independent from the verb and taking on the function of serving as a frame or as a topic for the following sentence – a use that appears to have been preserved in Present-Day French, as in the following example:

(12)   French (Prévost 2011: 398, (12))
        A propos de Paul, j'ai rencontré sa soeur hier au cinéma
        "As for Paul, I met his sister in the train yesterday."[4]

The second expression, *à ce propos*, is first attested in the fourteenth century, being used more frequently than *à propos de*, both occurring in preverbal and postverbal position, most often functioning as a verbal complement and being associated with a speech act verb, cf. (13).

(13)   French (1360 J. Daudin, *De la erudition*, 1360; Prévost 2011, (14))
        A laquele chose vault moult ajouster exemples manifestes, selonc le dit de Varron: "Tres clere maniere de enseignier est ajouster exemples." A ce **propos** *dist Aristote ou premier livre de Methafisique: . . .*

---

[3] The earliest meaning of the noun *propos* was "subject," "matter" (Prévost 2011: 401).
[4] The correct meaning is presumably "in the cinema" rather than "in the train."

"We should add to this many obvious examples, following Varron: 'in order to teach well, give examples.' **On this subject** Aristotle says in the first book of Metaphysics ..."

The first unambiguous example of *à ce propos* as a coopted unit stems from the end of the sixteenth century, cf. (14).

(14)   French (P. d'Alcrippe, *La Nouvelle fabrique des excellents traicts de verité*, 1580–96; Prévost 2011: 399, (16))
*On voit coustumierement qu'à ces foires et marchez sont plusieurs coupeurs de bourses, qui ne font autre chose qu'espier leur belle, et regarder les moyens d'en avoir. A **ce propos**, un jour de marché, à Lyons, estoit un bon simple homme baissé assez bas, lequel marchandoit des naveaux estant contre terre sur du foirre, comme on les estalle.*
"We often see in those fairs and markets many thieves who do nothing else than observe women and try to gain access to them. **By the way**, on a market day in Lyon, there was a good and simple man who had gone down quite low ..."

As expressions of sentence grammar, *à ce propos* and *à propos$_1$* often took on the same verbal complement function. An early example of *à propos$_2$* is dated 1542, presented in (15), where it no longer forms a verbal complement or constituent of a sentence but rather appears to have the features of a DM.

(15)   French (1542 F. Rabelais, *Pantagruel*, 1542; Prévost 2011: 403–4, (25))
A quoy elle respondit: Quant est de moy, je ne vous hays poinct, car, comme Dieu le commande, je ayme tout le monde.
*– Mais, **à propos**, (dist il), n'estez vous amoureuse de moy?*
"She answered: As for me, I don't hate you, since I love everybody, as God commands it.
– But, **by the way**, he said, aren't you in love with me?"

The diachronic relationship between *à ce propos* and *à propos$_2$* as DMs is not entirely clear. According to the analysis by Prévost (2011: 406, 409), the latter is derived from the former either via analogical formation or via morphological reduction, that is, via erosion of the demonstrative expression *ce*, but she considers the former to be the more plausible hypothesis. Subsequently, *à propos$_2$* progressively replaced *à ce propos* in certain contexts, and it also developed in contexts signaling a more abrupt discourse shift.

Placed at the left periphery of a sentence, both *à ce propos* and *à propos$_2$* assumed the properties to be expected from a thetical, cf. (16).

(16)   Thetical properties of French *à ce propos* and *à propos$_2$* (see Prévost (2011)
a Meaning: They assumed a new meaning (e.g., "incidentally"), and *à propos$_2$* lost its conceptual meaning in favor of a procedural one.
b Function: They also acquired a new function "on the pragmatic level," signaling a discourse shift, specifying that the segment introduced has to be interpreted relative to the prior sequence (Prévost 2011: 395–96).

    c Syntax: They became syntactically independent from the verb.
    d Prosody. They seem to have been set off prosodically from the following
       sentence, as the frequent use of commas suggests.[5]
    e Semantic–pragmatic scope: With their shift from manner adverb with
       narrow scope to DM, their scope widened, extending "over stretches of
       discourse beyond the sentence" (Prévost 2011: 409).

There is, however, no information on how cooptation affected the placement of *à propos₁*, other than that the DM *à propos₂* is now firmly established in preverbal position.

To conclude, the difference between *à propos₁* and *à propos₂* highlighted in the introduction to this section can overwhelmingly be described as being the result of cooptation, even if one of the six criteria, namely possible constraints on placement, may not apply; more information is needed on this issue.

The description by Prévost (2011) suggests that grammaticalization also played a role in the development of *à propos*. In particular, loss of lexical or conceptual meaning in favor of procedural meaning appears to be strongly suggestive of a grammaticalization process of desemanticization. However, when exactly this process set in is hard to establish on the basis of the data available.

4.2.3   *French* Alors[6]

The French expression *alors* belongs to the most common DMs of contemporary spoken French, its main functions being to mark re-perspectivization or reorientation, foregrounding, or results or conclusions; see Hansen (1997: 184) for a network of related meanings.

In their discussion of the development of DMs, Degand and Evers-Vermeul (2015: 74–75) assert that the development of DMs "falls within the scope of grammaticalization" and that DMs "are a part of the grammar." Neither of these conclusions is questioned here. Where we differ, however, is in arguing, first, that that development cannot be reduced to grammaticalization and, second, that their account does not explain why DMs have the properties they have, most of all the ones listed in (26) of Section 2.6.

Both points can be illustrated with the very example that Degand and Evers-Vermeul (2015) and Degand and Fagard (2011) propose in support of their

---

[5] Prévost cautiously observes on this point: "Another criterion is the presence of a pause, generally a comma. However this criterion should only be used very sparingly, because we know that the punctuation of medieval texts is largely the work of modern editors" (Prévost 2011: 400). We have discussed this issue in Section 2.1.

[6] We are grateful to Maj-Britt Mosegaard Hansen and Liesbeth Degand for valuable comments on an earlier version of this section.

grammaticalization hypothesis, namely the French marker *alors*, glossed in dictionaries as an adverb meaning "then, now." The following brief account rests on the data provided by them (Degand and Fagard 2011; Degand and Evers-Vermeul 2015: 75–77) but proffers an alternative interpretation of their data.[7]

The expression *alors* is commonly associated with three primary meanings, namely temporal, causal, and discourse-structuring meanings. Example (17) illustrates the temporal and (18) the discourse-structuring meanings. Both the meaning and the structure of *alors* in (17) are suggestive of those of an adverb of sentence grammar. But the first and the last occurrences of *alors* in (18), both combining with the connective *mais* "but," are best interpreted as instances of a DM, being neither semantically nor syntactically integrated in their host sentence and apparently serving the organization of the text.

(17)   French (twentieth century novel; Degand and Fagard 2011, (2))
          il était rentré en cinq jours de Valladolid à Saint-Cloud, crevant au galop on
          *ne sait combien de chevaux. Lui qui dormait **alors** dix heures par nuit et deux*
          heures dans son bain, grâce à ses revers en Espagne et à cette nouvelle
          équipée, il retrouvait d'un coup son endurance et sa force.
          "It took him five days to come back from Valladolid to Saint-Cloud, running
          who knows how many horses to death on the way. He who *alors* slept ten
          hours a night and two more in his bath, all of sudden, thanks to his setbacks in
          Spain and to this new adventure, recovered his endurance and his strength."

(18)   French (twentieth century spoken discourse; Degand and Fagard 2011, (12))
          *… mais **alors** ce qui était marrant c'est que euh / tout à coup il s'arrêtait / et*
          ***alors** euh / assez vite alors xx se disait maintenant vous vous dirigez vers telle*
          *porte // mais **alors** …*
          "… but *alors* the funny thing was that er / suddenly he stopped / and *alors* er /
          quite quickly *alors* xx was saying now you go toward the door // but
          alors …"

Analyzed by Degand and Fagard (2011) as a compound of *à* "at" and *lors* "then," *alors* goes back to the Latin prepositional phrase *ad illam horam* "at that hour" or the ablative form *illa hora* (Hansen 1997: 163). In Old French of the twelfth century, *alors* appeared as a prefixed variant of *lors* "then," being grammaticalized to a sentence adverbial in the twelfth century as an integrated adjunct of the sentence restricted to clause-internal position and having temporal usages (Degand and Evers-Vermeul 2015: 76). This situation strongly suggests that it was a constituent of sentence grammar.

This situation does not appear to have changed when *alors* underwent further grammaticalization at the end of the thirteenth century, being extended

---

[7] Note, however, that the interpretation offered in this section must be taken with care, for the following reason: With their emphasis on semantic reconstruction, Degand and Fagard (2011) employ a framework of analysis that does not always allow relating the categories used by them unambiguously to the notions used in this chapter (see Chapter 2 for the latter framework).

to contexts where causal meanings evolved (cf. the parameter of context extension; Section 2.2.2), and from the fourteenth century on also occasionally conditional meanings. Note that changes from temporal to causal and conditional meanings are paradigm instances of grammaticalization (see Kuteva et al. 2019 for examples).

The data at our disposal do not allow establishing when exactly cooptation took place for the first time.[8] But beyond any reasonable doubt this must have happened at the latest in the fifteenth or sixteenth century in Middle French. Thus, Degand and Fagard (2011, section 5.2) note that "*alors* jumps from medial position in Old French to initial position from Middle French onwards." It turned into what Degand and Fagard (2011) call a conversation-structuring marker introducing new discourse units and hinting at the relevance of upcoming discourse.

From this time on, *alors* exhibits the grammatical hallmarks of a DM (see (40) of Chapter 1.5), like those in (19).

(19)   Properties suggestive of cooptation in the development of French *alors* (cf. Degand and Fagard 2011; Degand and Evers-Vermeul 2015)

    a Meaning: *Alors* is no longer part of the meaning of the sentence, it can be omitted without changing the semantic content, and it no longer establishes a temporal relation (Degand and Fagard 2011, Section 3.2).[9]

    b Function: It acquired "metadiscursive" functions typical of theticals, such as assuming a connective function not restricted to connecting adjacent clauses.[10] And it was used to express coherence relations between adjacent clauses and to work as a discourse-structuring device.

    c Syntax: It turned from a syntactically integrated clause-internal adverbial into a non-integrated conjunct "outside the core syntactic clause" (Degand and Evers-Vermeul 2015: 75).

    d Prosody: There is no information on the prosodic form of coopted *alors*.

    e Semantic–pragmatic scope: Its scope was extended beyond the clause it was associated with.

    f Placement: It acquired positional flexibility, now being preferably placed clause-initially and, distinctly less commonly, also clause-finally.[11]

---

[8] This does not apply to non-coopted uses of *alors*, which continued to be employed as a sentence grammar unit. Conceivably, uses of coopted *alors* can be traced back to the fourteenth century, where *alors* is already found in initial position, set off by a comma from the following sentence (see Degand and Fagard 2011, ex. (18)).

[9] Diana Lewis (personal communication of June 16, 2019) suspects, however, that when *alors* moved to initial position it remained purely temporal for a while.

[10] Parameters used by Degand and Fagard (2011, section 3.2) to define *alors* as a metadiscursive marker are: (a) It does not establish a temporal or argumentative relation, (b) it can be left out without changing the semantic content, and (c) it can be glossed by other French topic shifters such as *bon* "well," or transition markers, such as *et puis* "and then."

[11] Degand and Fagard (2011) note that from Middle French on, the majority of cases of *alors* are found in initial position, with a slow rise of occurrences in final position from Classical French onwards. See also Beeching (2016: 224).

There are unfortunately no appropriate text examples in the data at our disposal to show when and how exactly cooptation took place, our interpretation therefore rests entirely on the description provided by Degand and Fagard (2011) and Degand and Evers-Vermeul (2015). But it would seem that the undated example in (20) reflects an early use of *alors* suggestive of cooptation in the sense of (19).

(20)   French (Earlier French of unknown date; Degand and Fagard 2011, (18))
         *Or actendez, monseigneur, ce dit elle. Et maintenant vous me voiez bien, faictes pas? – Par Dieu! m'amye, nenny, dit monseigneur, comment vous verroie je? vous avez bouché mon dextre oeil, et l'autre est crevé passé a dix ans. – **Alors**, dist elle, or voy je bien que c'estoit songe voirement qui ce rapport m'a fait.*
         "Wait a minute now, my Lord, she said. Now you can see me well, can't you? – By God! My dear, no, said his Lordship, how could I see you? You have blocked my right eye, and the other one has been dead for ten years now. – *Alors*, she said, now I can see that it was really all a dream."

Subsequent to cooptation, *alors* underwent another round of grammaticalization from conjunct to DM, perhaps most dramatically in the twentieth century when it acquired metadiscursive meanings as a topic shifter and transition marker. Thus, the overall development of *alors* seems to be compatible with the scenario in (21).

(21)   Main stages in the development of discourse markers (Heine 2013: 1238–39)
         (Grammaticalization >) cooptation > grammaticalization

In accordance with (21), cooptation can come in at any stage in the development of a grammaticalizing expression. Conceivably it is expressions that are used recurrently that are particularly well suited for cooptation leading to DMs, but this is an issue that is in need of further analysis (see also Section 8.2.1).[12] Note that after cooptation, the earlier expression will not disappear; rather, it is likely to continue to be used, as it appears to have happened with *alors*, whose use as a temporal adverb was continued up to Present-Day French; of the 268 examples of *alors* that Hansen (1997: 171) found in her text corpora, only one was a temporal one. Not uncommonly therefore, the coopted and the non-coopted units co-occur in the synchronic state of the language concerned, being distinguishable on the basis of the features listed in (40) of Section 1.5.

To sum up, the development of *alors* from adverbial, clause-internal use to discourse-structuring, peripheral (clause-initial and clause-final) use in spoken Present-Day French, or from "core grammar" to "discourse grammar" (Degand

---

[12] We are grateful to Alexander Haselow (personal communication of May 20, 2019) for having made this suggestion.

and Evers-Vermeul 2015: 77), can hardly be reduced to grammaticalization (see Section 2.2.2 on the criteria of grammaticalization), even if one were to adopt a wider notion of grammaticalization.[13]

In the view of Degand and Evers-Vermeul (2015) it was word order change, rather than cooptation, that was responsible for the rise of DMs like French *alors*, cf. (22), and Degand and Fagard (2011, section 6.2) conclude: "Put more strongly, syntactic change would be a prerequisite for semantic change." Extension of placement to the left- or the right-periphery of a sentence, which would be in accordance with the cooptation hypothesis, is well motivated, serving in particular information structuring functions (Beeching and Detges 2014: 2). But to establish that syntactic change is a prerequisite for semantic change is a hypothesis that would seem to be in need of further evidence.

(22)   Rather, a new syntactic position (clause-initial) gave rise to new meanings, requiring syntactic scope extension over the host clause in the case of the clausal conjunct, and over potentially more than the host clause in the case of the DM.

                                        (Degand and Evers-Vermeul 2015: 77)

There is no doubt that the left-periphery of a sentence or utterance is the favored position of English DMs (see, e.g., Schiffrin 1987: 31–32, 328; Traugott 1995: 5–6; Brinton 1996: 33–35; Hansen 1997: 156; Jucker and Ziv 1998; Schourup 1999: 233; Maschler 2009: 44; Rysová 2017: 13), and the same applies to some other languages (Onodera 2011). Accordingly, Aijmer (2002: 29) concludes that initial position "functions as a clue to discourse particle status."

This is an important observation; still, not all English DMs show such a preference for the left-periphery. For example, *I mean* originated in subordinate clauses in final position (Brinton 2008; Traugott 2018: 38), and the emergence of the DM *after all* was also strongly associated with final rather than initial position (see Traugott 2018: 38). Furthermore, there are also other languages where this does not generally seem to be the case. For example, Dér and Markó (2010: 144–45) found that of the 14 most frequently used Hungarian DMs, only 39.6 percent occur in a turn-initial position while 40.2 percent occurred turn-medially, 8.3 percent turn-finally, and 11.9 percent were stand-alones. In short, rather than their position it seems to be their function that is the primary determinant of the placement of DMs.

Ignoring such observations, there are also other problems with the claim in (22). First, French *alors* is not and *was* not restricted to initial position; it also

---

[13] Maj-Britt Mosegaard Hansen (personal communication of January 24, 2020) suggests that this problem might not exist if one were to replace grammaticalization by pragmaticalization.

occurred occasionally in final position in its use as, what Degand and Evers-Vermeul (2015) call, a conjunct. And second, there are DMs that do not and never did occur in clause-initial position. This applies, for example, to the Japanese DM *wake* (Suzuki 1998; see Section 5.2.8), or the Korean DM *ttak* (Section 6.1), or to the English DM *as it were*, as the reconstruction work by Brinton (2008: 171–75) suggests: Neither in its rise nor in its subsequent development or in its present use was *as it were* associated noticeably with initial position, and one may wonder how the hypothesis in (22) would account for such cases.

To conclude, we surmise that movement of French *alors* to clause-initial position more likely was an epiphenomenal effect of cooptation, as predicted by the generalization in (40f) of Section 1.5: Once deployed as a thetical, *alors* could be placed not only within the sentence but also at its left and right periphery. And since DMs "prototypically introduce the discourse segments they mark" (Hansen 1997: 156), it comes as no surprise that the left-periphery of an utterance tends to be a favored position of DMs.

4.2.4   French En fait *and* Au fait

In a comparative paper on the synchrony and diachrony of DMs, Defour et al. (2010) discuss the French expressions *en fait*, *de fait*, and *au fait* jointly with the English DM *in fact*. These expressions are all etymologically related and have to some extent similar, or even overlapping functions, and all except *de fait* have developed uses as DMs in the course of the last centuries (Simon-Vandenbergen and Willems 2011: 356). We are restricted here to two of them, namely *en fait* and *au fait*, for the following reason: While the two have much in common in their history, they developed in different directions of discourse processing.

4.2.4.1 En fait

Defour et al. (2010) distinguish three different uses of *en fait* (lit. "in fact"). The first, illustrated in example (23), is a lexical one, where *en fait* occurs as an adverbial phrase composed of the preposition *en* "in" and the noun *fait* "fact," having the literal meaning "in the (actual) fact(s)" and expressing a contrast between *en fait* and *en principe*.

(23)   French (1851 G. Sand; Defour et al. 2010: 437, (6))
         *Je resterai pauvre **en fait**, libre en principe.*
         "I will stay poor *en fait*, but free in principle."

In its second use, *en fait* is a contrastive epistemic adverb, having a double function, marking a contrast with the preceding part of discourse, on the one hand, and emphasizing the perspective of the speaker, on the other. Example (24) illustrates this adversative function, where *en fait* marks the contrast between *truand* "crook" and *policier* "policeman," with *en fait* being "explicitly embedded in a situation where a contrast in expectations is expressed" (Defour et al. 2010: 437).

(24)   French (LM 2006; Defour et al. 2010: 437, (7))
         *Une prostituée tombe amoureuse d'un truand qui est **en fait** un policier.*
         "A prostitute falls in love with a crook who is *en fait* a policeman."

The third use of *en fait* is that of a DM which can be used with an additive meaning, supporting the preceding assertion. In example (25), for instance, *en fait* serves text-structuring functions, introducing an elaboration or precision.

(25)   French (LM 2006; Defour et al. 2010: 438, (9))
         *Un groupe de gardes rouges venu des environs a encerclé le lieu de réunion du village qui était **en fait** la boutique de ma mère et j'ai eu très peur pour elle.*
         "A band of Red guards coming from the outskirts has encircled the meeting point of the village which was *en fait* the shop of my mother and I was really scared for her."

En fait in its sentence grammar meaning is attested from the fourteenth century onward, showing a significant increase in frequency after 1600. Before 1500, *en fait* only occurs in its lexical form in the frame of a prepositional phrase, as in example (26), where *en fait* expresses a contrast between what is factual and what is said.

(26)   French (1370 DMF; Defour et al. 2010: 457, (50))
         *Et donquez quant les gens se descordent **en fait** de ce qu'ils disent.*
         "And thus, when people differ *en fait* from what they say ('when they differ in acts and words')."

Between 1500 and 1700 there are two sentence grammar constructions involving *en fait*: On the one hand, it is frequently used in the prepositional form *en fait de* ("concerning"), as in *en fait de penitence* "concerning penitence," or *en fait d'amour* "concerning love." In the second construction it occurs as the complement of certain action verbs, as in *poser en fait* or *mettre en fait* "prove, propose as being true, lay down as a fact." The prepositional construction of *en fait de* "concerning" becomes even more frequent between 1800 and 1850.

These two constructions with *en fait*, functioning either as a prepositional unit (*en fait de* "concerning") or as a complement of action verbs (e.g., *mettre en fait* "lay down as a fact"), might have contributed to the cooptation of *en fait* as a syntactically independent discourse unit developing into a DM. There is no information to suggest a plausible pathway of a process of grammaticalization gradually leading from the former two to the latter, nor from the epistemic adverb (cf. (24)) to the DM.

On the basis of the data that there are, cooptation must have taken place around the middle of the nineteenth century: In 1855 *en fait* starts appearing as a separate unit ("in reality"), having either contrastive, connective meaning, as in example (27), or strengthening meaning of elaboration.[14]

(27)   French (1855 Frantext, G. Sand, *Histoire de ma vie*; Defour et al. 2010: 457, (52))
         *Enfin, à l'exception de deux ou trois paysans dont il avait sauvé la vie et refusé l'argent selon sa coutume, il n'y eut guère que moi au monde qui pleurai le grand homme, et encore dus-je m'en cacher pour n'être pas raillée et pour ne pas blesser ceux qu'il avait trop cruellement blessés. Mais, **en fait**, il emportait avec lui dans le néant des choses finies toute une notable portion de ma vie, tous mes souvenirs d'enfance, agréables et tristes, tout le stimulant, tantôt fâcheux, tantôt bienfaisant, de mon développement intellectuel.*
         "Well, except for the two or three peasants whose life he had saved and whose money he refused, as was his custom, there was scarcely anyone but me who mourned for the great man, and still I had to hide it in order not to be mocked and not to hurt those whom he had hurt too cruelly. But *en fait* he carried with him in the emptiness of finite things an important part of my life, all my childhood memories, pleasant as well as sad, the whole stimulus, sometimes bad, sometimes beneficial, of my intellectual development."

The limited grammatical data that are available on the development of the rising DM *en fait* in the mid-nineteenth century suggest that already in its first attestation in 1855 it appears to have shown the main hallmarks of cooptation, as reconstructed in (28).

(28)   Properties suggestive of cooptation in the development of French *en fait* (see Defour et al. 2010)
         a Meaning: It is not a semantic part of the sentence it is associated with, expressing semantic contrasts and elaboration.
         b Function: It has a metatextual function relating to the organization of texts.
         c Syntax: It is not a syntactic constituent of its host sentence.
         d Prosody: It appears to be set off prosodically, as is suggested by the frequent use of commas and other punctuation marks (but see also Section 2.1).
         e Semantic–pragmatic scope: It has variable scope beyond the sentence it is associated with.
         f Placement: It is placed predominantly though not exclusively in the clause-initial position but may be preceded by conjunctions like *mais* "but" or *et* "and."

Grammaticalization seems to have involved two processes of decategorialization, both having taken place prior to cooptation. On the one

---

[14] It remains unclear how exactly the remark by Defour et al. (2010: 461) is to be interpreted that from 1600 onwards "the (pragmatic) use of *en fait* starts to increase."

hand, it led from adverbial phrase as the head of a possessive construction (*en fait de* "in fact of") to the prepositional expression *en fait de* "concerning" between 1500 and 1700. On the other hand, it led to univerbation whereby two morphemes, namely the preposition *en* "in" and the noun *fait* "fact," fused into the invariable contrastive epistemic adverb *en fait* as illustrated in (24). When exactly the latter process took place remains unclear on the basis of the existing data, but it presumably provided the source for the DM *en fait*.

Finally there was a third process, coinciding with or following cooptation, whereby *en fait* lost its lexical meaning and acquired text-structuring functions as a DM, introducing elaboration or precision.

4.2.4.2 Au fait

Compared to *en fait*, *au fait* occurs fairly rarely as a DM in Present-Day French. Literally meaning "to/at the fact," *au fait* occurs in various combinations as a sentence grammar expression, including a number of recurrent or idiomatic collocations, such as *être au fait de* "to know, to be informed about." As a DM it occurs in roughly 80 percent of its uses in questions, as in example (29), where *au fait* is found in a question that introduces elaboration. The question functions as the starting point for a new sub-topic and *au fait* in this usage serves as a link between what precedes and what is to follow.

(29)   French (LM 2006; Defour et al. 2010: 443, (20))[15]
         Certains utilisent même des cages. Là encore, il est difficile de s'y opposer ... Le
         fonctionnaire est reparti, la cage est restée. Mais la salle a dû fermer, plus tard,
         *pour raisons financières. Pourquoi des cages, **au fait**? Pour le spectacle. Mais*
         pas seulement. "Cela réveille des instincts primaires. Moi, je me sens bien
         dedans", confie Jean-François Lenogue, un autre free fighter français, ...
         "Some even use cages. There again, it is difficult to be opposed ... The
         official has left, the cage has remained. But the room needed to be closed,
         later on, for financial reasons. Why cages, *au fait*? For the show. But not only
         this. 'It awakens primitive instincts. As for me, I feel good inside', confesses
         Jean-François Lenogue, another French free fighter, ...'"

A similar text-structuring use also appears in interrogative sentences, where *au fait* is used to take up an expression from the preceding context as a new topic, cf. example (30).

(30)   French (Frantext, Dormann Geneviève /*La Petite main*/ 1993, pp. 169–71;
         Defour et al. 2010: 444, (22))
         Elle revenait ensuite rue du Bac pour surveiller le départ des enfants
         qu'accompagnait Françoise et prendre un second petit déjeuner avec
         *Sylvain. **Au fait**, pourquoi ne l'a-t-il pas réveillée, ce matin?*

---

[15] Our use of bold print, marking only the expression concerned, differs from that of Defour et al. (2010).

"She then came back to the rue du Bac to watch the departure of the children accompanied by Françoise and to have a second breakfast with Sylvain. *Au fait,* why did he not wake her this morning?"

From its earliest stages of development on, *au fait* was used less frequently than *en fait*, although it acquired some currency between 1700 and 1900, but it remained restricted to sentence grammar usage.

This changed in the second half of the eighteenth century, when cooptation must have taken place: *Au fait* turns into an independent unit mostly placed in utterance-initial position with the meaning "in reality." Its discursive use is often contrastive, preceded by the conjunction *mais* "but," as illustrated in example (31), where *mais au fait* points out a contrast between what is said and what is actually the case (Defour et al. 2010: 459).

(31)   French (1755 Frantext, Mirabeau marquis Victor de, *L'Ami des hommes ou Traité de la population* 1755; Defour et al. 2010: 459–60, (54))
*[C]royez-vous que cet homme ait de revenu? Mais, dis-je, il passe pour avoir quatre-vingt mille livres de rente. Il le croit aussi, reprit le notaire, mais **au fait** il en a quatorze.*
"Do you think that that man has an income? But, said I, he is supposed to have an allowance of eighty thousand pounds. He also believes it, the solicitor resumed, but *au fait,* he has only fourteen pounds."

Furthermore, after 1750 *au fait* also occurs as a stand-alone in exhortations like *Au fait!* "To the point!," or in imperative forms like *Venons au fait!* "Let's come to the point!" The model for this cooptation was presumably provided by recurrent sentence grammar collocations that were in common use around 1750 or earlier, like *mettre quelqu'un au fait* "to inform someone" or *venir/ aller au fait* "come/go to the heart of the matter" or "come/get to the point" (Simon-Vandenbergen and Willems 2011: 354–55).

Prior to 1750, there are no examples of *au fait* occurring in questions (see Defour et al. 2010, Table 9). This changed when *au fait* turned into a DM: From 1782 onward it was increasingly combined with interrogative sentences up until Present-Day French, where [*au fait* + question] consti- tutes the clearly predominant construction associated with *au fait* usage. The following is the first attestation of this usage in Defour et al.'s (2010) data.

(32)   French (1782 Frantext, Choderlos de Laclos Pierre, *Les Liaisons dangereuses*: 1782; Defour et al. 2010: 460, (55))
*Au **fait** quand il ne pourra plus douter de sa déconvenue, quand elle sera bien publique et bien notoire, que nous importe qu'il se venge, pourvu qu'il ne se console pas?*

"*Au fait* when he can no longer doubt his misfortune, when it becomes public
and well-known, what will it matter if he avenges himself, as long as he does
not find any consolation?"

In the second half of the nineteenth century, sentence grammar uses of *au fait*
began to decrease while that of the DM expanded, establishing itself as the
main function of *au fait* uses. The fact that it was often translated by "oh, by
the way" suggests that one of its functions came to be that of introducing topic
change (Defour et al. 2010: 460).

With its cooptation presumably in the second half of the eighteenth century,
au fait appears to have acquired the salient properties characterizing DMs,
such as the ones in (33).

(33)   Properties suggestive of cooptation in the development of French *au fait*
        (Defour et al. 2010)
        a Meaning: It is not a semantic part of the sentence it is associated with,
           expressing functions like contrast or elaboration.
        b Function: It has metatextual functions, such as expressing topic change.
        c Syntax: It is not a syntactic constituent of its host sentence.
        d Prosody: It appears to be set off prosodically, as is suggested by the
           frequent use of commas and other punctuation marks (but see also
           Section 2.1).
        e Semantic–pragmatic scope: Its scope extends beyond the sentence it is
           associated with.
        f Placement: It is placed predominantly but not exclusively in clause-initial
           position but may be preceded by the conjunction *mais* "but."

As in the case of *en fait*, grammaticalization involved, on the one hand,
decategorialization leading to univerbation: Three morphemes, namely the
preposition *à* "to, at," the definite article *le* and the noun *fait* "fact" (where *à*
+ *le* > *au*) fused into the invariable thetical *au fait*, as illustrated in (31).
Univerbation must have been concluded before *au fait* was coopted in the latter
half of the eighteenth century. On the other hand, cooptation was followed by
semantic change, leading to the rise of a new function, namely that of a marker
of a topic shift, used to call the hearer's attention to the upcoming question
(Defour et al. 2010: 461).

The development of *au fait* differs from that of *en fait* especially in two
repects. First, its rise as a DM started almost a century earlier than that of *en
fait*, the latter having been coopted apparently not earlier than in the second
half of the nineteenth century (see Section 4.2.4.1). And second, it was more
strongly employed for purposes of speaker–hearer interaction than *en fait*, as is
suggested by the fact that it had a predilection for use in dialogs and plays.
Defour et al. (2010: 461) therefore observe that this might explain its preference for being combined with questions.

4.2.5   *French* Enfin[16]

The French expression *enfin* ("at last") is described by Hansen (2005a: 63, figure 1) in terms of a prototype network having a range of interrelated senses or uses; Hansen (2005a) distinguishes altogether 14 different uses of *enfin*. The expression is in some contexts largely interchangeable with the expression *finalement* (Hansen 2005b: 53).

Of interest to the present discussion are two contrasting kinds of uses of *enfin*: On the one hand, it is a temporal adverb, being truth-conditional and contributing to the propositional content of its host clause – hence, it is a unit of sentence grammar, illustrated in (34a). On the other hand, it consists of a set of at least twelve uses lacking propositional content and having discourse marking functions, having the appearance of a DM,[17] even if Hansen (2005a; 2005b) does not refer to it as a "discourse marker."[18] (34b) shows one of these uses, where *enfin* has a reformulative function.

(34)   French (Hansen 2005a: 38, (1), (4))
   a *Pierre a éteint la télé, il s'est brossé les dents, il s'est déshabillé, et **enfin** il s'est couché.*
      "Pierre turned off the TV, he brushed his teeth, undressed, and in the end he went to bed."
   b *Cédric est grand, beau, intelligent, spirituel, **enfin**, parfait, quoi!*
      "Cédric is tall, handsome, intelligent, witty, in a word, perfect!"

Ultimately derived from Latin *in fine* (in end.ABL) "in the end," *enfin* occurs in the oldest French texts mostly written in two words, apparently a prepositional phrase often containing the feminine determiner *la*: *en (la) fin*, also occurring as *an fin*. The variation between temporal *en la fin*, *en fin*, and *enfin* lasted for roughly 400 years, and there are examples where more than one variant could occur within the same paragraph (Maj-Britt Mosegaard Hansen, personal communication of September 12, 2019). Subsequently it grammaticalized into the temporal adverb *enfin* "in the end," occasionally also translatable as "forever" in Old French (Hansen 2005a: 45).

A fairly dramatic change appears to have taken place toward the end of the sixteenth century of Middle French when *enfin* acquired uses as a synthetizing

---

[16] We are grateful to Maj-Britt Mosegaard Hansen for valuable comments on an earlier version of this section.

[17] See our definition of "discourse marker" in (7) of Section 1.1.2.

[18] We are ignoring here an epistemic use of *enfin*, first attested in 1544 (Hansen 2005a: 50–51, (20)). The grammatical status of this use does not become entirely clear on the basis of the data available. While epistemic *enfin* has wider scope than the temporal adverb *enfin*, it might constitute a new functional use suggestive of a grammaticalized extension of the temporal adverb of sentence grammar.

and listing marker (e.g., "at last"), the latter illustrated in (35). Conceivably though there were transitional uses in the semantic development from sentence-level adverb *enfin* to the discourse-level DM *enfin*, as is suggested by (36), which might be a bridging example between the temporal and the listing sense of *enfin* (Maj-Britt Mosegaard Hansen, personal communication of September 12, 2019).

(35)   French (1587 Pierre de Lestoile, *Registre-journal du règne de Henri III*,
        vol. 5, from *Frantext*; Hansen 2005a: 47, (14))
        ... Et **enfin** n'estoit il pas en elle de resserrer tellement et si estroictement
        qu'elle ne peust venir à bout de ce qu'elle pretendoit?
        "... And, lastly, did she not have it in her to reign herself in this way and so
        tightly that she could not attain what she desired?"

(36)   French (1587 Pierre de Lestoile, *Registre-journal du règne de Henri III*,
        vol. 5, from *Frantext*; Hansen 2005a: 48–49, (17))

        . . .
        Le Parlement passe Tout,
        Le Duc Desparnon gaste Tout,
        La religion couvre Tout,
        Le Pape pardonne Tout,
        *Le Diable **enfin** portera Tout.*
        "... The Parliament passes everything,
        The Duke of Esparnon spoils everything,
        Religion covers everything up,
        The Pope pardons everything,
        The Devil at last will take everything."

We suggest that already in uses such as (35) and (36) at the end of the sixteenth century, *enfin* was a coopted form, a thetical, for the following reasons: First, no longer clearly having temporal significance, it is non-truth conditional and its meaning relates to the organization of the discourse rather than being a semantic part of its host sentence. Second, it has a metadiscursive function, signaling that "its host utterance is the last expression in a particular discourse sequence," providing instructions on how to integrate the interpretation of its host utterance into a developing mental representation of the discourse (Hansen 2005a: 47, 50). Third, it does not appear to be a constituent of the sentence it was associated with, and fourth, it has distinctly wider semantic–pragmatic scope, comprising the speech act level rather than the propositional level of the utterance (Hansen 2005a: 49).

Interestingly, early sixteenth century uses such as (35) were apparently restricted to utterance anchored theticals – that is, Hansen (2005a: 65, fn. 7) found no early examples of constituent anchored expressions marking only sub-clausal units (cf. similar observations that have been made in the history of a number of other DMs, such as English *I mean*, *if you will*, or *no doubt* (see Section 8.3).

Subsequently, *enfin* developed a range of new uses. Mention may be made, for example, of uses arising in the seventeenth century such as that of an aspectual, or phasal marker signaling the transition from a prior to a subsequent state of affairs or sporadically of an interjectional marker (e.g., *Mais enfin?* "Well? [But then what?]"; Hansen 2005a: 53, 57). As can in fact be observed in a number of theticals, *enfin* also acquired the ability to occur as an interjectional stand-alone, as in the following Victor Hugo example from the nineteenth century:[19]

(37)   French (1885 Victor Hugo, *Correspondence*, vol. 4, from *Frantext*; Hansen 2005a: 61, (39))
         *Vous allez nous arriver. **Enfin!** Savez-vous qu'il y a deux ans tout à l'heure de votre dernière visite!*
         "You will be coming to see us. Finally! Do you know that it has been two years just now since your last visit!"

In the twentieth century, *enfin* experienced an increase in its hedging, interjectional and intersubjective uses, and in situations of hesitation, where *enfin* signals that what follows it is the formulation finally chosen (Hansen 2005a: 62).

In accordance with the principle of persistence of Hopper (1991: 22), *enfin* continued, side by side with its use as DM, to occur as a temporal adverb up until Present-Day French, presently constituting the most frequent use of *enfin* in narrative fiction (Hansen 2005a: 65).

The semantic development of *enfin* into a network of interrelated senses was a long, gradual process, as demonstrated in the rich analysis by Hansen (2005a). The data available suggest that cooptation of *enfin* toward the end of the sixteenth century, if not earlier, resulted in a new kind of expression acquiring the properties listed in (38). This change does not seem to have involved a longer process within the history of *enfin* where one of the properties in (38) would have emerged gradually one after the other. Rather, as is to be expected in cooptation, most or all of the properties jointly appear to have been in place within a relatively short timespan.

(38)   Properties suggestive of cooptation in the development of French *enfin* (based on Hansen 2005a; 2005b)
         a Meaning: It no longer clearly has temporal meaning. Having no propositional content and being non-truth conditional, it is not a semantic part of its host sentence.
         b Function: Its function is "metadiscursive," described as constituting a metalinguistic comment on another stretch of discourse (cf. Hansen 2005a: 42).

---

[19] An anonymous reviewer notes that *enfin* in this example can still be understood in a temporal sense.

c Syntax: It is not a syntactic constituent of its host sentence.
d Prosody: While there is no direct evidence, the occasional use of punctuation marks preceding and following *enfin* suggests that it is or can be set off prosodically, and it can carry an exclamative intonation (cf. Hansen 2005a: 42).
e Semantic–pragmatic scope: It has distinctly wider scope than the temporal adverb from which it is derived.
f Placement: Occurring predominantly at the left-periphery of a sentence, it is also occasionally found sentence-internally, and it also occurs as a stand-alone, forming an utterance of its own.

As described in some detail by Hansen (2005a), grammaticalization, only interrupted by cooptation, was involved in all phases of the development of *enfin*. Early grammaticalization concerned most of all the change from the lexical, contentful prepositional phrase *en (la) fin* "in (the) end" to the temporal adverb *enfin* via desemanticization and decategorialization. Late grammaticalization following cooptation in the second half of the sixteenth century involved most of all context extension and the emergence of a range of new discourse functions. Finally, there was also optional erosion since the DM *enfin* can be reduced to *'fin*, being frequently denasalized and realized as [(a)fɛ] (Hansen 2005b: 168).

4.3   Discussion

On the basis of our interpretation of existing publications, the French DMs examined differ greatly from one another in the way they evolved. Nevertheless, in their rise as DMs they seem to show the same general pattern of development, and this development appears to be in support of the hypothesis proposed in (26) of Section 2.6. First, their emergence marked a distinct stage in the history of the DM concerned between the fifteenth and the nineteenth centuries. The reconstructed dates of their cooptation are listed in Table 4.1.

Second, with their cooptation, the expressions acquired all or most of the grammatical properties characterizing DMs, namely the ones listed in (26b) of Section 2.6. Note, however, that the evidence available to determine these properties is not entirely robust in some cases, but the reason for this is to be sought in an insufficient database rather than necessarily in an absence of the property concerned.

Third, these properties seem to have appeared all at once, that is, there is no compelling evidence to assume that they evolved gradually one after the other. And, fourth, the properties have remained largely unchanged up until Present-Day French.

Grammaticalization also played an important role in the development of French DMs, but it seems that it did not substantially affect the six properties

Table 4.1 *Hypothesized dates of cooptation of some*
French DMs

Discourse marker	Approximate date of cooptation
alors	Fifteenth or sixteenth century, if not earlier
à propos	Sixteenth century or earlier
enfin	End of sixteenth century
à la rigueur	Early eighteenth century, if not earlier
au fait	Second half of the eighteenth century
en fait	Mid-nineteenth century

characterizing the DMs. As described in detail by the authors cited in the chapter, grammaticalization had in particular two effects on the development of DMs: On the one hand, DMs lost part or all of their earlier lexical meaning and thus their sensitivity to truth conditions and, on the other hand, they acquired a range of new discourse functions.

5   Japanese Discourse Markers

5.1   Introduction

The Japanese language has been the subject of a plethora of studies on DMs (e.g., Matsumoto 1988; Onodera 1995; 2000; 2011; Suzuki 1998; 2006; Traugott and Dasher 2002; Shinzato 2017; Shibasaki 2018a; 2018b; 2019; 2020), and there is also a monograph devoted to DMs in this language (Onodera 2004). For the purposes of the present study, what is most important, however, is the fact that some of this work was not restricted to description but has also aimed at looking for historical explanations for why DMs are structured the way they are. The Japanese language offers a variety of exciting DMs that were possible candidates for analysis in the present chapter. But, unfortunately, a database that would have been needed for detailed reconstruction work was not available for many of them.

5.2   Case studies

The case studies presented below constitute but a small part of all the DMs that exist in Japanese. They are:

5.2.1 *Dakedo*
5.2.2 *Demo*
5.2.3 *Douride*
5.2.4 *Ga*
5.2.5 *Jijitsu*
5.2.6 *Na*
5.2.7 *Sate*
5.2.8 *Wake*

5.2.1   *Japanese* Dakedo[1]

Sentence-initial *dakedo* "but" is a conjunction, an independent word, historically derived from *da + kedo*. Japanese *kedo* is a clause-final conjunctive bound

---

[1] We are grateful to Noriko Onodera for valuable comments on an earlier version of this section.

form having a contrastive function, attached to a verb (or adjective), frequently agglutinated to *da* (or *d*), a copula or linking verb whose main function is that of a pro-verb standing for some verb in the preceding discourse.

The historical process leading to the rise of the DM *dakedo* is described by Onodera (1995: 415–22; see also Aoki 2019) in terms of two stages. It is at Stage I, which extends from the eighteenth to the early twentieth century, that the clause-final construction [V + *kedo*] first appeared. An example of the oldest example documented is found in (1), where the construction has an ideational, concessive function.

(1)   Japanese (*Chuushin kana tanzaku* 1732; Onodera 1995: 416, (8))
        Inakamono   *ja*   *to*   *iwa*   *nsu*   **kedo,**   . . .
        countrywoman   COP   QT   say   HON   but,
        "Although (you) call (me) a countrywoman, . . ."

The [V + *kedo*] construction continued to be used when sentence-initial *dakedo* emerged in the early twentieth century at Stage II, which covers the period from the early twentieth century to the present. In the Taishoo era (1912–1926), [V + *kedo*] was in common use, but now the unit-initial *dakedo* construction appears for the first time (Onodera 2004: 104). *Dakedo* is a content word consisting of the morphemes *da* and *kedo*, where the linking verb *da* stands for a predicate appearing in the prior discourse. Like [V + *kedo*], it has an ideational function but in addition it also has a textual function, linking portions of discourse across sentences, as in (2) (Onodera 1995: 418).

(2)   Japanese (*Anya kooro* 1922; Onodera 1995: 418, (10))[2]
        Moshi   *watashi*   *no tame*   *deshitara*   *doka*   *moo*
        if   me   LK   COP-if   please   no more
        "If it is for me please do not
        otanomi   *ni*   *naranaide itadakimasu.*
        ask-HON NEG   receive
        hire another one (nurse) again.
        Dakedo,   *watashi*   *hitori*   *de*
        but,   me   alone   COP-GER
        But, if you think that only me is not
        gofujiyuu   *da*   *to*   *oboshimesu*
        inconvenient   COP   QT   think HON
        n   *deshitara betsu*   *desu*   *kedo.*
        NOM   COP-if   other   COP   but
        enough, do it yourselves, though."

Thus, the shift from the sentence grammar unit [V + *kedo*] to the DM *dakedo* seems to have coincided with the introduction of its textual function.

---

[2] Non-alignment of some glosses adopted from the original.

Subsequently, *dakedo* increasingly assumes also an expressive function and it serves the following functions: (a) Point-making, (b) changing the sub-topic, and (c) claiming the floor, as well as opening a conversation. Onodera (1995: 426) observes, however, that already at its first appearance in the early twentieth century, *dakedo* had an expressive function without serving an ideational function. The "expressive function" apparently relates most of all to the attitudes of the speaker ("the speaker's own subjective point of view/ attitude/belief-state").

The transition from sentence grammar [V + *kedo*] to *dakedo*, attributed by Onodera (1995: 428) to "strategic convenience in interactional discourse," exhibits the main features to be expected from cooptation, cf. (3). It seems to have been fairly abrupt: There is no information to suggest that the change from Stage I to Stage II took place gradually, involving stages as they characterize grammaticalization and, as far as the evidence provided by Onodera suggests, the changes in (3) appear to have occurred rather simultaneously.

(3)   Grammatical changes suggestive of cooptation: Japanese *dakedo*
       a Meaning: In addition to the ideational meaning expressed by [V + *kedo*],
          dakedo, being a DM, acquired textual and expressive meanings.
       b Function: It changed from sentence-internal to inter-sentential text
          function, acquiring "expanded pragmatic functions" (Onodera 1995: 424).
       c Syntax: It changed from sentence-internal connective to a connective
          linking portions of discourse, such as the preceding sentence with the
          following sentence (Onodera 2004: 106).
       d Prosody: With its shift to the sentence-initial position, *dakedo* became an
          "opening bracket" (Onodera 1995: 424). The fact that *dakedo* is set off
          from the preceding and the following text by punctuation marks (full-stops
          before and commas after *dakedo*) might suggest that there is some
          prosodic boundary separating it from its text environment.[3]
       e Semantic–pragmatic scope: Its scope shifts from subordinate clause to
          scope beyond a sentence or sentences; thus, the scope widens from the
          sentence level to the discourse level (Onodera 1995: 422; 2004: 106).
       f Placement: With its cooptation, *dakedo* shifts from clause-final to
          sentence-initial position.

Subsequent to its cooptation, that is, to its turning into a sentence-initial thetical, there is also evidence for grammaticalization. On the one hand, there still was a morpheme boundary between *da* and *kedo*, where *da* functioned as a kind of auxiliary. With the loss of a boundary between the two morphemes via internal decategorialization, univerbation into the "monomorphemic word" *dakedo* took place (Onodera 1995: 427). On the other hand, there also was

---

[3] Reijirou Shibasaki (personal communication of January 25, 2020) reminds us, however, that comma marking in earlier Japanese writings is not reliable, varying from one author to the other (see also Section 2.1).

apparently context extension, giving rise to the new textual and expressive functions mentioned earlier in this section.

To conclude, *dakedo* is the joint product of cooptation and grammaticalization. Nevertheless, we argue that the main features characterizing its present status as a DM, such as the ones in (3), are overwhelmingly the result of cooptation.

5.2.2   *Japanese* Demo[4]

There is a family of connectives in Japanese, called the "*demo* type connectives" in Onodera (2000; 2004: 119), or d-connectives in Onodera (2007: 257–58), "which seem to have undergone the same kind of pragmatic change and positional shift from the final to initial position" (Onodera 2004: 119). This group, which is characterized by prefixing the copula *d*, includes *da*, *daga*, *dakara*, *datte*, *demo*, and *denakereba*. Our interest in this section is restricted to *demo*.

Present-Day Japanese has two contrasting and seemingly unrelated forms and constructions to express adversative contrasts. One consists of the clause-final expression [V-*te* + *mo*] (or [V + *de* + *mo*]) "but," where V is a verb, -*te* (or *da/de*) is a copula marking the gerundive form of the verb (V), and *mo* is a clause-final adversative particle "but;" Onodera (2004:115) describes *da* or *de* as a predicative marker, a linking verb, or a "pro-predicative." The second form is the connective particle *demo*, placed sentence-initially, linking sentences or larger discourse units. As the analysis by Onodera (1993; 1995; 2004; see also Aoki 2019) shows, the two are etymologically related in that the latter is derived from the former, and the following is a short summary of this development.

Onodera divides the development into three stages. At Stage I (eleventh to sixteenth centuries), there was only the unit-final expression [V-*te* + *mo*] (or [V + *de* + *mo*]) used as a connecting device, being a bound form (Onodera 2000: 30). The device is intra-sentential, linking the preceding subordinate clause with the following main clause. The expression appeared first in the eleventh century, (4) is an example from the fourteenth century.

(4)   Japanese (*Jinenkoji* (before 1384); Onodera 1995: 404)
Mi	*o*	*kokkani*	*kudakite*	*mo,*		
body	DO	now	break	but		

"Although my body would fall apart,

kano	*mono*	*o*	*tasuken*	*tame*	*nari,* ...
that	person	DO	save	purpose	COP

it (my body falling apart) is to save that person ...""

---

[4] We are grateful to Noriko Onodera for valuable comments on an earlier version of this section.

At Stage II (sixteenth to early twentieth centuries), around the mid-sixteenth century, [V-*te* + *mo*] (or [V + *de* + *mo*]) appears as the conjunction *demo*, shifting from clause-final to sentence-initial position, cf. (5). Whereas [V-*te* + *mo*] is a sentence-internal connective, *demo* connects sentences. It now serves textual purposes as a DM, having the contrastive function of refutation, as well as the expressive function of strengthening the speaker meaning and serving speaker–hearer interaction (Onodera 1995: 405–6, 412, Table 2). What this suggests is that at Stage II, *demo* changed from bound to free form, acquiring a metatextual function. Note that there is no historical information to the effect that the change from [V-*te* + *mo*] (or [V + *de* + *mo*]) to *demo*, taking place somewhere between the eleventh and the mid-sixteenth centuries, was due to a gradual process.

(5)   Japanese (*Nokyoogen: Suehirogari* (around the mid-sixteenth century); Onodera 1995: 405)[5]

Lord:	*Sore*	*o*	*motomete*	*kuru*		
	it	DO	get	come		
	"You shouldn't have brought it back."					
	to.iu.koto	*ga*	*aru*	*mono*	*ka.*	
	QT.say.NML	SB	exist	thing	FP	
Retainer:	***Demo***	*miyako*	*no*	*mono*	*ga*	
	but	capital	LK	people	SB	
	"But, because people in the capital					
	"suehirogari"	*ja*	*to*	*mooshita*		
	fan	COP	QT	say-PAST		
	told me it was *suehirogari* (a fan)					
	ni yotte	*motomete*	*maitta.*			
	because	get-GER	come-PAST			
	I brought it back."					

There is no significant change in the meaning of *demo* between the mid-sixteenth and the late eighteenth century (Onodera 1995: 406–7).

At Stage III of Present-Day Japanese (early twentieth century to the present), *demo* acquired additional functions, namely (a) point-making, (b) claiming the floor, (c) opening a conversation, and (d) changing the topic (Onodera 1995: 409). On the whole, however, there is no significant change in the structure of *demo*.

Obviously, the change from Stage I to Stage II was dramatic, leading from an expression [V-*te* + *mo*], which was firmly integrated in the meaning and the structure of the sentence, to an independent marker *demo* serving metatextual functions of discourse organization, speaker–hearer interaction, and the attitudes of the speaker. There is no information to show that the transition from

---

[5] Non-alignment of some glosses adopted from the original.

Stage I to Stage II was a continuous or gradual one, that is, of a kind that would be suggestive of grammaticalization.

What appears to have happened in the mid-sixteenth century or earlier was that a linguistic expression, [V-*te* + *mo*], was coopted and acquired the features in (6) defining cooptation.

(6)   Grammatical changes suggestive of cooptation: Japanese *demo*
    a   Meaning: In addition to the earlier adversative meaning, *demo* expresses "refutation" of an earlier position. And in addition to its ideational meaning, *demo* acquired textual and expressive meanings, "marking mostly the speaker's action of refuting the other's idea" (Onodera 1995: 423).
    b   Function: It changes from sentence-internal to inter-sentential text function, e.g., linking the prior discourse with upcoming discourse (Onodera 1995: 406, 411; 2004: 117–19).
    c   Syntax: It changes from a sentence-internal connective device to a connective between pieces of discourse such as sentences or turns.
    d   Prosody: There is no reliable information, but the use of punctuation marks (full-stops before and occasionally commas after *demo*) suggests that the marker was prosodically set off from its text environment (but see also Section 2.1).
    e   Semantic–pragmatic scope: Its scope shifts from subordinate clause to scope beyond a sentence or sentences.
    f   Placement: With its cooptation, *demo* became "movable" (Onodera 1995: 424), shifting from clause-final to sentence-initial position.

Note, however, that there is also an alternative reconstruction according to which *demo* is not to be traced back directly to [V-*te* + *mo*] (or V + *de* + *mo*) but rather is a truncated form of the sentence-initial connective *soredemo* ("that" + *demo*) (Noriko Onodera, personal communication of July 21, 2019). Whether or how this reconstruction affects the analysis proposed by Onodera (1995; 2004) is an issue that is in need of further research.[6] Noriko Onodera observes in this connection:

Nonetheless, even more recently, the development of "d-connectives" from a sentence-internal connecting device (e.g. V-*te* + *mo*) to a sentence-initial and discourse marker is supported by Aoki (2019, personal communication of March 4, 2020 by Noriko Onodera). Aoki (personal communication) reports that the "forerunners" of "d-connectives," *nareba/naredomo*, *jaga/jahodoni*, had also undergone the process similar to *demo/dakedo*, i.e., from sentence-internal connecting particles (devices) to sentence-initial conjunctions (discourse markers). (Noriko Onodera, personal communication of March 23, 2020)

In addition to cooptation, there were also at least two changes in the history of *demo* that are suggestive of grammaticalization (see also

---

[6] If this alternative reconstruction should in fact be correct, then the question arises where the expression *demo* in *soredemo* comes from.

Onodera 2000: 32). First, the change from the segment *-te mo* to *demo* must have involved decategorialization leading to univerbation (cf. Lehmann [1982] 2015: 161), whereby the two forms *-te* and *mo* lost their morphological distinctiveness and merged into an unanalyzable new morpheme *demo* (internal decategorialization). It remains unclear, however, when univerbation took place, other than that it was concluded by the mid-sixteenth century.

The second change, or series of changes, concerned late grammaticalization and the parameter of context extension. When coopted at Stage II, *demo* expressed essentially only one discourse function, namely refutation. Subsequently at Stage III from the early twentieth century on, *demo* gradually acquired the following new "expressive" functions: (a) point-making, (b) claiming the floor, (c) opening a conversation, and (d) changing the topic or subtopic (Onodera 1995: 423; 2000: 34). Being a coopted unit, that is, a thetical, these new functions were not primarily anchored in the sentence to which *demo* was attached but rather in the situation of discourse in which it occurred, that is, in the organization of texts, speaker–hearer interaction, and the attitudes of the speaker.

To conclude, grammaticalization also had a noteworthy impact on the development of *demo*. Nevertheless, it would seem that the semantic, syntactic, and prosodic structure that this DM of Present-Day Japanese exhibits cannot reasonably be explained without recourse to the mechanism of cooptation, which accounts not only for the features listed in (6) but also for the fact that the segment *-te mo* was cut out of the sentence structure and moved from its clause-final position to the initial position of the sentence for purposes of discourse processing. To be sure, the grammaticalization parameter of context extension entails that linguistic expressions are extended to new contexts, but – as also observed by Onodera (2000: 34) – it is hard to find another established case of grammaticalization where a kind of change comparable to that of Japanese *demo* has been documented.[7]

5.2.3   *Japanese* Douride

The Japanese noun *douri* (or *doori* or *dōri*) "reason, truth" occurs in a wide range of different constructions. In particular, it is found in two etymologically related expressions, namely its nominal use, on the one hand, and its use in the DM *douride* (or *dooride*), on the other, the latter

---

[7] Note, however, that Korean has a number of connective adverbials which also serve as DMs that had been clipped from verbs (involving the light verb *-ha*), followed by a dependent connector (Seongha Rhee, personal communication of August 9, 2020); see Section 8.2.3.

being translatable as "no wonder." An example of the former is presented in (7), where *douri* acts as a nominal predicate, the phrase *douri ga nai* being translatable as "no matter how one thinks about something, there is no reason to accept it," (8) illustrates the "adverbial use" of *douride* as a pragmatic marker (DM) translatable as "of course, that makes sense/that must be why,"[8] The latter is described by Shibasaki (2018b: 384–85) as a projector since its function is to make hearers or readers anticipate the upcoming discourse.

(7)   Japanese (Group Jammassy; Shibasaki 2018b: 384, (1))
    konna   *mutsukasii*   *hon*   *ga*   *kodomo*   *ni*   *yomeru*
    such   difficult   book   NOM   child   DAT   read.can
    douri   *ga*   *nai.*
    reason   NOM   be.not
    "It's absurd to think that a child should be able to read such a difficult book."

(8)   Japanese (Group Jammassy; Shibasaki 2018b: 384, (2))
    A: *kanojo*   *no*   *ryooshin* *wa*   *gakusha*   *da*   *yo*
        she   GEN   parents   TOP   scholars   COP   FP
        "Both of her parents are scholars."
    B: ***douride***   *kanojo* *mo*   *atamagaii* *hazu-da.*
        no.wonder   she   too   be.smart   must-COP
        "So that explains why she's so smart too."

The following account rests on the analysis provided by Shibasaki (2018b; see also Shibasaki 2019). The noun *douri* "reason, truth" is first recorded in 718. As a nominal predicate it appears in 1053. *Douride* is documented much later, namely as an "adverbial connector" in 1749, cf. (9), being composed of the noun *douri* and the adnominal copula form *-de*.

(9)   Japanese (1749 *Yorokobigarasu*; Kitahara 2006; Shibasaki 2018b: 385, (4))
    douride   *mago*   *ga*   *me-ni-kakari*   ...
    no.wonder   grandchild   NOM   eye-in-hang
    "No wonder, (one) caught sight of (his/her) grandchild and ..."

The case of *douride* is not an isolated one in the history of Japanese. As described by Shibasaki (2018b: 386), a group of nominal predicates gave rise to "adverbial expressions" from the middle of the eighteenth century on. A second wave occurred around the turn of the twentieth century; a couple of examples are presented in (10).

---

[8] Heiko Narrog (personal communication of February 23, 2020) argues that *douride* (or *dooride*) in this usage is a sentence-initial adverb expressing a conclusion.

(10)   Changes from nominal predicate to "adverbial expressions" in Japanese
         (Shibasaki 2018b: 385–86)

Nominal predicate	Gloss	Meaning	"Adverbial"	Meaning
kihon-teki-ni (1947)	basis-SUF-PT	"basically"	kihon (2002)	"basically"
gensoku-teki-ni ieba (1925)	principle-SUF-PT saying	"generally speaking"	gensoku (2001)	"in principle, as a rule"

Douri as a nominal predicate combined with a range of copulas reduced to the copula form *-de* in the "adverbial," In the second half of the nineteenth century, *douri* on its own occurred as an "adverbial," later on giving way to the invariable expression *douride*. Shibasaki (2018b: 391–94) distinguishes four stages in the development of *douride*:

At Stage I, the predicate nominal (*douri-da*) forms the head of a biclausal sentence, it is preceded by an embedded clause ending in the nominalizer *no,* and followed by the topic marker *wa*. In terms of information structure, the embedded clause formed the theme and the nominal predicate the rheme. At Stage II, *douri* is followed by the conjunction *ga* "but" and the nominalizer, and the topic marker can be omitted; thus, the preceding clause is no longer clearly an embedded clause.

At Stage III, *douri* is part of the independent adverbial phrase *sayoona-douri-dearu-kara* (such/left-reason-COP-because) "for this reason," and "the theme–rheme relation is expanded from a biclausal construction to a sequenced-sentence construction" (Shibasaki 2018b: 393). Occurring now at the beginning of a sentence, it has the appearance of a thetical, an independent expression coopted as a "projector" for relating two sentences to one another. Finally, at Stage IV, *douride* turns into a largely fossilized sentence-initial "adverb" serving as a projector between sentences or clauses and having features of a DM, as in (11) (see also (8)).

(11)   Japanese (1990 Tagen'uchu; BCCWJ; Shibasaki 2018b: 392, (10))
         Douride   eigo   ga   tassha-na   hazu.da.
         no.wonder   English   NOM   good-be   AUX.COP
         "No wonder, (he) speaks English fluently."

A question that cannot clearly be answered on the basis of the data available is: What provided the source for the cooptation of *douride*? While the Stage III expression *sayoona-douri-dearu-kara* may have served as a structural model for the sentence-initial thetical, the most plausible source seems to have been the *douri-da* construction of Stage I since it has the same constructional format: [noun-COP *da/de*]. This is an issue, however, that is in need of more research.

Interestingly, *douride* was first written with Chinese characters (*kanji*), but when it surfaced as a thetical ("adverb") it was transcribed with *hiragana* characters – possibly suggesting that the transition from nominal predicate to thetical ("adverb") was conceived by speakers as introducing a new quality. Note that content words are generally written in Japanese in *kanji* and function words in *hiragana*.

To conclude, *douri* seems to have given rise to two separate theticals, namely, on the one hand, as part of the independent adverbial phrase *sayoona-douri-dearu-kara* "for this reason" (Stage III) and, on the other hand, as the DM *douride* (Stage IV). We are restricted here to the latter, which shows the features of cooptation listed in (12).

(12)   Grammatical changes suggestive of cooptation: Japanese *douride* (see Shibasaki 2018b)

    a Meaning: It changed from an expression having lexical meaning (*douri* "reason, truth") to a discourse-pragmatic meaning as a projector, that is, serving to make the addressee anticipate the upcoming discourse.

    b Function: It changed from sentence-internal to inter-sentential text function, connecting the preceding with the following discourse.

    c Syntax: It changed from sentence-internal connective to a syntactically independent connective linking portions of discourse.

    d Prosody: Turning into a sentence-initial marker, *douride* was presumably set off prosodically from the preceding sentence: In Shibasaki's (2018b) English translation, there is a comma in example (11), which might be suggestive of a prosodic break between *douride* and the following sentence.[9]

    e Semantic–pragmatic scope: It changed from sentence-internal scope to wider scope over the preceding discourse and the following sentence.

    f Placement: With its cooptation, *douride* shifted from clause-final to sentence-initial position.

The question then is what the role of grammaticalization was in this overall development. First, as observed by Shibasaki (2018b: 385), there is a common pathway of grammaticalization leading from nominal to adverbial forms and conjunctions (see Heine and Kuteva 2007: 111). This process may have been responsible for the transition from nominal predicate to "adverbial," that is, an invariable thetical. Most likely, the process followed cooptation, but the evidence on this is not conclusive. Second, there was internal decategorialization: The two morphemes involved, *douri* and *-de*, lost their morphological distinctiveness, leading from the compound form *douri-da* to the invariable marker *douride*.

---

[9] Modern punctuation had not yet been fully established around the turn of the twentieth century (Reijirou Shibasaki, personal communication of January 23, 2020); see also Section 2.1.

The four-stage scenario proposed by Shibasaki (2018b: 392–93) captures what appears to be a structural development from one construction type to another. But one may wonder whether this development was the result of grammaticalization. What is fairly obvious is that Stages I and II represent constructions located in sentence grammar, but the morphological structure of Stage III is different from that of Stage I to the extent that it seems hard to account for this difference in terms of grammaticalization.

Stages III and IV mark a fairly pronounced change in the history of the erstwhile noun *douri* "reason, truth": The noun is now part of discourse structuring devices that occur sentence-initially, and they have semantic–pragmatic scope and express a theme–rheme relation beyond the sentence in which they occur – that is, both are suggestive of thetical connectives. But again, it is hard to see that the DM *douride* of Stage IV could have evolved directly from the Stage III adverbial phrase *sayoona-douri-dearu-kara* "for this reason" via grammaticalization.

In sum, we hypothesize that the DM *douride* was coopted at some stage in the eighteenth century from a construction akin to that characterizing Stage I.

5.2.4   Japanese Ga

In order to argue for a wider concept of grammaticalization, Traugott (1995: 4) invokes Matsumoto's (1988) description of the clause-final clitic *-ga* of Japanese as providing supporting evidence. This clitic, exemplified in (13a), is part of a paradigm of Japanese enclitic particles connecting two clauses of a sentence and occurring in final position of the first clause (Matsumoto 1988: 2). But there is also a second use of the form, illustrated in (13b). Rather than a clitic, the latter appears to be a free form.

(13)   Present-Day Japanese (Matsumoto 1988: 2)
       a *Taro-wa   wakai-**ga**,   yoku yar-u(-yo).*
         Taro-TOP young-but   well   do-PRES(-PTC)
         "Taro is young, but he does a good job."
       b *Taro-wa   wakai(-yo).*   ***Ga,***   *yoku yar-u(-yo).*
         Taro-TOP young(-PTC) But   well do-PRES(-PTC)
         "Taro is young. But he makes a good job."

We will refer to the enclitic *-ga* in (13a) as *ga$_1$* and to *ga* in (13b) as *ga$_2$*. The two expressions exhibit a fairly contrastive behavior. According to Matsumoto (1988), the difference can be summarized in the following way:

(a) Whereas *ga$_2$* is restricted to adversative meaning, *ga$_1$* also has non-adversative meanings (Matsumoto 1988: 347–48).

(b) Whereas the function of *ga$_1$* is part of the meaning of the sentence, *ga$_2$* appears to function on the discourse level, "it can be used to start a new discourse, with no related preceding utterance" (Matsumoto 1988: 3).

(c) Whereas ga_1 connects clauses within a sentence, ga_2 is a connective beyond the sentence, linking two independent sentences to one another. Furthermore, ga_1 is a bound form, an enclitic; ga_2, by contrast, is a free form, which can start a new turn in discourse.

(d) Whereas ga_1 usually forms an "accentual unit" with the preceding word, ga_2 is separated from the preceding sentence by a long pause, that is, it is prosodically distinct.

(e) Whereas the scope of ga_1 is restricted to the sentence in which it occurs, that of ga_2 extends beyond the sentence.

(f) Whereas ga_1 occurs clause-finally, ga_2 is placed sentence-initially.

This expression -ga/ga is not the only one in Japanese to show features such as the ones just listed (see Matsumoto 1988), but we are restricted here to the present case. There is no doubt that ga_1 and ga_2 are etymologically related and, *prima facie*, the data just presented are seemingly suggestive of a canonical process of grammaticalization leading from ga_2 to ga_1, for the following reasons: As would be predicted by grammaticalization theory, there is a widespread process leading from semantically free forms, as ga_2 is, to the semantically restricted forms, like ga_1 (desemanticization), from morphosyntactically free form to clitic (external decategorialization), and from prosodically distinct to prosodically integrated form (erosion). Traugott (1995: 4) in fact argues that the changes involving -ga/ga are due to grammaticalization. But – perhaps somewhat surprisingly – she argues for a grammaticalization process in the opposite direction, namely from ga_1 to ga_2.

There is information to show that the change was in fact one from ga_1 to ga_2. According to Matsumoto (1988: 5), the earlier history of ga_1 was one of grammaticalization: Starting as a genitive and subject (nominative) marker in certain kinds of subordinate clauses in Old Japanese, ga_1 developed into a connective particle around the late eleventh century.

We have no information on what happened to ga_1 in ensuing centuries of Japanese history. But around the seventeenth century, ga_2 emerged as a connective, apparently derived from ga_1. This shift from ga_1 to ga_2 resulted in changes such as the ones listed in (14).

(14)   Grammatical changes in the shift from ga_1 to ga_2 in Japanese
    a Meaning: From meaning as part of the sentence to "discourse/pragmatics-oriented meaning"
    b Function: From sentence-internal to metatextual function: "the function . . . changed from the domain of syntax to that of discourse" (Matsumoto 1988: 345).
    c Syntax: From clause-final clitic to syntactically "detached connective" at the left periphery of a sentence.
    d Prosody: From enclitic that was normally prosodically integrated in the preceding word to less integrated or unintegrated particle.

Table 5.1 *Contrasting changes typically observed in expressions undergoing cooptation and grammaticalization*

	Grammaticalization	Cooptation
Meaning	Change of meaning within the sentence	From meaning as part of the sentence to meaning outside the sentence
Function	Increasing functional dependence within the sentence	From function within the sentence to metatextual function
Syntax	Increasing syntactic integration within the sentence	From integrated to detached syntax
Prosody	Decrease in prosodic distinctiveness	Increase in prosodic distinctiveness
Semantic–pragmatic scope	Scope may change within the sentence	From scope within the sentence to variable scope beyond the sentence
Placement	Decrease in freedom of placement	Increase in freedom of placement

Note: This table is the same as Table 2.2 of Section 2.5.1.

    e Semantic–pragmatic scope: From restricted scope within the sentence to scope beyond a sentence.
    f Placement: From clause-final to sentence-initial placement.

The changes listed in (14) are hard to reconcile with findings made in studies of grammaticalization, being at variance with parameters of grammaticalization as they have been described in Section 2.2.2. At the same time, they are fully compatible with cooptation, suggesting that at some stage, presumably in the seventeenth century, there was a shift whereby the use of ga_1 was extended to the level of discourse monitoring, giving rise to ga_2. This is suggested by the following observations. In Table 2.2 of Section 2.5.1 we identified a catalog of six types of changes that distinguish cooptation from grammaticalization. That table, re-printed here for convenience as Table 5.1, shows that the shift from ga_1 to ga_2 represents roughly the opposite from what one would expect in grammaticalization but is fully compatible with cooptation (see (14)).[10]

Matsumoto (1988: 344) suggests that the shift from final to initial position in combinations of two clauses may be due to rebracketing where the final expression of the first clause (ga_1) was reinterpreted as the initial expression of the second clause (ga_2). While this may have been a contributing factor, it is

[10] There is one partial exception, namely one concerning placement ((14f)): Rather than increase in the freedom of its placement, ga_2 shows a change from clause-final to sentence-initial position. This exception, however, does not contradict the general directionality of the change leading from semantically, syntactically, and prosodically integrated clitic of sentence grammar to grammatically unattached DM ga_2.

unlikely that it was responsible for all the grammatical changes listed in (14), for the following reasons: It would not explain why ga_2 acquired the set of new grammatical features listed in (14), nor why this set is essentially the same as we observe it in other cases of cooptation, nor why similar cases of cooptation have been identified where the unit coopted was not placed clause-finally but rather clause-initially (see Section 5.2.1 on *dakedo* and Section 5.2.2 on *demo*).

Hopper and Traugott (1993: 184–85; 2003: 210) treat the present case as a "counterexample to the unidirectionality in clause combining," and for Norde (2009: 199–201) it is a case of debonding, a subtype of degrammaticalization, that is, the opposite of grammaticalization. Thus, insisting on grammaticalization as an explanatory notion for ga_2, as Traugott (1995: 4) in fact does, would require an understanding of "grammaticalization" that vacuously applies, e.g., to both changes from free form to clitic and from clitic to free form. In sum, the discussion in this section may have shown why the history of the DM ga_2 cannot reasonably be reduced to grammaticalization.

5.2.5   Japanese Jijitsu "In Fact"[11]

Japanese has a range of DMs, the history of which is well described (e.g., Onodera 2004; 2011). The following account rests entirely on the insightful analysis by Shibasaki (2018a).

Japanese *jijitsu* "fact" belongs to the group of nouns that were borrowed from Chinese around the sixth century (Shinzato 2017: 314). It commonly occurs in a nominal predicate clause followed by a copulative verb and preceded by another clause, and the two clauses are connected by the topic marker *wa*, as illustrated in (15).

(15)   Japanese (2001 *The art of spirited away*; BCCWJ; Shibasaki 2018a: 334, (2))

Dejitaru-ni-natte,	*shigoto*	*no*	*haba*	*ga*	*hirogatta-no*	*wa*	*jijitsu-desu.*
digital.PTC-become	job	GEN	range	NOM	widen.PAST-NML	TOP	fact-COP.POL
Tada,	*amari*	*hiroge*	*sugiru*	*to*	*betsuno*	*genba*	*no*
but	too	broaden	a.bit.much	if	another	field	GEN

shigoto	*ni*	*hurete-shimau.*
job	PTC	be.an.obstacle-AUX

"In the digital era, (it) is [a] fact that the range of (our) jobs became wider. Yet if (we) increase the range (of our jobs) too much, it turns out that (such increased workload) will bring about obstacles to jobs in another field."

---

[11] We are grateful to Reijirou Shibasaki for valuable comments on an earlier version of this section.

But the item *jijitsu* also occurs as a DM, commonly glossed "in fact," called a pragmatic marker by Shibasaki (2018a). In this capacity, it is usually placed sentence initially. Its main function is that of a "projector," that is, an expression whose function it is to anticipate upcoming discourse. At the same time, *jijitsu* also relates the upcoming discourse to the preceding information (Shibasaki 2018a: 348). It thus has a dual function, namely linking an utterance to the previous discourse and guiding the hearer's expectations to the subsequent stretch of discourse (Shibasaki 2018a: 348). This usage is illustrated in (16).

(16)   Japanese (2004 *Hebi ni Piasu*; BCCWJ; Shibasaki 2018a: 334, (1))

Kekkon	*nanteno*	*mo,*	*hitori*	*no*	*ningen*	*o*	*shoyuu. suru*
marriage	so-called	also	one. person	GEN	human	ACC	possess. do
toiu	*koto*	*ni*	*naru*	*no-daroo*	*ka.*	***jijitsu,***	*kekkon*
so-called	COMP	PTC	become	NML-may.be	QP	fact	marriage
o	*shinaku*	*temo*	*nagaku*	*tsukiatte-iru*	*to*	*otoko*	*wa*
ACC	do.not	even. if	long	go. together	if	man	TOP

oubou-ni-naru.
high-handed-PTC-become
"Speaking of marriage, (I wonder if it means) that one is in the possession of another. In fact, even if (people) do not get married, men become highhanded if (they) go together for a prolonged period."

Henceforth, we will refer to *jijitsu* in its uses such as in (15) as *jijitsu₁* and to the one in (16) as *jijitsu₂*.

Jijitsu₁ is considered to have started its life as part of a nominal predicate in the early eleventh century. Its use is illustrated in (17), where *jijitsu₁* takes the copulative verb *-nari* to form a sentence.

(17)   Japanese (c1017 [July 7] *Midookanpakuki*; Shibasaki 2018a: 336, (4))

Udaishoo	*no*	*tokoro*	*tikaki*	*ni*	*aru*	*niyori,*
duty.position	GEN	place	nearby	PTC	exist	because
annai	*wo*	*tofa.simu.*	***Jijitsu**-nari.*			
guide	ACC	ask.make	fact-COP			

"Since Udaishoo's Palace is in the vicinity (of my place), (I) ordered (my subordinates) to guide (me). (It) is the fact."

In subsequent centuries, *jijitsu* and the nominal predicate construction of which it was a part were used sparingly, and this was also the case when it gave rise to a new construction – a change that is the subject of the following paragraphs.

It took about nine centuries for *jijitsu₂* to emerge. Usually occurring sentence initially, *jijitsu₂* appears to have arisen in the late nineteenth century (Shibasaki 2018a: 336), the first attested example being from 1901 (Shibasaki 2018a: 345, Table 5). The following example of its early usages stems from 1914.

(18)   Japanese (c.1914 *Inaka Ishi no Ko*; Kitahara 2006, Vol. 6: 655; Shibasaki 2018a: 336, (5))

Soshite	***jijitsu,***	*tookyoo*	*de*	*wakai*	*ookuno*	*onna*	*no*
and	fact	Tokyo	in	young	many	female	GEN

o-tomodachi	*mo*	*oari*	*no*	*koto*	*de*	*atta.*
PREF-friend	too	exist	GEN	COMP	COP	PAST

"And in fact, (it) turned out that (he) has lots of young girlfriends in Tokyo."

Two factors may have contributed to the appearance of *jijitsu₂*. One factor is what Shibasaki calls a process of "colloquialization":

... the adverbialized *jijitsu* in the late nineteenth century onward seems to have stemmed from the impact of the spoken mode on the written mode, reformulating discourse sequential relations. (Shibasaki 2018a: 337)

The second factor is analogy. Thus, Shibasaki (2018a: 348–49) observes that the rise of *jijitsu₂* was presumably triggered by analogy with the structurally and functionally similar development of other connective particles such as *(da) ke(re)do(mo)* "but" and the stand-alone *dakara* "so," which also developed from clause-final predicate uses, turning into DMs sentence initially (Shibasaki 2018a: 335).

Occurring only rarely at the beginning of the twentieth century, the use of *jijitsu₂* increased remarkably in the course of that century, even if it never attained the popularity of its predecessor *jijitsu₁*.

Jijitsu₁ retained the structural format it had since the eleventh century; what changed was simply the kind of copulative verbs it associates with. *Jijitsu₁* not only survived the rise of *jijitsu₂* but even acquired a higher frequency of use. After roughly 1975, both increased to be used at much the same rate, but *jijitsu₁* retained overall a higher text frequency than *jijitsu₂* (see Shibasaki 2018a: 339, Tables 4, 5, 8, and 9).

To conclude, the change from *jijitsu₁* to *jijitsu₂* took an extremely short time to materialize, apparently no more than a few decades. The effects of this change are discussed in this section; suffice it here to summarize it on the basis of the characterizations proposed by Shibasaki (2018a). One main effect of the change can be seen in fairly drastic formal and functional changes, such as from sentence-final nominal predicate use (*jijitsu₁*) to sentence-initial DM, and moving from the inside of the sentence to the outside of the sentence (*jijitsu₂*).

Another main effect was that it imposed a larger discourse frame on *jijitsu*, where the discourse following *jijitsu₂* provides a piece of evidence for, or additional information on the discourse preceding *jijitsu₂*. Thus, the two parts of discourse constitute obligatory components of one and the same discourse frame (cf. Shibasaki 2018a: 340).

How to explain this fairly abrupt shift in the history of Japanese? Observing that grammaticalization theory is hard-pressed to volunteer a reasonable answer, Shibasaki (2018a) decides to draw on Construction Grammar to account for the structural change from *jijitsu₁* to *jijitsu₂* and, in fact, he is able to describe the major lines of this transition in terms of constructional change and constructionalization drawing on Traugott and Trousdale (2013). The present account is meant to supplement his analysis by relying on the framework of discourse grammar and cooptation as a processing strategy.

Based on the generalizations proposed in the preceding chapters we will expect the shift from *jijitsu₁* to *jijitsu₂* to crucially have been shaped by cooptation, that is, to be in accordance with the hypothesis proposed in (26) of Section 2.6.

This hypothesis also holds water for the present case, as is suggested by various observations made by Shibasaki, such as the following:

> In other words, for a better understanding of the functions of commentary inductive adverbs [such as *jijitsu₂*; a.n.], we need to widen our view from the sentence level to the discourse level, which means that it is necessary to consider the preceding context. (Shibasaki 2018a: 339)

We will now look into the criteria listed in (26b) of Section 2.6 in turn with a view to testing the cooptation hypothesis.

(a) Meaning: *Jijitsu₁* had the meaning of a noun in the predicate construction of a sentence, being an integral part of the sentence meaning, as example (17) illustrates. *Jijitsu₂*, by contrast, acquired new meanings/functions beyond that of the sentence, such as guiding the hearer's expectations to the subsequent stretch of discourse (Shibasaki 2018a: 348).

(b) Function: The function of *jijitsu₂* changed from that of forming the main predication of the sentence to that of a connective marker linking the preceding discourse to the following discourse. In terms of sentence grammar, the shift from *jijitsu₁* to *jijitsu₂*, as described by Shibasaki (2018a: 349), resulted in a shift from sentence-final predicate to sentence-initial projector and DM. And much the same can be said about the information structure involved, which can be represented in a simplified format as in (19): There was a change from *jijitsu* as part of the Rheme constituent to a constituent connecting the Theme with the Rheme.

(19)   Shift in information structure from *jijitsu₁* to *jijitsu₂* (based on Shibasaki (2018a: 349; NML = nominalized, TOP = topic)

Theme	*Rheme*	*Kind of discourse function*
Clause$_{\text{NML}}$ +	***jijitsu₁*** -	Part of the sentence-internal
wa$_{\text{TOP}}$	COP	predicate
> Sentence 1	***jijitsu₂*** Sentence 2	Discourse connective beyond the sentence

(c) Syntax: Perhaps most spectacular is the shift from sentence constituent to syntactically unattached status. Shibasaki (2018a: 349) characterizes this shift in short as one that proceeded "from the inside to the outside of the sentence": While *jijitsu₁* was an inherent part of the sentence, *jijitsu₂* moved outside the sentence.

(d) Prosody: Being taken from corpora of written Japanese, the data available do not clearly allow for generalizations on how cooptation affected the prosodic structure of *jijitsu*. However, assuming that the use of punctuation marks might be indicative of some kind of prosodic feature, one is led to assume that *jijitsu₂* tends to be set off from the rest of the sentence. Shibasaki summarizes the situation thus:

> While commas are sometimes inserted between *jijitsu* and the following sentence, they do not necessarily mean any intonational break or pause, especially in the written texts; rather, this seems to reflect the writer's own preference for particular punctuation styles. (Shibasaki 2018a: 340)

More information on whether *jijitsu₁* and *jijitsu₂* are prosodically distinguished is urgently needed.

(e) Semantic–pragmatic scope: The scope of *jijitsu₁* was restricted to within the sentence. That of *jijitsu₂*, by contrast, widened beyond the sentence, extending from the preceding to the following piece of discourse. Accordingly, Shibasaki (2018a: 348) notes: "In a nutshell, the syntactic change of *jijitsu* involves an increase in structural scope, i.e. from a bi-clausal sentence to a sequenced-sentence construction."[12]

(f) Placement: The most spectacular change in placement was the shift from final sentence position of *jijitsu₁* to sentence-initial position or, perhaps more appropriately, to the position of a connective between two pieces of discourse. Whether this change entailed a decrease in constraints on placement of *jijitsu₂* is an issue that is in need of more research.

To conclude, the shift from *jijitsu₁* to *jijitsu₂* is largely in support of the cooptation hypothesis, even if more information is needed on the criteria (d) and (f).

---

[12] It would seem that Shibasaki's term "structural scope" is equivalent to Lehmann's ([1982] 2015) use of the term; that is, it is different from uses of the term in syntactic models, including that of Tabor and Traugott (1998); see Section 1.3.2.1 for a discussion.

Table 5.2 *Century of first attestation of* na *elements in the history of Japanese*

Element	Sentence-final	Sentence-internal	Interjection
na	eighth	eighth	twelfth
noo	fourteenth–sixteenth	fourteenth–sixteenth	fourteenth
no	sixteenth	nineteenth (?)	nineteenth
naa	fourteenth–sixteenth	?	nineteenth
ne	eighteenth	nineteenth	twentieth
nee	eighteenth	eighteenth	nineteenth

(Onodera 2000: 35, Table 3)

The preceding discussion raises a number of questions, such as the following: (i) Was *jijitsu* coopted as such, or else (ii) did cooptation involve a larger segment that included, e.g., the following copulative verb, which was later on ellipted? The data at our disposal do not allow for a clear answer. However, in the absence of any evidence that would be in support of an "ellipsis" hypothesis in terms of (ii), (i) appears to be the more plausible hypothesis.

The changes summarized above appear to have taken place jointly and fairly abruptly towards the end of the nineteenth century or at the beginning of the twentieth century. There is no evidence that they were the result of a long process involving intermediate stages as they are commonly observed in grammaticalization. Rather, all changes seem to have been concluded within a period of between 30 and 50 years (cf. Shibasaki 2018a: 351).

Presumably on account of this short time span, *jijitsu₂* does not show any noticeable traces of grammaticalization.

5.2.6   *Japanese* Na

There is a family of elements having a range of similar discourse functions which Onodera (2004: 157) refers to as the *na* group or the *na* elements, consisting of the particles *na, naa, ne, nee, no, nono,* and *noo*. Their general function is characterized by Onodera (2007: 241) as "expressive," but they also play an important role as "involvement markers." The elements have three contrasting usages depending on whether they are used in sentence final, internal, or initial position, and when used in initial position they are called by Onodera "interjections." As Table 5.2 shows, these usages arose at different periods of Japanese history.

The sentence-internal elements of the *na* family appeared around the same time as the sentence-final elements, in some cases slightly later though. The initial (interjection) *na* elements, by contrast, are almost invariably found later in the texts, being historically derived from the final and internal elements. Thus, final *na* is attested first in 712 of the Nara period (710–784), whereas initial *na* is found only in 1171 of the late Heian period (794–1192) (see later in this section). According to Onodera (2000: 36; 2004) there is a general pathway leading from final via internal to initial *na* elements.

For space reasons we will largely focus on the first-named element *na*; the reader is referred to the detailed synchronic and diachronic study by Onodera (2004) on the remaining elements. But, wherever generalizations are possible, we will also include the other *na* elements in our discussion.

In accordance with Table 5.2, the history of these elements is described by Onodera thus:

... the development of *na* elements does not involve grammaticalization. It is the path from a non-grammatical sentence final particle to a non-grammatical sentence internal particle to a non-grammatical interjection. However, the developmental path of *na* elements displays a pragmaticalization process. (Onodera 2000: 35)

This is an important conclusion, which is also supported by our analysis of the data: First, the *na* elements differ from the other DMs surveyed in this chapter in that they did not start out clearly as sentence constituents in the sense of forming arguments of the sentence. And second, in their known history they never had the ideational functions to be expected from expressions of sentence grammar; rather, they served the expression of the attitudes of the speaker from their earliest occurrence onwards (Onodera 2004: 187, 192) – that is, they seem to be anchored in the situation of discourse rather than in the structure of their host sentence. Thus, they exhibit features of DM-like theticals rather than of elements of sentence grammar.

Our main concern in this section is not with determining the original grammatical structure of *na* and the other elements of the family, for which see Onodera (2004); rather, our interest is with what happened to the family after it first appeared in the history of Japanese in the eighth century. One of the earliest attestations of sentence final *na* is found in (20).

(20)   Japanese (712, *Kojiki*; Onodera 2000: 39, (6))
          . . .

Akara	*otome*	*o*
red faced	girl	DO
izasaba	*yorashi*	*na.*
invite.if	good	FP

"If you invite that beautiful girl, it will be good."

Sentence final *na* in (20) expresses the writer's exclamation on the content of the preceding clause. As Onodera (2000: 39–40) points out, it has no ideational meaning, no propositional function, nor any sentence-grammatical function, and without it the sentence would still be grammatically appropriate.

Like sentence-final *na*, sentence-internal *na*, first attested in the same year, 712, also expresses the attitude of the speaker, even if less pronouncedly than final *na*.

A distinctly new situation arises with the appearance of sentence-initial interjection *na* in the twelfth century, which we hypothesize to be a case of cooptation. One of the first attested examples of *na* as a coopted unit and DM is reproduced in (21), where *na* has an expressive, vocative-like function, focusing on the following information unit, now "indicating the speaker's action of summons" (Onodera 2000: 41). Perhaps most conspicuous is the fact that initial *na* serves two new functions, namely speaker–hearer interaction as well as text organization, filling the gap between the preceding text (marked by . . . in (21)) and the current utterance, which addresses the hearer.

(21)   Japanese (1171, *Ryoojin Hishoo*; Onodera 2004: 175, (18))
        . . .

Na,	*iza*	*tamae*	*hijiri*	*koso,*
hey	come on	please	come	monk
ayashi	*no*	*yoo*	*nari*	*tomo,*
poorly	LK	state	COP	athough
warawara	*ga.*	*shiba no*		
us	GEN	wooden		
iori	*e,*			
cottage	to			

"Hey, sir (addressing the monk), please come to our wooden cottage although it is only a shabby place."

With its shift to initial position, now referred to as an interjection, *na* acquired most, if not all of the properties characteristic of cooptation to a DM, as shown in (22) (Onodera 2004: 174–75). It is now "acting as initial brackets," which Onodera (2004: 174) takes to be a defining feature of Japanese DMs (but see also Section 5.2.8 on *wake*). And in addition to the expressive functions that final and internal *na* have, it acquired a textual function.

(22)   Effects of cooptation hypothesized for the shift from final and internal *na* to initial *na* in Japanese
        a Meaning: While retaining an earlier expressive meaning, *na* now serves speaker–hearer interaction as an interjection, typically expressing summons.
        b Function: It acquired a metatextual function of marking discourse cohesion and involving the hearer.
        c Syntax: From sentence-final or internal particle to syntactically detached DM at the left-periphery of a sentence.
        d Prosody: The particle appears to be prosodically set off from the preceding text, as is suggested by the use of punctuation marks in some of the examples (e.g., Onodera 2004: (18a); but see also Section 2.1).

   e Semantic–pragmatic scope: Its scope now extends over the preceding and the following text piece.

   f Placement: From sentence-final or internal to sentence-initial placement.

That the shift of *na* to initial position coincides with or, more likely, is a result of the cooptation of the *na* elements is described by Morita (1973) in short as follows:

> As for this group of interjections (such as *na, naa, noo, noo noo* and *nayo*), the equivalent sentence-final particles were detached [from the rest of the sentence] and occurred sentence-initially as independent elements. (Morita 1973: 197; cited from Onodera 2004: 157)

This shift is described by Onodera (2000; 2004: 157–95) as one of pragmaticalization and, in fact, the properties of cooptation that initial *na* exhibits also relate to the ones that students of pragmaticalization have pointed out to characterize the rise of DMs, as we saw in Section 1.2.2. Her conclusion that the DM *na* is the result of pragmaticalization is therefore on the whole compatible with the hypothesis proposed here.

It would seem that following its cooptation as a sentence-initial interjection, more recently *na* also underwent some late grammaticalization (see Section 2.5.2), acquiring new discourse functions via context extension, such as signaling the announcement of upcoming new information, reinforcement, affirmative response, and calling attention (Onodera 2000: 42).

5.2.7   Japanese Sate

The main function of the Japanese DM *sate* is to connect sentences, presenting a new topic, and it may also express a mild hedge, similar to English *well*, frequently introducing a turn in a conversation. Note that it can also occur as a stand-alone, that is, as an utterance of its own, as in (23). It has no truth-functional or lexical meaning and occurs mainly in initial position, rarely in clause-internal position.

(23)   Japanese (Traugott and Dasher 2002: 178, (49))
        A: *Sensee, doo nasai-masu-ka?*
           teacher how do (RESP)-POL-Q
           "What will you [respected teacher] do?"
        B: **Sáte!**   ...   *(doo   si-masyo-o).*
           well   ...   how   do-POL-PROB
           "*Well!* ... (What shall I do ...)."

Traugott and Dasher (2002) distinguish the five stages of development listed in Table 5.3.

Table 5.3 *Stages in the semantic development of Japanese* sate[13]

Stage	Function	Time of attestation
I	Deictic manner adverb	Eighth century
II	Discourse marker connective	Early tenth to early eleventh centuries
III	Pragmatic marker signaling the beginning of a new topic	Early tenth to early seventeenth centuries
IV	Exclamatory lexeme	Fourteenth century
V	Epistolary formula	Between seventeenth century and present

(Traugott and Dasher 2002: 186)

The DM is historically derived from the clause-internal deictic manner adverb *sate* "thus, in that (sort of) way," but this meaning is no longer available today. Its earliest attestation at Stage I dates back to before 759 in Old Japanese, where it occurred in sentence-internal position. At that stage it was an adverb of sentence grammar, having participant status within the sentence and expressing contentful meaning which is part of the sentence meaning.

At Stage II, in Late Old Japanese (800–1100), there is a noteworthy change: *Sate* is now found most frequently in clause-initial position expressing new, text organizing functions. While its earlier manner meaning is retained in some examples, it may now impose a kind of conditional schema on the relation between two pieces of discourse (p, q), strengthening the nuance of q as the inevitable outcome of what has just been said in p. Alternatively, it can establish an additive relation between p and q, as it does in (24). Note that, unlike *sate* at Stage I, that of Stage II now refers to the event p as a whole rather than to a part of it.

(24)   Japanese (c1006, Genji Monogatari [Abe et al. 1970: 280.6]; Traugott and Dasher 2002: 181, (53))
Kiyoge-naru   otona   hutari   bakari,
elegant-looking- adult   two:people   just/only
COP
"[There were] just two elegant-looking adults,
sate   *ha*   *warahabe*   *zo*   *ide-iri-asobu.*[14]
and (in addition) TOP   children-   EMPH   go:out-go:in-play
also children were playing running in and out [of the room]."

Traugott and Dasher (2002: 186) note that *sate* at Stage II is a DM having connective functions. While the database available on grammatical change

---

[13] The dates proposed in the last column are ours, based on the dates of attestation of the examples provided.

[14] Heiko Narrog (personal communication of February 23, 2020) observes that the topic maker "ha" was presumably pronounced *fa* in the eleventh century.

between Stage I and Stage II is scant, there are a number of clues suggesting that at some point in Late Old Japanese cooptation had in fact taken place. These clues are in particular: First, the meaning of *sate* no longer seems to be a part of the meaning of its host sentence. Second, unlike its uses at Stage I, *sate* now performs clearly metatextual functions. Third, it is no longer a syntactic constituent of its host sentence. Fourth, it has wider scope beyond the clause, and finally, its position is now established at the left boundary of a sentence, that is, in a slot that tends to be favored by DMs.

Stage III seems to continue or even to run parallel to Stage II – both stages are first attested around the same time in the early tenth century. The stage is characterized by context extension leading to the emergence of new discourse functions. *Sate* now operates at a global discourse level as a scene shifter (Traugott and Dasher 2002: 182–84).

Stage IV is attested in the fourteenth century, and like Stage III it shows no pronounced changes in the grammatical status of *sate*: Change appears to have been essentially restricted to the meaning of the DM, now called a "pragmatical particle" by Traugott and Dasher (2002: 184–85). New meanings arising at Stage IV concern most of all exclamatory and hedging uses, on the one hand, and that of a "global pragmatic marker," on the other.

The final Stage V marks another kind of context extension to the domain of letter writing. Possibly to be traced back to conventions already present in the early seventeenth century, *sate* becomes one of the standard formulaic expressions used to mark the beginning of the body of a letter immediately following the sentence of formal greetings. How this new function exactly relates to earlier stages of development is not entirely clear; the extension is classified by Traugott and Dasher (2002: 186) as an instance of marking topic shift.

To conclude, the insightful analysis by Traugott and Dasher (2002) provides a detailed profile of the semantic–pragmatic development of *sate*. There is, however, little information on other aspects of grammaticalization. In particular, the way in which *sate* changed from an adverbial expression of sentence grammar to a marker having discourse structuring functions is largely opaque considering that there are no appropriate data for grammatical reconstruction. However, we concur with Traugott and Dasher (2002: 184) in assuming that by the year 1000 AC in Late Middle Japanese, *sate* must have become a DM, and this entails that by that time or earlier it had undergone cooptation.

There is no evidence to the effect that *sate* acquired the grammatical properties of a DM just listed as a result of grammaticalization. In the centuries to follow, however, *sate* underwent massive grammaticalization, acquiring a range of metatextual functions, and grammaticalization was apparently largely restricted to the meaning and functions of the DM. Nevertheless, as predicted by the hypothesis in (26) of Section 2.6, the main grammatical properties of a

DM that *sate* appears to have acquired roughly a millennium ago have survived relatively unchanged up until Present-Day Japanese.

5.2.8   *Japanese* Wake

The Japanese expression *wake* has a number of different usages (see Suzuki 2006) among which there are two main, contrasting ones. On the one hand, *wake* is a noun meaning "reason," as in (25), where it occurs in the position determined by its status as a patient argument placed before the verb, marked for case; note that Japanese is a verb-final (SOV) language.

(25)   Japanese (Suzuki 1998: 68, (2); 2006: 37, (1))
       gakkoo-ni   tikoku-si-ta   wake-o   iu.
       school-to   late.coming-do-PAST   reason-ACC   say
       "(I) gave the reason why (I) was late for school."

On the other hand, it is a DM, called "pragmatic particle" by Suzuki (1998), illustrated in (26), where it occurs utterance-finally after the predicate, although it may be followed by a copula and/or another DM. Unlike the noun *wake* in (25), it is uninflected, its main function being to express the speaker's "explanatory" attitude toward the utterance (see Suzuki 1998: 69–71 for more detailed discussion).

(26)   Japanese (Suzuki 1998: 68, (3))
       T-san-wa   nanka,   zibun-tosite-wa   ne,
       (Name)-TOP   HESI   self-as.for-TOP   PTC
       *tunezune   tatiba-o   hakkirisasete-ki-ta   tte   iu   **wake** yo.*
       consistently   standpoint-   clear.make.continue-   QUO   say   *wake*   PTC
                      ACC   PAST
       "T-*san* says (to me) that (he) has been consistently making (his) standpoint clear, you see *wake*."

Suzuki (1998) divides the history of the DM into five stages. Prior to 1830, no uses of the DM were observed. Derived from the verb *wakeru* "to divide," the derived noun *wake* had the meanings "left over division of food" and "a prostitute's splitting her earnings with her master" from the fifteenth to the seventeenth centuries. More abstract meanings evolved from the sixteenth century onward, such as "difference," "meaning of a word or a situation," and "how the present situation has come about," It is only in the early nineteenth century that the senses "situation (with a reason behind it)" and "reason" emerged, almost always preceded by a modifying clause (Suzuki 2006: 47–48).

Suzuki's Stage I is located in the 1830s, when *wake* occurred in combination with the predicate formative *da*, and this usage is typically characterized as an utterance-final auxiliary signaling the speaker's "explanatory" attitude (Suzuki

2006: 48). Around that time, Suzuki found 21 tokens of lexical *wake* and two tokens of *wake* as a pragmatic particle. The latter occur at the end of a cause-effect sequence of two clauses, where the first clause indicates a reason and the second "the outcome." Example (27) illustrates this innovation, where it is followed by the copula or linking verb *da* (or the polite copula *desu*) and the DM *mono*.

(27)   Japanese (1832; Suzuki 1998: 73, (9))
         ano-toori-no   kisyoo-no   toosan-da-kara
         that-way-GEN   character-GEN   (Name)-COP-because
         mikakete   *tanon-da*   **wake**-da mono.
         trust   ask-PAST   *wake*-COP PTC
         "Because Toosan's character is that way, (I) trusted (him) and asked (him) [for] a favor *wake*."

One may wonder if *wake* in example (27) qualifies as a DM in accordance with our definition in Section 1.1.2, but we argue that cooptation had already taken place at Stage I, for reasons given in (28). Accordingly, Suzuki (2006: 48) calls *wake* in such usages of the 1830s a pragmatic marker.

(28)   Effects of cooptation hypothesized for the rise of the Japanese DM *wake* in the 1830s (see Suzuki 1998; 2006 for details)
         a Meaning: *Wake* apparently no longer has lexical content, expressing a meaning that is not part of the sentence semantics.
         b Function: Its function is now metatextual, presenting the speaker's reasoning on the semantic relationship between the two clauses in (27).
         c Syntax: *Wake* is no longer a participant of the clause, having no more a syntactic function within the clause *mikakete tanon-da* in (27).[15]
         d Semantic–pragmatic scope: *Wake* now has scope that extends over both clauses and appears to be anchored in the situation of discourse, more specifically in the attitudes of the speaker and the organization of the text.
         e Placement: The placement of *wake* is no longer determined by its syntactic function within the sentence; rather, *wake* has apparently been taken out of the sentence and moved to the end of the utterance.

Even if there is no information on the prosodic form of *wake*, there is thus reason to maintain that *wake* became a thetical by 1830 or earlier, having the procedural function of monitoring the production of the text, providing an instruction on how to interpret the text. And the grammatical properties summarized in (28) that *wake* acquired around that time appear to have largely been retained up until Present-Day Japanese.

The ensuing history of *wake* after Stage I is mainly one of grammaticalization. On the one hand, the noun *wake* "reason" or the nominal predicate construction *wake-da* (reason-COP) underwent desemanticization, losing most of its lexical

---

[15] Heiko Narrog (personal communication of March 23, 2020) suggests, however, that *wake* is syntactically integrated here.

meaning, even if part of the reason semantics was apparently retained in the causal function of the pragmatic particle in Stage I uses.

On the other hand, grammaticalization led to substantial context extension resulting in the rise of new discourse functions. After 1880, two new functions emerged. One involved new usages of *wake* in conditional sentences (Suzuki's 1998: 73–74, Stage II). In another kind of usage, arising apparently slightly later, *wake* expresses paraphrases of what has just been said, where the *wake* clause presents a re-phrasing of the content of the preceding clause (Suzuki 1998: 74, Stage III).

Before 1930, the functions of *wake* concerned primarily the organization of texts. From Stage IV, from the 1930s onward, it developed new uses relating to the attitudes of the speaker, indicating "that the speaker is engaged in the act of reasoning/inferring" (Suzuki 1998: 75). It allows presenting the speaker's evaluation of the content of the text, translatable as "no wonder."

Finally, from the 1980s on, two main directions of grammaticalization can be observed, both involving loss of integrity (see Section 2.2.2). On the one hand, *wake* seems to lose its functional specificity, developing in the direction of a functionally reduced particle. On the other hand, it gradually develops into an invariable DM that can occur without being followed by the copula *da* or any other copula form and/or some discourse particle. For example, before the 1930s *wake* was almost invariably followed by a copula. From 1980 on, by contrast, *wake* is fairly commonly used as an unanalyzable form without any morphological trappings. Thus, in nearly half of the documented uses of the DM *wake* in the 1980s and 1990s, *wake* is found only in its bare form (see Suzuki 1998: 83, Table 1). This usage of *wake* as a bare form gradually increased subsequently, and in Present-Day Japanese it represents clearly the most popular form of *wake* (Suzuki 2006: 47).

Loss of the erstwhile predicative formative appears to have been accompanied by a slight change in function, in that this loss correlates with a weakening or even the absence of the speaker's evaluative judgment towards the content of the utterance, at the same time expressing stronger involvement of the hearer (Suzuki 2006: 47–49). Example (29) illustrates this use, where *wake* occurs on its own and apparently lacks any of the functions it had earlier.

(29)　Japanese (1981 Suzuki 1998: 76, (14))
　　　[M tells Y how he met his girlfriend]
　　　M: *itido*　　*boku-no*　*ie-ni*　　*asobi-ni-ki-ta*　*koto-ga*　*atte*　*ne,*
　　　　　once　　I-GEN　　house-　visit-to-come-　event-　exist　PTC
　　　　　　　　　　　　　to　　PAST　　　　　NOM
　　　　　boku-wa　*kanozyo-no*　*koto-o*　*kiniitte*　　*simat-ta*　**wake.**
　　　　　I-TOP　　she-GEN　　entity-　be.fond.of　COMP-　*wake*
　　　　　　　　　　　　　ACC　　　　　　　PAST
　　　"(She) came to my house once, and I became fond of her *wake*."

To conclude, with its rise in the 1830s or earlier, *wake* acquired its thetical grammatical properties, most of which have survived in its history virtually unchanged into Present-Day Japanese. *Wake* thus is a fairly young DM. Nevertheless, it has undergone a remarkable amount of late grammaticalization, that is, changes taking place almost entirely after its cooptation. Perhaps most conspicuously, there was erosion in that the earlier *wake da* was reduced to *wake*, and desemanticization, resulting in a decline of earlier discourse functions and an increase in the role of *wake* to contributing to speaker–hearer interaction ("intersubjectivity"), as described in more detail in Suzuki (2006).

5.3   Discussion

One major theme in the rise of Japanese DMs is that it frequently led to a change from clause-final or sentence-final position to placement in sentence-initial position of a sentence. The prevalent slot for placement of DMs in Japanese appears to be the sentence-initial position (see Onodera 2000; 2011), and this applies to almost all DMs surveyed in this chapter; note that, for Onodera (2011: 617), initialness is a universal feature of DMs. There are, however, exceptions crosslinguistically, and a Japanese exception is provided by the DM *wake* (Section 5.2.8), which was apparently taken out of the sentence and moved to the end of the utterance (Suzuki 1998; 2006).

There is also another case that is different from the remaining DMs examined in the present chapter, namely that of the family of *na* elements discussed in Section 5.2.6: Unlike the remainder of DMs, their sources of cooptation were not pieces of sentence grammar but rather particles that have the appearance of theticals, expressing functions of speaker attitudes. Onodera (2000: 35; 2004) therefore concludes that this is a case of pragmaticalization without grammatialization.

The DMs treated differ greatly from one another, not only in their etymological sources but also in how and when they evolved. Furthermore, the database for reconstructing the transition from expressions of sentence grammar to expressions anchored in the situation of discourse is of varying quality. It is weakest in the case of the DM *sate*, where there is highly detailed information on functional developments but hardly any details on syntactic, morphological or phonetic changes (Traugott and Dasher 2002). Nevertheless, there is on the whole converging evidence in support of the cooptation hypothesis proffered in Section 2.6.

First, cooptation can be reconstructed back to some stage in the development of the DMs. One main effect of it can be seen in fairly drastic formal and functional changes, such as a shift from clause-final or sentence-final usage to DM at the left periphery of the sentence in a number of the DMs surveyed.

Cooptation is located in different time periods of the history of Japanese: It dates back to Late Old Japanese of the early tenth century in the case of *sate*

Table 5.4 *Hypothesized dates of cooptation of some Japanese DMs*

Discourse marker	Approximate date of cooptation
sate	Early tenth to early eleventh centuries
na	Twelfth century
demo	Mid-sixteenth century
ga	Seventeenth century
douride	Eighteenth century
wake	1830s
jijitsu	Late nineteenth century
dakedo	Early twentieth century

(Traugott and Dasher 2002), the mid-sixteenth century in *demo* (Onodera 1995; 2004), the seventeenth century in *ga* (Matsumoto 1988), the eighteenth century in *douride* (Shibasaki 2018b), the early nineteenth century in *wake*, the late nineteenth century in the case of *jijitsu* (Shibasaki 2018a: 336), and the early twentieth century in *dakedo* (Onodera 1995; 2004). In some cases it is not possible to determine some specific date for this stage, which seems to be due mainly to lack of more detailed historical information. Table 5.4 lists the approximate dates when the Japanese DMs surveyed must have been coopted, extending over a time span of nearly 1,000 years.

Second, once the evolving DMs had reached this stage, they acquired all or most of the grammatical properties characterizing DMs, namely the ones listed in (26) of Section 2.6. The evidence available to determine these properties, however, may not be highly robust in a given case but, once again, the reason for this would seem to lie in an insufficient database rather than necessarily in an absence of the property concerned.

Third, rather than being suggestive of a gradual process of grammaticalization, the properties appear to have evolved fairly abruptly, and rather than conforming to the criteria of grammaticalization discussed in Section 2.2.2, they are at variance with such criteria.

Fourth, in spite of all the contextual and functional extensions that Japanese DMs experienced in the course of their subsequent history, the thetical properties that they acquired following their cooptation have largely been retained up to Present-Day Japanese.

And finally, there were also effects of grammaticalization, most of all involving the parameters of desemanticization and context extension (see Section 2.2.2): The DMs appear to have lost their sensitivity to truth conditions and part or all of their earlier lexical meaning, on the one hand, and to have acquired a range of new discourse functions, on the other.

6   Korean Discourse Markers

6.1   Introduction

Reconstruction work on the rise of DMs is contingent on the availability of detailed historical information. Such information is, unfortunately, not available for most languages. But historical information in itself is not sufficient for the present purposes. What is equally important is that that information be specific enough to reconstruct the situation in the past that may have provided the basis for the emergence of a DM. This observation was central for our selection of case studies to be included in the present chapter.

The Korean language exhibits an extraordinary wealth of DM structures. Whether this is due to the pioneering work done by Korean scholars or is a characteristic of the structure of this language is not entirely clear. There is in fact a large number of studies on DMs in Korean (e.g., Lee 1996; Kim 2000; Rhee 2004; 2013; 2015; 2018a, 2018b, 2018c, 2018d; 2019; Choi 2007; Kim 2000; Kim and Lee 2007; Sohn and Kim 2008; Ahn 2012; Ahn and Yap 2013; Koo and Rhee 2018; Rhee and Koo 2019).

But Korean DMs also stand out with regard to the wide range of functions they express. For example, there is a family of what Rhee (2019) calls *kule-*DMs, derived from *kule* "be so" (*kulay, kulssey, kuntey, ku(le)n(i)kka,* and *kulem*; see Table 6.1), for which altogether forty-seven discourse functions have been identified (Rhee 2019).

Another interesting feature of Korean can be seen in the fact that it has developed a range of DMs from interrogative constructions via rhetorical questions, that is, questions that do not seek information or require an answer (Rhee 2004: 413). For example, the question words *way* "why?" and *eti* "where?" acquired uses as markers for emphatic confirmation ("yes") and disconfirmation ("no"), respectively, as illustrated in (1).

(1)   Korean (Rhee 2004: 418, (10a))
          A: [Didn't you have much trouble?]
          B: *way?   kosayng   cengmal   manh-ass-ci.*
             why?   trouble   really   be:much-PAST-END
             "Absolutely! We had lots of trouble." (Lit. "Why? (We) had lots of trouble")

DM	1 Meaning: Sentence-external	2 Function: Metatextual	3 Syntax: Non-constituent	4 Prosody: Set off	5 Scope: Larger	6 Position: Variable (L = left periphery, M = medial, R = right periphery)
camkkan (< "duration of eye-blinking")	+	+	+	+	+	L
cengmal (< "correct word")	+	+	+	+	+	L, M, R
cham (< "true, truth, truly")	+	+	+	+	+	L, M, R
chammal (< "true word")	+	+	+	+	+	L, M, R
chammallo (< "with/in true words")	+	+	+	+	+	L, M, R
cincca (< "real thing")	+	+	+	+	+	L, M, R
com (< "a little"; Mikyung Ahn, personal communication)	+	+	+	+	+	L, M, R
eti (< "where?")	+	+	+	+	+	L, M, R
eti poca (< "where, let's see")	+	+	+	+	+	L, M, R
isscanha ("doesn't it exist?"; Mikyung Ahn, personal communication)	+	+	+	+	+	L, M, R
kaman (< ideophone for quietness)	+	+	+	+	+	L
kalay (< "(as) it is so")	+	+	+	+	+	L, R
kalem (< "it is so")	+	+	+	+	+	L, (M,) R
kulenikka (< "while it is so")	+	+	+	+	+	L, M, R
kuman! (< "that much; enough!")	+	+	+	+	+	L, M
kulssey (< "while it is so")	+	+	+	+	+	L, M, R
kuntey ("at it being so")	+	+	+	+	+	L, M, R
kunyang (< "that shape")	+	+	+	+	+	L, M, R
mak (< "coarse(ly)")	+	+	+	+	+	L, M, R
mwe (< "what?")	+	+	+	+	+	L, M, R
sasilun (< "the fact is")	?	?	?	+	+	L
ta (< "all")	?	?	?	+	+	(L,) M, R
ttak (< ideophone)	+	+	+	+	+	M
tul (< PL suffix)	+	+	+	+	+	L, M, R
way ("why?")	+	+	+	+	+	L, M, R

(Seongha Rhee, personal communication of August 25, 2019, based on Koo and Rhee 2018; Rhee 2015; 2018a, 2018b, 2018c, 2018d; 2019; Rhee and Koo 2019; Mikyung Ahn, personal communication of January 13, 2020)

197

The DMs found in Table 6.1 are far from representing all the DMs that exist in the Korean language; for example, three of the four DMs examined in this chapter are not contained in Table 6.1.[1] And some of the items in the list stand for families of etymologically related DMs. For example, side by side with *kuman!* "that much; enough!" (< *ku* "that" + *man* "amount") there are the following related DMs having similar functions: *kumanhay* "Stop!"(< *kuman ha-y* "that.much do-END") and *kumantwe* "Stop!" (< *kuman twu-e* "that.much leave.it-END") (Rhee 2018a: 4).

In general terms, Table 6.1 shows that, with the partial exception of *ta* and *sasilun*, all DMs conform essentially to the list of properties that are expected to be found in DMs (see (40) of Section 1.5). But the table presents a highly simplified account of all the diversity and variation that characterizes Korean DMs. We will now look at each of the six properties in turn.

1 *Meaning*: The Korean DMs have non-lexical sentence-external meanings, with the exception of *sasilun* and *ta*, whose meaning is close to that of their corresponding sentence grammar meanings.
2 *Function*: With the exception of *ta*, DMs have metatextual functions of organizing discourse. But in medial position, a few are ambiguous between their sentence grammar and their DM functions.
3 *Syntax*: The DMs have no syntactic constituent status, but a few are syntactically ambiguous in medial position.
4 *Prosody*: All DMs are in some way or other marked off prosodically. But prosody exhibits a complex situation and a great amount of variation – in the wording of Seongha Rhee (personal communication of August 25, 2019), "prosody is crucial but its analysis is difficult and elusive." One important observation, also made in DMs of other languages, concerns a difference between the left- and the right-periphery: DMs tend to prosodically merge with the preceding text at the right-periphery but not or less so at the left periphery. This applies in particular to the following DMs, which are often bound with the preceding material: *kulay*, *kulem*, *kulenikka*, *kulssey*, *kuntey*, and *mwe*.

Prosodic marking appears to strongly correlate with the respective functions expressed by a given DM. The following are a few general observations:

(a) Some DM functions are signaled by uniform prosody, and this applies, for example, to the functions of floor-holding, assertion, summary/conclusion, feigned surprise, and self-affirmation.
(b) The following DM functions tend to be associated with short duration and fast speed: Agreement, elaboration request, disregard for emphasis, emphatic reassertion, topic initiation, topic shift, and surprise.

---

[1] The present section rests overwhelmingly on information kindly volunteered by Seongha Rhee and Mikyung Ahn, to whom we wish to express our deeplyfelt gratitude. More detailed information is found in the studies mentioned in the remainder of this section.

Table 6.2 *Quantitative distribution of placement slots occupied by twenty-five Korean DMs*

Possible slots of placement	Number of DMs	Percentage
L	3	12
M	1	4
L, M	1	4
L, R	1	4
L, M, R	19	76
Total	*25*	*100*

Note: L = left-periphery, M = medial position, R = right-periphery.
(Seongha Rhee, personal communication; Mikyung Ahn, personal communication)

(c) Long duration and slow speed tend to be associated with the functions of uncertainty, pause-filling, reluctance/hesitance, and upcoming disalignment.

(d) Falling intonation is associated with the functions of agreement, elaboration, and request.

(e) Falling–rising intonation is associated with surprise, discontent, and protest.

(f) Level-elongated intonation is associated with uncertainty, pause-filling, reluctance/hesitance, and upcoming disalignment.

(g) A preceding/following pause is associated with uncertainty, pause-filling, reluctance/hesitance, preface to dispreferred information, topic initiation, and topic shift.

(h) No preceding/following pause is found with agreement, disregard for emphasis, emphatic reassertion, surprise, discontent, and protest.

5 *Semantic–pragmatic scope*: The scope of all DMs is wider than that of the corresponding sentence grammar units from which they are derived, frequently extending over the situation of discourse.

6 *Placement*: There is some positional variation among some DMs. Table 6.2 provides quantitative details on the nature of the variation exhibited by the DMs.

According to Table 6.2, DMs can predominantly occur in all three major positions of a sentence: For three quarters of all DMs this appears to be somehow the default pattern of Korean DMs. Furthermore, of all the slots, the left-periphery is most frequently found with these DMs (ninety-six percent). This is an observation that is in accordance with observations also made in other languages; for Onodera (2011: 617), for example, "the initialness of discourse markers is universal." There is, however, no pronounced difference in Korean compared to the other two positions, considering that the majority of DMs can occur both in medial position and at the right periphery. Perhaps interestingly, none of the twenty-five DMs is restricted in its occurrence to the right-periphery. Considering that the number of the items listed is small, however, this observation is of limited value. A number of the DMs show constraints on placement. In particular, *camkkan*, *kaman*, and *sasilun* occur only at the left-periphery, and *ttak* has been found only in medial position.

To conclude, Korean DMs exhibit overall characteristics that can also be found in DMs of other languages, and these characteristics are in accordance with the generalizations proposed in (40) of Section 1.5.

6.2   Case Studies

The selection of the DMs for the case studies to be presented here was determined most of all by the availability of appropriate data on their early development. For a language like English, such data are sufficiently available, as we saw in Chapter 3. For Korean, by contrast, the database for historical text analysis is fairly restricted: The number of Korean DMs for which there are detailed historical reconstructions is limited; the present chapter therefore is a relatively short one, being restricted to the following DMs:

6.2.1   *Icey*
6.2.2   *Makilay*
6.2.3   *Maliya*
6.2.4   *Tul*

But there were also other reasons that played a role in addition in our selection of case studies. For example, the expression *tul* was picked for inclusion in Section 6.2.4 because it represents the highly unusual case of a suffix rather than a free expression giving rise to the growth of a DM.

6.2.1   *Korean* Icey

The Korean expression *icey* (or *incey*) is composed of the proximal deictic morpheme *i-* and *cey*, historically a noun meaning "time," the meaning of *icey* therefore being "this time" (Kim and Lee 2007). *Icey* has two main uses and structures. On the one hand, it is a deictic temporal adverb meaning "now," making reference to the speaker's time of utterance, cf. (2a). It is frequently used interchangeably with the adverb *cikum* "right now," the latter denoting a temporal point whereas *icey* expresses both a temporal point and temporal extent.

On the other hand, *icey* is a DM, signaling the speaker's stance on the utterance, illustrated in (2b). We will refer to *icey* as a temporal adverb in (2a) as *icey$_1$* and to the DM, as in (2b), as *icey$_2$*.

(2)   Korean (Kim and Lee 2007: 28, (1), (2))
        a *cal ka-a   ne icey ka-nun ke(s)-i-a?*
        well go-IMP you now go-REL NML-COP-Q1
        "Good-bye, are you going now?"

        b *icey, sengcek-ul kongkayha-l   sikan-i   tolao-ass-supnita.*
        now grade-ACC go:public-REL time-NOM return-PAST-PE
        "Now, it is time to make your grades open."

In historical texts, *icey₁* is most frequently used in contexts expressing a temporal contrast or transfer of states or events, e.g., when the first clause expresses that an activity ceases and the second clause introduces a new activity (Sohn and Kim 2008: 187, 191).

There is no doubt that *icey₂* is historically derived from *icey₁* but there is no detailed information on when exactly and how the transition from *icey₁* to *icey₂* took place. The DM *icey₂* is attested already in the early sixteenth century, where it no longer expressed a temporal contrast but highlighted the stance of the speaker or writer as well as connecting a previous with an upcoming piece of discouse, as in (3).

(3)   Korean (1517, Nokeltay (Vol. I) – 63; Sohn and Kim 2008: 192–93, (7). Underlining in the original)
        A: *musum tyohan namasay is-ketun cyeki kac-ye-o-la.*
        any   good   vegetable exist-if little bring-CONN-come-IMP
        "If you have good vegetables (side dish), bring it to us."

        B: *ile-myen   kan   thi-n   oy   is-nani   icey*
        like.this-if seasoning put-ATTR cucumber exist-CRCM icey
        cukcay   kac-ye-o-ma.
        immediately bring-come-CONN-PROM
        "Then, I have pickled cucumber and let me bring it right away."

A reason for *icey₁* providing the basis for the emergence of *icey₂* as a DM can presumably be seen in the fact that *icey₁* served already as a frequently used sentence connective (Sohn and Kim 2008: 200). Cooptation therefore simply involved a shift of a connective from the level of the sentence to that of discourse. The thetical properties that *icey₂* appears to have acquired as a result of this shift are listed in (4) (Kim and Lee 2007; Sohn and Kim 2008).

(4)   Grammatical changes hypothesized to have accompanied the cooptation of Korean *icey*
        a Meaning: As a DM, *icey* has no more temporal reference and it no longer contributes to the propositional content of its host utterance (Kim and Lee 2007: 41).
        b Function: It has a range of metatextual discourse functions like expressing the speaker's attitudes and sequential relations, as a topic changer, as an attention getter (Kim and Lee 2007: 41), and it serves to secure the hearer's attention.

c Syntax: It has a high degree of syntactic independence from the rest of the sentence.

d Prosody: When used as a hedge, there are pauses before and after *icey* (Mikyung Ahn, personal communication of August 17, 2019).

e Semantic–pragmatic scope: It seems to have distinctly wider scope than the temporal adverb, extending beyond the clause it is associated with.

f Placement: It is not restricted to one position; rather it can appear freely in any position without restrictions (Kim and Lee 2007: 46).

Grammaticalization appears to have taken place, on the one hand, prior to cooptation, when the noun phrase *i-cey* "this time" merged into an invariable marker via internal decategorialization. On the other hand, it also followed cooptation when, subsequent to turning into a DM, *icey$_2$* was grammaticalized into a hedge marker and filler, with the effect that its use can now be repeated several times within an utterance, "indicating the speaker's avoidance of direct confrontation with the hearer" (Kim and Lee 2007: 45, (30)).

6.2.2   *Korean* Makilay

A feature of some Korean DMs, more so than DMs in many other languages, is that they tend to pattern into families of etymologically related markers (see Section 3.1). One such family looked at now consists of a group of forms based on the source adverbial *makwu* "randomly, coarsely, carelessly, in an unrefined manner." The group includes forms such as *makcelay, makilay, makilayyo, makileko,* and *makyolay,* henceforth referred to as the *makilay*-DMs. Of these, *makilay* is the one most frequently used, followed by *makileko.* Through the use of these DMs, having mitigating function, the discourse stance of interlocutors is constantly evaluated and negotiated.[2]

In contemporary Korean, *makilay*-DMs are very popular among youngsters – to the extent that between 2011 and 2017 there was a children's TV show in South Korea named the *Makilay Show* (Seongha Rhee, personal communication of September 26, 2019). The use of this variant is illustrated in (5), which was uttered by a female speaker who places the DM as an addendum to her utterance, evidently to mitigate her uneasiness.

(5)   Korean (Rhee 2013: 481, (1a))
        na-n   cengmal   chakha-ko   ippu-e   **makilay.**
        I-TOP   really   be.nice-and be.pretty-SFP DM
        "I am really nice and pretty. (DM: (She) says this recklessly.)"

---

[2] The present section is entirely based on Rhee (2013). We wish to express our gratitude to Seongha Rhee for all his cooperation.

The *makilay*-DMs are transparently derived from clause-like constructions – a process whereby constructions like that illustrated in (6) turned into a set of more or less unanalyzable forms.

(6)   Korean (Rhee 2013: 482, (2a))
        makwu   ilehkey   ha-e(yo)   > *makilay(yo)*
        reckless like.this say-SFP(POL)   DM

The source adverbial *makwu* "randomly, coarsely, carelessly, in an unrefined manner," being part of all DMs of the family, is first attested in newspaper articles of *The Independence* in 1896. It goes back to the fifteenth and sixteenth centuries, that is, to Late Middle Korean *mako* (*mak-* "block/seal" + *-o* CONV) "in the manner of blocking/sealing" (Rhee 2020b). There are no occurrences of *makilay*-DMs recorded prior to the end of the nineteenth century, and the analysis of historical corpus data extending from the fifteenth to the latter half of the twentieth century yields no attestations of *makilay*-DMs. This suggests that these DMs must have evolved from the adverbial *makwu* not earlier than by the end of the twentieth century or later and that cooptation of the DMs most likely took place at some point in the twentieth century. If this interpretation is correct then there is maximally one century between the first appearance of the adverb and the rise of the DMs.

The shift from compositionally analyzable sentence grammar expressions to expressions for metatextual functions might have been facilitated by the use of proximal (*i/yo* "this") and distal-visible demonstratives (*celco* "that") while no genuine distal demonstrative is found in the expressions. This might suggest that the entity referred to, that is, the preceding utterance, is brought to the addressee as something that deserves his or her attention (Rhee 2013: 483).

With the use of these DMs, the speaker adopts an imaginary third-person's evaluative viewpoint. The speaker aims to foil the addressee becoming displeased by the utterance by quickly intervening with the hypothetical third party's evaluation expressed by the DMs to the effect that the remark was reckless and thus should not be taken seriously. The meaning of the DMs can be paraphrased roughly by "I know I am shameless to say this (so you don't need to blame me for that)," the strategy being to tone down the illocutionary force of the assertion or request made. By using *makilay*-DMs the speaker switches his or her perspective, attempting "to seduce the addressee into believing the content of the proposition" (Rhee 2013: 484). A central function of *makilay*-DMs thus is to take a metatextual (or "meta-discursive") stance by monitoring the self's utterance, and to make an evaluative judgment.

When placed at the right periphery of an utterance, Korean DMs tend not to be clearly separated from the prosodic contour of the preceding utterance. But this does not apply to the family of *makilay*-DMs: While uttered without a preceding pause, they are clearly set off from the intonation contour of the preceding utterance. The main grammatical changes leading to the rise of *makilay*-DMs are summarized in (7), suggesting that these changes are essentially in accordance with observations made in the development of other DMs of Korean or of other languages.

(7)   Effects of cooptation hypothesized for Korean *makilay*-DMs (cf. Rhee 2013)
  a Meaning: *Makilay*-DMs are not propositionally bound to the host utterance, their meaning is no longer part of the sentence meaning.
  b Function: Their function is metatextual, relating to the strategy of the speaker to monitor his or her own utterance.
  c Syntax: They do not form syntactic constituents of the sentence.
  d Prosody: Occurring at the right periphery of an utterance, they are distinctly set off from the utterance.
  e Semantic–pragmatic scope: Their scope extends beyond the utterance over the situation of discourse that characterizes speaker–hearer interaction.
  f Placement: They seem to be positionally fixed at the right periphery of an utterance.

As demonstrated in detail by Rhee (2013), grammaticalization involved mainly two kinds of processes. On the one hand, it had the effect that clause-like constructions, like the one illustrated in (5), underwent two main changes, namely internal decategorialization, leading to the loss of formal identity of the morphological expressions involved, and erosion, that is, loss of phonetic substance (e.g., *makwu ilehkey ha-e(yo) > makilay(yo)*). The end product thus was univerbation, resulting in largely unanalyzable DMs (see Rhee 2013: 482, (2)). When exactly this process took place is not entirely clear on the basis of the data available. Most likely, this happened in the twentieth century immediately following cooptation.

On the other hand, the process also involved context extension leading to the loss of lexical and other semantic features (desemanticization) and the rise of a new discourse function, namely one enabling the speaker to attenuate "the illocutionary force of the self's talk by protecting the face of the addressee as well as that of the speaker in a potentially face-threatening act" (Rhee 2013: 485). The latter process of functional shift possibly preceded the former process leading to univerbation in time but the evidence available is not conclusive on this issue. More research is needed, most of all on when exactly a set of morphologically complex constructions acquired the properties they now have, in particular those listed in (7).

6.2.3   *Korean* Maliya[3]

The Korean DM *maliya* is best portrayed as a common ground marker, having a wide range of discourse functions. These functions are described in detail in

[3] We are grateful to Mikyung Ahn for valuable comments on an earlier version of this section.

the seminal study of Ahn and Yap (2013), and the reader is referred to this study for more information.

The DM can be traced back to the predicative expression *mal-i-ya*, which is composed of the noun *mal* "word," the copula *i* and the sentence-final particle *-ya* (Ahn and Yap 2013: 45). Lexical uses of *mal-i-ya* are attested from as early as the eighteenth century, as in (8).

(8)   Korean (Imhwacengyen, eighteenth century; Ahn and Yap 2013: 45, (17))
        olh-un   *mal-i-ya*   *mos-ha-liiska?*
        be.right-ADN   word-COP-SFP   NEG-do-SFP
        "(Why) can't (we) say a right word?"

A construction that may have provided the model for the rise of the DM is the following. In the eighteenth century, *mal-i-ya* was used in an emphasizing function as a sentence final particle in a focus construction, as in (9). Note, however, that *mal-i-ya* was apparently morphologically still compositional and syntactically integrated, functioning as a clausal complement.

(9)   Korean (Kiminhyangcen, eighteenth century; Ahn and Yap 2013: 46, (20);
        bold print in the original)
        *sinpyeng-i kiph-ess-ni   i-lul   cangcha esci ha-ca-n   **mal-i-ya***
        illness-   deep-   this-   in.the.   how do-HOR-   NML-be-
        NOM   PAST-as   ACC   future   ADN   SFP
        "As (my brother's) illness is serious, **what is it that** I will do in the future?"

By the late eighteenth century, *maliya* turned into a DM (pragmatic marker). It signals the introduction of "the topic as common ground to both speaker and hearer, and further invites the hearer to participate in the discourse," even though this does not exhaust its functions:

Moreover, as seen in (21) [= (10); a.n.], *maliya* could already begin to also express the speaker's emotion, including negative feelings such as sarcasm or discontent toward the addressee. This illocutionary usage of *maliya* appears to stem from its strong emphatic marking function, and its ability to single out the topical referent for censure as the speaker expresses incredulity or disbelief that the addressee would consider doing something contrary to the speaker's expectation. (Ahn and Yap 2013: 46)

(10)   Korean (Sukungka, nineteenth century; cited in Ahn 2012: 106; Ahn and Yap
        2013: 46, (21))
        canay maliya co (h)-nay-manun   kule-khi-ka   swi-wulswu-nka.
        2.SG DM   be.good-EVID-though so.do-NML-NOM   easy-can-SFP
        "Though it is good, is it easy for you to do so?" (Lit.: "You! Though it is
        good, is it easy to do so?")

The rise of *maliya* as a DM appears to have entailed the grammatical changes in (11).

(11)   Effects of cooptation hypothesized for the Korean DM *maliya* (see Ahn and Yap 2013)
        a   Meaning: *Maliya* turned from a referential into a non-referential expression as a common ground marker, its meaning no longer being part of the sentence meaning.
        b   Function: Its function is metatextual, relating to the attitudes of the speaker and speaker–hearer interaction.
        c   Syntax: It appears to have become syntactically unattached, no longer being a constituent of the sentence.
        d   Prosody: When used as a hedge, there are pauses before and after *maliya* (Mikyung Ahn, personal communication of August 17, 2019).
        e   Semantic–pragmatic scope: Its scope extends over a larger part of the discourse.
        f   Placement: It seems to be positionally fairly flexible.

There is no information to suggest that these structural changes were gradual, e.g., following one another.

Furthermore, *maliya* underwent univerbation, losing its internal boundaries and becoming an invariable marker (= internal decategorialization leading to bonding; see Section 2.2.2), but at which stage exactly this process took place does not become clear from the data available; conceivably, it coincided with the transition of *mal-i-ya* from sentence grammar unit to DM (*maliya*).

Subsequent to becoming a DM, *maliya* underwent several rounds of grammaticalization. In the early twentieth century, its functions were extended to include that of "a pragmatic hedger," serving as "a politeness marker to defuse any potentially offending bluntness in the speaker's utterance," and more recently it assumed a counter-expectation marking and a negative emotion marking function (Ahn and Yap 2013: 47–48; see also Figure 2).

6.2.4   Korean Tul[4]

The Korean DM *tul* poses a number of problems for the cooptation hypothesis advocated here, it has therefore been included here, based on the study by Rhee (2018d). The functions of the DM *tul* are discussed in great detail by Rhee (2018d), suffice it here to mention three more general functions, namely those of mirativity ("I am surprised"), irritation ("I am annoyed"), and friendliness ("We are equal and in good terms"). Its development is sketched by Rhee as in (12).

(12)   The development of Korean *tul* (Rhee 2018d: 243)
        Object (noun) > grammar/text (plural suffix) > discourse/stance (DM)

---

[4] We are grateful to Seongha Rhee for valuable comments on an earlier version of this section.

The DM *tul* can be traced back to the Old Korean noun *tAl(h)* "others (of a similar kind)" or "these (just listed)" (Rhee 2018d: 223). Already in Late Middle Korean of the fifteenth and sixteenth centuries, *tAl(h)* is attested as a plural suffix of [-Honorific] nouns, cf. (13), later on changing into *-tAl* and finally into *-tul*. The development from noun to plural marker is a paradigm process of grammaticalization (see, e.g., Kuteva et al. 2019, CHILDREN, PEOPLE > PLURAL). As a noun it no longer exists in present-day Korean.

(13)   Korean (1447 *Sekposangcel* 6:2b; Rhee 2018d: 224)
         MWUN-tAlh
         door-PL
         "doors"

In Early Modern Korean (seventeenth to eighteenth centuries), its host class was further expanded to include adverbs, other case-marked nouns, and connective particles. Another round of dramatic host class expansion is witnessed in the nineteenth century when the categorial status of *-tul* became blurred. It turned into a variable marker that could be affixed also to various kinds of sentential constituents. Conceivably, this is the time when cooptation took place, resulting in a reanalysis of the plural suffix *-tul*, turning into a "floating" expression that could occur in multiple locations in a sentence. It acquired diverse stance-marking discourse functions but retained its semantic property of signaling plurality as a layering feature (Hopper 1991: 25–29).

In the twentieth century, its versatility greatly increased. As a stance marker that can host non-nominal constituents, its status as a plural suffix became unclear, as it is in the second and third occurrences of *-tul* in (14). Note that in examples such as (14), *-tul* has the appearance of an optional agreement marker.

(14)   Korean (Rhee 2018d: 226, (7); question marks signal unclear categorial
         status)
         *yay-**tul**-a*   *kamanhi-**tul***   *iss-kela-**tul**.*
         child-PL-VOC   quietly-PL(?)   exist-IMP-PL(?)
         "Children, stay still!"

The development of the DM *tul* is unusual in a number of ways. For example, Rhee (2018d) observes:

It is also noteworthy that as a DM, its phonological dependence (typical for suffixes) is variable; it may be uttered as dependent on the preceding form or as independent (often utterance-initially as well.). (Rhee 2018d: 234)

Thus, *tul* became reanalyzed as a marker the function of which is on the one hand that of a pluralizer and on the other hand that of a DM expressing functions of speaker–hearer interaction and the speaker's attitudes. The following example shows that it can in fact occur sentence-initially.

Furthermore, it can appear after the termination of a sentence (Rhee 2018d: 226–27). Being a DM, its use is optional: If *tul* were omitted in (15), this would simply be an information-seeking interrogative sentence, that is, the discourse functions would be absent in the sentence.

(15)   Present-Day Korean (Rhee 2018d: 227, (8a))
       tul   *way*   *tul*   *ila-y*   *tul?*
       PL   why   PL   do.this-END   PL
       "Why are you guys doing this?" [irritated protest]

The problems raised by the development of *tul* are of three kinds. First, it presents the unusual case where the source of a DM is provided by a bound morpheme, namely the plural suffix *-tul*, even if the use of the latter is often optional (Rhee 2018d: 222). Second, it is associated with two morphosyntactic formats, either being phonologically dependent on the preceding form or being an independent expression that often occurs sentence-initially. And third, the nature of the transition from sentence grammar unit, i.e., the plural suffix, is far from clear. Rhee describes it as a more or less gradual transition and, in fact, on the basis of the limited diachronic data available, no clear point of shift can be identified. What is obvious, however, is that *tul* acquired essentially the whole range of properties characterizing DMs, as can be seen in (16).

(16)   Properties characterizing the Korean DM *tul* (based on Seongha Rhee, personal communication of August 25, 2019)
    a Meaning: It is not part of the meaning of the sentence, even if its plural meaning is retained. It can be omitted without affecting the meaning of the sentence.
    b Function: Its functions are metatextual.
    c Syntax: It is not a syntactic constituent of the sentence in which it occurs.
    d Prosody: It is marked off prosodically (Rhee 2018d: 240).
    e Semantic–pragmatic scope: It has a distinctly wider scope than the plural suffix.
    f Placement: It can either be placed at the left- or the right-periphery of a sentence or in medial position.

To conclude, prior to turning into a DM, *tul* experienced a common process of early grammaticalization from noun to number suffix (cf. Section 2.5.2). Its transition into a discourse-structuring device in the nineteenth century is described by Rhee (2018d) as a case of degrammaticalization, whereby a bound form developed into a free form – in accordance with Norde's (2009: 186–227) degrammaticalization type of debonding. It would seem, however, that this case constitutes another instance of a shift from a sentence grammar expression to the plane of discourse monitoring. What makes this a highly unusual case, however, is that the source of cooptation was provided not by an unbound expression, such as a word, a phrase, or a (reduced) clause, but rather by an affix.

Finally, subsequent to its rise as a DM, *tul* entered a new phase of grammaticalization, extending its range of functions from mirativity to feigned mirativity and sarcasm, from irritation to protest and reprimand, and from friendliness to imploration (Rhee 2018d: 233, (16).

6.3   Discussion

There is only a limited amount of historical data that could be consulted on the development of Korean DMs. The four markers examined arose at different periods of Korean history within the last 500 years. Clearly the oldest is *icey*, which can be traced back to the early sixteenth century, followed by *maliya* in the late eighteenth century and *tul* in the nineteenth century, while the *makilay* group of DMs is of very recent origin, arising only towards the end of the twentieth century; see Table 6.3.

Differences also exist with regard to the sentence grammar sources of the DMs: Whereas *makilay* and *maliya* go back to clausal constructions, *icey* has an adverbial source and *tul* can be reconstructed back to a nominal plural suffix. These, however, represent only a fraction of all the historical sources of Korean DMs: As we saw in Table 6.1, there is a fairly broad spectrum of sentence grammar expressions that were recruited, including interrogative expressions and an ideophone (*kaman*).

In spite of all the differences that there are among Korean DMs, however, their rise and development seem to be generally in accordance with the cooptation hypothesis proposed in (26) of Section 2.6. First, the evidence that there is allows identifying a specific phase in the history of each of the DMs when cooptation must have taken place. Second, with their cooptation the expressions concerned acquired essentially the whole set of grammatical properties listed in (26b) of Section 2.6.

Third, there is little support for a grammaticalization hypothesis according to which the set of properties emerged one after the other over an extended period of time. This can be demonstrated most conspicuously with the example

Table 6.3 *Hypothesized dates of cooptation of some Korean DMs*

Discourse marker	Approximate date of cooptation
icey	Early sixteenth century or earlier
maliya	Late eighteenth century
tul	Nineteenth century
makilay	End of twentieth century

of the *makilay* group of DMs, which all appeared with the whole range of grammatical properties around the end of the twentieth century. And fourth, the thetical properties that the DMs acquired with their cooptation have largely been retained up to Present-Day Korean.

Note, however, that with these observations we are ignoring the semantic developments that Korean DMs underwent following cooptation, leading in particular to loss of sensitivity to truth conditions and of part or all of their earlier lexical meaning, on the one hand, and to the rise of a wide range of new discourse functions, on the other. As we observed in Section 6.1, for example, Rhee (2019) identified altogether 47 different discourse functions expressed by the set of *kule*-DMs. These developments were the result of grammaticalization processes, as aptly pointed out and described by the authors cited in the chapter.

7   Discourse Markers in Language Contact

A generalization surfacing in the preceding chapters is that, in spite of all the diversity that we observed, interlocutors across languages exploit the pool of discourse options available to them in a similar way to design new DMs. In order to test this generalization, we will look in this chapter into a different domain of language use, namely that of language contact.

The chapter differs from the preceding chapters in a number of ways. Rather than with the situation within a given language, it is concerned with situations involving two or more different languages. And rather than with language-internal reconstruction, it deals with generalizations across languages; hence, it looks at DMs from the perspective of comparative typology rather than from that of language-internal description. At the same time, the chapter does not provide the kind of diachronic depth that we were able to provide in the preceding chapters, for an obvious reason: With few exceptions, the reconstruction of DM use in earlier situations of language contact is still plagued with a lack of substantial historical information.

The concern of the preceding chapters was with identifying a general line of development leading to the rise of DMs. This line turned out to be on the whole fairly uniform across different DMs and languages, but it does not represent the only way in which new DMs can arise in a given language. Building on Heine (2016a), the present chapter argues that there is a fairly common alternative way, namely via contact between different languages. Thus, in addition to the development of DMs sketched in (24) of Section 1.2.4, reprinted here as (1a), this chapter proposes a second scenario, namely that in (1b).

(1)   Two pathways hypothesized for the development of discourse markers
        a   (Grammaticalization >)   cooptation   >   grammaticalization
        b   borrowing   >   (grammaticalization)

In the remainder of this chapter, our concern is exclusively with the scenario in (1b).

7.1   Borrowing versus Contact-Induced Replication

More than most other grammatical categories, DMs are deeply entrenched in the socio-cultural environment and the discourse organization of a language. It may therefore seem surprising that DMs can be affected by language contact more than many other kinds of linguistic expressions, as we will see in the present chapter. "Being affected" normally involves either of the following two mechanisms: borrowing or contact-induced replication.

Borrowing means that a DM is taken as a form-meaning unit from one language and inserted in another language. Replication, including loan translation ("calquing"), is a more complex mechanism which involves meaning and/or structure but not form (see Heine and Kuteva 2005 for discussion and exemplification). Replication takes place when speakers of language A design a new meaning or structure on the model of some expression in language B by using the morphosyntactic material available in language A. This may have been the case, for example, when speakers of French (A) designed the word *grate-ciel* (scratch-sky) on the model of *skyscraper* of English (B).

In many European languages, including English, discourse patterns have been influenced in particular by Latin in the course of their history, and the Latin model also seems to have played some role in the contact-induced replication of DMs. For example, Latin *id est* "that is" provided the model for replicating *esto es* "that is" in Spanish. *Esto es* appeared as a DM in Spanish around 1200, first used only in legal texts such as last wills, after 1250 extending to new types of texts such as translations from Arabic or Greek into Romance languages (Pons Bordería 2018: 7). In a similar fashion, the rise of the English DM *so to say/so to speak*, like that of French *pour ainsi dire* (lit. "to so say") and German *sozusagen* (lit. "so to say"), was conceivably influenced by the Latin model *ut ita dicam* (lit. "as so I.should.say") via contact-induced replication (loan translation) (Claridge 2013: 173).

In the case of English, language contact with French also had some impact on the replication of DMs. For example, the rise of the DM *no doubt* and related expressions, such as *out of doubt* and *without doubt*, is likely to have been due to contact-induced replication of the early French expression *saunz doute* "without doubt," which first occurred in English between 1250 and 1350 (Simon-Vandenbergen 2007); note that the noun *doubt* (or *doute*) was borrowed in Middle English from French, where it meant "fear," "hesitation," or "doubt" (Simon-Vandenbergen 2007: 31).

Both borrowing and replication are commonly involved in the rise of new DMs, and both may be employed simultaneously in a situation of language contact. For example, the study by Garachana (2018) suggests that both appear to have been employed in the rise of the Spanish concessive DMs *no obstante*, *no contrastante*, and *no embargante* on the model of Latin, Catalan, and Aragonese.

Contact-induced replication is notoriously difficult to reconstruct, and quite a number of DMs that have been claimed to be the result of replication are controversial to some extent. This is different with borrowing, which is as a rule fairly easy to identify. Furthermore, borrowing of DMs seems to be distinctly more common than replication, and our main interest in the remainder of the chapter is with borrowing.

Contact-induced transfers of DMs from one language to another have been discussed either in terms of borrowing or of code-switching (or code-mixing),[1] or of both, and the boundary between the two is far from clear in many cases (Lipsky 2005; Andersen 2014: 21): Does a given instance of a DM really qualify as a case of borrowing or is it more appropriately analyzed in terms of code-switching? This question is discussed controversially (see Salmons 1990; de Rooij 2000: 464). Since DMs are not integrated in the syntax of their host sentence, it is frequently hard to tell whether they are the result of borrowing or code-switching.[2] And since some of the authors cited in this chapter do not clearly distinguish the two, we will also have to deal with the latter (see Heine 2016a).

In the literature on the borrowing of DMs there is no generally agreed upon convention on what a DM is and which kinds of expressions qualify for the status of DM. Accordingly, the term for such markers is not the same with all authors. What Poplack (1980), Maschler (1994), de Rooij (2000), Schreiber (2014), and others call "discourse markers" is called "discourse particles" by Salmons (1990), and Matras (1998: 293) also refers to them as "utterance modifiers." Common to most of the authors is that they subsume a fairly wide range of units under their respective term. For Poplack (1980), for example, "discourse marker" is a cover term that includes the thetical categories of question tags, interjections, and fillers in her account of the contact situation of New York City. Maschler (1994: 334) calls DMs metalingual "because their realm of operation is, first of all, framing various parts of the text, not referring to the extralingual world."

Our interest here is exclusively with expressions that correspond to the definition of DMs in (7) of Section 1.1.2. We will therefore deal with categories of borrowed expressions as they have been proposed by the authors cited in

---

[1] Code-switching occurs when a speaker alternates between two or more languages or language varieties in the context of a single conversation (see e.g., Sankoff and Poplack 1981; Woolford 1983; Winford 2003).

[2] The two are distinguished by Poplack (2018) in the following way: In borrowing, the item is imbued with the morphology and syntax of the recipient language. In code-switches, by contrast, the morphosyntax of the donor language is retained.

this chapter only to the extent that the expressions can be assumed to relate to that definition.

Most cases of DMs that have been transferred from one language to another have been borrowed as such, that is, they were already DMs in the donor language prior to their transfer to the recipient language. But there are some examples suggesting that an expression of sentence grammar in the donor language may appear as a DM in the recipient language, that is, that borrowing may coincide with cooptation. For example, the English text piece *as if* is typically associated with sentence grammar uses; yet, it was borrowed in Norwegian as a DM to signal emphatic rejection (Andersen 2014: 18) – in other words, cooptation did not take place in the donor language English but rather appears to have occurred when *as if* entered the Norwegian language as a borrowing.

Such a case has also been reported by de Rooij (2000) with an example from Shaba Swahili in Lubumbashi, capital of the Shaba province in the southeast of the Democratic Republic of the Congo. Shaba Swahili, a creolized form of the East African lingua franca Swahili, is the main language of Lubumbashi, while French is the official language. Speakers of Shaba Swahili have borrowed the French causal subordinate conjunction *puisque* "since" as a DM in Shaba Swahili, as the example in (2) shows. The excerpt is taken from a conversation between two men, Papa Tshibangu (T) and Papa Dikuyi (D), both migrants from the Kasai region, who have learned Shaba Swahili as a second language and have attained near-native fluency in it. T starts with a French formula (*voyez bien* "Keep that in mind"). Then D uses *puisque* as a turn taker, successfully claiming a new turn with the intention of supporting Papa Tshibangu's observation and providing a comment on it (de Rooij 2000: 450).

(2)   Shaba Swahili (Papa Dikuyi/DM86; excerpt from de Rooij 2000: 449–50, (1))

    ...
    T: *voyez*   *bien*
       see.IMP.2.PL   well
       "Keep that in mind."

    D: ***puisque,***   *sa(w)a*   *u-na-ona*   *ba-:*   *ba-Kasayi*
       since   as   you-TMA-see   NC2-   NC2-Kasaian
       ya   *(h)umu (0.5)* *ba-na-anza*   *(h)u-mu*   *mw-etu*
       CONN   DEM-LOC   they-TMA-begin   DEM-LOC   LOC-1.PL
       mu   *Shaba*   *ba-na-ita*   *ki-ntu.=*
       LOC   Shaba   they-TMA-call   NC-thing
    ...

    "*Puisque* ('cause), as you see the Kasaians over here, here with us in Shaba call (it) *kintu*."

As the description by de Rooij (2000) suggests, *puisque* conforms in essentially all respects to the definition of DMs (see Section 1.1.2). It clearly functions as a DM, usually appearing turn- and utterance-initially, separated prosodically from what follows, and differing syntactically from the subordinating conjunction *puisque* of French, signaling a knowledge-based causal relation at the metatextual level.[3]

The evidence available suggests, however, that cases like this Shaba Swahili example are rare compared to cases where DMs were borrowed ready-made from another language, and cases of the former kind are ignored in the sections to follow. As a rule therefore one is led to conclude that a language typically acquires a DM either via cooptation, as in (1a), or via borrowing, as in (1b) – that is, in the latter case there is no cooptation involved since it had taken place already in the donor language prior to borrowing.

7.2   Borrowing: An Overview

Borrowing DMs from another language is by no means exceptional (cf. Brinton and Traugott 2005: 160); it has been documented in some form or other in a range of studies of bilingual situations in various parts of the world. The following are representative of these studies: Poplack (1980); Berk-Seligson (1986); Brody (1987; 1993); Olshtain and Blum-Kulka (1989); Salmons (1990); Maschler (1994; 2000); Backus (1996); Matras (1998); de Rooij (2000); Moyer (2000); Goss and Salmons (2000); Torres (2002; 2006); Lipsky (2005); Hlavac (2006); Stolz (2007); Specker (2008); Torres and Potowski (2008); Ruhi (2009); Grant (2012); Flores-Ferrán (2014); Schreiber (2014); and Fiorentini (2017). Matras (2009: 193–97) draws attention to the "almost epidemic status of discourse markers" in bilingual situations, DMs being included in his group of "unbound function words" that are "contact-vulnerable" in Romani, the language studied by him in detail (Matras 1998: 293–94).

It would seem in fact that DMs are amongst the first grammatical items that speakers borrow or code-switch in situations of intense language contact, frequently but not always from the language of the more dominant or "prestigious" group involved (Matras 1998; Grant 2012). The following examples illustrate the magnitude of DM borrowing (Heine 2016a: 246–47):[4]

---

[3] But see also Detges and Gévaudan (2018) on insubordinate *puisque* in French. Maj-Britt Mosegaard Hansen (personal communication of January 24, 2020) notes in fact that *puisque* arguably occurs also as a DM in French as well – that is, an expression which cannot mark causal relations at the strictly propositional level.

[4] The percentages provided in the following list must be taken with care since it frequently does not become entirely clear what exactly the statistical value is on which they are based. Furthermore, the term DM is used by some authors in a fairly generous fashion. Whenever there are reasons to suspect that use of the term is not fully compatible with our definition of it in Section 1.1.2 this is pointed out by using "discourse marker" instead of the acronym DM.

- Many German Americans in Texas, Indiana, etc. have borrowed an English system of discourse marking in their German dialect. Thus, English DMs such as *anyhow, anyway, of course, well, you know*, are used in German conversations among German–English bilinguals in Texas and elsewhere (Salmons 1990: 462, 468).
- In a study of code-switching of Puerto-Rican Spanish–English bilinguals in New York City, Poplack (1980: 602) found that twenty-nine percent of all code switches in her corpus, that is, the majority of all switches, were "discourse markers." Among these Puerto-Rican speakers of New York City, "discourse markers" are "the first category for which exposure to English is echoed by active replication of English items in Spanish discourse" (Matras 1998: 288).
- Torres (2002) found English and Spanish dominant Puerto Ricans in New York to employ English DMs in their Spanish narratives, regardless of their language dominance (see also Torres and Potowski 2008).
- The Spanish DM *entonces* "then, therefore, thus" has been borrowed in a wide range of languages spoken in the former Spanish empire (Stolz 2007).
- In second generation Dutch of Turkish immigrants in the Netherlands, it is in particular Turkish DMs, such as *ama* "but," *falan* "etc.," *doğru* "right," *sey* "thing," and *niye* "why," that are commonly switched into Dutch discourse (Backus 1996: 316).
- The Italian DM *allora* "then, at that time" was borrowed in language regions where Italian is spoken as a dominant language, like Maltese, (Italo-) Albanian, Cimbrian, and Molise Slavic (Stolz 2007).
- The bilingual community (*llanito*) of Gibraltar has massively code-switched DMs, such as *no* ("no") or *mira* ("look!"), from Spanish into the local variety of English (Goria 2016; 2017).
- In the region of Trentino-South Tyrol of northern Italy, speakers of the Rhaeto-Romance language Ladin have borrowed a range of DMs from Italian (Fiorentini 2017).
- In the English speech of Hebrew–English bilinguals in Jerusalem, the majority of DMs used are switched from Hebrew. Maschler (1994: 352) found altogether forty-six DMs switched from Hebrew into the English discourse of these bilinguals.
- In American Israeli family interactions, the largest category of code-mixes (sixty percent was found to be that of nouns, but the second largest category was what Olshtain and Blum-Kulka (1989: 68–69) term "discourse fillers," accounting for fourteen per cent of the code-mixes. The latter category consists essentially of tags, interjections, exclamatives, etc.
- Among immigrants in Judeo–Spanish and Hebrew bilinguals in Jerusalem, the largest number of code-switches involves single nouns (forty per cent) followed by thetical categories of exclamatives, idioms, tags, and

Table 7.1 *Spanish* entonces *"then, therefore, thus" borrowed as a DM in some Amerindian and Austronesian languages*

Borrowing language	Genetic affiliation	Where spoken	Form
Guaraní	Amerindian, Guaraní-Tupi	Paraguay	*e<n>tónse*
Hiligaynon	Austronesian, Philippinian	Philippines	*intonsis*
Rapanui	Austronesian, Polynesian	Easter Island	*entonces*
Totonac	Amerindian, Totonac-Tepehuan	Mexico	*entonces*

(Stolz 2007: 77–78)

interjections (twenty-one percent of all Spanish-to-Hebrew switches; Berk-Seligson 1986).

- In the Eastern Mande language Samo of Burkina Faso and Mali, salient DMs were borrowed from French, the official language, and Jula, the local lingua franca (Schreiber 2014).
- In Siberian Yupik, an Eskimo-Aleut language, DMs and other function words account for more than half the total of loans from the more prestigious Chukchi language (Grant 2012: 311).
- A number of Mayan languages have borrowed DMs from Spanish (Brody 1987; 1993).

These are but a few of the cases that have been described in studies of language contact, for many more examples see Andersen (2014) – suffice it to also mention the English DM *okay*, which, according to Görlach (2001: 217), is among the most widespread anglicisms worldwide.

The following observations made in two Romance languages may show the magnitude of spread of DMs in language contact. As a result of the Hispanicization of Latin America and parts of the Pacific region, Spanish has either replaced or strongly influenced languages spoken in those regions. One prominent effect of this influence can be seen in the borrowing of discourse-structuring material, most of all of the Spanish DM *entonces*, derived from the adverb *entonces* "then, therefore, thus" (Stolz 2007: 77–78; see Table 7.1, see also Section 7.3.2).

A similar situation can be observed in central southern Europe under the influence of Italian as an important second language. Once again, DMs played an outstanding role, most of all the Italian DM *allora*, derived from the temporal adverb *allora* "then, at that time" and serving in particular consecutive, causal and temporal functions. Thus, Stolz (2007: 75) found that in languages spoken in Italy or neighboring countries, "the discourse particle *allora* stands out as the most widespread Italian loan." Table 7.2 lists some of the languages concerned; for sentence examples, see Stolz (2007: 87–90; see also Section 7.3.2).

Table 7.2 *Italian* allora *"then, at that time" borrowed as a DM in some languages*

Borrowing language	Genetic affiliation	Where spoken	Form
(Italo-)Albanian	Indo-European, Albanian	Italy	*allura*
Cimbrian	Indo-European, Germanic	Italy	*alóra*
Maltese	Afroasiatic, Semitic	Malta	*allura*
Molise Slavic	Indo-European, Slavic	Italy	*lor*

(Stolz 2007: 77–78)

As some of the examples mentioned may indicate, pronounced borrowing is by no means restricted to DMs; rather, it is a phenomenon that extends beyond DMs to the whole gamut of formulaic theticals, including interjections, exclamatives, expletives, question tags, and formulae of social exchange. In accordance with the general theme of this book, however, our main interest here is with the behavior of DMs.

Borrowing may involve one or only a few DMs, but it may as well affect the entire repertoire of such markers. Thus, it has been observed that languages in long-term contact with English in the USA lost much of their own native DM system, borrowing key English DMs (Goss and Salmons 2000: 482; see also Flores-Ferrán 2014: 78).

That DMs belong to the most attractive material in the process of borrowing and code-switching is also suggested, e.g., by the following observations. First, the borrowing of DMs can be a reciprocal process. For example, Texas Chicanos often use English DMs in Spanish, but they may also use Spanish DMs such as *pero* "but" and *pues/pos* "well" in English conversations (Salmons 1990: 475).

Second, this is also suggested by the existence of borrowing chains, where borrowed DMs are borrowed once again in another language. For example, speakers of the Eastern Mande language Samo in the border area of Burkina Faso and Mali borrowed DMs, e.g., from the local lingua franca Jula (Manding, Western Mande), and a part of these DMs was earlier borrowed by Jula speakers from Arabic (Schreiber 2014).

And third, in a number of contact situations, borrowed markers are replacing, or have already replaced, existing indigenous DMs. For example, Schreiber (2014) reports that markers earlier borrowed from Arabic and the local lingua franca Jula now tend to be replaced by DMs of French origin in the style of mobile and younger speakers.

There are many studies suggesting that the meaning of a borrowed DM is not the same as that of the donor language (see Andersen 2014 for examples). Furthermore, a borrowed expression may undergo a grammaticalization process that cannot be observed in the donor language. For example, the English vocative interjection *hallo* has been borrowed in Norwegian as *hallo* and has subsequently been grammaticalized into a DM whose function is to signal dismay at an utterance or state-of-affairs that the speaker finds to be unacceptable, incorrect, irrelevant, or the like (Andersen 2014: 20).

Typically, the transfer of DMs means that the speakers concerned have a good knowledge of both the donor and the recipient languages, and not uncommonly these speakers have a near native-speaker competence of both. But this is by no means a requirement. Samo speakers in West Africa commonly use French DMs, such as *wala* (< French *voilà*), *foo* (< French *il faut (que)* "it is necessary"), *mɛ* (< French *mais* "but"), or *bɔ* (< French *bon* "good"), yet most of these speakers have no command of French. For example, the marker *wala* is not used by French speaking Samo people, while Samo speakers not competent in French make extensive use of it (Schreiber 2014: 260).

These observations raise the following question: Why are DMs frequently taken from one language and inserted in texts of another language? We will discuss this question in Section 7.3. Our interest in this chapter is mainly with DMs, but as shown by Goria (2016) the contribution of other thetical categories is far more extensive in language contact than can be dealt with in the present chapter.

7.3   Functions: The Situation of Discourse

What motivates people to insert DMs of one language in a text designed in another language instead of following the pathway of internal development described in Chapters 3–6? This question is the topic of the present section. A partial answer can already be derived from the terminology and general characterizations used for such DMs: They have been referred to as utterance modifiers that regulate linguistic–mental processing activities (Matras 1998; 291) or emblematic switches (Poplack 1980; Salmons 1990), or as serving backflagging, that is, signaling the traditional ethnic or cultural identity of the speaker (Muysken 2013). The complexity of their meanings is captured by Baker's (1980: 7) characterization of DMs and other "emblematic switches" as being "not very translatable."

A comparative survey suggests that it is most of all the following kinds of factors that are named in some form or other to account for the role played by DMs in bilingual situations, being either responsible for or conducive to borrowing DMs:

(a) Formal linguistic factors
(b) Text organization
(c) Attitudes of the speaker
(d) Speaker–hearer interaction

With the exception of (a), all factors listed concern functional components of the situation of discourse,[5] and it would seem that most of the functions of code-switched or borrowing DMs can in fact be accounted for with reference to the situation of discourse as defined in the framework of discourse grammar (see Kaltenböck, Heine, and Kuteva 2011: 861). We will now look at each of the factors in turn.

7.3.1   Formal Linguistic Factors

Among the formal linguistic factors that have been invoked to account for the prominent role played by DMs in bilingual language use, it is most of all the following that have been argued to play a role in borrowing:

(a) Their syntactically unattached status,
(b) Their internal structure, that is, their short and formulaic (unanalyzable) form, and
(c) Their text frequency.

Here (a) concerns the external syntax of DMs: Being theticals, frequently marked off in writing by means of commas, etc., DMs are by definition syntactically unattached (see (7) of Section 1.1.2). They are therefore easy both to identify in text material of the donor language and to integrate in the receiver language.

Matras argues that the reason for the particular status of DMs in terms of linguistic cognition is their "detachability" (Matras 2009: 193–97), that is, their extra-clausal or extra-sentential status, and, according to Stolz and Stolz (1996: 111), Spanish DMs (discourse particles) are borrowed in Mesoamerican languages because they do not entail problems in structural adaptation. Similar observations have been made in studies of code-switching.

One reason for the remarkable role played by DMs in code-switching in fact appears to be their status as unattached information units in the donor language, which facilitates their identification and transfer into the receiver language. And the fact that they tend to be prosodically set off and, hence, easy to incorporate in the receiver language might also contribute to making DMs suitable for code-switching and borrowing. De Rooij (2000: 455) found that 84.3 percent of the uses of the eight French DMs *alors, bon, donc, et puis, mais, non, parce que,* and *puisque* in Shaba Swahili were accompanied by pauses and/or prosodic cues. And in the English discourse of Hebrew–English bilinguals in Jerusalem, Maschler (1994: 354) observed that the DMs switched from Hebrew into English tended to be separated from both the preceding and the following phrases.

---

[5] See (7) of Section 1.1.2 for a definition of "situation of discourse."

(b) The second factor concerns the *internal* morphosyntax of DMs: DMs are short and unanalyzable and might therefore be easier to manipulate than morphologically complex expressions. They are therefore considered to be prone to switching or borrowing because of their fixed, unanalyzable, morphological form (Matras 2009: 193–97): Interlocutors need not be concerned with any particular morphological requirements to integrate them in another language.

(c) A final factor that has been invoked for the prominent role of DMs in contact-induced transfer is their high frequency of occurrence in speech (Goss and Salmons 2000; Matras 2009: 193–97): They are therefore easy to retrieve and to be deployed for new purposes.

Whether, or to what extent, the linguistic factors mentioned can account for the contribution of DMs to bilingual discourse is still largely unclear and in need of more research. In the following sections, attention will also be drawn to the metatextual role in shaping the language use of bilinguals. By being anchored in the situation of discourse rather than in the structure of a sentence, DMs allow interlocutors to view discourse in a wider context and relate it to the entire pragmatic space of linguistic communication. For example, in the borrowing of Spanish DMs in Mayan languages it is not only their detachable nature but also their general function of structuring discourse that is said to make Spanish DMs eligible for borrowing (Brody 1987: 513).

A survey of the literature on bilingual discourse suggests that it is almost invariably the following functional components of the situation of discourse listed in Kaltenböck, Heine, and Kuteva (2011: 861) that are sensitive to language contact: Text organization, attitudes of the speaker, and speaker–hearer interaction. This tripartite division of components largely correlates with an alternative terminological distinction proposed by some authors (e.g., Fedriani and Sansò 2017: 2; Goria 2017: 440), according to which markers devoted to text organization tend to be referred to as DMs, those related to speaker–hearer interaction as pragmatic markers (PMs), while markers related to the attitudes of the speaker tend to be referred to as modal particles (MPs).[6]

7.3.2   Text Organization

Work on DMs has been shaped to quite some extent by Schiffrin (1987), who defines the English particles *oh, well, and, but, or, so, because, now, then,*

---

[6] For example, Goria (2017: 440) writes: "PMs are related to the management of an ongoing interaction, and include markers like attention getters and turn yielding devices. DMs have the function of expressing textual and 'intra-discourse' (Ghezzi 2014: 15) relations between utterances; they include for example quotation markers. With MPs we refer to a set of markers whose function is to express the speakers' stance towards the utterance ..."

I mean, and *y'know* as "sequentially dependent expressions which bracket units of talk" (Schiffrin (1987: 31). And like Schiffrin, many subsequent authors discuss DMs almost exclusively in terms of the component of text organization. Thus, Maschler (1994: 333) describes DMs in her work on Hebrew–English bilinguals as "utterances occurring at verbal-activity boundaries which are metalingual at the level of discourse."

Research on borrowing and code-switching suggests the following main text organizing functions of theticals (see Heine et al. 2013):

(a) To set the frame of discourse,
(b) To relate text segments to one another,
(c) To mark boundaries, and
(d) To provide further information for an understanding of the text.

These functions are now looked at in turn. Note that these are overlapping functions that are hard, if not impossible, to separate from one another.

(a) *To set the frame of discourse.* Based on Berk-Seligson (1986), Matras (1998: 289) argues that the use of discourse particles such as *avál* "but" and *az* "so," switched from Hebrew into Spanish discourse in Jerusalem, is "part of the functional–operational frame of the discourse," and "language alternation is seen as a way of highlighting the function of DMs in framing units of talk" (Matras 1998: 289). In a similar fashion, Maschler (1994: 325) observes that code-switched DMs are employed in Hebrew–English bilingual conversation "to metalanguage the frame of the discourse, clustering at discourse unit boundaries." This also appears to be a major function of two Romance DMs that have been found to play a prominent role in situations of language contact, namely of Spanish *entonces* "then, therefore, thus" and Italian *allora* "then, at that time," and the two seem to be largely equivalent in their borrowed discourse functions.

As we saw in Section 7.2, Spanish *entonces* was borrowed in a wide range of languages where Spanish was spoken as the language of the Spanish empire, such as Amerindian languages (e.g., Yucatec Mayan, Totonac of Mexico, Guaraní of Paraguay), Austronesian languages (e.g., Hiligaynon of the Philippines, Rapanui of Easter Island), as well as some African languages (Stolz 2007: 77–79). The main function that the borrowed DMs serve is to establish consecutive connections between two clauses or utterances, in particular causal relations, as *intonsis* (< *entonces*) does in the following example:

(3)   Hiligaynon (Austronesian, Philippinian; Wolfenden 1971: 79–80; Stolz 2007: 78)

Madamo	*ang*	*bulak*	*dira'*	***intonsis***
many	DET	flower	at.there	therefore

manguha	*kita.*
FUT.get	1.PL

"There are lots of flowers there, **so** let's get some."

The Italian DM *allora* appears to be coopted from the temporal adverb *allora* "then, at that time" (see Stolz 2007: 80). It has been borrowed as a DM in (Italo-)Albanian, Cimbrian, Molise Slavic, and Maltese, that is, in languages being in close contact with Italian. Its functions concern mainly though not only discourse regulation, including the expression of temporal, causal, and consecutive relations, emphatic imperatives, emphatic questions, and turn-taking. Like the borrowed Spanish DM *entonces, allora* is mostly placed utterance-initially, exceptions such as the DM *lor* (< *allora*) of Molise Slavic in the following example being rare:

(4)   Molise Slavic (Breu and Piccoli 2000: 422; Stolz 2007: 88)
        tvoj^a divojik^a **lor**   je   ndelidžend
        your.F   daughter.F   *allora*   be.3.SG   intelligent
        "Thus, your daughter is intelligent!"

Among Ladin speakers in the region of Trentino-South Tyrol of northern Italy, the most frequent DM with metatextual function is Italian *perché* "because," usually having argumentative and justifying functions (Fiorentini 2017: 426).

(b) *To relate text segments to one another.* DMs are described by Schiffrin (1987: 326) as "contextual coordinates of talk." In his analysis of French DMs in Shaba Swahili in the city of Lubumbashi (Democratic Republic of the Congo), de Rooij (2000) treats them as a special kind of contextualization cue that ties parts of a discourse to each other, thereby creating and strengthening discourse coherence, and they are used instead of their Swahili equivalents.

As Brody's (1987: 513) work on language contact between Spanish and Mayan languages and the borrowing of DMs suggests, it is the general function of structuring discourse that is transferred from one language to another when borrowing takes place. The DMs that Mayan languages have borrowed from Spanish serve to establish links between segments of discourse ranging from phrases to paragraphs (Brody 1987; 1993).

Relating text segments to one another appears to be the main function of a set of Hebrew DMs in English discourse used by Hebrew–English bilinguals in Jerusalem. Termed referential markers by Maschler (1994: 339), these markers provide either the cause for a later point (*kì* "because"), or express a contrast (*'axshav* "now," *kan* "here," *'aval* "but," *lehefex* "on the contrary"), or a consequential relationship with the preceding verbal activity (*'az* "so").

A fairly commonly employed tool for achieving text cohesion is provided by fillers (or interjective hesitators, or hesitation fillers), such as English *uh, um*); they were classified in Section 1.1.2 as a marginal group of DMs (see Section 8.5). Acquiring native-like competence of filler use when learning another language is arguably one of the most difficult tasks that bilinguals face (cf. Maschler 1994: 348). One might therefore expect that they are particularly resistant to transfer from one language to another. But, perhaps surprisingly, fillers are quite commonly transferred in language contact. For example, Clark and Fox Tree (2002: 93) observe:

> Speakers of English as a second language often import the fillers from their first language – we have heard examples from native French, Hebrew, Turkish, and Spanish speakers – and that is one reason they continue to be heard as non-native speakers.

In the English discourse of Hebrew–English bilinguals in Jerusalem, the Hebrew hesitation fillers *'e* and *'em* (pronounced with a front, half-open vowel [ɛ]), corresponding to English *uh* and *um*, respectively, are often found at verbal–activity boundaries (Maschler 1994: 343, 347).

Fillers ("hesitations") also play an important role in borrowing processes observed in other bilingual situations, such as that of Puerto Ricans in New York City (Poplack 1980: 605–8), or of Spanish and speakers of Mayan languages, where fillers such as *este* "um" and *bueno* "good" have been transferred from Spanish into Mayan languages (Brody 1987: 510).

(c) *To mark boundaries.* Relating text segments to one another and marking boundaries can conceivably be interpreted as different sides of the same coin. Among the many functions that Hebrew DMs switched into the English discourse fulfill is to mark boundaries between major parts of a text, e.g., for switching from one topic of discourse to another. For example, the Hebrew feminine second-person singular imperative form *xaki* "wait (a moment)" is placed at a verbal–activity boundary to separate a main verbal activity from an unrelated, minor activity, thereby temporarily interrupting the discourse (Maschler 1994: 344). Similarly, moving to a new verbal activity can be signaled by the DM *'agav* "by the way" switched from Hebrew into English discourse (Maschler 1994: 345).

Using borrowed DMs for shifting from one topic to another has also been reported from other bilingual situations. Salmons (1990) discusses example (5) from German Americans where the speaker shifts topic in mid-sentence from a general discussion to a specific case, using the English DM *well* in an otherwise German text.

(5)   American German (Salmons 1990: 458)
        *Gerade 'ne Maße davun is **well** wie, sach, wie meine Frau …*
        "The whole lot of that is, well, just like, say, with my wife …"[7]

(d) *To provide further information.* A final factor that is important for text organization is to place a message in a wider context by adding further

---

[7] The correct translation should possibly be "like my wife" rather than "with my wife." No glosses are provided by the author.

information that is believed to be relevant for a better understanding of the message. This can be achieved, e.g., by means of comments, modifications, or elaborations, and in particular by reformulations. That this factor might play a role in inducing speakers to insert theticals in another language is suggested by some research reports. For example, Maschler (1994: 325) observes that code-switched DMs of one language can serve as commentaries in another language involved in the contact situation.

Providing further information may also serve to repair a preceding piece of text, as in the following case of conversational repair made by a middle-aged Texas German speaker, using the English DM *well* in German discourse:

(6)   Texas American German (Salmons 1990: 458)
         *Das war nach, **well**, die Ws sin alle verwandt . . .*
         "That was after, well, the Ws [the speaker's family] are all related . . ."

7.3.3   Attitudes of the Speaker

This component of the situation of discourse includes a range of functions served by discourse, in particular the expression of

(a) Emotional states,
(b) Cognitive states,
(c) Socio-economic values, and
(d) Emblematic status.

(a) Emotional states. A paradigm linguistic category that crosslinguistically serves the expression of emotional attitudes of the speaker is that of interjections having a discourse marker function and, in fact, interjections belong to the linguistic material that tends to be borrowed or code-switched in contact situations. For example, the interjection *'a* "oh" is switched from Hebrew into English discourse of Hebrew–English bilinguals in Jerusalem, serving to provide information about a shift in the speaker's cognitive processes at a verbal–activity boundary. In a similar way, the Spanish interjection *ay* is used at the beginning of a turn in Latino–English discourse recorded in an educational television program in the USA:

(7)   Latino–English discourse (Specker 2008: 114)
         Maya: *It was the only way, Mama.*
         Rosa: *¡**Ay!**, Maya, you're taking this too far.*

(b) Cognitive states. A second function of this component is to signal the cognitive state of the speaker. And here it is most of all comment clauses (e.g., *I think*) that are involved. For example, in the spoken discourse of Hebrew–English bilinguals, the DM *klomar* "I mean" is switched from Hebrew into English discourse, providing information about the speaker's cognitive processes, realizing the need to modify her/his prior talk (Maschler 1994: 342).

(c) Socio-economic values. A third function concerns social aspirations of the speaker and the socio-economic value attributed to some language that has been claimed in some form or other to offer a motivation for drawing on DMs from another language in situations of language contact. According to Stolz and Stolz (1996: 112), for example, speakers of Mesoamerican languages rely on the role ascribed to Spanish as a "prestige language" in grammatical borrowing. Spanish markers in the discourse of speakers of Mesoamerican languages are interpreted by these authors as *prestige signals* that allow building a prestigious register.

Enhancing one's social status also appears to be a motivating force for speakers of the Mande language Samo in West Africa: Using DMs from a language that is considered to be more prestigious may serve one's own prestige. It can be "a feature indicating power and personal identity in discourse," as appears to be the case with Samo speakers borrowing DMs from French and Jula, another second language. DMs have a high symbolic value in verbal interaction for Samo speakers, and whereas French is associated with a modernist and Jula with commercial-bourgeoisie identity, Samo stands for a traditionalist identity (Schreiber 2014: 259).

(d) Emblematic status. An alternative aspect of speaker attitudes in bilingual situations is captured by what Poplack (1980: 614) refers to as "emblematic switches" of DMs or Muysken (2013) as "backflagging." The former relates to the borrowing or code-switching of DMs and other theticals such as question tags or interjections. Emblematic symbols are found for instance in some linguistic routines that have been maintained in German among many German Americans, some barely bilingual. German interpolations in English discourse serve to mark speakers as Texas Germans or Indiana Germans, but in addition to speaker attitudes, they also involve speaker–hearer interaction: It is mainly formulae of social exchange that appear to be involved, namely greetings, farewell taking, thanking, or welcoming. Such sequences often take place in German, even when the rest of the interaction takes place in English (Salmons 1990: 471).

Backflagging is selected by speakers to signal their traditional ethnic identity even though they themselves may have shifted to a dominant non-ethnic language (Muysken 2013). To this end, the Moroccan Arabic conjunction *wella* "or" is inserted in (8) in an otherwise Dutch utterance, the latter being an L2 (second language) of the speaker community involved.[8]

---

[8] Whether *wella* in this example really is a thetical must remain questionable on the basis of the data available.

(8)   Insertion of heritage language DMs in Dutch L2 discourse of Moroccan
          Arabic speakers (Muysken 2013: 2)
          Q: *What will you be when you grow up?*
          A: *Ik   ben   doctor   **wella**   ik   ben   ingenieur.*
             I   am   doctor   or   I   am   engineer
          "I will become a doctor or an engineer."

Similarly, in a chat in a Suriname community website, Sranan *no mang* "no man" was inserted as a DM for "backflagging" into an otherwise Dutch comment (Muysken 2013).

7.3.4   Speaker–Hearer Interaction

Fiorentini (2017: 434) found that in the contact situation of Trentino-South Tyrol of northern Italy, speakers of the Rhaeto-Romance minority language Ladin are less likely to borrow DMs of speaker subjectivity from Italian, whereas markers of speaker's intersubjectivity (i.e., speaker–hearer interaction), signaling acknowledgment of and attention to the addressee, are more easily borrowed. And of all the forty-six Hebrew DMs that Maschler (1994) found in the English discourse of Hebrew–English bilinguals in Jerusalem, twenty-five, that is more than half, involved shifts in the interpersonal realm.

In the English discourse of Hebrew–English bilinguals in Jerusalem described by Maschler (1994), DMs switched from Hebrew include the following interpersonal functions: Confirming a comment made by the addressee (*ken* "yes," *bidyuk* "exactly," *naxon* "true, right," *betax* "sure," and *beseder* "all right"), disagreement (*tir'i* "look"), as well as other functions (e.g., *tishme'i* "listen," *'at mevina?* "[do] you understand?," *bo'i navin* "let's understand," *ta'amini li* "believe me," *ted'i lax* "let me tell you," and *'at yoda'at* "you know"). Maschler (1994: 341) describes these functions as facilitating "the negotiation of interpersonal closeness vs. distance between participants." Note that this group of markers includes a number of imperative-like forms (cf. Section 8.4).[9]

Analyzing the use of the Spanish DM *no?* in Spanish–English bilingual conversations, Moyer (2000) concludes that this marker serves the negotiation of agreement and disagreement in discourse, having two main functions: Either as a yes/no request where a speaker seeks information s/he does not possess from the hearer, or as a device employed by the speaker to check information with the hearer and obtain his/her acquiescence. She finds that the employment of *no?* by a speaker "constitutes a move to situate the

---

[9] For most Hebrew verbs, the future (rather than the imperative) is the tense most often used to convey the imperative sense in speaking (Maschler 1994: 362).

interpersonal relationship between speaker and hearer in a more informal or friendly domain."

That the use of code-switched or borrowed DMs is contingent on the social context is suggested for instance by the following observation. During his research among the Samo of West Africa, Schreiber (2014: 263) found that all speakers showed a higher rate of French DMs in the presence of the researcher, while most of the speakers showed a lower rate of French borrowings when no outsiders were present. One important function of borrowed DMs in French–Samo language contact in West Africa is "to marshal interaction, functioning as speaker–hearer signals, e.g. as cues to prompt turn-taking, rather than adding to the predicational core of an utterance" (Schreiber 2014: 259).

Matras (1998: 288) argues that the code-switching of DMs and related items of the dominant (or majority) language – such as Spanish-to-Hebrew switches in Jerusalem – starts "in the domain of expressions that modify utterances as interactional events."

Speaker–hearer interaction is also one of the functions of the English DM *well*, not only in monolingual but also in bilingual discourse. For example, *well* is inserted in German discourse taking place in the USA in a discussion where the speaker was beginning to counter a point that the author of the paper (Joseph Salmons) had previously made:

(9)   German discourse in the USA (Salmons 1990: 458)
        ***Well**, sie baue eine, eine Car ... bei Oldsmobile ...*
        "Well, they build one, a car, at Oldsmobile ..."

In addition to DMs, essentially all kinds of theticals are transferred from one language to another for the purpose of speaker–hearer interaction, with the partial exception of vocatives. Vocative expressions, such as *Waiter!* and *Ladies and Gentlemen!*, are a paradigm category of speaker–hearer interaction but are rarely mentioned in the literature on borrowing and code-switching. Nevertheless, they are found occasionally, as in the following example of Dutch–Sranan code-switching, where the Sranan expression *mang* "man" is inserted in an otherwise Dutch discourse for what Muysken (2013) calls "backflagging" (see Section 7.3.3).

(10)   Insertion of heritage language DMs in Dutch L2 discourse of a Suriname
        community (Muysken 2013: 14)
        *No **mang** vrouw- tje,   vind   juist   z'n   accent   hinderlijk*
        no   man   woman- DIM,   find.1.SG just   his   accent   irritating
        "No, woman, I just find his accent irritating."

7.3.5   An Interlocking System

The preceding paragraphs were meant to answer the question of what motivates people to insert DMs and related theticals such as interjections and tags in a text designed in some other language. Overall, the functions identified are similar to those fulfilled by DMs in monolingual speech (see Chapters 3–6).

The functions were described in terms of three major components of the situation of discourse, namely text organization, attitudes of the speaker, and speaker–hearer interaction. At the same time, these components are usually not neatly separated; rather, a given DM can, and frequently does express functions relating to more than one of these semantic components. In the English discourse of Hebrew–English bilinguals in Jerusalem described by Maschler (1994: 336–39), the temporal adverb *'axshav* "now," borrowed (or codeswitched) from Hebrew, serves on the one hand as a DM to express the speaker's disagreement with the previous speaker. On the other hand, it also serves to mark progression through discourse time by displaying attention to what is coming next.

Among the thetical categories that are commonly borrowed or codeswitched, the thetical category of imperatives plays an important role. The catalog of what appear to be Hebrew DM-like imperative forms presented by Maschler (1994: 350) include the following items, apparently used for interpersonal functions: *tagidi li* "tell me," *ta'amini li* "believe me," *lenasi* "try," *ti'ri* "look," *tishme'i* "listen," and *xaki* "wait a second." But imperatives are not only employed in their canonical function as a tool of speaker–hearer interaction, they also serve the organization of texts. For example, Maschler (1994: 344) describes the Hebrew imperative form *xaki* "wait," switched from Hebrew into English discourse in Jerusalem, as a boundary marker used to separate a main verbal activity from an unrelated minor activity, thereby temporarily interrupting the discourse.

The following example suggests that use of borrowed DMs can simultaneously serve the presentation of a text and enhance the prestige of the speaker: Among the Samo of West Africa, borrowed DMs can be considered on the one hand as a social symbol of speaker identity in that "the added social capital may be seen to strengthen the position of the speaker by referring symbolically to prestigious and powerful languages in linguistic interaction." On the other hand, they also serve text presentation, being considered as a rhetorical means of supporting a statement (Schreiber 2014: 266).

Maschler (1994: 350) concludes that, to some extent, all Hebrew DMs figuring in the English discourse of her Hebrew–English bilinguals in Jerusalem involve "shifts in aspects of all contextual realms" even though some particular realm may be more prominent in a given case. This finding is in accordance with observations made in many studies that there are on multi-functionality in DMs, which suggest that the usage of these markers tends to simultaneously involve more than one of the three components distinguished, even if one component may be foregrounded in a given DM or a given context.

7.4   Borrowing and the Areal Dimension: Arabic *Yaa'ni*

Borrowing of DMs is somehow a ubiquitous phenomenon, to be observed in some form or other in all major regions of the world, and in some cases it has reached an areal dimension, having spread across groups of languages and across continents. Paradigm examples have already been mentioned in the preceding sections (Sections 7.2 and 7.3.2), provided most of all by the Spanish DM *entonces* "then, therefore, thus" and the Italian DM *allora* "then, at that time."

In the present section we are restricted to a non-European language, namely Arabic, which has provided the source of massive borrowing across languages spoken in the Islamic world, and DMs have been a part of the borrowing processes. For example, Persian, Swahili, and Turkish are genetically unrelated languages, spoken far away from each other, Persian being an Indo-European language spoken in Iran, Swahili a Niger-Congo (Bantu) language spoken in East Africa, and Turkish a Turkic language of Turkey. Nevertheless, all three contain a DM having a similar form and function, namely *yæ'ni* "that is" in Persian (cf. (11)), *yaani* "that is, that is to say, I mean" in Swahili (12), and *yani* "that is, in other words" in Turkish (13):

(11)   Persian (Noora and Amouzadeh 2015: 99)
         Ali! **yæ'ni,**   *âqâye Ahmadi, ketabe-   toon.*
         Ali, meaning Mr.   Ahmadi book.EZ- your
         "Ali! I mean, Mr. Ahmadi, here is your book!"

(12)   Swahili (own data)
         Ali, **yaani** *Bwana Ahmadi, kitabu   chako   kipo   hapa.*
         Ali, that.is Mr   Ahmadi NC7.book NC7.your NC7.be.LOC here
         "Ali! I mean, Mr. Ahmadi, here is your book!"

(13)   Turkish (Ruhi 2009: 288)[10]
         Adamin evi, arabasi, yati var; **yani** *para babasi.*
         "The man's got a house, a car, a yacht; in other words, he's a money bag."

There are compelling similarities between these three DMs: First, all can be classified as what Blakemore (2007) calls "that is"-parentheticals. Second, all are instances of borrowing and, third, all can be traced back to Arabic as the

---

[10] No interlinear glosses are provided by the author.

donor language, and borrowing is likely to have taken place independently in the course of roughly the last millennium in connection with the spread of Islamic religion and culture.

Presumably the ultimate donor of Persian *yæ'ni*, Turkish *yani*, and Swahili *yaani* is Classical Arabic *yaa'ni* [jaʕni], which originally appears to have been a verbal expression *(jaʕni (ʔanna)* "[this] means (that)"). In "modern Arabic," *yaa'ni* ([jæʕni] or [jaʕni]) is the third-person masculine singular imperfective of the defective verb عَنَى *('anā)* "he means." But this form is fixed, noncompositional, it is no longer inflected for tense and is "used to focus the speaker's modification of his/her talk" (see Noora and Amouzadeh 2015: 96–97 for detailed discussion). Arabic *yaa'ni* appears to be a DM (or a "that is"-parenthetical) coopted from the homophonous sentence grammar form *yaa'ni*. Cognates of the marker are also found in modern Arabic dialects. In Libanese, Syrian, and Palestinian Arabic, for example, the reflex is [jæʕne], serving as a DM to signal functions such as reformulations, corrections, and background repairs (Kanaan 2012).

What these observations suggest is that Arabic *yaa'ni* was borrowed in languages such as Persian, Swahili, or Turkish as a formulaic, i.e., unanalyz-able DM rather than as a compositional form of sentence grammar. The borrowed DM appears to be flexible in its placement behavior in all languages concerned. For example, the Turkish reflex *yani* can be used both inserted in various positions of an utterance and even as a stand-alone in an utterance of its own. Thus, in the following dialog between A and B, *yani* is used by speaker B both utterance-finally and twice as a stand-alone: With the first *yani* in (b), having a rising intonation, B is inquiring about the consequence of A's statement and the second *yani* in (c) may then be glossed "Wasn't that to be expected?"

(14)   Turkish (Ruhi 2009, (3))[11]
         A: *Emre Ali'ye yenildi*
            "Emre lost [the match] to Ali"
         B: a   *Artık turnuvayı terk etti* **yani**
                  "So [he] is out of the tournament [you mean]"
            b   **Yani?**
         c   **Yani!**

In its functions, the DMs in all the three languages exhibit features of all the main components of the situation of discourse discussed in Section 7.3, as the following observations suggest.[12]

---

[11] No interlineal glosses are provided by the author.
[12] No mention of Swahili is made in the following notes, since no analysis of its DM *yaani* exists so far.

Text organization. The meaning of the borrowed DMs is commonly rendered as "that is, in other words, meaning, I mean" or "what it means is that." And in all three languages it can be described as being multifunctional, expressing a range of contextually defined meanings, but its central meaning appears to be that of a reformulation marker in the sense of Blakemore (2007) – that is, the DM concerns first and above all text organization.

Thus, the Persian marker *yæ'ni* includes the following discourse functions among its meanings (Noora and Amouzadeh 2015): (a) filler or hesitation marker indicating ongoing planning, (b) repair, serving as a "mistake editor," or marker of (self)-initiated (self)-repair of a preceding utterance, used to prevent misunderstandings, (c) elaboration, clarification, expansion, explanation, or reformulation of the preceding utterance, (d) a voluntary marker of "imprecision," an expression of "*like*-ness," (e) non-equivalence, where what the speaker says and what he has in mind are not well matched, (f) presenting a "further instance" where the general is made more specific, (g) summing up ("the point is"). The following example illustrates the reformulation use of *yæ'ni*:

(15)   Persian (Noora and Amouzadeh 2015, (4))
     yâdæm   nemiyâd   kæsi   in   hæme
     memory.1.SG   NEG.IMP.come   person this all

     bâhâm hærf zædeh   baŝe   yæ'ni,
     to.me   talk   beat.3SG be.SUBJ.3.SG meaning

     behem   tævædʒoh   kærde   baŝ.
     to.me   attention   do.PAST.3.SG   be.SUBJ.3.SG
     "(Sana says to her mother): I can't remember anyone has talked to me so much, in other words, who gave me so much attention."

Turkish *yani* and Swahili *yaani* exhibit similar functions. The former is used in particular to place constraints on the interpretation of the referent in the preceding constituent, to present summaries, results, expansions, or to strengthen a proposition (Ruhi 2009: 288).

Speaker–hearer interaction. But these DMs also serve the interaction among interlocutors, helping to "increase, establish, or restore harmony between interlocutors functioning for an interactive, cooperative, hearer-oriented and intersubjective purpose" (Noora and Amouzadeh 2015: 98). And one of the functions of Persian *yæ'ni* is to regulate relations between speaker and hearer, being used as a softener or "compromiser" to lessen the assertive force, or as a mitigator. And it is also used for politeness to encode "the speaker's appreciation and recognition of the addressee's social status" (Noora and Amouzadeh 2015).

In a number of its uses, such as the following, Turkish *yani* stimulates the
addressee to re-conceptualize the referent of the preceding noun phrase:

(16)   Turkish (Ruhi 2009: 295, (16))
         ... *mafyayla,* **yani** *bir ülkenin iliğini kemiğini sömürerek para kazanan*
         insanlarla ...
         "... with the mafia, **that is**, with people who gain money by ripping off a
         country to its bones ..."

Attitudes of the speaker. Finally, the borrowed DMs also involve functions
relating to the attitudes of speakers. For example, among the functions of
Persian *yæ'ni* there is one "expressing the speaker's subjective attitude toward
the relevant information or the addressee," e.g.,

(17)   Persian (Noora and Amouzadeh 2015, (13))
         Ali: *bæĉæ-m   diŝæb   tæb-e   bædi   dâŝt.*
         child.my last.night fever. EZ   bad   have.PAST.3.SG
         "My child had a severe fever last night."

         Mother: *væ   xânum.-et   **yæ'ni**   pæræstâr-eh!*
                  and woman-EZ.2.SG   meaning   nurse.is
         "And your wife is a nurse, indeed!"

Similarly, both Turkish *yani* and Swahili *yaani* may create an emotive effect
on the interpretation of the referent in the preceding constituent (Ruhi
2009: 288).

To conclude, the functions of borrowed DMs, such as those derived
from Arabic *yaa'ni* discussed in this section, are complex, they can be
described in terms of a network of the components text organization,
speaker–hearer interaction, attitudes of the speaker, and the relations holding among these components. Which of the components is highlighted is
contingent on the context in which the marker is used. In the case of the
markers borrowed from Arabic *yaa'ni*, text organization is highlighted,
figuring at least to some extent in all the uses of these markers. An
important question that cannot be answered at the present stage of research
is to what extent the various discourse functions discussed were there
already in Arabic prior to borrowing or else arose independently in the
languages concerned.

7.5   Conclusions

The main goal of the chapter was to test the generalization proposed at the
beginning of the chapter, namely that the way in which interlocutors design

new DMs by exploiting the pool of discourse options available to them is similar across languages. The observations made in this chapter can be taken as support of this generalization. However, interlocutors are not necessarily restricted to the resources of their own language; rather, they also may and commonly do draw on the resources available in other languages for this purpose, using cooptation in the former but borrowing in the latter case. Based on a crosslinguistic-typological perspective rather than language-internal reconstruction, the chapter showed that the general path of development described in Chapters 3–6 is not the only one in which DMs may arise; rather, language contact provides an important alternative pathway. The chapter thus contributes to a more comprehensive understanding of the behavior of DMs.

The DMs described in the preceding sections must, with few exceptions such as the ones mentioned in Section 7.1, have been transferred straight from language A to language B, and once they have entered B they usually exhibit the grammatical properties of DMs. And the functions they express appear to be of the same kind as those of DMs not having a record of pronounced language contact, like those described in Chapters 3–6, but more research is needed on this issue.

As the scenario of development depicted in (1a) shows, grammaticalization is an important determinant of the history of DMs. It may or may not affect an expression prior to its cooptation, but once cooptation has taken place, grammaticalization shapes the particular form and functions of the evolving DM. In the case of DMs arising in language contact, by contrast, its role is far from clear (cf. the scenario in (1b)). These DMs have been borrowed in language B ready-made from language A and their prior history is presumably of little import to speakers of language B. There is hardly any information on the role played by grammaticalization in their ensuing development in language B. Most likely, context extension and functional diversification are involved in this development, as is suggested in particular by the insightful description of the Persian DM *yæ'ni* by Noora and Amouzadeh (2015), but more research is urgently required on this issue.

One reason why DMs are so frequently taken from one language and inserted in texts of another language can be seen in their formulaic nature and, more specifically, in their "detachability" (Matras 2009: 193–97). DMs and other theticals, such as interjections, formulae of social exchange, and frozen imperatives are as a rule syntactically unattached, prosodically set off, and not a semantic part of sentence structure. They thus contrast with words or constituents of sentence grammar, such as noun phrases, verb phrases, etc., which are syntactically, prosodically, and semantically integral parts of sentence structure, functioning as predicates, arguments, etc. Accordingly, compared to the latter, DMs are technically much easier to manipulate and to integrate in another language.

In their grammatical structure, DMs used in bilingual interaction do not differ essentially from the DMs that were discussed in Chapters 3–6. For example, the analysis by de Rooij (2000) shows that French DMs borrowed in Shaba Swahili of the Democratic Republic of the Congo are syntactically detached from the rest of the utterance, usually preceded and followed by Shaba Swahili material, and they are also prosodically set off, in that they "tend to be preceded and/or followed by pauses and produced with a characteristic high–low falling or low falling pitch contour"; de Rooij (2000: 455) found that 84.3 percent of the uses of the eight French DMs *alors*, *bon*, *donc*, *et puis*, *mais*, *non*, *parce que*, and *puisque* in Shaba Swahili were accompanied by pauses and/or prosodic cues.

If there is a difference between the DMs looked at in the preceding chapters and those discussed here beyond their contrasting origin then it might concern their function. Observations made in the preceding sections, especially in Section 7.3.3, suggest that a DM arising in language contact tends to remain psychologically linked in some way to its donor language: Its use may evoke cultural and/or emotional features believed to characterize the donor language community. It is therefore not surprising that some authors portray borrowed DMs as signaling "emblematic switches" (Poplack 1980: 614) or "backflagging" (Muysken 2013), but more research is needed on this issue.

The present chapter was not meant to do justice to the rich literature that exists on borrowing and code-switching. There are many questions that could not be answered, either because of lack of sufficient information or because the questions are beyond the immediate concern of the chapter, which was with the nature of the use of DMs in and as a consequence of language contact. One problem concerns the distinction between borrowing and code-switching, which is notoriously controversial yet which is crucial for exactly understanding the mechanism underlying language processing in bilingual interaction (but see also Poplack 2018). Another problem to be addressed in future research is whether there are more general principles of discourse management that guide interlocutors in deciding on DMs rather than using other material when structuring their linguistic discourse.

8   Discussion

The present chapter is reserved for issues that surfaced in previous chapters but for some reason or other could not be discussed there in any detail. We saw in Chapters 1 and 2 that DMs exhibit a set of peculiar grammatical properties but, as was also pointed out there – especially in Section 2.4 – they are not the only linguistic categories exhibiting such properties. In Section 8.1 it is argued that this observation has some wider implications for the status of DMs, namely that linguistic discourse has a dualistic organization. Section 8.2 then is devoted to the factors that induce speakers to draw on cooptation to structure their discourses.

Our interest in the preceding chapters was with providing an account of some major lines in the development of DMs, ignoring more restricted patterns. There are in particular two topics that did not receive the kind of attention they deserve, namely the rise of constituent anchored DMs and the role played by imperative expressions as a source of DMs. These topics are looked at in more detail in Sections 8.3 and 8.4, respectively. Finally, in Section 8.5 we will deal with the fringes of the DM domain and more specifically with what tend to be referred to as fillers or hesitation markers.

8.1   Dual Process Models

In the introduction to this book, DMs were defined as having a metatextual function ((7) of Section 1.1.2; see also (40) of Section 1.5), and we saw in Section 2.4 that DMs are not the only linguistic category having such a function.[1] The term "metatextual" implies that, in addition to a "textual" level there is a second level of discourse processing. In fact, we saw in Section 2.4 that in the framework of discourse grammar a basic distinction is made between two levels or domains, namely between sentence grammar and thetical grammar, where the former relates to textual and the latter to metatextual functions of discourse processing.

---

[1] As observed in Section 1.1.2, the term "metatextual" stands in more general terms for a statement whose topic is the text itself (see Genette 1982; Witosz 2017: 108).

But discourse grammar is not the only framework exhibiting such a distinction. In the course of the past decades, a range of other frameworks – or models – have been proposed to argue for a dualistic organization of linguistic discourse. The models, summarily referred to as dual process models, assume in some form or other that linguistic discourse can be analyzed with reference to a distinction between what is described by Heine (2019) and Heine et al. (2020) as one between a microstructure and a macrostructure of discourse, where the former corresponds to sentence grammar and the latter to thetical grammar.

Microstructure is based on knowledge of the propositional–semantic format of text pieces expressing events, states, or relations, most commonly taking the form of sentences, clauses, or phrases. Macrostructure, by contrast, is based on the communicative intents of the speaker and on knowledge of discourse processing at large, relating the text to the situation of discourse. The two structures complement and interact with one another, both being needed for successful linguistic communication.

A related distinction surfaces, for example, in neurolinguistic research on processing (Van Lancker Sidtis 2009; 2012), in linguistic work on syntax (Debaisieux 2007; 2018; Deulofeu 2017), on performance (Clark 1996; Clark and Fox Tree 2002), on discourse analysis (Van Dijk 1980; Johnstone 2002; Haselow 2017), on discourse grammar (Kaltenböck, Heine, and Kuteva 2011; Heine et al. 2013), on speech-act formulas (Pawley 1992; 2009), on bilingualism (Maschler 1994; 2009), on text comprehension (e.g., Gernsbacher, Varner, and Faust 1990; Prat, Long, and Baynes 2007), on written discourse (e.g., Hyland 1998; 2017), or on pragmatics (Cap 2011).

These studies have been discussed in more detail in Heine (2019); suffice it to illustrate the distinction with an example not mentioned in Heine (2019), namely that of work on metadiscourse (e.g., Hyland 1998; 2005; 2017; Ädel 2006; Mauranen 2010; Zhang 2016; see also Section 1.1.2). Using data from written discourse such as academic writing, Hyland (1998), for example, proposes a distinction between propositional discourse (microstructure) and metadiscourse (macrostructure). The latter deals with "discourse about discourse," it is defined by Hyland thus (where "writer" and "reader" correspond to "speaker" and "hearer," respectively, in the framework of discourse grammar):

Metadiscourse refers to aspects of a text which explicitly organise the discourse, engage the audience and signal the writer's attitude ... Its role in establishing and maintaining contact between the writer and the reader and between the writer and the message also makes it a central pragmatic concept. (Hyland 1998: 437)

There seem to be few restrictions on the linguistic shape that metadiscourse units may take. They include linguistic expressions consisting of particles, words, phrases, clauses, as well as reduced phrases and clauses. And they include in the same way units of sentence grammar (e.g., *my purpose is, you can see that*) and theticals (e.g., *in addition, thus*; Hyland 2017: 20). Paradigm examples of metadiscourse units serving the organization of texts are what is called "phoric markers" (e.g., *above, following, first*), "discourse labels" (e.g., *aim, answer, speak*), and "code glosses" (e.g., *namely, i.e.*) (see Ädel 2006: 98; Zhang 2016: 2005–6).

The significance of metadiscourse lies in its role of explicating a context for interpretation, "making linguistic choices which that audience will conventionally recognise as persuasive" (Hyland 1998: 438). The concept of "metadiscourse" is compatible with most of the other approaches on the macrostructure of discourse, relating the text to the situation of discourse, that is, to (a) the organization of texts, (b) the attitudes of the speaker, and (c) speaker–hearer interaction.

The distinction between microstructure and macrostructure is not only supported by evidence from a wide range of data and different research traditions, it is also supported by neurolinguistic findings: Some of the studies mentioned show that there is a clear correlation between discourse processing and brain activity relating to the lateralization of the human brain (Heine, Kuteva, and Kaltenböck 2014; Heine et al. 2015; Haselow 2019; Heine 2019). This correlation has been summarized in the following way: Whereas the microstructure implicates mainly left hemisphere activity, building a macrostructure of discourse is a task that cannot be achieved without participation of the right hemisphere (Heine et al. 2015: 15; Heine 2019: 434).[2] Capabilities associated with activity in the right cerebral hemisphere appear to be essential for building a macrostructure of discourse, involving in particular the interrelated tasks in (1):

(1)   Some capabilities strongly associated with right hemisphere activity (Heine 2019: 426–33; see also Haselow 2019)
       a To construct a coherent model for a text,
       b to provide instructions on how to interpret the text, and
       c to relate the text to the situation of discourse.

DMs are linguistic expressions functioning on the level of macrostructure (e.g., Heine, Kuteva, and Kaltenböck 2014; Heine et al. 2015; Haselow 2019; Heine 2019), serving the three metatextual tasks mentioned in (1). Accordingly, they are hypothesized to show the same neurolinguistic behavior as other expressions serving macrostructural functions and, as Haselow

[2] Maj-Britt Mosegaard Hansen (personal communication of January 24, 2020) asks whether this is a matter of degree, and the answer is clearly in the affirmative (see Heine et al. 2015; Heine 2019).

(2019) demonstrates, there is in fact some neurolinguistic evidence in favor of this hypothesis. Analyzing the frequency of occurrence of turn-initial DMs by means of experimental data on the spontaneous speech of unilaterally brain-damaged speakers of English, Haselow found significant differences between left-hemisphere damaged and right-hemisphere damaged speakers in that the latter used distinctly fewer DMs than the former. He takes this observation to lend support to findings suggesting that an unimpaired right hemisphere is strongly associated with processing on the level of macrostructure.

This is an important generalization, converging with observations made in Heine, Kuteva, and Kaltenböck (2014; see also Heine et al. 2015); nevertheless, more neurolinguistic data are needed to define the role played by DMs in lateralization-related brain activity.

8.2 What Serves As the Input of Cooptation?

We observed in Section 8.1 that microstructure (sentence grammar) and macrostructure (thetical grammar) complement and interact with one another. One salient form of interaction was a central topic of the preceding chapters, namely cooptation, whereby a chunk of sentence grammar, such as a word, a phrase, a reduced clause, or a full clause, is deployed for use on the metatextual level of discourse monitoring (see (8) of Section 2.3). This raises the question of which "chunks" exactly qualify for cooptation.

A comprehensive answer to this question would need a separate study and the observations made in this chapter are more of an impressionistic nature – for an obvious reason: There are so far no appropriate quantifiable data on which crosslinguistic generalizations could be built. The purpose of this section therefore is first and above all to point out topics that are in need of further investigation.

We will be dealing with factors that induce people to design new DMs and with factors that might be conducive for cooptation in Section 8.2.1. Section 8.2.2 will then be concerned with the kind of text segments that are picked for cooptation, and Section 8.3 will remind us that there are also limits to cooptation.

8.2.1 What Motivates the Rise of DMs?

There is little information on what motivates speakers to introduce new DMs. Obviously, motivations involved in spoken language are presumably not the same as in writing, and this is true for the DMs employed. Furthermore, there are indications suggesting that DMs occur more frequently in informal than in formal situations.

It would seem that specific socio-cultural situations can be conducive to the rise of DMs, and such situations can also involve written language use. In South Korea of the early twentieth century, a new genre of pre-modern novels arose, called *sinsosel* "new novel" and written between 1894 and 1917. The *sinsosel* literary genre, being influenced by Western literary styles, bridged the gap between classical novels and modern novels. It was the first Korean literary genre to use colloquial language, and it would seem that this fact contributed to the emergence of new kinds of DMs.[3] For example, Korean has a set of DMs expressing agreement, marking consensus or agreement with what the previous speaker has said, such as *kulem* ("if it is so"), *amwulyem* ("if it is whatsoever") and *kulenikka* ("because it is so") (Rhee 2015: 10, 15). Most of these DMs date back exactly to the period of *sinsosel* in the early twentieth century, which appears to have provided a favorable environment for designing such new DMs.

A different kind of socio-cultural situation appears to have contributed to the rise of the Early Modern English DM *marry*. Arising as what appears to be a vocative use in the context of religion it is first attested in the second half of the fourteenth century, going back to the name of Virgin Mary used as an oath or an invocation. In the sixteenth century *marry* freed itself of the religious context, becoming a mere interjection, having DM functions in certain contexts, no longer being perceived as a religious invocation. By the nineteenth century its use became obsolete (Jucker 2002: 227).

Socio-cultural factors seem to be important; for a succinct overview of research on sociolinguistic factors influencing the development and use of DMs, see Fedriani and Sansò (2017: 20–22; see also Jucker and Taavitsainen 2000, as well as the contributions in Pons Bordería and Loureda Lamas 2018). But they are not the only ones that may be instrumental to the rise of new DMs. A survey of the relevant literature suggests that there are a number of other factors that might also be held responsible for a text segment to be eligible to being picked for transfer to the metatextual level of discourse, namely those listed in (2).

(2)   Factors that might be conducive to cooptation
        a Recurrent use,
        b Suitability for expressing specific discourse functions, and
        c Morphosyntactic status.

We will now look at each of these factors in turn.

(a) *Recurrent use.* Arguably the most attractive factor that one may wish to think of as contributing to the selection of text segments for cooptation is frequency of use: Expressions occurring time and again in speech or

---

[3] Maj-Britt Mosegaard Hansen (personal communication of January 24, 2020) suggests that it seems considerably more plausible to assume that this was simply the first written genre in which these DMs could be felicitously used.

written texts are likely to have relatively high discourse salience and therefore to be picked easily for deployment as metatextual units, eventually turning into DMs.[4]

There is in fact a bit of evidence to this effect, even if that evidence is not based on quantitative data. For example, Waltereit (2002: 988; 2006: 68) proposes the notion "overuse," or being employed "abusively" to account for the rise of DMs.[5] Accordingly, with regard to the imperative form *guarda!* "Look!" of Italian he observes:

[... it came to be] used more and more frequently because it provided speakers with an excellent justification for self-selection at turn-taking, even at non-transition-relevance places. The result of this strategical overuse was the reanalysis of the imperative as a DM with the function "Listen to me, I have something important to say!" (Waltereit 2002: 988)

There are in fact a number of examples indicating that frequency of use might have been a contributing factor for cooptation. For example, that the temporal adverb *icey* "now" of Korean gave rise to the emergence of the DM *icey* is possibly due to the fact that the adverb already served as a frequently used connective on the level of sentence grammar (Sohn and Kim 2008: 200). Thus, with its cooptation, *icey* simply shifted from the level of sentence grammar to that of discourse processing.

Overall, however, the evidence for frequency of use as a motivating factor does not seem to be compelling. Take the example of the Japanese noun *jijitsu* "fact" that was discussed in Section 5.2.5. Arising in the nineteenth century as a unit of sentence grammar in a nominal predicate construction ("it is a fact (that)"), it took about nine centuries for *jijitsu* to emerge as a thetical and DM ("in fact"). During all this time, *jijitsu* was used sparingly, also when cooptation must have taken place in the late nineteenth or early twentieth century, and the DM never attained the frequency of use of the sentence grammar expression *jijitsu*, from which it is historically derived (Shibasaki 2018: 337). Thus, high frequency of use does not appear to have been a contributing factor in the rise of the DM *jijitsu*.

(b) *Suitability for expressing specific discourse functions.* It would seem that in order to encode some specific discourse function, speakers browse through their repertoire of grammatical constructions in search of an expression that would be most conducive to conveying that function. In

---

[4] We are grateful to Alexander Haselow (personal communication of May 20, 2019) for having drawn our attention to this observation.

[5] Richard Waltereit (personal communication of February 7, 2020) notes that he owes this interpretation to Ulrich Detges, who uses it in a number of his publications.

fact, in a number of studies it is argued that it is first and above all the suitability of a text segment for expressing some particular discourse function that determines its selection, possibly also the rise of a DM.

For example, Claridge (2013: 170) observes that there were already early uses of the English text segment *so to speak* in sentence grammar, such as (3), which carried a meaning very similar to the distancing and hedging function of the DM *so to speak* that arose in the seventeenth century (see Section 3.2.10, *so to say/so to speak*). What this situation might suggest is that certain uses of the sentence grammar unit turned out to have provided an option that may have been semantically most conducive for deployment as an expression for a discourse function on the metatextual level.

(3)   English (a1640, J. Ball Answ. to Can. I (1642) 101, OED); Claridge (2013: 170, (14a))
        *The Conformists (I use that Word because you are pleased **so to speake**.)*

In a similar way, the rise of the English DM *well* may have been facilitated by the availability of suitable text segments of sentence grammar, inviting an interpretation with reference to specific discourse functions. Simon-Vandenbergen and Willems (2011: 652) observe that *well* as an adjective, as in *that is well*, or as an adverb with the meaning "in accordance with a good or high standard," contained a positive core of approval which may have played a role in recruiting *well* as a DM in Middle English.

(c) *Morphosyntactic status.* There are at least some observations suggesting that (c) can play a role as a motivating factor. A number of case studies indicate that main clause segments seem to be favored over segments from subordinate clauses. For example, the segments picked for the cooptation of English *I think*, *I admit*, etc. appear to have been uses of these expressions as main clause predicates taking first person singular subject referents. In a similar way, the selection of the Japanese noun *jijitsu* "fact" was apparently influenced by its use as part of the main clause predicate of the sentence (see Section 5.2.5).

But there are also data that are not in support of such a generalization. First, rather than main clause segments, text segments to be coopted can be, and not uncommonly are, also taken from subordinate clauses, as we will see in Section 8.2.2.[6] Second, and even more importantly, a common source for cooptation is provided by adverbs, English *well* being a case in point. Having the function of arguments or adjuncts of a clause, adverbs do not seem

---

[6] We are grateful to Laura Brinton (personal communication of January 20, 2020) for feedback on this point.

to have a highly prominent discourse status in a clause. Yet on the basis of what we know about the development of DMs crosslinguistically, adverbs seem to provide the most frequent source for DMs. It is locative adverbs ("there") and, even more commonly, temporal adverbs meaning "now" or "then" that have been recruited and developed into DMs in languages across the globe. English has contributed *now* and *then*, French *alors* "now, then," Italian *allora* "then, at that time," Spanish *entonces* "then, therefore, thus," etc. (e.g., Stolz 2007; Borreguero Zuloaga 2018); see Section 8.2.2 for more details.

And third, coopted chunks can also be recruited from morphosyntactically complex text segments that do not form grammatically defined units. Striking examples are provided most of all by the rise of some Japanese DMs (see Section 5.2). For instance, the DM *dakedo* appears to have been coopted from a text piece consisting of the clause-final conjunctive *kedo*, a bound form having a contrastive function attached to a verb or adjective, and the copula or linking verb *da* (or *d*) to which this conjunctive was frequently agglutinated (Onodera 1995: 415–22).

In sum, it is hard to find a morphosyntactic denominator common to all or most of the text segments recruited for the cooptation of and subsequent development into DMs. An interesting hypothesis is proposed by Traugott (in press b, section 4.3; personal communication of January 19, 2020) according to which the rise of new DMs could be influenced by morphosyntactic changes in the structure of a language. Note that the development of so many DMs and discourse management markers in the sixteenth and seventeenth centuries correlates with the fact that during this period English experienced remarkable systemic syntactic change.

To conclude, the overall evidence for identifying motivations for the selection of text segments of sentence grammar to be recruited for cooptation is far from satisfactory, and more research is needed on this issue. A question to be looked into in such research is, for example: Are there certain social groups of speakers or genres of texts that may play a special role in the creation of DMs?

For example, analyzing the text frequency of 20 DMs in the Southern Nilotic language Akie of north-central Tanzania, Heine, König, and Legère (2017: 159–60) found that men not only show a higher rate of DM tokens but also distinguish a larger number of types of DMs. The authors found that some DMs were restricted to male, others to female speakers. And there is a clear difference between descriptive texts, such as procedural and biographical descriptions, on the one hand, and fictional narrative texts, on the other: The former are distinctly richer in the occurrence of both tokens and types of DMs, and there are also some DMs that appear in the former but not in the latter, and vice versa.

However, whether such observations allow for any generalizations beyond the people and the language examined and, more importantly, whether they are of any value for contributing to our understanding of what motivates people to create new DMs remains an open question.

8.2.2   The Expressions Coopted

There is an old hypothesis, to be traced as far back as Wackernagel (1897: 21–27), according to which DMs are the result of diachronic processes, having "main clauses" as their source (see Schneider 2007b: 38). As we saw in Section 8.2.1, however, the situation is more complex in that in addition to main clauses there are a variety of other text segments serving as the input for cooptation, and these segments include not only main clauses but also subordinate clauses (see later in this section). For Fraser (1988: 24; 1990: 388), for example, the main historical sources of English DMs are provided by verbs, adverbs, adjectives, conjunctions, interjections, prepositional phrases, and (elliptical) clauses.

An even more impressive list of sources is provided by Brinton (2017: 13–23). Distinguishing a number of syntactic pathways leading to the development of DMs (pragmatic markers in her terminology), she proposes the following main sources for DMs:

(a) Adverbial sources (e.g., *indeed, after all*),
(b) Main-clause-like comment clauses (e.g., *you know, I think*),
(c) Adverbial comment clauses (e.g., *as you know, as I can see*), and
(d) Nominal relative comment clauses (e.g., *that is to say > that is, what is more*).

While the classifications just mentioned are limited to the development of English DMs, Table 8.1 provides a catalog of sources that appear to be cross-linguistically widespread. The source constructions listed in Table 8.1 merely represent the tip of the iceberg of all the types of expressions that may serve as the input for cooptation. In this table, only a few examples are provided to illustrate each of the types of sources distinguished. DMs are for the most part presented without meaning glosses, for the following reason: DMs are typically highly polysemous and it is in many cases hard, if not impossible, to determine which of the meanings or functions can be assumed to be the "basic" or the "core," or the "underlying" one – if there is one at all. Details on the meanings or functions of the DMs listed can be found in the references in the last column of the table. Source expressions are listed alphabetically.

Table 8.1 shows that there is a wide range of text segments that are recruited for cooptation in the development of DMs, and it is hard to find a common denominator for all of them.

It would seem that there are two main sources that can be expected in some form or other to give rise to uses as DMs in a given language, namely temporal

Table 8.1 *Common source expressions of DMs*

Text segment	Example of source expression	DM	References
Adverb	E. *well*	E. *well*	(Jucker 1993; 1997)
	G. *bloß* "only"	G. *bloß*	(Auer and Günthner 2003)
	K. *ceki* "over there"	K. *ceki*	(Park 2001)
Adverbial phrase	E. *in dede* "in action"	E. *indeed*	(Traugott 1995: 8)
	Latin *ad illam horam* (or *illa hora*) "at that hour"	F. *alors*, I. *allora*	(Degand and Fagard 2011)
Affix	K. *i-cey* "this time" > *icey* "now"	K. *icey*	(Kim and Lee 2007)
	K. *-tul* (nominal plural suffix)	K. *tul*	(Rhee 2018d: 223)
Clause, conditional protasis	E. *if you like, if you will*	E. *if you like, if you will*	(Brinton 2017: 23)
Clause, infinitival	E. *so to speak*	E. *so to speak*	(Claridge 2013: 177)
Clause, (reduced) main	E. *I think (that), you know (that)*	E. *I think, you know*	(Kaltenböck 2010)
	G. *ich meine* "I mean"	G. *(ich) mein(e)*	(Auer and Günthner 2003)
	K. *sasilun* "the fact is"	K. *sasilun*	Seongha Rhee, personal communication
Clause, negative	E. *there is no doubt*	E. *no doubt*	(Davidse, De Wolf, and Van linden 2015)
Clause, relative	E. *that is to say*	E. *that is*	(Brinton 2017: 23)
Clause, non-finite subordinate	E. *that having been said, that being said*	E. *that said*	(Brinton 2017: 23)
Clause marker, relative	G. *wobei* "where"	G. *wobei*	(Auer and Günthner 2003)
Clitic	J. *-ga*, connecting enclitic	J. *ga*	(Matsumoto 1988: 2)
Complex segment	J. *V-te + mo*, unit-final expression	J. *demo*, sentence-initial DM	(Onodera 1995: 404; 2004; V = verb)
Conjunction, coordinating	G. *und* "and"	G. *und?*	(Auer and Günthner 2003)
Conjunction, subordinating	G. *weil* "because"	G. *weil*	(Auer and Günthner 2003)
Demonstrative	E. *thus*	E. *thus*	(Traugott and Dasher 2002: 180)
Hortative	K. *eti poca* "where, let's see"	K. *eti poca* "well, let's see"	(Rhee 2020a)

245

Table 8.1 (*cont.*)

Text segment	Example of source expression	DM	References
Ideophone	K. *kaman*, ideophone for quietness	K. *kaman*	(Seongha Rhee, personal communication of August 25, 2019)
Imperative	E. *listen!, look!*	E. *listen, look*	(Brinton 2017: 23)
	Hebrew *tir'i* "look"	Hebrew *tir'i*	(Maschler 1994)
	G. *komm!* "come!"	G. *komm*	(Auer and Günthner 2003)
Negation marker	K. *anita* ('not:be') "no"	K. *ani*	(Rhee 2003; Koo 2008)
Noun (phrase)	J. *wake* "reason"	J. *wake*	(Suzuki 1998: 2006)
Preposition	E. *like*	E. *like*	(Romaine and Lange 1991; Streeck 2002; D'Arcy 2017)
Pseudo-cleft	E. *what I am saying is*	E. *what I am saying*	(Brinton 2017: 23)
Question, polar	E. *do you see?, do you hear?*	E. *see, hear*	(Brinton 2017: 23)
	K. *iss-ci?* "does (it) exist?"	K. *iss-ci?* "Look!"	(Rhee 2004: 414)
	Akie *arisowé íra?* "have you seen today?"	Akie *arisowéira*	(Heine, König and Legère 2017: 153)
Question word	E. *what else?, why?*	E. *what else, why*	(Brinton 2017)
	K. *eti/mwe* "where?," "what?"	K. *eti, mwe* "well," mitigating DMs	(Rhee 2004: 416)
Verb	L. *precor* "(I) pray, beg"	I. *prego* "please"	(Ghezzi and Molinelli 2014: 62)
	Romanian *mă rog* "I ask (for)"	Romanian *mă rog*	(Livescu 2014)
Vocative noun	Mexican Spanish *güey* "ox"	Mexican Spanish *güey, wey*	(Kleinknecht and Souza 2017)
	G. *Alter* "old man"	Colloquial G. *alter, alla*	(Kleinknecht and Souza 2017)

Note: E. = English, F. = French, G. = German, I. = Italian, J. = Japanese, K. = Korean, L. = Latin, P. = Portuguese, S. = Spanish.

246

adverbs for "now" and/or "then," and imperative forms of perception verbs for "look," "see," and "listen" (for the latter source, see also Section 8.4). Note that both sources are deictic in nature, referring to the here-and-now of the situation of discourse in which they are employed. In the course of their grammaticalization into DMs, they lose their lexical semantics in favor of discourse structuring functions, turning from temporal deictics into discourse deictics (Levinson 2006) or indexicals (Aijmer 2002; Furkó 2014: 292).

In the San language !Xun, spoken by traditional hunter-gatherers in south-western Africa, the DM *kūndò'à*, derived from the adverb *kūndò'à* "there, then," is used by some speakers in almost every sentence in tale telling as a marker of text cohesion, appearing six times in the following example, taken from a tale of the jackal and the hyena, cf. (4).

(4)   !Xun (W2 dialect, Kx'a ("Northern Khoisan"); Christa König, personal communication; König and Heine 2019)

tà	*/àālè*	***kūndò'à***	*g/ù-ā*	*hä*	*tà*	*/àālè*	***kūndò'à***	*kwèé* ...
and	jackal	DM	refuse-T	NC1	and	jackal	DM	say
kūndò'à	*má*	*kāhɳ́*	***kūndò'à***	*n!hàè*	***kūndò'à***	*úkā*	*hä*	*kē*
DM	TOP	when	DM	lion	DM	where	NC1	PAST
ú	*tcāō*	*má*	*hä*	*má*	*ú*	*hòhò*	*dàbà*	*kā*
far.away	awake.SG	TOP	NC1	TOP	far.away	find	child	and
dàbà	***kūndò'à***	*kwàlā.*						
child	DM	be.absent						

"But the jackal refused [the hyena] and said: ... Then, when the lion awoke, he realized that the child was not there."

Table 8.2 provides examples of temporal adverbs in a range of languages; for a survey of perception verbs, see Table 8.4 of Section 8.4.

As we saw in Section 7.2 (Tables 7.1 and 7.2), DMs derived from deictic temporal adverbs are not only found within a given language; rather, they are also commonly transferred to other languages in situations of language contact.

Other kinds of adverbs are also found, though less frequently, among the sources for DMs, in particular manner adverbs and demonstratives, like English *thus*, German *so* "thus, so," or Japanese *sate* "thus, in that way" (Traugott and Dasher 2002: 180), and evaluative adverbs, like English *well*, Spanish *bién* "well," or Persian *khob* "well" (Mohammad Amouzadeh, personal communication),

One may wonder why there is no segment "adjective" among the sources for DMs in Table 8.1. In fact, in some cases it appears to be adjectives rather than adverbs that were recruited. This applies, for example, to the French adjective *bon* "good" (Hansen 1998a), and the history of the English DM *right* might ultimately be traced back to the Old English adjective *riht* "straight, not bent" rather than to the adverb *riht-e* "straight; in a direct course or line" (Méndez-Naya 2006: 147). Compared to adverbs, however, adjectives would seem to be a rare source of DMs.

Table 8.2 *Deictic temporal adverbs as sources for DMs in some languages*

Language	Adverb	DM	Source
Akie	kɔrtɔ "now"	kɔrtɔ	(Heine, König, and Legère 2017: 153)
	koto "then"	koto	(Heine, König, and Legère 2017: 153)
	ɪra "today"	ɪra	(Heine, König, and Legère 2017: 153)
Denjongke	t'a "now"	t'a	(Yliniemi 2019: 134)
	tɛ "then, so"	tɛ	(Yliniemi 2019: 134)
English	now	now	(Aijmer 2002)
	then	then	(Haselow 2011)
Finnish	nyt "now"	nyt	(Hakulinen 1998)
French	alors "now, then"	alors	(e.g., Degand and Fagard 2011)
	puis "then"	puis	(e.g., Dostie 2009)
Portuguese	então "then"	então	(Ghezzi 2014: 25)
Lingala	ébóngó "now, then"	(é)bóngó	(Nzoimbengene 2016: 18)
Italian	allora "then, at that time"	allora	(Stolz 2007)
Korean	icey "now"	icey	(Kim and Lee 2007)
Persian	hala "now"	hala	(Mohammad Amouzadeh, personal communication)
Spanish	entonces "then, therefore, thus"	entonces	(Stolz 2007; Borreguero Zuloaga 2018)
Swahili	sasa "now"	sasa	(own data)
!Xun	kūndò'à "there, then"	kūndò'à	(König and Heine 2019)

Another fairly common source is provided by imperative expressions. They differ from many other expressions in that their development into DMs does not involve cooptation. We will therefore deal with them in a separate section (Section 8.4).

Furthermore, DMs in a number of different languages can be reconstructed back to both word questions and polar questions. An example of the former, namely English *what else*, was discussed in Section 3.2.12. With regard to polar questions, it seems that most frequently it is rhetorical questions or question tags that may turn into DMs, and there seems to be a common pathway of grammaticalization leading from expressions for rhetorical questions to DMs. Thus, the questions expressed in the following examples from Korean have given rise to DMs serving as discourse initiators, both translated by Rhee (2004: 414) with "Look!":

(5)   Korean rhetorical questions (Rhee 2004: 414, (1))
       a *iss-ci?*
          exist-Q
          "Look!" (Lit. Does (it) exist?)

Table 8.3 *Korean insubordinate DMs*

Sentence grammar source	Literal meaning	DM	Approximate meaning
amu-lye-ha-myen anything-ADVZ-be-if	"if (it is) whatsoever"	*amwulyem*	"Right!"
ku-le-ha-myem that-ADVZ-be-if	"if (it is) so"	*kulem*	"Right!"
kuleha-nikka be.so-because	"because (it is) so"	*kulenikka*	"Right!"

(Rhee 2015: 11)

    b *iss-c-anh-a?*
       exist-NF-NEG-Q
       "Look!" (Lit. Doesn't (it) exist?)

Perhaps surprisingly, there is one category in the list of sources in Table 8.1 that one might expect to be represented more pronouncedly, namely that of verbs. For example, Ghezzi and Molinelli (2014: 2) conclude that, side by side with adverbials, verbal expressions constitute privileged sources for DMs in Romance languages. In fact, verbs figure in some form or other fairly prominently among the sources of DMs in many languages. The reason for their poor representation in Table 8.1 is that they are listed as parts of other grammatical categories, like imperatives or (reduced) main clauses.

On the other hand, the list contains also two somewhat unexpected kinds of expressions, namely insubordinate clauses, on the one hand, and clitics and affixes, on the other. Insubordinate clauses, like English *if you will*, are prima facie subordinate clauses without corresponding main clauses (Evans 2007; Heine, Kaltenböck, and Kuteva 2016; Kaltenböck 2016). These are for the most part, though not only, conditional protasis clauses, that is, *if*-clauses without apodosis main clauses. A list of Korean DMs to be traced back to insubordinate clauses is found in Table 8.3.

English examples include the pragmatic markers *as it were*, *if you will*, and *if you like* of Claridge (2013) or the indirect elliptical *if*-clauses of Brinton (2014), belonging to the larger set of forms called "disjunct adverbial clauses" by Espinal (1991: 726–27), "supplements" by Huddleston and Pullum (2002: 1350), or "adverbial clauses/clausal adjuncts" by Kaltenböck (2007: 30). An example is provided in (6).

(6)   English (BNC FMP: 718; Claridge 2013, (1a))
        *newts seem to be **as it were** very choosy in where they er go, bearing in mind*
        the existence of at least three other ponds in Skelton, . . .

The second unexpected kind of expressions concerns clitics and affixes. Waltereit (2006: 76) notes that "syntactic independence (or any other property) of the source construction as such is not a requirement for recruitment to a DM," and it would seem in fact that morphological independence is not a requirement either. Text segments to be recruited for cooptation, as a rule, honor word boundaries, being, e.g., words, phrases or (reduced) clauses. But there are exceptions. First, we saw in Section 5.2.4 that the Japanese DM *ga* was coopted from the clause-final clitic -*ga*, a form that is part of a paradigm of Japanese enclitic particles connecting two clauses of a sentence and occurring in clause-final position of the first clause (Matsumoto 1988: 2).

And second, there is at least one example suggesting that DMs can also be derived from affixes. As we saw in Section 6.2.4, the source of the Korean DM *tul* is the nominal plural suffix -*tul*. While the suffix itself can be traced back to the Old Korean noun *tAl(h)* "others (of a similar kind)" or "these (just listed)," Rhee (2018d: 223) demonstrates that it was not the noun but rather the suffix which provided the source for the emergence of the DM.[7]

According to Waltereit (2006: 76), items of any word class can acquire uses as DMs. Table 8.1 shows that the range of possible source expressions is even wider: The text segments recruited for cooptation include both main clauses without subordinate clauses and subordinate clauses without main clauses, conjunctions without conjunct clauses and conjunct clauses without conjunctions, they also include all major speech acts, that is declaratives, interrogatives, and imperatives, and they are not restricted to free forms.

8.2.3   Possible Constraints

Considering the enormous diversity of text segments that can serve as a source for DMs it would seem that speakers are fairly unconstrained in their selection of expressions for metatextual functions of text monitoring. The only conceivable factors that might constitute constraints on cooptation are the ones in (7).

(7)   Possible constraints on the choice of sources for discourse markers
  a The text segment must be such that it can be accepted by the hearer as a relevant contribution to the interpretation of the discourse concerned.
  b It need not be and frequently is not syntactically and semantically complete as long as the meaning of the missing part is recoverable from the situation of discourse (the "context").
  c The text segment typically honors word boundaries but this is not a requirement.

---

[7] Maj-Britt Mosegaard Hansen (personal communication of January 24, 2020) draws attention to the fact that the phonetic level can also be involved. For example, epenthetic schwa in Parisian French functions much as something like a DM.

One may wonder, however, what the actual significance is of the generalizations in (7). (7a) is deliberately phrased in a fairly general format. In spite of all the seminal work that has been done on this issue by students of Relevance Theory, there still are many open questions (see Schourup 1985; 1999; 2001; 2011; Blakemore 1987; 1988; 2002; 2007, Ifantidou-Trouki 1993; Unger 1996). As long as it remains largely unclear what empirical significance exactly the phrasing "can be accepted by the hearer as a relevant contribution" has, (7a) is not very helpful.

(7b) alludes to the fact that text segments recruited as DMs frequently consist of parts of clauses or sentences and, hence, tend to be referred to as "elliptical" expressions.

(7c) is based on the observation that paradigm instances of documented DMs have been coopted from text segments of sentence grammar that are separated from surrounding linguistic material by word boundaries. As we saw in Section 8.2.2 with reference to the Japanese DM *ga* and the Korean DM *tul*, however, word boundaries are by no means an obstacle for cooptation.

Fedriani and Sansò (2017: 17) rightly observe that it is more difficult to identify restricted pools of sources and recurrent scenarios across languages in the case of DMs than it is in grammaticalization. To be sure, the pool of sources to be found in grammaticalization is larger than is widely believed (see Kuteva et al. 2019); nevertheless, both the number and the kind of source expressions are highly constrained in grammaticalization, as noted in Section 2.2: There are for the most part only a few sources from which a grammatical category can historically be derived. Such constraints are absent in cooptation and, accordingly, there are few limits to what can serve as a source for the development of DMs: Speakers seem to be fairly free in drawing on the resources available in sentence grammar when creating new expressions for metatextual processing.

That speakers are in fact fairly free in their choice of source expressions can be illustrated perhaps most succinctly with the following examples from Korean and Japanese. As Seongha Rhee (personal communication of August 11, 2020) demonstrates, there was a Korean construction of the kind presented in (8a) that was responsible for the rise of the DM *hana* "but," illustrated in (8b).

(8)　　Korean (Seongha Rhee, personal communication of August 11, 2020)
　　　a *ku-lul　　salangha-na　naysayk-ul　　an　　ha-n-ta.*
　　　　he-ACC　　love-**but**　　display-ACC　not　do-PRES-DEC
　　　　"(She) loves him, but (she) does not show it."

　　　b *ku-lul　　salangha-n-ta.　　**hana**　naysayk-ul　　an　　ha-n-ta.*
　　　　he-ACC　　love-PRES-DEC　　**But**　display-ACC　not　do-PRES-DEC
　　　　"(She) loves him. But (she) does not show it."

Rhee (personal communication) argues convincingly that the connective adverbial *hana* in (8b), which is analyzed here as a DM in accordance with our definition in (7) of Section 1.1.2, can be traced back historically to the combination *-ha* and *-na* in (8a), printed in bold. The element *-ha* is a light verb meaning "do, say, be" suffixed to the noun *salang* "love," while *-na* "but" is a clause-final connective particle. This combination changed into the expression *hana* in (8b), occurring sentence-initially as an independent word that connects independent sentences. What appears to have happened on the way to the rise of the DM *hana* is that *-ha* was clipped off from the word *salangha* and combined with the particle *-na* to create an independent connective.

Thus, the source expression for the DM in this example was neither a word nor a phrase nor a clause but rather a chunk consisting of the combination of a part of a word plus a particle, and the two were merged to create a new "word." This chunk did not honor word boundaries, nor presumably morpheme boundaries – note that speakers may not even be aware of the grammatical function of the erstwhile light verb *-ha* occurring in words like *salangha-na* in (8a) or *salangha-n-ta* in (8b).

This case might seem peculiar or even unique; as a matter of fact, however, it is not. First, *hana* is not the only Korean DM that arose in this way; rather, there is a range of other discourse connectives that underwent the same kind of development, namely *haciman* "but," *hani* "so," *hantey* "but," *hataka* "if" (now obsolete), *haye* "so," etc. (Seongha Rhee, personal communication; Rhee 1996). And second, there are a range of items in Japanese that appear to have gone through essentially the same process from morphosyntactically disparate clause-final chunk to sentence-initial DM. Two Japanese examples of this kind were discussed in Chapter 5, namely *dakedo* (Section 5.2.1) and *demo* (Section 5.2.2). By way of illustration, we are restricted here to a brief summary of the development of the latter; for a detailed analysis, see Onodera (1995; 2000; 2004).

The sentence-initial discourse connective *demo* "but" of Japanese is historically derived from the complex clause-final chunk [V-*te* + *mo*] (or [V + *de* + *mo*]) "but," where V was a verb, *-te* (or, more likely, *de*) was a copula or predicative marker with a quite general meaning, marking the gerundive form of the verb, and *mo* was a clause-final adversative particle "but" (see Onodera 2004: 213, figure 7.9). The change from the latter complex to *demo* took place presumably around the mid-sixteenth century, when the clause-final chunk [-*te* + *mo*] (or [*de* + *mo*]) must have been coopted to give rise to the form *demo*. The change may have been facilitated by the fact that when *-te* (or *de*) merged with *mo* it had "pro-predicate" function referring to some part of the preceding discourse (Noriko Onodera, personal communication of September 8, 2020). With the shift, *demo* changed from clause-final to sentence-initial expression, from adversative connective between clauses to connective between sentences or even larger discourse units, and it subsequently acquired a number of new DM functions.

Ignoring minor details, the overall process appears to have been much the same: Speakers recruited a morphosyntactically disparate chunk consisting of two elements occurring at the end of the first of two clauses, where the first element was cut off from the preceding word and the second a connective particle. And the result of the process was also the same, namely the emergence of a new, invariable DM used mainly but not only for text organization beyond the sentence.

An explanation of this phenomenon, to be observed in two different languages, is urgently required but would need to be based on a larger corpus of historical text data in the critical periods when the relevant changes in Korean and Japanese took place. Such data are presently not available. But here we are restricted to the question of whether there are constraints on what can serve as a source for the creation of new DMs, and it would seem in fact that the two examples just presented can be taken to lend support to the generalization proposed in (7c), namely that text chunks recruited for cooptation may cut across word boundaries, and conceivably even morpheme boundaries.

8.3   Constituent Anchored Discourse Markers

Among the grammatical changes typically associated with cooptation, as listed in (9) of Section 2.3, two are seemingly problematic, namely that cooptation leads from restricted to wider semantic–pragmatic scope (9e) and from positionally constrained to less constrained placement (9f).[8] These generalizations are in need of qualification. In Heine et al. (2017: 823), a distinction is made between utterance anchored and constituent anchored coopted units (theticals), where semantic–pragmatic scope relates, respectively, to either the utterance as a whole or to some part of it.[9] Constituent anchored theticals usually have phrasal scope (Kaltenböck 2008; 2009: 52; 2013); they operate over one segment of the host utterance rather than the utterance as a whole. This constituent is typically a noun phrase, or an adverbial phrase, or even a clause within a sentence. And the scope may even be restricted to a single word (Furkó 2014: 294; see also Van Bogaert 2011: 325, fn. 1).

Constituent anchored DMs are most commonly placed immediately before their host constituent, although they may also follow it. For example, the DM *if*

---

[8] Concerning "semantic–pragmatic scope," see Sections 1.3.2 and 1.4.5.
[9] In addition, there are two further types, which need not concern us here, namely context anchored coopted units having a host, and context anchored coopted units without a host (Heine et al. 2017: 823).

you like precedes its host constituent *of tribes* in (9), while in (10) the DM follows its host *middle-aged*.

(9)   English (Walter Bagehot, 1872; Claridge 2013: 174, (22b))
       *As I have said, I am not explaining the origin of races, but of nations, or, **if you like**, of tribes.*

(10)   English (1909 W. H. Hudson *Afoot in Eng*. ii.20, OED; Claridge 2013: 174, (22d))
       *"What!" I exclaimed. "Lady Y –: that funny old woman!" "No – middleaged," he corrected ... "Very well, middle-aged **if you like**."*

Our interest in this book was mainly with utterance anchored DMs: They seem to constitute the majority of DM uses and the generalizations we proposed apply exclusively to them. But DMs quite commonly show both kinds of uses. There is, however, some evidence to suggest that the historical development of the two is not the same, and in the remainder of this section we will be concerned with this evidence.

Our first example concerns the English DM *I mean*. Early attestations of *I mean* provided by Brinton (2008: 119–20) date back to the end of the fourteenth century, and they are utterance anchored. Thus, *I mean* (*I mene*) in (11) appears to have scope over the utterance rather than over one of its constituents.

(11)   English (1392–1400; Chaucer, *The Canterbury Tales*; Brinton 2008: 127, (28c))
       *Medleth namoore with that art, **I mene**, / For if ye doon, youre thrift is goon ful clene.*
       ["meddle no more with that art, **I mean**, for if you do, your success will be gone completely"].

Unequivocal examples of constituent anchored *I mean*, used in an appositional, self-repair or mistake-editing sense, do not occur until the Early Modern English period in the seventeenth century (Brinton 2008: 121). Thus, in example (12), the writer uses *I mean* (*I meane*) as a constituent anchored marker to replace the incorrect word *use* by its antonym *abuse* (Brinton 2008: 121).

(12)   English (1653 Robinson, *Certain Proposals in Order to a new Modelling of the Laws* 1 [LC]; Brinton 2008: 120, (16c))
       *The chiefe use, **I meane** abuse, of Oaths, is as afore I have said in our Courts of Justice.*

The second example concerns the DM *if you will* (cf. Section 3.2.5). The data provided by Brinton (2008; 2017: 168–71, (8), (9)) suggest that it was essentially an utterance anchored thetical in Old and Middle English. Instances of constituent anchored *if you will* can only be found much later in the modern period from the mid-sixteenth century onward. Thus, example (13) from a seventeenth century text suggests that *if you will* is anchored in and has scope over the noun *Quatrumvirate* rather than the whole utterance, in that the "landing site" of the thetical seems to be provided not by a sentence but rather by a noun phrase.

(13)   English (1684 Goddard, *Plato's Demon; or the State-physician Unmaskt* 53 [*OED*]; Brinton 2017: 171)
         *The whole Triumvirate, or **if you will**, Quatrumvirate are included.*

A third example is provided by the English DM *no doubt*, which occurs in a number of different constructions (see Section 3.2.8). As the reconstruction by Davidse, De Wolf, and Van linden (2015) shows, utterance anchored *no doubt* of the DM, with scope over the sentence as a whole, arose in Middle English in the period between 1350 and 1420. Its function was to express either certainty, or less than full certainty. In Late Modern English (1710–1920), the use of *no doubt* was extended to contexts where its semantic–pragmatic scope was restricted to one constituent of the sentence – that is, where it acquired uses as a constituent anchored DM in specific contexts. Thus, Davidse, De Wolf, and Van linden (2015: 49) argue that in (14), *no doubt* focuses mainly the adverbial *in part* rather than the utterance as a whole.[10]

(14)   English (CLMETEV, 1847 Cottle, *Reminiscences of Samuel Taylor Coleridge and Robert Southey*; Davidse, De Wolf, and Van linden 2015: 49, (53))
         *She [Mrs. Hannah More] is, indisputably, the first literary female I ever met with. In part, **no doubt**, because she is a Christian.*

Such cases of change of utterance anchored DMs to also allow for constituent anchored uses do not seem to be restricted to English. As the reconstruction work by Hansen (2005a; 2005b) suggests, the French temporal adverb *enfin* (lit. "at last") gave rise to the thetical *enfin* toward the end of the sixteenth century of Middle French,[11] with *enfin* acquiring uses as a synthetizing and listing marker (e.g., "at last") around the end of the sixteenth century. Now, Hansen (2005a: 65, fn. 7) points out that she found no early examples of "listing" *enfin* as a constituent anchored expression, that is, uses of the DM marking only "sub-clausal units" seem to have evolved only in a later phase of development (see Section 4.2.5).

On the basis of the little evidence presented here it would be premature to postulate any general directionality. Note that there is also one case where a DM appears to have been restricted to constituent anchored uses from its

---

[10] Elizabeth Traugott (personal communication of January 19, 2020), however, disagrees with this interpretation of scope range.

[11] Note, however, that Hansen (2005a; 2005b) does not refer to *enfin* as a "discourse marker."

beginnings in the first half of the nineteenth century, namely English *if you like* (see Section 3.2.4).

The three cases mentioned are presumably results of late grammaticalization (see Section 2.5.2.1), that is, they involve changes following cooptation, when the use of DMs was extended to new contexts allowing for an interpretation with reference to only restricted semantic–pragmatic scope. These cases are of more general interest, for the following reasons. On the one hand, they lead to scope reduction. And on the other hand, they also lead to a decrease in syntactic variability: Utterance achored DMs are typically fairly flexible in their placement in the sentence. Constituent anchored DMs, by contrast, are restricted to placement immediately before or after the constituent providing the anchor.

To conclude, it remains unclear how exactly the kind of scope reduction looked at in this section is to be accounted for. More data beyond the few cases examined here are needed to establish whether in fact we are dealing with a more general pattern in the development of DMs.

8.4   Imperative-based Discourse Markers

We saw in Section 8.2 that DMs derived from second person imperative forms, in short, imperative-derived DMs, are crosslinguistically fairly common (e.g., Lamiroy and Swiggers 1991; Brinton 2001; Waltereit 2002; Fagard 2010). It is especially imperative forms of perception verbs for "look," "see," and "listen" that tend to be recruited for discourse structuring purposes, such as calling for the addressee's attention, emphasizing thematic progression and/or enabling or facilitating turn-taking (Fagard 2010; see also Lamiroy and Swiggers 1991).[12] In fact, English expressions like *look, listen,* etc. have been described as serving discourse organizing functions typical of DMs (Takahashi 2012). Table 8.4 provides examples from a number of different languages.

Crosslinguistically, imperatives exhibit a wide range of structures, and our concern here is restricted to "canonical imperatives," that is, positive singular imperatives addressing a singular referent as a hearer (or reader or signee), expressing commands or requests directed at the hearer, and being non-finite and short forms (cf. Aikhenvald 2010: 18). Canonical imperatives, like English *go!, wait!,* can be observed in many, but by no means all languages of the world; they usually have the thetical properties listed in (15).

---

[12] Elizabeth Traugott (personal communication of January 12, 2020) points out that there is no evidence that "look" arose in imperatives in the way suggested by Waltereit (2002) for Italian *guarda*.

Table 8.4 *Canonical imperatives of perception verbs as sources for DMs in some languages*

Language	Verb	DM	Source
Akie	*suwɛ-n* "look (ye)!"	*suwɛn*	(Heine, König, and Legère 2017: 153)
Catalan	*mira* "look!"	*mira*	(Fagard 2010)
Dutch	*kijk* "look!"	*kijk*	(Fagard 2010)
English	*listen*	*listen*	(Brinton 2017: 23)
	look	*look*	(Brinton 2017: 23)
French	*regarde* "look!"	*regarde*	(Fagard 2010)
French	*écoute donc!* "so listen!"	Quebequian French *coudon*	(Dostie 2004)
Galician	*mira* "look!"	*mira*	(Fagard 2010)
	olla	*olla*	(Lamiroy and Swiggers 1991; Fagard 2010)
Italian	*guarda* "look!"	*guarda*	(Waltereit 2002: 984)
	senti! "listen!"	*senti*	(Fuschi 2013)
Lingala	*tálá* "look!"	*tálá*	(Nzoimbengene 2016: 71)
Portuguese	*olha* "look!"	*olha*	(Lamiroy and Swiggers 1991; Fagard 2010)
Polish	*patrz* "look!"	*patrz*	(Fagard 2010)
Romanian	*uite* "look!"	*uite*	(Fagard 2010)
Spanish	*mira* "look!"	*mira*	(Goria 2017)

(15)   Thetical properties characterizing canonical imperatives (cf. Fagard 2010; Heine 2016b: 249–52)

   a Meaning: The meaning of bare imperatives is not normally part of the meaning of sentences they may be associated with, even if they can be interrelated, e.g., by means of coreference.

   b Function: Their function is metatextual, that is, rather than in the structure of a text they are immediately anchored in the situation of discourse, and more specifically in speaker–hearer interaction.

   c Syntax: They have been portrayed as "syntactic orphans." Being unattached, they cannot normally be embedded in other clauses.

   d Prosody: They are set off prosodically from surrounding utterances.

   e Semantic–pragmatic scope: They have variable scope, but generally their scope extends over the situation of discourse in which they are used, more specifically over the relation between speaker and hearer.

   f Placement: Typically being stand-alones, they form utterances of their own, that is, they need no placement slot. But when grammaticalized into DMs they are flexible in their placement behavior depending on their discourse function.

The reason for treating imperative-derived DMs separately in this section is that their development differs from that of many other DMs in one important aspect: Imperatives are by definition theticals (Heine 2016b) on account of the

Table 8.5 *Variation in some Romance DMs derived from "look" imperatives*

	Singular		Plural	
	Informal	Formal	Informal	Formal
Spanish	*mira*	*mire*	*mirad*	
Catalan	*mira*	*miri*		*mirin*
Italian	*guarda*	*guardi*	*guardate*	
Romanian		*uite*	*uitați*	

(Waltereit 2002; Fagard 2010)

grammatical properties in (15) they typically exhibit.[13] Accordingly, their development into DMs, which at least some of them experience, no longer involves cooptation; rather, this development is essentially restricted to late grammaticalization (Section 2.5.2), whereby they gradually turn into text structuring devices.

Imperative-derived DMs have been particularly well described in Romance languages (e.g., Lamiroy and Swiggers 1991; Waltereit 2002; Fagard 2010) and one feature characterizing these DMs is that they show an alternation between two or even more variants based on differences in number and/or formality. However, neither the etymology nor the extent to which degrees of formality are conventionalized are the same in these languages, as Table 8.5 shows. The Italian DM *guarda* "look!" for example, has three variants, distinguishing formality in the singular but not in the plural (Waltereit 2002: 984). Excluded from the listing in Table 8.5 is the French imperative form *regarde!* "look!," which Fagard (2010) portrays as a weakly grammaticalized DM.

Paradigm processes of grammaticalization exhibited by imperatives developing into DMs, such as the Romance DMs presented in Table 8.5 are, in accordance with the parameters listed in Section 2.2.2 (see also Fagard 2010):

Context extension, whereby the imperatives are placed in specific contexts highlighting their potential as discourse structuring devices: Typically, imperatives are syntactic stand-alones whose use is extended to structure larger portions of discourse. For example, Waltereit (2002: 1000) interprets the development of imperatives like Italian *guarda!* as a case where "the imperative 'look!' invokes a higher-order 'force majeure' right that occasionally may justify an interruption."

---

[13] The hedge "typically" draws attention to the fact that there are a few exceptions to this generalization. For example, Maj-Britt Mosegaard Hansen (personal communication of January 24, 2020) rightly points out that examples such as the following are not in accordance with (14): *If you want me to help you, then be quiet and listen to what I say.*

Desemanticization means that the lexical meaning of a verb denoting "look" is backgrounded, in that there is a shift from one kind of speaker–hearer interaction, e.g., a command, to another ("I have something important to say that justifies interrupting you"). Desemanticization does not necessarily mean, however, that the semantics of the perception verbs concerned will be lost entirely; more likely some of the semantic features tend to be retained. For example, Brinton (2001: 181) found that all of the English imperative *look*-forms have retained some of their meaning (see also Fagard 2010).

Decategorialization leads to internal loss of morphosyntactic features. On the one hand, it concerns loss of the ability to take complements, such as patient arguments – a process that has apparently been concluded in most of the DMs surveyed by Fagard (2010: 12). In fact, the inability to take complements may be taken to be criterial for determining that an imperative form has changed into a DM. On the other hand, it involves the morphological structure of the verb, which changes, e.g., from inflected verb to some particle-like invariable form (cf. Waltereit 2002: 999).

Erosion, that is, loss of phonetic features, has been recorded sporadically in imperative-derived DMs. For example, when French *écoute donc* "so listen!" turned into a DM it was reduced to *coudon* in Quebequian French (Dostie 2004; Bolly 2014: 30). And English imperatives like *look ye/look thee* were reduced to *lookee*, or *say to me/say to us* to *say* (Brinton 2017: 30). But pronounced erosion does not seem to be highly widespread in imperative-derived DMs.

To conclude, the transition from the thetical category of imperatives to DM involves central parameters of grammaticalization. Imperative verbs have lexical content, they can be modified, and take arguments. Grammaticalization is most pronounced in the change from conceptual to procedural meaning (desemanticization) and from complement taking verb to unanalyzable particle (decategorialization), and weakest in the reduction of phonetic substance (erosion). However, many imperative-derived DMs that have been studied in some detail exhibit a continuum extending from weakly to strongly grammaticalized usages. Note, for example, that the Romance DMs listed in Table 8.5 have not (yet) been grammaticalized to the extent that they were reduced to one unalyzable form, in accordance with our definition of DMs in (7) of Section 1.1.2.

A general effect of desemanticization is that the conceptual meaning of a perception verb gradually gives way to functions relating to the organization of the text, speaker–hearer interaction ("intersubjectification"), and/or the attitudes of the speaker ("subjectification"). For all the Romance imperative DMs analyzed by Fagard (2010), these functions include (a) topic management, (b) evaluation by the speaker of what is said, and (c) discourse organization, such as turn taking. (a) can be illustrated with example (16) from Romanian (see also Waltereit 2002: 1001), where the speaker proposes a change in topic. An example of (b) can be seen in the function of English *look*-DMs of conveying, for example, the speaker attitude of impatience (Brinton and Traugott 2005: 138; Fagard 2010: 13).

(16)   Romanian (A. Ștefănescu, personal communication; Fagard 2010, (5))
        *Mie nu îmi plac mașinile. **Uite**, motocicletele sunt mai ieftine.*
        "I don't like cars. **Look**, motorcycles are cheaper."

More specifically, Waltereit (2002: 1001) argues that use of the Italian DM *guarda!* "look!" has at least five "side-effects" for the structure of discourse: First, a speaker change occurs and the imperative marks the boundary between two speakers in the overall sequence of discourse. Second, since the speaker now has the floor, the other conversation partners will believe that the speaker has something highly relevant to say. Third, the speaker has some time to think about the formulation of what s/he wants to say. Fourth, there is a topic shift, and the topic of the ensuing discourse will be one that the conversation partners have not touched upon in the preceding discourse. And fifth, the topic of the ensuing discourse is highlighted as particularly important and interesting.

With regard to the general theme of the present book, one of the main observations to be made in modern imperative-derived DMs is that they inherited most of the grammatical properties that they had as imperative theticals, namely those listed in (15) – that is, properties also observed in other thetical categories. There is, however, one noteworthy exception: Whereas imperatives are frequently stand-alones, forming utterances of their own, imperative-derived DMs, like other DMs, have some host within the text they are associated with, and while being strongly associated with the left periphery of a clause, many can also be inserted in various slots within a clause.

To conclude, imperative-derived DMs differ greatly from most other kinds of DMs that were discussed in the preceding chapters in that they start out as theticals and their subsequent development is restricted to grammaticalization, giving rise to a set of particular functions of discourse processing.

8.5   Fillers

Fillers, or hesitation markers or hesitators, are among the kinds of expressions that conform to our definition of DMs in (7) of Section 1.1.2:[14] They are (a) invariable expressions which are (b) semantically and syntactically

---

[14] The term "filler" must be distinguished from many other uses of the term for elements filling up gaps of some kind, as in syntactic theory, where it refers for example to the pre-posed element that fills in the gap in *wh*-movement constructions.

independent from their environment, (c) typically set off prosodically from the rest of the utterance in some way, and (d) their function is metatextual, being anchored in the situation of discourse and serving the organization of texts, the attitudes of the speaker, and/or speaker–hearer interaction.

Still, fillers received little attention in the preceding chapters, for the following reasons: First, their status as a grammatical category has been discussed controversially (see later in this section) and the concern of this book is most of all with "canonical" instances of DMs. And second, in many languages, including English, fillers are etymologically opaque, that is, their history is essentially unknown. Accordingly, in a book devoted to the history of DMs there is not really a place for them. The reason for nevertheless devoting this final section to them is that they exhibit a number of features that are of interest for more generally understanding the behavior of DMs.

English has a range of elements that have been classified as fillers (see O'Connell and Kowal 2008: 126–27) but there are two that are generally considered as paradigm exemplars of fillers, namely *uh* ([ʔə(:)]) and *um* ([ʔə(:)m]), usually transcribed *er* and *erm*, respectively, in British English (e.g., Biber et al. 1999: 1092; Clark and Fox Tree 2002; O'Connell and Kowal 2004; 2005; Tottie 2011; 2014; 2015; 2016; see also the contributions in Amiridze, Davis, and Maclagan 2010). Also called filled pauses (Maclay and Osgood 1959: 21), pause fillers, hesitation fillers, hesitation markers, hesitators, interjective hesitators, and the like, they form a crosslinguistically fairly common discourse-structuring device. The example in (17) illustrates the English filler *uh*, occurring three times in one utterance (cf. (16) of Section 2.4).

(17)   English (ICE-GB: s1b-075-68)
        *We did feel **uh** union council was two or three weeks ago when this was put to us that **uh** the increase from seven to sixteen **uh** was actually a very good idea.*

What is more, fillers are frequently borrowed in situations of language contact, as we saw in Section 7.3.2. The place of fillers in language use is characterized aptly by O'Connell and Kowal (2008: 127) thus:

Spontaneous spoken discourse just happens to be the only natural habitat of fillers; they can be found nowhere else in such abundance. The other side of this coin is the consistent finding that fillers are perhaps the most valid indicators of the genuine spontaneity of spoken discourse. The only occasion for fillers to be used in written discourse is the simulation of spontaneous spoken discourse in the written mode . . .

The goal of the present section is to determine the status of fillers with reference to what was observed on DMs in the preceding chapters. The term "filler," if taken literally, may be somewhat misleading since it does not very well reflect the functions that such expressions have. These functions have been associated in particular with monitoring the flow of the production of an utterance or, more generally, with progressivity of linguistic interaction. It is most of all the following functions, or tasks, that are mentioned in the relevant literature (e.g., Clark and Fox Tree 2002; Hansen 2005a; Hayashi and Yoon 2006; O'Connell and Kowal 2008: 127–29; Watanabe 2010; Tottie 2014; 2015):

(18)   Functions frequently associated with fillers in speech
   a Pause filling
   b Marking of hesitation and/or delay
   c Searching for what to say next, or prefacing a new conversational move
   d Correcting (e.g., self-repair)
   e Signposting speaker turns (turn-taking, turn-holding, turn-yielding)
   f Inviting the hearer to reply
   g Commenting on preceding discourse
   h Breaking the continuity with preceding discourse (e.g., topic change)
   i Preparing the hearer for what is going to happen next
   j Attracting attention or highlighting
   k Mitigating undesirable effects of the message
   l Being polite

Students of fillers differ greatly from one another in how to classify them, but the stances listed in (19) seem to be the ones surfacing most frequently in the relevant literature.

(19)   Common stances expressed on the classification of fillers
   a They are interjections (e.g., Biber et al. 1999: 1054; Clark and Fox Tree 2002: 76–80; Norrick 2009).
   b They are DMs (e.g., Hayashi and Yoon 2010: 43; Tottie 2011; 2014; 2015; 2016).

Which of the stances in (19) is more appropriate is contingent on the perspective and the definition one may wish to adopt. As we observed in Section 1.1.2, fillers conform essentially to our definition of DMs, and we follow Tottie (2014: 21) in adopting (19b), arguing that fillers ("UHMs" in Tottie's terminology) can actually serve the same functions as *bona fide* DMs such as *well, I mean, you know*, and *like*. Like "canonical" DMs, fillers are used to monitor the flow of the delivery of an utterance (Hayashi and Yoon 2010: 58) and, unlike interjections, both fillers and DMs are usually anchored in some piece of text, that is, they are not normally found as "stand-alones." The boundary between "canonical" DMs and fillers are frequently fuzzy, and one and the same expression not uncommonly serves both functions. For example, the DMs *t'a* and *tɛ* of the Tibetic language Denjongke of northeastern India can also do service as fillers, e.g., when the speaker is not yet sure what to say (Yliniemi 2019: 134).

While there is frequently no clear boundary between interjections and fillers either, O'Connell and Kowal (2004: 469–70; 2005: 571–72) and O'Connell,

Kowal, and Ageneau (2005) note that fillers need to be distinguished from interjections not only in their inability to occur as free-standing turns but also in their placement, in prosodic features, and in their lack of affective and emotional significance.

Properties relating fillers to DMs can be illustrated with the example of English *uh* in (20). Fillers are mostly a feature of spoken language but, as this example shows, they can also be observed occasionally in writing, and they may occur in headlines, as it does in (20).

(20)   English (*The Los Angeles Times*, December 17, 2009; Tottie 2015, (13))
        *Ashley Dupre: From prostitute-to-politicians to, **uh**, paid journalist*

With reference to the properties of DMs proposed in (40) of Section 1.5, the filler *uh* can be described as in (21).

(21)   Grammatical properties typically to be expected in fillers
        a   Meaning: Their meaning is not part of the sentence meaning – that is, the semantic content of the text piece in (20) would not change if *uh* were omitted.
        b   Function: Their function is metatextual, e.g., signaling ironic euphemism in (20).
        c   Syntax: They are not a syntactic constituent of the sentence in which they occur, they do not combine with other expressions in syntactic constructions (Clark and Fox Tree 2002: 99).
        d   Prosody: They are likely to be set off prosodically from the rest of the sentence, as is suggested, e.g., by the use of commas preceding and following *uh* in (20). O'Connell and Kowal (2005: 567) found no evidence that the English fillers *uh* and *um* occur typically between silent pauses, but according to Clark and Fox Tree (2002), they tend to be prosodically separated in some way from other parts of an utterance.
        e   Semantic–pragmatic scope: They have variable scope which relates to the here-and-now of the situation of discourse, in example (20) to the attitudes of the speaker. More specifically, *uh* in (20) is a constituent anchored DM (Section 8.3), that is, its immediate scope extends over the following noun phrase *paid journalist*.
        f   Placement: Depending on their discourse function they are highly flexible in their placement behavior. Not uncommonly they are inserted within a phrase, as in (20), where *uh* cuts across an adverbial phrase.

Crosslinguistic observations suggest that two kinds of fillers can be distinguished, namely primary and secondary ones – a distinction that has been made in a similar form for interjections (Ameka 1992; Norrick 2009). Primary fillers, such as English *uh* and *um*, are not transparently related to any units of sentence grammar, they are etymologically opaque. Secondary fillers by contrast have identical or similar expressions in sentence grammar, and all evidence that there is suggests that they are historically derived from the latter.

There are languages that are largely or entirely restricted to primary fillers, English (*uh, um*), Dutch (*uh, um*), German (*äh, ähm*), and French (*eu, euh, em, eh, oe, n, hein*) being examples of such languages (see Clark and Fox Tree 2002, Table 8.1).

Other languages again draw overwhelmingly or entirely on secondary fillers. The main sources of the latter are provided by demonstrative pronouns, question words, and adverbs. In the languages of East Asia it is demonstrative pronouns that appear to be the main source. Japanese uses the adnominal form of the distal demonstrative *ano* "that," Korean the adnominal forms of the medial (*ku*), the distal (*ce*), and the locative demonstratives (*ceki* "that (far away)"), and Mandarin Chinese speakers the proximal demonstrative (*zhe-ge*) and the distal demonstrative (*na-ge*) as common fillers. Thus, in the following example, Hayashi and Yoon point out that the Japanese demonstrative-derived filler *ano* has a function similar to English *um*:

(22)   Japanese (Hayashi and Yoon 2010: 43; excerpt only)
         iya   *konkai*   ***ano***   *hashittemo [. . .].*
         well   this.time   DEM   run:even.if
         "Well, this time, ***ano*** [= um], even if ((you)) run ((in a race)), . . ."

But there are also languages combining both primary and secondary fillers. Spanish appears to be such a language: As the data in Clark and Fox Tree (2002, Table 8.1) suggest, there are, on the one hand, the primary fillers *eh* and *em* and, on the other hand, secondary ones, namely *este* (< *este* "this") and *pues* (< *pues* "then"); see also Hansen (2005a) on French *enfin*, which was the subject of Section 4.2.5.

There is so far little historical information on the rise and development of fillers. Obviously, this applies most of all to primary fillers, which are not immediately accessible to historical reconstruction. Nevertheless, Tottie (2015) proposes the following developmental scenario for fillers ("UHMs") such as English *uh* and *um*:

I would propose that UHM operates on a gradient, originating in spoken language as a symptom of processing difficulty or need for planning time, and proceeds via uses as a pragmatic marker to occasional specialized and deliberate use as a signal with quasi-word status. As a word, UHM is then used in writing, where it can have meanings of ironic euphemism or polite disagreement, as well as others. (Tottie 2015: 43)

This is a plausible hypothesis but diachronic information is needed to verify the sequence of developmental stages postulated by Tottie (2015).

Secondary fillers, by contrast, are more readily accessible to reconstruction since they can be assumed to be historically derived from some units of sentence grammar, most commonly from demonstratives. Hayashi and Yoon (2010: 58) propose what they call "pragmaticization" as the process whereby grammatical items, such as adnominal demonstratives in East Asian languages, evolve into DMs ("pragmatic markers"). These markers lack the salient grammatical properties characterizing their etymological sources:

We suggest that, as a result of the pragmaticization of their function as discourse particles used to monitor the flow of the delivery of an utterance, hesitator demonstratives [i.e., fillers; a.n.] have lost several key features of demonstrative reference, such as referentiality and syntactic participation in the structure of an ongoing utterance. (Hayashi and Yoon 2010: 58)

The account by Hayashi and Yoon (2010) thus is by and large in accordance with what other authors call pragmaticalization, as we saw in Section 1.2.2. In fact, secondary fillers do not seem to differ substantially in their development from "canonical" DMs: They are the joint product of cooptation and grammaticalization. In accordance with what we observed in Section 1.5, effects of cooptation in fillers such as Korean *ceki* or Japanese *ano* can be summarized as in (23).

(23)   Grammatical changes hypothesized to characterize the cooptation of
        demonstratives as fillers
        a From meaning as locative or temporal deictics within the sentence to
           meaning outside the sentence
        b From function as nominal modifier or pronominal clausal participant to
           metatextual function
        c From syntactic constituent of the sentence to syntactically unattached
           status
        d From prosodically integrated to unintegrated or less integrated status
        e From semantic–pragmatic scope within a noun phrase or a clause to wider
           scope
        f From positionally constrained to largely unconstrained placement

By being transferred from demonstrative unit of sentence grammar to filler, the item concerned loses its ability to participate syntactically, resulting in more distributional freedom.

For example, Japanese *ano* as a distal demonstrative of sentence grammar contributes to the sentence meaning and is restricted to the syntactic environment of a nominal constituent, often in a slot directly before the head noun. But as a filler it is not part of the sentence meaning, it can appear anywhere in an utterance, and it does not behave as a grammatical item at all in the sense of participating in the morphosyntactic structure of the utterance-in-progress (Hayashi and Yoon 2010: 58, 59).

The notion of pragmaticization of Hayashi and Yoon (2006; 2010) comes close to what in the framework of Discourse Grammar is called cooptation. These authors observe, for example, on Japanese *ano* and other fillers:

[They] do not behave as grammatical items at all in the sense that they do not participate in the morphosyntactic structure of the utterance-in-progress. Rather, their occurrences are motivated by pragmatic considerations such as monitoring the flow of the delivery of an utterance. (Hayashi and Yoon 2010: 59)

Once coopted, the expression concerned will undergo grammaticalization on the way to developing into a filler, turning from a conceptual into a procedural unit via context extension and desemanticization: Their use is extended to contexts where their semantic content gives way to new, discourse-specific functions. This appears to have happened in the development from coopted demonstrative to secondary filler in Korean and Japanese. For example, the locative form of the distal demonstrative *ceki* "that (far away)" of Korean has a spatial and a referential function and these functions were desemanticized and lost in the homophonous filler, giving rise to text structuring functions, now serving "to preface certain kinds of conversational moves that the speaker is about to launch into" (Hayashi and Yoon 2010: 58).

To conclude, the pathway leading from demonstrative or other expression to secondary filler is in accordance with the one that we observed in the development of "more canonical" DMs. This hypothesis, however, is in need of appropriate historical evidence, which is so far not available.

9   Conclusions

The main goal of the present book was to look for an answer to the following question: Why do discourse markers have the grammatical properties they have, such as the ones discussed in Sections 1.5 and 2.6?

On the perspective adopted in this book, language users are creative agents who may, and quite commonly do employ the linguistic resources available to them in novel ways. To this end they may extend the use of some expression to new contexts for specific cognitive–communicative purposes, gradually grammaticalizing that expression into another expression serving new functions. Alternatively, they may via cooptation extend the use of some element of sentence grammar to the metatextual level of discourse processing, resulting in some cases in the rise of new discourse markers.

While contrasting sharply with grammaticalization, cooptation is not a unique kind of operation. We saw in Section 2.3.1 that English word class conversion provides a structurally similar case – for example, when speakers transfer nouns (e.g., *email*) to be also used as verbs (*to email*). But whereas in word class conversion speakers switch their perspective from one part of grammar to another, in cooptation the switch is from one domain of discourse processing to another.

The authors of the book are all students of grammaticalization, having spent a larger part of their research reconstructing grammatical forms and constructions. But after approaching the study of discourse markers they became aware that grammaticalization theory reaches its limits when it comes to answering the question raised at the beginning of this chapter, and to understanding how discourse markers evolve. On the basis of the analyses presented in the preceding chapters, the general conclusion reached is the following: As was observed in Chapter 1, discourse markers as they are found in the languages of the world are mainly the joint product of two distinct mechanisms, namely grammaticalization, which accounts for most of their grammatical properties, and cooptation, which accounts most of all for the wealth of metatextual functions they express.

As also demonstrated by students of pragmaticalization, the rise of discourse markers cannot be reduced to grammaticalization (see Section 1.2.2). The account proposed here is in fact largely compatible with the pragmaticalization hypothesis but differs from the latter in two important aspects: First, rather than one unitary mechanism, the present account assumes that there are two distinct mechanisms involved, that is, cooptation followed by grammaticalization. And second, the pragmaticalization hypothesis has been designed essentially to account for the development of DMs. The cooptation hypothesis, by contrast, has a wider explanatory potential: It is based on a more extended perspective of discourse management – one that accounts not only for discourse markers but also for other kinds of metatextual grammatical categories, such as comment clauses, reporting clauses, non-restrictive relative clauses, as well as formulaic categories like interjections, formulae of social exchange, question tags, expletives, exclamatives, etc. (Heine 2013: 1217–19; 2018a: 32; see Section 2.4).

We saw in Section 2.3 that cooptation differs remarkably from grammaticalization, and this is also reflected in the kind of source expressions that each of the two mechanisms employs. Unlike cooptation, grammaticalization typically requires specific contexts to evolve, and both the number and the kind of source expressions are highly constrained. This means that there are as a rule only a few sources from which a given grammatical category can historically be derived (see Kuteva et al. 2019). Such constraints are not found in cooptation and, accordingly, there are hardly any limits on what can serve as a source for DMs. Thus, according to Table 8.1 of Section 8.2.2, DMs can be traced back to virtually any word category, such as nouns, verbs, adverbs, adpositions, demonstratives, adpositions, and conjunctions, to all kinds of full or reduced clausal structures, to all three major types of speech acts (declaratives, interrogatives, and imperatives), and their sources include even clitics and affixes.

Grammaticalization in discourse markers is essentially of the same kind as elsewhere – that is, it can be described in terms of the criteria presented in Section 2.2.2, and this applies in the same way to their early grammaticalization and their late grammaticalization (see Section 2.5.2 for this distinction). But being also the product of cooptation, discourse markers differ from other grammaticalizing material in fundamental ways; Table 9.1 highlights salient differences between the two in a simplified format (see also Table 2.2 of Section 2.5.1).

The contrasting effects of grammaticalization and cooptation can be illustrated with the following example. According to a crosslinguistically fairly common pathway of grammaticalization, main clause structures develop into subordinate clauses, whereby lexical material like nouns (e.g., "place," "time"), verbs (e.g., "say," "give"), demonstratives (e.g., "that"), etc. are grammaticalized into markers of clause subordination (Hopper and Traugott 2003: 184–90; Heine and Kuteva 2007: 236–61; Givón 2009; Kuteva et al.

Table 9.1 *Grammatical changes typically to be expected in grammaticalization and cooptation*

Feature	Grammaticalization	Cooptation
Semantic independence	Decrease	Increase
Functional independence	Decrease	Increase
Syntactic independence	Decrease	Increase
Prosodic autonomy	Decrease	Increase
Semantic–pragmatic scope	Within the sentence	Beyond the sentence
Freedom of placement	Decrease	Increase

2019). In contrast, rather than from main clauses to subordinate clauses, cooptation quite commonly has somehow the opposite effect, in that subordinate clauses can become syntactically and semantically independent expressions (Günthner 1999: 438; Heine, Kaltenböck, and Kuteva 2016; Kaltenböck 2016), English examples being provided by insubordinate discourse markers like *as it were*, *if you like*, and *if you will* (see Sections 3.2.4 and 3.2.5). As we saw in the course of the preceding chapters, the contrasting features described in Table 9.1 are due to the specific history of discourse markers, which can be characterized as one leading to transfer of linguistic material from the level of sentence grammar to that of discourse monitoring. As a result of this transfer, the expressions giving rise to discourse markers move outside the structure of a sentence and acquire functions that structure discourses rather than sentences. Accordingly, Waltereit portrays discourse markers thus:

Given that they are themselves syntactically independent and complete, they cannot contract syntagmatic relations that are dictated by categories of sentence grammar. (Waltereit 2002: 1007)

We observed in Section 2.1 that the framework used in this book includes both a diachronic and a typological perspective. In accordance with the general theme of the book, the former perspective constituted the basis of analysis, involving language-internal reconstruction work. The typological perspective was reserved for Chapters 7 and 8, where we were concerned with regularities in the behavior of discourse markers across languages. Combining the two different perspectives of analysis made it possible to provide a broader understanding in the study of discourse markers. At the same time, it also yielded two contrasting kinds of findings: The reconstructions presented in Chapters 3–6 are suggestive of language-internal developments. In Chapter 7, by contrast, we saw that there are also discourse markers having their origin in language-external factors: Discourse markers are quite commonly borrowed in situations of language contact, being transferred ready-made from one language to another.

Considering the language-specific character that discourse markers generally exhibit, this observation may seem surprising; as a matter of fact, however, it is not. Similar observations have also been made in other kinds of grammatical change. For example, grammaticalization processes commonly take place internally within a given language, but there is massive evidence to show that they can also be the result of external forces in situations of language contact (see, e.g., Aikhenvald 2002; Heine and Kuteva 2005). English has acquired a range of new grammatical forms via grammaticalization, developing its numeral for "one" into an indefinite article or the demonstrative *that* into a complementizer and relative clause marker. But it has also borrowed grammatical forms from Latin or later offsprings of it to form new grammatical categories, such as derivational prefixes like *ex-* and *de-* or suffixes like *-al* or *-ation*.

What this suggests is that, in spite of the specific features that characterize their rise and development, discourse markers do not behave substantially differently from other linguistic material used for expressing novel grammatical functions: Speakers commonly employ the resources that are available in their own language, but they may as well draw on material or concepts from other languages for this purpose. And as we saw in Chapter 7, language contact provides especially conducive conditions for the rise of new discourse markers.

The main concern of the book was with earlier states of language use. These states are no longer directly accessible and, hence, can be accessed only via hypotheses based on historical reconstruction. The extent to which such hypotheses capture features of earlier states of language use depends, on the one hand, on the database that is available. For the reconstruction of discourse markers, the database that could be used in this book was on the whole satisfactory. Nevertheless, there remain many gaps in it, which means that we frequently had to draw on hedges like "it seems" or "apparently" to bridge the gaps in the reconstruction of earlier states of the use of discourse markers.

On the other hand, it is also the quality of the hypotheses proposed that determines successful reconstruction work. Work on how discourse markers evolved has generated a range of hypotheses, the main ones of which were sketched in Chapter 1. These hypotheses are generally based on sound evidence, and they all have contributed greatly to our understanding of the rise of discourse markers. Nevertheless, the question is: Which of them is best suited to interpret and describe the historical processes leading to this rise?

No genuine evaluation of the hypotheses was attempted here (but see Heine 2018a). Rather, our interest was with accounting for the six salient grammatical properties listed in (40) of Section 1.5 that characterize discourse markers crosslinguistically, and with whether these properties can be explained with reference to what we know about their history. The general conclusion reached was that of all the hypotheses that there are, the one expounded in this book, called in short the "cooptation hypothesis," provides the most plausible explanation.

Taking Ockham's razor as a heuristic, this is not the most parsimonious hypothesis (cf. Heine 2019). To be sure, grammaticalization can be and has fairly successfully been accounted for in terms of a single mechanism for a wide range of grammatical phenomena. But discourse markers cannot reasonably be reduced to such an account, as is nowadays conceded even by some scholars that previously were strong proponents of the "all-grammaticalization hypothesis" outlined in Section 1.2.1.1 (Elizabeth Traugott, personal communication of March 29, 2020). As can be seen in the scenario depicted in (1), discourse markers are in fact shaped on the one hand by grammaticalization, like other grammatical markers such as tense and aspect markers, articles, conjunctions, adpositions, case markers, etc. But, on the other hand, they also require the mechanism of cooptation that enables them to take on the metatextual functions they have to monitor the flow of delivery of texts and to provide instructions on how to interpret the texts.

(1)   Hypothesized development of discourse markers (repeated from Section
        1.2.4; Heine 2018a: 41)
        (Grammaticalization >) cooptation > grammaticalization

Studies in grammaticalization have a long history, going back to the early nineteenth century. While the term "grammaticalization" was coined only in the twentieth century (Meillet ([1912] 1958), there was on the whole agreement on the general nature of this mechanism. Loss of grammatical autonomy (Lehmann 2004: 155), or discourse autonomy (Hopper 1991: 22), have implicitly or explicitly always been cornerstones of this research tradition, and the concept of unidirectionality is in some form or other an inherent part of most definitions of grammaticalization – a position also adopted in other research traditions devoted to the study of grammaticalization, such as Cognitive Grammar (e.g., Langacker 2011) or formal syntax (e.g., Roberts 1993; van Gelderen 1993; 2004; Roberts and Roussou 2003). Accordingly, when we observe in the development of discourse markers an increase rather than decrease of autonomy, as seems to uncontroversially be the case (see Table 9.1), then this observation is hard to reconcile with what grammaticalization is actually about. Extending the term to this kind of development would not only turn "grammaticalization" into a largely vacuous concept, roughly equivalent to "grammatical change," but it would also deprive it of its significance to capture a wide range of grammatical regularities and to serve as an important tool of historical reconstruction.

To be sure, the development of discourse markers also involves grammaticalization, but it cannot be reduced to it, as has also been demonstrated in the rich work on pragmaticalization: Grammaticalization theory reaches its limits when it comes to accounting for paradigm properties of discourse markers such as the ones listed in (40) of Section 1.5 and discussed in the preceding chapters. Notions of "wider" or "expanded" grammaticalization as they have been proposed in the preceding decades (see Section 1.2.1) have greatly informed our understanding of grammatical change, but they have also contributed to our awareness of the limits of grammaticalization as one of the main fields of historical linguistics that it has been in some form or other over roughly the last two centuries.

As we saw in Section 2.4, accounting for the properties of discourse markers requires a wider perspective of discourse processing, namely one that also includes other kinds of linguistic expressions showing these properties, namely thetical categories such as exclamatives (*How beautiful!*), expletives (*Good Lord!*, *shit!*), formulae of social exchange (*Good morning!*), vocatives (*Ladies and gentlemen!*), and the like (see Kaltenböck, Heine, and Kuteva 2011; Heine et al. 2013; 2017). Like discourse markers, they are the result of cooptation, having been transferred from the level of sentence grammar to the level of discourse management. Accordingly, they all share most of their properties with discourse markers, not only the thetical properties listed in Section 2.4 but also the fact that, first, they are immediately anchored in the situation of discourse (Heine et al. 2017), second, their functions are restricted to the here and now of that situation, third, they tend to have the appearance of "elliptical" expressions and, fourth, and for the purposes of the present book most important, their development cannot be explained exhaustively as being the result of grammaticalization.

The issues raised in the book concern only a small fraction of questions that a student of discourse markers may have, and many of those questions could not be addressed in the present study. Suffice it to mention one question that we notoriously ignored in the preceding chapters, namely whether or how discourse markers are related to the expressions from which they are historically derived, where "relationship" concerns the grammatical status of the expressions concerned. For example, do English discourse markers like *now*, *still*, *then*, or *well* belong to the same general grammatical category as the corresponding adverbs from which they are historically derived? This is an issue that has been discussed controversially and we have little to contribute to it, for the following reason: Our main interest in this study was with the historical development of discourse markers from their genesis to their present state. Accordingly, the implications that this development has for the synchronic structure of the languages concerned raises theoretical questions of grammatical and semantic taxonomy that are beyond the scope of the present study.

References

Abraham, Werner 1991. The grammaticization of the German modal particles. In Elizabeth Closs Traugott and Bernd Heine (eds.), *Approaches to Grammaticalization*, volume 2 (Typological Studies in Language, 19). Amsterdam: John Benjamins. Pp. 331–80.

Ädel, Annelie 2006. *Metadiscourse in L1 and L2 English*. Amsterdam: John Benjamins.

 2012. "What I want you to remember is...": Audience orientation in monologic academic discourse. *English Text Construction* 5, 1: 101–27.

Ahn, Mikyung 2012. A pragmatic role of Korean *maliya* in discourse. *Discourse and Cognition* 19, 1: 103–18.

Ahn, Mikyung and Foong Ha Yap 2013. Negotiating common ground in discourse: A diachronic and discourse analysis of *maliya* in Korean. *Language Sciences* 37, 1: 36–51.

Aijmer, Karin 1997. "I think" – An English modal particle. In Toril Swan and Olaf J. Westvik (eds.), *Modality in Germanic Languages. Historical and Comparative Perspectives*. Berlin: Mouton de Gruyter. Pp. 1–47.

 2002. *English Discourse Particles: Evidence from a Corpus*. Amsterdam: John Benjamins.

 2013. *Understanding Pragmatic Markers: A Variational Pragmatic Approach*. Edinburgh: Edinburgh University Press.

 2016. Pragmatic markers as constructions: The case of *anyway*. In Gunther Kaltenböck, Evelien Keizer, and Arne Lohmann (eds.), *Outside the Clause* (Studies in Language Companion Series, 178). Amsterdam: John Benjamins. Pp. 29–57.

Aijmer, Karin, Ad Foolen, and Anne-Marie Simon-Vandenbergen 2006. Pragmatic markers in translation: A methodological proposal. In Kerstin Fischer (ed.), *Approaches to Discourse Particles*. Amsterdam: Elsevier. Pp. 101–14.

Aijmer, Karin and Anne-Marie Simon-Vandenbergen 2003. The discourse particle "well" and its equivalents in Swedish and Dutch. *Linguistics* 41, 1: 1123–61.

 2009. Pragmatic markers. In Jan-Ola Östman and Jef Verschueren (eds.), *Handbook of Pragmatics*. Amsterdam: John Benjamins. Pp. 1–29.

Aikhenvald, Alexandra Y. 2002. *Language Contact in Amazonia*. Oxford: Oxford University Press.

 2010. *Imperatives and Commands* (Oxford Studies in Linguistic Theory). Oxford: Oxford University Press.

Ameka, Felix 1992. Interjections: The universal yet neglected part of speech. *Journal of Pragmatics* 18, 2–3: 101–18.

Amiridze, Nino, Boyd H. Davis, and Margaret Maclagan (eds.) 2010. *Fillers, Pauses and Placeholders* (Typological Studies in Language, 93). Amsterdam: John Benjamins.

Andersen, Gisle 2001. *Pragmatics Markers and Sociolinguistic Variation. A Relevance-Theoretic Approach to the Language of Adolescents* (Pragmatics & Beyond, New Series, 84). Amsterdam: John Benjamins.

    2014. Pragmatic borrowing. *Journal of Pragmatics* 67, 1: 17–33.

Andersen, Henning 2006. Grammation, regrammation, and degrammation. *Diachronica* 23, 2: 231–58.

Aoki, Hirofumi 2019. Setsuzokushi to bunpooka – Chusei kooki 'shoomono shiryou' o chuushin ni [Conjunctions and grammaticalization – With special focus on the Late Medieval "Shoomono data"]. *Paper presented at the Workshop on Grammaticalization (GJNL-4)*, Tohoku University, 2019.

Arroyo, José Luis Blas 2011. From politeness to discourse marking: The process of pragmaticalization of *muy bien* in vernacular Spanish. *Journal of Pragmatics* 43: 855–74.

Asher, Nicholas 2000. Truth conditional discourse semantics for parentheticals. *Journal of Semantics* 17: 31–50.

Auer, Peter 1996. The pre-front field position in spoken German and its relevance as a grammaticalization position. *Pragmatics* 6: 295–322.

Auer, Peter and Susanne Günthner 2003. Die Entstehung von Diskursmarkern im Deutschen – ein Fall von Grammatikalisierung? *Interaction and Linguistic Structures* 38: 1–30.

    2005. Die Entstehung von Diskursmarkern im Deutschen – ein Fall von Grammatikalisierung? In Torsten Leuschner, Tanja Mortelmans, and Sarah De Groodt (eds.), *Grammatikalisierung im Deutschen* (Linguistik – Impulse & Tendenzen 9). Berlin: Walter de Gruyter. Pp. 335–62.

Backus, Angus 1996. *Two in One: Bilingual Speech of Turkish Immigrants in the Netherlands*. Tilburg: Tilburg University Press.

Baker, Opal Ruth 1980. *Categories of Code Switching in Hispanic Communities: Untangling the Terminology* (Sociolinguistic Working Papers 76). Austin: Southwest Educational Development Laboratory.

Barth-Weingarten, Dagmar and Elizabeth Couper-Kuhlen 2002. On the development of final *though*: A case of grammaticalization? In Ilse Wischer and Gabriele Diewald (eds.), *New Reflections on Grammaticalization*. Amsterdam: John Benjamins. Pp. 345–61.

Bax, Stephen 2011. *Discourse and Genre: Analysing Language in Context*. Basingstoke: Palgrave Macmillan.

Beeching, Kate 2016. *Pragmatic Markers in British English*. Cambridge: Cambridge University Press.

Beeching, Kate and Ulrich Detges (eds.) 2014. *Discourse Functions at the Left and Right Periphery: Crosslinguistic Investigations of Language Use and Language Change*. Leiden: Brill.

Beijering, Karin 2012. Expressions of Epistemic Modality in Mainland Scandinavian: A Study into the Lexicalization–Grammaticalization–Pragmaticalization Interface. Dissertation, Rijksuniversiteit Groningen, Groningen.

Bell, David M. 2009. Mind you. *Journal of Pragmatics* 41: 915–20.

Berk-Seligson, Susan 1986. Linguistic constraints on intrasentential code-switching: A study of Spanish/Hebrew bilingualism. *Language in Society* 15: 313–48.

Biber, Douglas, Stig Johansson, Geoffrey Leech, Susan Conrad, and Edward Finegan 1999. *Longman Grammar of Spoken and Written English*. London: Longman.

Blakemore, Diane 1987. *Semantic Constraints on Relevance*. Oxford: Blackwell.

1988. *So* as a constraint on relevance. In R. Kempson (ed.), *Mental Representation: The Interface between Language and Reality*. Cambridge: Cambridge University Press. Pp. 183–95.

1996. Are apposition markers discourse markers? *Journal of Linguistics* 32, 2: 325–47.

2002. *Relevance and Linguistic Meaning: The Semantics and Pragmatics of Discourse Markers* (Cambridge Studies in Linguistics, 99). Cambridge: Cambridge University Press.

2007. "Or"-parentheticals, "that is"-parentheticals and the pragmatics of reformulation. *Journal of Linguistics* 43: 311–39.

Blass, Regina 1990. *Relevance Relations in Discourse: A Study with Special Reference to Sissala*. Cambridge: Cambridge University Press.

Bolly, Catherine 2014. Gradience and gradualness of parentheticals: Drawing a line in the sand between phraseology and grammaticalization. *Yearbook of Phraseology* 5: 25–56.

Bolly, Catherine and Liesbeth Degand 2013. Have you seen what I mean? From verbal constructions to discourse markers. *Journal of Historical Pragmatics* 14, 2: 210–35.

Börjars, Kersti, Nigel Vincent, and George Walkden 2015. On constructing a theory of grammatical change. *Transactions of the Philological Society* 113, 3: 363–82.

Borreguero Zuloaga, Margarita 2018. The evolution of temporal adverbs into consecutive connectives and the role of discourse traditions: The case of Italian *allora* and Spanish *entonces*. In Salvador Pons Bordería and Óscar Loureda Lamas (eds.), *Beyond Grammaticalization and Discourse Markers: New Issues in the Study of Language Change* (Studies in Pragmatics, 18). Leiden: Brill. Pp. 231–70.

Boye, Kasper and Peter Harder 2007. Complement-taking predicates: Usage and linguistic structure. *Studies in Language* 31, 3: 569–606.

2012. A usage-based theory of grammatical status and grammaticalization. *Language* 88: 1–44.

Breban, Tine 2015. Refining secondary grammaticalization by looking at subprocesses of change. *Language Sciences* 47: 161–71.

Breban, Tine & Svenja Kranich 2015. Introduction to what happens after grammaticalization? Secondary grammaticalization and other late stage processes. *Language Sciences* 47: 129–31.

Breu, Walter and G. Piccoli 2000. Dizionario croato molisano di Acquaviva Colleroce. Campobasso, typescript.

Brinton, Laurel J. 1995. Pragmatic markers in a diachronic perspective. In J. Ahlers, L. Bilmes, J. S. Guenter, B. A. Kaiser, and J. Namkung (eds.), *Proceedings of the Twenty-First Annual Meeting of the Berkeley Linguistics Society, February 17–20, 1995. General Session and Parasession on Historical Issues in Sociolinguistics/ Social Issues in Historical Linguistics*. Berkeley: Berkeley Linguistics Society. Pp. 377–88.

1996. *Pragmatic Markers in English: Grammaticalization and Discourse Functions* (Topics in English Linguistics, 19). Berlin: Mouton de Gruyter.

2001. From matrix clause to pragmatic marker: The history of *look*-forms. *Journal of Historical Pragmatics* 2: 177–99.

2006. Pathways in the development of pragmatic markers in English. In Ans Van Kemenade and Bettelou Los (eds.), *The Handbook of the History of English.* Oxford: Blackwell. Pp. 307–34.

2008. *The Comment Clause in English: Syntactic Origins and Pragmatic Development* (Studies in English Language). Cambridge: Cambridge University Press.

2010a. The development of *I mean*: Implications for the study of historical pragmatics. In Susan M. Fitzmaurice and Irma Taavitsainen (eds.), *Methods in Historical Pragmatics.* Berlin: Mouton de Gruyter. Pp. 37–80.

2010b. From performative to concessive disjunct: *I/you admit* and *admittedly*. In Merja Kytö, John Scahill, and Harumi Tanabe (eds.), *Language Change and Variation from Old English to Late Modern English: A Festschrift for Minoji Akimoto* (Studies in Language and Communication 14). Bern: Lang. Pp. 279–302.

2014. *If you choose/like/prefer/want/wish*: The origin of metalinguistic and politeness functions. In Marianne Hundt (ed.), *Late Modern English Syntax in Context.* Cambridge: Cambridge University Press. Pp. 271–90.

2017. *The Evolution of Pragmatic Markers in English: Pathways of Change.* Cambridge: Cambridge University Press.

Brinton, Laurel J. and Elizabeth C. Traugott 2005. *Lexicalization and Language Change.* Cambridge: Cambridge University Press.

Brody, J. 1987. Particles borrowed from Spanish as discourse markers into Mayan languages. *Anthropological Linguistics* 29: 507–21.

1993. Borrowing the "unborrowable": Spanish discourse markers in indigenous American languages. In Carmen Silva-Corvalán (ed.), *Spanish in Four Continents.* Washington, DC: Georgetown University Press. Pp. 132–47.

Bybee, Joan L., Revere D. Perkins, and William Pagliuca 1994. *The Evolution of Grammar: Tense, Aspect, and Modality in the Languages of the World.* Chicago, IL: University of Chicago Press.

Campbell, Lyle 1991. Some grammaticalization changes in Estonian and their implications. In Elizabeth C. Traugott and Bernd Heine (eds.), *Approaches to Grammaticalization*, volume 1. Amsterdam: John Benjamins. Pp. 285–99.

Cap, Piotr 2011. Micropragmatics and macropragmatics. In Wolfram Bublitz and Neal R. Norrick (eds.), *Foundations of Pragmatics* (Handbook of Pragmatics 1). Berlin: De Gruyter Mouton. Pp. 51–75.

Carter, Ron and Michael McCarthy 2006. *Cambridge Grammar of English.* Cambridge: Cambridge University Press.

Choi, Jane Boyun 2007. *A corpus-based discourse analysis of Korean discourse markers: An analysis of spoken and written use.* PhD dissertation, University of California, Los Angeles.

Cinque, Guglielmo 1999. *Adverbs and Functional Heads: A Cross-Linguistic Perspective.* Oxford: Oxford University Press.

Claridge, Claudia 2013. The evolution of three pragmatic markers: *As it were, so to speak/say* and *if you like*. *Journal of Historical Pragmatics* 14, 2: 161–84.

Claridge, Claudia and Leslie Arnovick 2010. Pragmaticalisation and discursisation. In H. Jucker and Irma Taavitsainen (eds.), *Historical Pragmatics* (Handbook of Pragmatics, 8). Berlin: de Gruyter Mouton. Pp. 165–92.

Clark, Herbert H. 1996. *Using Language.* Cambridge: Cambridge University Press.

Clark, Herbert H. and Jean E. Fox Tree 2002. Using *uh* and *um* in spontaneous speaking. *Cognition* 84: 73–111.

Claudi, Ulrike and Bernd Heine 1986. On the metaphorical base of grammar. *Studies in Language* 10, 2: 297–335.

Coulmas, Florian 1979. On the sociolinguistic relevance of routine formulae. *Journal of Pragmatics* 3: 239–66.

Craig, Colette G. 1991. Ways to go in Rama: A case study in polygrammaticalization. In Elizabeth C. Traugott and Bernd Heine (eds.) *Approaches to Grammaticalization*, volume 2. Amsterdam: John Benjamins. Pp. 455–92.

Crible, Ludivine 2017. Towards an operational category of discourse markers: A definition and its model. In Chiara Fedriani and Andrea Sansò (eds.), *Pragmatic Markers, Discourse Markers and Modal Particles* (Studies in Language Companion Series, 186). Amsterdam: John Benjamins. Pp. 99–124.

Croft, William 2001. *Radical Construction Grammar.* Oxford: Oxford University Press.

Cuenca, Maria Josep 2008. Pragmatic markers in contrast: The case of *well. Journal of Pragmatics* 40: 1373–91.

2013. The fuzzy boundaries between discourse marking and modal marking. In Liesbeth Degand, Bert Cornillie, and Paola Pietrandrea (eds.), *Discourse Markers and Modal Particles: Categorization and Description* (Pragmatics and Beyond, New Series, 234). Amsterdam: John Benjamins. Pp. 191–216.

D'Arcy, Alexandra 2017. *Discourse-Pragmatic Variation in Context: Eight Hundred Years of LIKE.* Amsterdam: John Benjamins.

Davidse, Kristin, Simon De Wolf, and An Van linden 2015. The development of the modal and discourse uses of *there/it is/I have no doubt* expressing modal and interactional meaning. *Journal of Historical Pragmatics* 16, 1: 25–58.

Davies, Mark 2008. *The Corpus of Contemporary American English (COCA): One Billion Words, 1990–2019.* Available at www.english-corpora.org/coca/. Last accessed October 2020.

2010. *The Corpus of Historical American English (COHA): 400 Million Words, 1810–2009.* Available at www.english-corpora.org/coha/. Last accessed October 2020.

de Rooij, Vincent A. 2000. French discourse markers in Shaba Swahili conversations. *International Journal of Bilingualism* 4, 4: 447–66.

Debaisieux, Jeanne-Marie 2007. La distinction entre dépendance grammaticale et dépendance macrosyntaxique comme moyen de résoudre les paradoxes de la subordination. *Faits de Langue* 28: 119–32.

2018. Utterances: One speaker but two resources, micro and macro syntax. Paper presented at the international workshop *One Brain – Two Grammars? Examining dualistic approaches to grammar and cognition*, Rostock, March 1–2, 2018.

Defour, Tine 2007. A Diachronic Study of the Pragmatic Markers *well* and *now*: Fundamental Research into Semantic Development and Grammaticalization by Means of a Corpus Study. PhD dissertation, University of Ghent.

Defour, Tine, Ulrique D'Hondt, Anne-Marie Simon-Vandenbergen, and Dominique
Willems 2010. *In fact, en fait, de fait, au fait*: A contrastive study of the synchronic
correspondences and diachronic development of English and French cognates.
Neuphilologische Mitteilungen 111, 4: 433–63.

2012. Degrees of pragmaticalization: The divergent histories of *actually* and
actuellement. In Peter Lauwers, Gudrun Vanderbauwhede, and Stijn Verleyen
(eds.), *Pragmatic Markers and Pragmaticalization: Lessons from False Friends*.
Amsterdam: John Benjamins. Pp. 37–64.

Defour, Tine and Anne-Marie Simon-Vandenbergen 2010. "Positive appraisal" as a
core meaning of *well*: A corpus-based analysis in middle and early modern English
data. *English Studies* 91, 6: 643–73.

Degand, Liesbeth, Bert Cornillie, and Paola Pietrandrea (eds.) 2013. *Discourse Markers
and Modal Particles: Categorization and Description* (Pragmatics & Beyond,
New Series, 234). Amsterdam: John Benjamins.

Degand, Liesbeth and Jacqueline Evers-Vermeul 2015. Grammaticalization or
pragmaticalization of discourse markers?: More than a terminological issue.
Journal of Historical Pragmatics 16, 1: 59–85.

Degand, Liesbeth and Benjamin Fagard 2011. *Alors* between discourse and grammar:
The role of syntactic position. *Functions of Language* 18, 1: 19–56.

Degand, Liesbeth and Anne-Marie Simon-Vandenbergen 2011. Introduction:
Grammaticalization and (inter)subjectification of discourse markers. *Linguistics*
49, 2: 287–94.

Dehé, Nicole 2014. *Parentheticals in Spoken English: The Syntax-Prosody Relation*
(Studies in English Language). Cambridge: Cambridge University Press.

Dehé, Nicole and Yordanka Kavalova 2006. The syntax, pragmatics, and prosody of
parenthetical *what*. *English Language and Linguistics* 10: 289–320.

(eds.) 2007. *Parentheticals* (Linguistics Today, 106). Amsterdam: John Benjamins.

Dehé, Nicole and Anne Wichmann 2010. Sentence-initial *I think (that)* and *I believe
(that)*: Prosodic evidence for use as main clause, comment clause and discourse
marker. *Studies in Language* 34, 1: 36–74.

Dér, Csilla Ilona 2010. On the status of discourse markers. *Acta Linguistica Hungarica*
57, 1: 3–28.

2013. Grammaticalization: A specific type of semantic, categorical, and prosodic
change. *Berliner Beiträge zur Hungarologie* 18: 160–79.

Dér, Csilla Ilona and Alexandra Markó 2010. A pilot study of Hungarian discourse
markers. *Language and Speech* 53, 2: 135–80.

Detges, Ulrich and Paul Gévaudan 2018. Insubordination, *Abtönung*, and the next move
in interaction: Main-clause-initial *puisque* in French. In Salvador Pons Bordería
and Óscar Loureda Lamas (eds.), *Beyond Grammaticalization and Discourse
Markers: New Issues in the Study of Language Change* (Studies in Pragmatics,
18). Leiden: Brill. Pp. 304–33.

Detges, Ulrich and Richard Waltereit 2007. Different functions, different histories:
Modal particles and discourse markers from a diachronic point of view. *Catalan
Journal of Linguistics* 6: 61–81.

2016. Grammaticalization and pragmaticalization. In S. Fischer and C. Gabriel (eds.),
Manual of Grammatical Interfaces in Romance (Manuals of Romance
Linguistics). Berlin: de Gruyter Mouton. Pp. 635–57.

Deulofeu, Josés 2017. La macrosyntaxe comme moyen de tracer la limite entre organisation grammaticale et organisation du discours. *Modèles Linguistiques* 2016: 135–66.

Diessel, Holger 2019. *The Grammar Network: How Language Structure is Shaped by Language Use*. Cambridge: Cambridge University Press.

Diewald, Gabriele 2006. Discourse particles and modal particles as grammatical elements. In Kerstin Fischer (ed.), *Approaches to Discourse Particles* (Studies in Pragmatics, 1). Amsterdam: Elsevier. Pp. 403–25.

2011a. Grammaticalization and pragmaticalization. In Narrog, Heiko, and Bernd Heine (eds.), *The Oxford Handbook of Grammaticalization*. Oxford: Oxford University Press. Pp. 450–61.

2011b. Pragmaticalization (defined) as grammaticalization of discourse functions. *Linguistics* 49, 2: 365–90.

Dik, Simon C. 1997. *The Theory of Functional Grammar, Part 2: Complex and Derived Constructions* (Functional Grammar Series, 21). Berlin: Mouton de Gruyter. Pp. 379–409.

Dostie, Gaetane 2004. *Pragmaticalisation et marqueurs discursifs: Analyse sémantique et traitement lexicographique*. Brussels: De Boeck & Larcier.

2009. Discourse markers and regional variation in French: A lexico-semantic approach. In Kate Beeching, Nigel Armstrong, and Francoise Gadet (eds.), *Sociolinguistic Variation in Contemporary French*. Amsterdam: John Benjamins. Pp. 201–14.

Emanatian, Michele 1992. Chagga "come" and "go": Metaphor and the development of tense-aspect. *Studies in Language* 16, 1: 1–33.

Emonds, Joseph 1973. Parenthetical clauses. In Claudia Corum, T. C. Smith-Stark, and A. Weiser (eds.), *You Take the High Node and I'll Take the Low Node*. Chicago, IL: Linguistic Society. Pp. 333–47.

Erman, Britt and Ulla-Britt Kotsinas 1993. Pragmaticalization: the case of *ba* and *you know*. *Studier i modern sprakvetenskap* 10: 76–92.

Espinal, M. Teresa 1991. The representation of disjunct constituents. *Language* 67: 726–62.

Evans, Nicholas 2007. Insubordination and its uses. In Irina Nicolaeva (ed.), *Finiteness: Theoretical and Empirical Foundations*. Oxford: Oxford University Press. Pp. 366–431.

Fagard, Benjamin 2010. *É vida, olha . . .*: Imperatives as discourse markers and grammaticalization paths in Romance: A diachronic corpus study. *Languages in Contrast* 10, 2: 245–67.

Fedriani, Chiara and Andrea Sansò 2017. Pragmatic markers, discourse markers and modal particles: What do we know and where do we go from here? In Chiara Fedriani and Andrea Sansò (eds.), *Pragmatic Markers, Discourse Markers and Modal Particles* (Studies in Language Companion Series, 186). Amsterdam: John Benjamins. Pp. 1–33.

Ferrara, Kathleen W. 1997. Form and function of the discourse marker *anyway*: Implications for discourse analysis. *Linguistics* 35: 343–78.

Fforde, Jasper 2003. *The Well of Lost Plots*. London: Hodder and Stoughton.

Fiorentini, Ilaria 2017. Italian discourse markers and modal particles in contact. In Chiara Fedriani and Andrea Sansò (eds.), *Pragmatic Markers, Discourse Markers and Modal Particles* (Studies in Language Companion Series, 186). Amsterdam: John Benjamins. Pp. 417–37.

Fischer, Olga 2007a. The development of English parentheticals: A case of grammaticalization? In Ute Smit et al. (eds.), *Tracing English through Time: Explorations in Language Variation: A Festschrift for Herbert Schendl on the Occasion of His 65th Birthday* (Austrian Studies in English, 95). Vienna: Braumüller. Pp. 103–18.

  2007b. *Morphosyntactic Change: Functional and Formal Perspectives*. Oxford: Oxford University Press.

Flores-Ferrán, Nydia 2014. So *pues entonces:* An examination of bilingual discourse markers in Spanish oral narratives of personal experience of New York City-born Puerto Ricans. *Sociolinguistic Studies* 8, 1: 57–83.

Frank-Job, Barbara 2006. A dynamic-interactional approach to discourse markers. In Kerstin Fischer (ed.), *Approaches to Discourse Particles*. Amsterdam: Elsevier. Pp. 359–74.

Fraser, Bruce 1988. Types of English discourse markers. *Acta Linguistica Hungarica* 38: 19–33.

  1990. An approach to discourse markers. *Journal of Pragmatics* 14, 3: 383–98.

  1996. Pragmatic markers. *Pragmatics* 6, 2: 167–90.

  1999. What are discourse markers? *Journal of Pragmatics* 31: 931–52.

  2009. Topic orientation markers. *Journal of Pragmatics* 41: 892–98.

  2015. The combining of discourse markers: A beginning. *Journal of Pragmatics* 86: 48–53.

Fried, Mirjam and Jan-Ola Östman 2005. Construction Grammar and spoken language: The case of pragmatic particles. *Journal of Pragmatics* 37: 1752–78.

Furkó, Bálint Péter 2007. *The Pragmatic Marker – Discourse Marker Dichotomy Reconsidered: The Case of "well" and "of course."* Debrecen: Debrecen University Press.

  2014. Cooptation over grammaticalization. *Argumentum* 10: 289–300.

  2018. The boundaries of discourse markers: Drawing lines through manual and automatic annotation. *Acta Universitatis Sapientiae, Philologica*, 10, 2: 155–70.

Fuschi, Laura 2013. Discourse Markers in Spoken Italian: The Functions of *senti* and *guarda*. PhD dissertation, University of Bielefeld.

Gaines, Philip 2011. The multifunctionality of discourse operator *okay*: Evidence from a police interview. *Journal of Pragmatics* 43: 3291–315.

Garachana, Mar 2018. New challenges to the theory of grammaticalization: Evidence from the rise of *no obstante, no contrastante* and *no embargante*. In Salvador Pons Bordería and Óscar Loureda Lamas (eds.), *Beyond Grammaticalization and Discourse Markers: New Issues in the Study of Language Change* (Studies in Pragmatics, 18). Leiden: Brill. Pp. 198–230.

Genette, Gérard 1982. *Palimpsestes: la littérature au second degré*. Paris: Seuil.

Gernsbacher, M. A., Varner, K. R., and Faust, M. E. 1990. Investigating differences in general comprehension skill. *Journal of Experimental Psychology: Language, Memory, and Cognition* 16, 3: 430–45.

Ghezzi, Chiara 2014. The development of discourse and pragmatic markers. In Chiara Ghezzi and Piera Molinelli (eds.), *Discourse and Pragmatic Markers from Latin to the Romance Languages* (Oxford Studies in Diachronic and Historical Linguistics). Oxford: Oxford University Press. Pp. 10–26.

Ghezzi, Chiara and Piera Molinelli (eds.) 2014. *Discourse and Pragmatic Markers from Latin to the Romance Languages* (Oxford Studies in Diachronic and Historical Linguistics). Oxford: Oxford University Press.

Giacalone Ramat, Anna and Caterina Mauri 2011. The grammaticalization of coordinating interclausal connectives. In Heiko Narrog and Bernd Heine (eds.), *The Oxford Handbook of Grammaticalization*. New York: Oxford University Press. Pp. 653–64.

Givón, T. 1971. Historical syntax and synchronic morphology: An archaeologist's field trip. *Chicago Linguistic Society* 7: 394–415.

1975. Focus and the scope of assertion: Some Bantu evidence. *Studies in African Linguistics* 6, 2: 185–207.

1979. *On Understanding Grammar*. New York: Academic Press.

1991. The evolution of dependent clause morpho-syntax in Biblical Hebrew. In Elizabeth C. Traugott and Bernd Heine (eds.), *Approaches to Grammaticalization*, volume 1. Amsterdam: John Benjamins. Pp. 257–310.

2009. *The Genesis of Syntactic Complexity: Diachrony, Ontogeny, Neuro-Cognition, Evolution*. Amsterdam: John Benjamins.

2015. *The Diachrony of Grammar*. Two volumes. Amsterdam: John Benjamins.

Gohl, Christine and Susanne Günthner 1999. Grammatikalisierung von *weil* als Diskursmarker in der gesprochenen Sprache. *Zeitschrift für Sprachwissenschaft* 18, 1: 39–75.

Goldberg, Adele E. 1995. *Constructions: A Construction Grammar Approach to Argument Structure*. Chicago: University of Chicago Press.

2006. *Constructions at Work: The Nature of Generalization in Language*. Oxford: Oxford University Press.

Gonen, Einat, Zohar Livnat, and Noam Amir 2015. The discourse marker *axshav* ("now") in spontaneous spoken Hebrew: Discursive and prosodic features. *Journal of Pragmatics* 89, 1: 69–84.

González, Montserrat 2004. *Pragmatic Markers in Oral Narrative: The Case of English and Catalan*. Amsterdam: John Benjamins.

Goria, Eugenio 2016. The role of extra-linguistic constituents in bilingual speech. In Gunther Kaltenböck, Evelien Keizer, and Arne Lohmann (eds.), *Outside the Clause* (Studies in Language Companion Series, 178). Amsterdam: John Benjamins. Pp. 273–301.

2017. Functional markers in *llanito* code-switching: Regular patterns in Gibraltar's bilingual speech. In Chiara Fedriani and Andrea Sansò (eds.), *Pragmatic Markers, Discourse Markers and Modal Particles* (Studies in Language Companion Series, 186). Amsterdam: John Benjamins. Pp. 439–58.

Görlach, Manfred 2001. *A Dictionary of European Anglicisms: A Usage Dictionary of Anglicisms in Sixteen European Languages, XXV*. Oxford: Oxford University Press.

Goss, Emily L. and Joseph C. Salmons 2000. The evolution of bilingual discourse marking system: Modal particles and English markers in German–American dialects. *International Journal of Bilingualism* 4: 469–84.

Gould, Stephen Jay and Elisabeth S. Vrba 1982. Exaptation: A missing term in the science of form. *Paleobiology* 8, 1: 4–15.

Grant, Anthony P. 2012. Contact, convergence, and conjunctions: a cross-linguistic study of borrowing correlations among certain kinds of discourse, phasal adverbial, and dependent clause markers. In Claudine Chamoreau and Isabelle

Léglise (eds.), *Cross-Linguistic Tendencies in Contact-Induced Change: A Typological Approach Based on Morphosyntactic Studies*. Berlin: Mouton de Gruyter. Pp. 311–58.

Grice, H. Paul 1989. *Studies in the Way of Words*. Cambridge, MA: Harvard University Press.

Günthner, Susanne 1999. Entwickelt sich der Konzessivkonnektor *obwohl* zum Diskursmarker? Grammatikalisierungstendenzen im gesprochenen Deutsch. *Linguistische Berichte* 180: 409–46.

    2000. From concessive connector to discourse marker: The use of *obwohl* in everyday German interaction. In Elizabeth Couper-Kuhlen and Bernd Kortmann (eds.), *Cause-Condition-Concession-Contrast: Cognitive and Discourse Perspectives*. Berlin: Mouton de Gruyter. Pp. 439–68.

Günthner, Susanne and Katrin Mutz 2004. Grammaticalization vs. pragmaticalization? The development of pragmatic markers in German and Italian. In W. Bisang, N. Himmelmann, and B. Wiemer (eds.), *What Makes Grammaticalization? A Look from its Fringes and its Components*. Berlin: Mouton de Gruyter. Pp. 77–107.

Haegeman, Liliane 1991. Parenthetical adverbials: The radical orphanage approach. In S. Chiba, A. Shuki, A. Ogawa, Y. Fuiwara, N. Yamada, O. Koma, and T. Yagi (eds.), *Aspects of Modern Linguistics: Papers Presented to Masatomo Ukaji on His 60th Birthday*. Tokyo: Kaitakushi. Pp. 232–54.

Haiman, John 1994. Ritualization and the development of language. In William Pagliuca (ed.), *Perspectives on Grammaticalization* (Amsterdam Studies in the Theory and History of Linguistic Science, 109). Amsterdam: John Benjamins. Pp. 3–28.

Hakulinen, Auli 1998. The use of Finnish *nyt* as a discourse particle. In Andreas H. Jucker and Yael Ziv (eds.), *Discourse Markers: Descriptions and Theory* (Pragmatics and Beyond, New Series, 57). Amsterdam: John Benjamins. Pp. 83–96.

Hancil, Sylvie 2013. Introduction. In: Sylvie Hancil and Daniel Hirst (eds.), *Prosody and Iconicity*. Amsterdam: John Benjamins. Pp. 1–31.

Hancil, Sylvie and Daniel Hirst (eds.). 2013. *Prosody and Iconicity*. Amsterdam: John Benjamins.

Hansen, Maj-Britt Mosegaard 1997. *Alors* and *donc* in spoken French: A reanalysis. *Journal of Pragmatics* 28: 153–87.

    1998a. *The Function of Discourse Particles. A Study with Special Reference to Spoken Standard French*. Amsterdam: John Benjamins.

    1998b. The semantic status of discourse markers. *Lingua* 104, 3–4: 235–60.

    1998c. La grammaticalisation de l'interaction, ou, Pour une approche polysémique de l'adverbe "bien." *Revue de Sémantique et Pragmatique* 4: 111–38.

    2005a. From prepositional phrase to hesitation marker: The semantic and pragmatic evolution of French *enfin*. *Journal of Historical Pragmatics* 6, 2: 37–68.

    2005b. A comparative study of the semantics and pragmatics of French *enfin* and *finalement*, in synchrony and diachrony. *French Language Studies* 15: 153–71.

    2008. *Particles at the Semantics/Pragmatics Interface: Synchronic and Diachronic Issues*. Oxford: Elsevier.

Haselow, Alexander 2011. Discourse marker and modal particle: The functions of utterance-final *then* in spoken English. *Journal of Pragmatics* 43: 3603–23.

2013. Arguing for a wide conception of grammar: The case of final particles in spoken discourse. *Folia Linguistica* 47, 2: 375–424.

2015. Left vs. right periphery in grammaticalization: The case of *anyway*. In Andrew D. M. Smith, Graeme Trousdale, and Richard Waltereit (eds.), *New Directions in Grammaticalization Research*. Amsterdam: John Benjamins. Pp. 157–86.

2016. A processual view on grammar: Macrogrammar and the final field in spoken syntax. *Language Sciences* 54: 77–101.

2017. *Spontaneous Spoken English. An Integrated Approach to the Emergent Grammar of Speech*. Cambridge: Cambridge University Press.

2019. Discourse markers and brain lateralization: Evidence for dual language processing from neurological disorders. *Lecture presented at the University of Düsseldorf*, December 15, 2019.

Haspelmath, Martin 2004. On directionality in language change with particular reference to grammaticalization. In Olga Fischer, Muriel Norde, and Harry Perridon (eds.), *Up and Down the Cline – the Nature of Grammaticalization* (Typological Studies in Language, 59). Amsterdam: John Benjamins, pp. 17–44.

2011. The gradual coalescence into "words" in grammaticalization. In Heiko Narrog and Bernd Heine (eds.), *The Oxford Handbook of Grammaticalization*. Oxford: Oxford University Press. Pp. 342–55.

Hayashi, Makoto and Kyung-Eun Yoon 2006. A cross-linguistic exploration of demonstratives in interaction: With particular reference to the context of word-formulation trouble. *Studies in Language* 30: 485–540.

2010. A cross-linguistic exploration of demonstratives in interaction: With particular reference to the context of word-formulation trouble. In Nino Amiridze, Boyd H. Davis, and Marboyegaret Maclagan (eds.), *Fillers, Pauses and Placeholders* (Typological Studies in Language, 93). Amsterdam: John Benjamins. Pp. 33–65.

Heine, Bernd 1992. Grammaticalization chains. *Studies in Language* 16, 2: 335–68.

2002. On the role of context in grammaticalization. In Ilse Wischer and Gabriele Diewald (eds.), *New Reflections on Grammaticalization* (Typological Studies in Language, 49). Amsterdam: John Benjamins. Pp. 83–101.

2003. On degrammaticalization. In Barry Blake, Kate Burridge, and John Taylor (eds.), *Historical Linguistics 2001*. Selected papers from the 15th International Conference on Historical Linguistics, Melbourne, August 13–17, 2001 (Amsterdam Studies in the Theory and History of Linguistic Science. Series IV: Current Issues in Linguistic Theory, 237). Amsterdam: John Benjamins. Pp. 163–79.

2013. On discourse markers: Grammaticalization, pragmaticalization, or something else? *Linguistics* 51, 6: 1205–47.

2016a. Language contact and extra-clausal constituents: The case of discourse markers. In Gunther Kaltenböck, Evelien Keizer, and Arne Lohmann (eds.), *Outside the Clause* (Studies in Language Companion Series, 178). Amsterdam: John Benjamins. Pp. 243–72.

2016b. On non-finiteness and canonical imperatives. In Claudine Chamoreau and Zarina Estrada-Fernández (eds.), *Finiteness and Nominalization* (Typological Studies in Language, 113). Amsterdam: John Benjamins. Pp. 245–70.

2018a. Are there two different ways of approaching grammaticalization? In Sylvie Hancil, Tine Breban, and José Vicente Lozano (eds.), *New Trends on Grammaticalization and Language Change*. Amsterdam: John Benjamins. Pp. 23–54.

2018b. Grammaticalization in Africa: Two contrasting hypotheses. In Heiko Narrog and Bernd Heine (eds.), *Grammaticalization from a Typological Perspective*. Oxford: Oxford University Press. Pp. 16–34.

2019. Some observations on the dualistic nature of discourse processing. *Folia Linguistica* 53, 2: 411–42.

Heine, Bernd and Ulrike Claudi 1986. *On the Rise of Grammatical Categories: Some Examples from Maa* (Kölner Beiträge zur Afrikanistik, 13). Berlin: Reimer.

Heine, Bernd, Ulrike Claudi and Friederike Hünnemeyer 1991. *Grammaticalization: A Conceptual Framework*. Chicago: University of Chicago Press.

Heine, Bernd, Gunther Kaltenböck, and Tania Kuteva 2016. On insubordination and cooptation. In Evans, Nicholas and Honoré Watanabe (eds.), *Insubordination* (Typological Studies in Language). Amsterdam: John Benjamins. Pp. 39–63.

Heine, Bernd, Gunther Kaltenböck, Tania Kuteva, and Haiping Long 2013. An outline of discourse grammar. In Shannon Bischoff and Carmen Jany (eds.), *Functional Approaches to Language*. Berlin: Mouton de Gruyter. Pp. 175–233.

2015. *On Some Correlations between Grammar and Brain Lateralization* (Oxford Handbooks Online in Linguistics). New York: Oxford University Press.

2017. Cooptation as a discourse strategy. *Linguistics* 55, 4: 1–43.

2020. On the rise of discourse markers. In Sylvie Hancil and Alexander Haselow (eds.), *Studies at the Grammar–Discourse Interface*. Amsterdam: John Benjamins. Pp. 23–55.

Heine, Bernd, Christa König and Karsten Legère 2017. A text study of discourse markers in Akie, a Southern Nilotic language of Tanzania. In Raija Kramer and Roland Kießling (eds.), *Mechthildian Approaches to Afrikanistik: Advances in Language-Based Research on Africa, Festschrift für Mechthild Reh*. Cologne: Rüdiger Köppe. Pp. 147–67.

Heine, Bernd and Tania Kuteva 2002. *World Lexicon of Grammaticalization*. Cambridge: Cambridge University Press.

2005. *Language Contact and Grammatical Change* (Cambridge Approaches to Language Contact, 3). Cambridge: Cambridge University Press.

2007. *The Genesis of Grammar: A Reconstruction* (Studies in the Evolution of Language, 9). Oxford: Oxford University Press.

Heine, Bernd, Tania Kuteva, and Gunther Kaltenböck 2014. Discourse grammar, the dual process model, and brain lateralization: Some correlations. *Language & Cognition* 6, 1: 146–80.

Heine, Bernd, Tania Kuteva, and Haiping Long 2020. Dual process frameworks on reasoning and linguistic discourse: A comparison. In Alexander Haselow and Gunther Kaltenböck (eds.), *Grammar and Cognition: Dualistic Models of Language Structure and Language Processing*. Amsterdam: John Benjamins. Pp. 59–89.

Heine, Bernd and Mechthild Reh 1984. *Grammaticalization and Reanalysis in African Languages*. Hamburg: Buske.

Hengeveld, Kees 2017. A hierarchical approach to grammaticalization. In Kees Hengelveld, Heiko Narrog, and Hella Olbertz (eds.), *The Grammaticalization of*

Tense, Aspect, Modality and Evidentiality: A Functional Perspective. Berlin: Mouton de Gruyter. Pp. 13–37.

Hengeveld, Kees and J. Lachlan Mackenzie 2008. *Functional Discourse Grammar: A Typologically-Based Theory of Language Structure*. Oxford: Oxford University Press.

2011. *Functional Discourse Grammar*. In Bernd Heine and Heiko Narrog (eds.), *The Oxford Handbook of Linguistic Analysis*. Oxford: Oxford University Press. Pp. 367–400.

Hilpert, Martin 2008. *Germanic Future Constructions: A Usage-Based Approach to Language Change* (Constructional Approaches to Language, 7). Amsterdam: John Benjamins.

2013. *Constructional Change in English: Developments in Allomorphy, Word-Formation, and Syntax*. Cambridge: Cambridge University Press.

Hilpert, Martin and David Correia Saavedra 2018. The unidirectionality of semantic changes in grammaticalization: An experimental approach to the asymmetric priming hypothesis. *English Language and Linguistics* 22, 3: 357–80.

Himmelmann, Nikolaus P. 2004. Lexicalization and grammaticalization: Opposite or orthogonal? In Walter Bisang, Nikolaus Himmelmann, and Björn Wiemer (eds.), *What Makes Grammaticalization? A Look from its Fringes and its Components*. Berlin: Mouton de Gruyter. Pp. 19–40.

Hirschberg, Julia and Diane Litman 1993. Empirical studies on disambiguation of cue phrases. *Computational Linguistics* 19: 501–3.

Hlavac, Jim 2006. Bilingual discourse markers: Evidence from Croatian–English codeswitching. *Journal of Pragmatics* 38: 1870–900.

Hooper, Joan B. 1975. On assertive predicates. In John Kimball (ed.), *Syntax and Semantics IV*. New York: Academic Press. Pp. 91–124.

Hopper, Paul J. 1991. On some principles of grammaticization. In Elizabeth Closs Traugott and Bernd Heine (eds.), *Approaches to Grammaticalization*, volume 1 (Typological Studies in Language, 19, 1). Amsterdam: John Benjamins. Pp. 17–35.

Hopper, Paul J. and Elizabeth C. Traugott 1993. *Grammaticalization*. Cambridge: Cambridge University Press.

2003. *Grammaticalization*, second, revised edition. Cambridge: Cambridge University Press.

Huddleston, Rodney and Geoffrey K. Pullum 2002. *The Cambridge Grammar of the English Language*. Cambridge: Cambridge University Press.

Hyland, Ken 1998. Persuasion and context: The pragmatics of academic metadiscourse. *Journal of Pragmatics* 30: 437–55.

2005. *Metadiscourse: Exploring Interaction in Writing*. London: Continuum.

2017. Metadiscourse: What is it and where is it going? *Journal of Pragmatics* 113: 16–29.

Ifantidou-Trouki, Elly 1993. Sentential adverbs and relevance. *Lingua* 90, 1–2: 69–90.

Johnstone, Barbara 2002. *Discourse Analysis*. Oxford: Blackwell.

Jucker, Andreas H. 1993. The discourse marker *well*: A relevance-theoretical account. *Journal of Pragmatics* 19, 5: 435–52.

1997. The discourse marker *well* in the history of English. *English Language and Linguistics* 1, 1: 91–110.

2002. Discourse markers in Early Modern English. In Richard Watts and Peter Trudgill (eds.), *Alternative Histories of English*. London: Routledge. Pp. 210–30.

Jucker, Andreas H. and Irma Taavitsainen 2000. Diachronic speech act analysis: Insults from flyting to flaming. *Journal of Historical Pragmatics* 1, 1: 67–95.

Jucker, Andreas H. and Yael Ziv 1998. Discourse markers: introduction. In Andreas H. Jucker and Yael Ziv (eds.), *Discourse Markers: Descriptions and Theory* (Pragmatics and Beyond New Series, 57). Amsterdam: John Benjamins. Pp. 1–12.

Kac, Michael B. 1970. Clauses of saying and the interpretation of *because*. *Language* 48, 3: 626–32.

Kaltenböck, Gunther 2007. Spoken parenthetical clauses in English. In Nicole Dehé and Yordanka Kavalova (eds.), *Parentheticals* (Linguistics Today, 106). Amsterdam: John Benjamins. Pp. 25–52.

2008. Prosody and function of English comment clauses. *Folia Linguistica* 42, 1: 83–134.

2009. English comment clauses: Positions, prosody, and scope. *AAA (Arbeiten aus Anglistik und Amerikanistik)* 34, 1: 51–77.

2010. Pragmatic functions of parenthetial *I think*. In Gunther Kaltenböck, Wiltrud Mihatsch, and Stefan Schneider (eds.), *New Approaches to Hedging*. Bingley: Emerald Publishers. Pp. 243–70.

2013. The development of comment clauses. In Bas Aarts, Joanne Close, Geoffrey Leech, and Sean Wallis (eds.), *The Verb Phrase in English: Investigating Recent Language Change with Corpora*. Cambridge: Cambridge University Press. Pp. 286–317.

2016. On the grammatical status of insubordinate *if*-clauses. In Gunther Kaltenböck, Evelien Keizer, and Arne Lohmann (eds.), *Outside the Clause* (Studies in Language Companion Series, 178). Amsterdam: John Benjamins. Pp. 341–77.

Kaltenböck, Gunther, Bernd Heine, and Tania Kuteva 2011. On thetical grammar. *Studies in Language* 35, 4: 848–93.

Kanaan, Layal 2012. *jæ*ʃ*ne*: un verbe parenthétique à la troisième personne? *Paper presented at the conference on Les verbes parenthtétiques: hypotaxe, parataxe or parenthèse?* Université Paris Ouest Nanterre, May 24–26, 2012.

Kavalova, Yordanka 2007. *And*-parenthetical clauses. In Nicole Dehé and Yordanka Kavalova, *Parentheticals (Linguistics Today, 106)*. Amsterdam: John Benjamins. Pp. 145–72.

Kerouac, Jack 1958. *The Subterraneans*. New York: Grove Press.

Kibiki, Magreth J. 2019. The functions of the pragmatic marker "*sawa*" in spoken Swahili. *Paper presented at the international conference on "Language – Culture – Literature: East African Perspective,"* University of Warsaw, May 23–24, 2019.

Kim, Myung-Hee and Jeonghwa Lee 2007. The role of subjectivity and intersubjectivity in the grammaticalization of *icey* in Korean. *Discourse and Cognition* 14, 2: 27–49.

Kim, Tae-Youb 2000. A type of discourse particle and changed discourse particle in Korean. *Urimalgeul* 19: 1–24.

Kitahara, Yasuo (editor in chief) 2006. *Nihon Kokugo Daiijiten* (The Dictionary of the Japanese Language). Tokyo: Shogakkan.

Klamer, Marian 2000. How report verbs become quote markers and complementisers. *Lingua* 110: 69–98.

Kleinknecht, Friederike and Miguel Souza 2017. Vocatives as a source category for pragmatic markers: From deixis to discourse marking via affectivity. In Chiara Fedriani and Andrea Sansò (eds.), *Pragmatic Markers, Discourse Markers and Modal Particles* (Studies in Language Companion Series, 186). Amsterdam: John Benjamins. Pp. 257–87.

König, Christa and Bernd Heine 2019. Discourse markers in !Xun (W2 dialect). In Klaus Beyer, Gertrud Boden, Bernhard Köhler, and Ulrike Zoch (eds.), *Linguistics across Africa: Festschrift for Rainer Vossen*. Cologne: Köppe. Pp. 207–19.

Koo, Hyun Jung 2008. Grammaticalization of negation markers in Korean. *Discourse and Cognition* 15, 3: 1–27.

Koo, Hyun Jung and Seongha Rhee 2018. On the emergence of polyfunctionality of discourse markers: The case of *kulay* "it is so" in Korean. *Paper presented at the 36th International Conference of the Spanish Society for Applied Linguistics (AESLA-2018)*, Universidad de Cádiz, Cádiz, Spain, April 19–21, 2018.

Kranich, Svenja 2015. The impact of input and output domains: Towards a function-based categorization of types of grammaticalization. *Language Sciences* 47: 172–87.

Kuteva, Tania, Bernd Heine, Bo Hong, Haiping Long, Heiko Narrog, and Seongha Rhee 2019. *World Lexicon of Grammaticalization*, second extensively revised and updated edition. Cambridge: Cambridge University Press.

Lamiroy, Béatrice and P. Swiggers 1991. Imperatives as discourse signals. In Suzanne Fleischman and L. R. Waugh (eds.), *Discourse-Pragmatics and the Verb: The Evidence from Romance*. London: Routledge. Pp. 121–46.

Langacker, Ronald W. 2011. Grammaticalization and cognitive grammar. In Heiko Narrog and Bernd Heine (eds.), *The Oxford Handbook of Grammaticalization*. Oxford: Oxford University Press. Pp. 79–91.

Lass, Roger 1990. How to do things with junk: Exaptation in language evolution. *Journal of Linguistics* 26: 79–102.

1997. *Historical Linguistics and Language Change*. Cambridge: Cambridge University Press.

Lee, Han-gyu 1996. The pragmatics of the discourse particle *kuray* in Korean. *Discourse and Cognition* 3: 1–26.

Lehmann, Christian 1982. *Thoughts on Grammaticalization. A Programmatic Sketch*, volume 1. *AKUP* 48 (Arbeiten des Kölner Universalien-Projekts). Cologne: Universität zu Köln, Institut für Sprachwissenschaft.

2004. Theory and method in grammaticalization. *Zeitschrift für germanistische Linguistik* 32, 2: 152–87.

[1982] 2015. *Thoughts on Grammaticalization*, third edition (Classics in Linguistics, 1). Berlin: Language Science Press.

Lenk, Uta 1998. *Marking Discourse Coherence: Functions of Discourse Markers in Spoken English*. Tübingen: Narr.

Lenker, Ursula 2000. *Soþlice* and *witodlice*: Discourse markers in Old English. In Olga Fischer, Anette Rosenbach, and Dieter Stein (eds.). *Pathways of Change. Grammaticalization in English*. Amsterdam: John Benjamins. Pp. 229–49.

Levinson, Stephen C. 2006. Deixis. In Laurence R. Horn and Gregory L. Ward (eds.), *The Handbook of Pragmatics*. London: Blackwell. Pp. 87–120.

Lewis, Diana M. 2000. *Some Emergent Discourse Connectives in English: Grammaticalization via Rhetorical Patterns*. PhD dissertation, University of Oxford, Faculty of English Language.

2007. From temporal to contrastive and causal: the emergence of connective *after all*. In Agnès Celle and Ruth Huart (eds.) 2007. *Connectives as Discourse Landmarks*. Amsterdam: John Benjamins. Pp. 89–99.

2011. A discourse-constructional approach to the emergence of discourse markers in English. *Linguistics* 49, 2: 415–43.

Li, Charles N. (ed.) 1975. *Word Order and Word Order Change*. Austin: University of Texas Press.

Li, Charles N. and Sandra A. Thompson 1974. An explanation of word order change SVO > SOV. *Foundations of Language* 12: 201–14.

Lipsky, John M. 2005. Code-switching or borrowing? *No sé so no puedo decir*, you know. In Lofti Sayahi and Maurice Westermoreland (eds.), *Selected Proceedings of the Second Workshop on Spanish Sociolinguistics*. Somerville, MA: Cascadilla Proceedings Project. Pp. 1–15.

Livescu, Michaela 2014. *Mă rog*: A pragmatic marker in Romanian. In Chiara Fedriani and Andrea Sansò (eds.), *Pragmatic Markers, Discourse Markers and Modal Particles* (Studies in Language Companion Series, 186). Amsterdam: John Benjamins. Pp. 86–108.

López-Couso, María José and Belén Méndez-Naya 2014. From clause to pragmatic marker: A study of the development of *like* parentheticals in American English. *Journal of Historical Pragmatics* 15, 1: 36–61.

Lyons, John 1977. *Semantics*, 2 volumes. Cambridge: Cambridge University Press.

Maclay, Howard and Charles E. Osgood 1959. Hesitation phenomena in spontaneous English speech. *Word* 15: 19–44.

Mann, William C. and Sandra A. Thompson 1987. *Rhetorical Structure Theory: A Theory of Text Organization* (ISI Report RS-87-190). Marina del Rey, CA: Information Sciences Institute, University of Southern California.

Maschler, Yael 1994. Metalanguaging and discourse markers in bilingual conversation. *Language in Society* 23: 325–66.

2000. What can bilingual conversation tell us about discourse markers? *International Journal of Bilingualism* 4, 4: 437–45.

2009. *Metalanguage in Interaction: Hebrew Discourse Markers*. Amsterdam: John Benjamins.

Matasović, Rolf 2008. Patterns of grammaticalization and the layered structure of the clause. In Rolf Kailuweit, Björn Wiemer, E. Staudinger, and Rolf Matasović (eds.), *New Applications of Role and Reference Grammar: Diachrony, Grammaticalization, Romance Languages*. Newcastle: Cambridge Scholars Publishing. Pp. 45–57.

Matras, Yaron 1998. Utterance modifiers and universals of grammatical borrowing. *Linguistics* 36: 281–331.

2009. *Language Contact* (Cambridge Textbooks in Linguistics). Cambridge: Cambridge University Press.

Matsumoto, Yo 1988. From bound grammatical markers to free discourse markers: History of some Japanese connectives. In Shelley Axmaker, Annie Jaisser, and

Helen Singmaster (eds.), *Proceedings of the Fourteenth Annual Meeting of the Berkeley Linguistics Society*. Berkeley, CA: Berkeley Linguistics Society. Pp. 340–51.

Matthews, P. H. 2007. *The Concise Oxford Dictionary of Linguistics*, second edition. Oxford: Oxford University Press.

Matzen, Laura 2004. Discourse markers and prosody: A case study of *so*. *LACUS Forum* 30: 73–94.

Mauranen, Anna 2010. Discourse reflexivity – A discourse universal? The case of ELF. *Nordic Journal of English Studies* 9, 2: 13–40.

Meehan, Teresa 1991. It's like "What's happening in the evolution of like?": A theory of grammaticalization. *Kansas Working Papers in Linguistics* 16: 37–51.

Meillet, Antoine [1912] 1958. *L'évolution des formes grammaticales*. *Scientia* (Rivista di Scienza) 12: 26, 6. Reprinted in Meillet, Antoine 1958. *Linguistique historique et linguistique générale* (Collection Linguistique publiée par la Société de Linguistique de Paris, 8.) Paris: Champion. Pp. 130–48.

Méndez-Naya, Belén 2006. Adjunct, modifier, discourse marker: On the various functions of *right* in the history of English. *Folia Linguistica Historica* 27, 1–2: 141–95.

2019. Of *right heirs, right idiots* and *bad data*: The diachrony of the intensifying adjective *right*. *Studia Neophilologica* 91, 3: 273–95.

Miyashita, Hiroyuki 2003. *Weil, obwohl, während und wobei*: Warum werden sie V2-Konjunktionen und nicht andere? *Energeia* 28: 59–81.

Mkhatshwa, Simon Nyana Leon 1991. Metaphorical extensions as a basis for grammaticalization. With special reference to Zulu auxiliary verbs. MA Thesis, University of South Africa, Pretoria.

Morita, Yoshiyuki 1973. Kandooshi no hensen (The change of interjections). In K. Suzuki and O. Hayashi (eds.), *Setsuzokushi.Kandooshi* (Conjunctions. Interjections) [Hinshibetsu Nihonbunpoo Kooza, 6]. Tokyo: Meiji Shoin. Pp. 177–208.

Moyer, Melissa G. 2000. Negotiating agreement and disagreement in Spanish–English bilingual conversations with *no*. *International Journal of Bilingualism* 4, 4: 485–504.

Müller, Max 1861. *Lectures on the Science of Language*, volume 1. London: Longmans, Green.

Muysken, Pieter 2013. Language contact outcomes as the result of bilingual optimization strategies. *Bilingualism: Language and Cognition Online* 2013: 1–22.

Nakayama, Toshihide and Kumiko Ichihashi-Nakayama 1997. Japanese *kedo*: Discourse genre and grammaticization. In Ho-min Sohn and John Haig (eds.), *Japanese/Korean Linguistics*, volume 6. Stanford: CSLI Publications. Pp. 607–18.

Narrog, Heiko 2020. Scope and Unidirectionality in Grammaticalization: The Anatomy and History of a Misunderstanding. *Lecture presented at Tohoku University*, Sendai, September 2020.

Nicolle, Steve 2012. Diachrony and grammaticalization. In Robert Binnick (ed.), *The Oxford Handbook of Tense and Aspect*. Oxford: Oxford University Press. Pp. 370–97.

Noora, Azam and Amouzadeh, Mohammad 2015. Grammaticalization of Yæ'ni in Persian. *International Journal of Language Studies* 9, 1: 91–122.

Norde, Muriel 2009. *Degrammaticalization*. Oxford: Oxford University Press.
    2012. Lehmann's parameters revisited. In K. Davidse, T. Breban, L. Brems, and
    T. Mortelmans (eds.), *Grammaticalization and Language Change: New
    Reflections*. Amsterdam: John Benjamins. Pp. 73–110.
Norde, Muriel and Karin Beijering 2014. Facing interfaces: A clustering approach to
    grammaticalization and related changes. *Folia Linguistica* 48, 2: 385–424.
Norrick, Neal R. 2009. Interjections as pragmatic markers. *Journal of Pragmatics* 41:
    866–91.
Nzoimbengene, Philippe 2016. Les "discourse markers" en lingála de Kinshasa oral:
    Étude sémantique et pragmatique sur base d'un corpus de lingála de Kinshasa oral.
    PhD dissertation, Université Catholique de Louvain.
Ocampo, Francisco 2006. Movement towards discourse is not grammaticalization: The
    evolution of *claro* from adjective to discourse particle in spoken Spanish. In Nuria
    Sagarra and Almeida Jacqueline Toribio (eds.), *Selected Proceedings of the 9th
    Hispanic Linguistics Symposium*. Somerville, MA: Cascadilla Proceedings
    Project. Pp. 308–19.
Olshtain, Elite and Blum-Kulka, Shoshana 1989. Happy Hebrish: Mixing and switching
    in American Israeli family interaction. In Susan M. Gass, Carolyn Madden, Dennis
    Preston, and Larry Selinker (eds.), *Variation in Second Language Acquisition*.
    Clevedon, UK: Multilingual Matters. Pp. 59–83.
Onodera, Noriko Okada. 1993. Pragmatic Change in Japanese: Conjunctions and
    Interjections as Discourse Markers. PhD dissertation, Georgetown University.
    1995. Diachronic analysis of Japanese discourse markers. In Andreas H. Jucker (ed.),
    Historical Pragmatics. Amsterdam: John Benjamins. Pp. 393–437.
    2000. The development of *demo* type connectives and *na* elements: Two extremes of
    Japanese discourse markers. *Journal of Historical Pragmatics* 1, 1: 27–55.
    2004. *Japanese Discourse Markers: Synchronic and Diachronic Discourse Analysis*
    (Pragmatics & Beyond New Series, 132). Amsterdam: John Benjamins.
    2007. Interplay of (inter)subjectivity and social norm. In Noriko Okada Onodera and
    Ryoko Suzuki (eds.), Historical Changes in Japanese. Special Issue of *Journal of
    Historical Pragmatics* 8, 2: 239–67.
    2011. The grammaticalization of discourse markers. In Heiko Narrog and Bernd
    Heine (eds.), *The Oxford Handbook of Grammaticalization*. Oxford: Oxford
    University Press. Pp. 611–20.
O'Connell, Daniel C. and Sabine Kowal 2004. The history of research on the filled
    pause as evidence of *The written language bias in linguistics* (Linell, 1982).
    Journal of Psycholinguistic Research 33: 459–74.
    2005. *Uh* and *um* revisited: Are they interjections for signaling delay? *Journal of
    Psycholinguistic Research* 34: 555–76.
O'Connell, Daniel C., Sabine Kowal, and C. Ageneau 2005. Interjections in interviews.
    Journal of Psycholinguistic Research 34: 153–71.
O'Connell, Daniel C. and Sabine Kowal 2008. *Cognition and Language: A Series in
    Psycholinguistics. Communicating with One Another: Toward a Psychology of
    Spontaneous Spoken Discourse*. Berlin: Springer Science + Business Media.
Palander-Collin, Minna 1999. *Grammaticalization and Social Embedding: I THINK
    and METHINKS in Middle and Early Modern English* (Mémoires de la Société
    Néophilologique, Tome LV). Helsinki: Société Néophilologique.

Park, Jung-ran 2001. Politeness: The Korean discourse marker *ceki*. *Pan-Pacific Association of Applied Linguistics* 5, 2: 297–319.

Pawley, Andrew 1992. Formulaic speech. In Bright, William H. (ed.), *Oxford International Encyclopedia of Linguistics*, volume 2. New York: Oxford University Press. Pp. 22–25.

   2009. Grammarians' languages versus humanists' languages and the place of speech act formulas in models of linguistic competence. In Roberta Corrigan, Edith A. Moravcsik, Hamid Ouali, and Kathleen M. Wheatley (eds.), *Formulaic Language. Volume 1: Distribution and Historical Change* (Typological Studies in Language, 82). Amsterdam: John Benjamins. Pp. 3–26.

Pinto de Lima, José 2002. Grammaticalization, subjectification and the origin of phatic markers. In Ilse Wischer and Gabriele Diewald (eds.), *New Reflections on Grammaticalization*. Amsterdam: John Benjamins. Pp. 363–78.

Pons Bordería, Salvador 2018. Introduction: New insights in grammaticalization studies. In Salvador Pons Bordería and Óscar Loureda Lamas (eds.), *Beyond Grammaticalization and Discourse Markers: New Issues in the Study of Language Change* (Studies in Pragmatics, 18). Leiden: Brill. Pp. 1–16.

Pons Bordería, Salvador and Óscar Loureda Lamas (eds.) 2018. *Beyond Grammaticalization and Discourse Markers: New Issues in the Study of Language Change* (Studies in Pragmatics, 18). Leiden: Brill.

Poplack, Shana 1980. Sometimes I'll start a sentence in English Y TERMINO EN ESPAÑOL: Toward a typology of code-switching. *Linguistics* 18, 7–8: 581–618.

   2018. *Borrowing: Loanwords in the Speech Community and in the Grammar*. New York: Oxford University Press

Prat, Chantel S., Debra L. Long, and Kathleen Baynes 2007. The representation of discourse in the two hemispheres: An individual differences investigation. *Brain and Language* 100, 3: 283–94.

Prévost, Sophie 2011. *A propos* from verbal complement to discourse marker: a case of grammaticalization? *Linguistics* 49, 2: 391–413.

Prévost, Sophie and Benjamin Fagard 2018. French *à la rigueur*: A sharp turn. *Journal of Pragmatics* 129: 220–32.

Quirk, Randolph, Sidney Greenbaum, Geoffrey Leech, and Jan Svartvik 1985. *A Comprehensive Grammar of the English Language*. London: Longman.

Ramat, Paolo 1992. Thoughts on degrammaticalization. *Linguistics* 30: 549–60.

Redeker, Gisela 1991. Linguistic markers of discourse structure. *Linguistics* 29: 1139–72.

Reinhart, Tanya 1983. Point of view in language: The use of parentheticals. In Gisa Rauh (ed.), *Essays on Deixis*. Tübingen: Narr. Pp. 169–94.

Rhee, Seongha 1996. *Semantic Verbs and Grammaticalization: The Development in Korean from a Crosslinguistic Perspective*. PhD dissertation, The University of Texas at Austin.

   2003. When "no" does not mean "no": Grammaticalization of discourse markers and auxiliaries from rhetorical negations. *Journal of Linguistic Science* 27: 269–90.

   2004. From discourse to grammar: Grammaticalization and lexicalization of rhetorical questions in Korean. In Gordon Fulton, William J. Sullivan, and Arle R. Lommel (eds.), *LACUS: Forum XXX: Language, Thought and Reality*. Houston: Lacus. Pp. 413–23.

2013. "I know I'm shameless to say this": Grammaticalization of the mitigating discourse marker *makilay* in Korean. *Procedia: Social and Behavioral Sciences* 97: 480–86.

2015. On the emergence of Korean markers of agreement. *Journal of Pragmatics* 83: 10–26.

2018a. On the emergence and pragmatic functions of discourse markers of interruption: A case in Korean. *Paper presented at the 22nd Sociolinguistics Symposium*, The University of Auckland, New Zealand, June 27–30, 2018.

2018b. On multiple determinants of discourse marker functions: Peripheral asymmetry revisited. *Paper presented at the 20th International Congress of Linguists*, Cape Town International Convention Center, South Africa, July 2–6, 2018.

2018c. On the emergence of discourse markers of emphasis in Korean. *Paper presented at the 26th Japanese/Korean Linguistics Conference*, University of California, Los Angeles, November 29–December 1, 2018.

2018d. Grammaticalization of the plural marker in Korean: From object to text to stance. *Journal of Language Sciences* 25, 4: 221–49.

2019. On determinants of discourse marker functions: Grammaticalization and discourse-analytic perspectives. *Paper presented at the 21st International Circle of Korean Linguistics Conference*, Monash University, Melbourne, July 10–12, 2019.

2020a. Pseudo-hortative and the development of the discourse marker *eti poca* ("well, let's see") in Korean. *Journal of Historical Pragmatics* 21, 1: 53–82.

2020b. On the many faces of coarseness: The case of Korean *mak* "coarsely." *Journal of Pragmatics* 170: 396–412.

Rhee, Seongha and Hyun Jung Koo 2019. On divergent paths and functions of "background"-based discourse markers in Korean. *Paper presented at the International Conference on Current Trends in Linguistics*, Université de Rouen, Mont-Saint-Aignan, France, March 28–29, 2019.

Rissanen, Matti. 2008. From "quickly" to "fairly": On the history of *rather. English Language and Linguistics* 12, 2: 345–59.

Roberts, Ian G. 1993. A formal account of grammaticalisation in the history of Romance futures. *Folia Linguistica Historica* 13: 219–58.

Roberts, Ian G. and A. Roussou 2003. *Syntactic Change: A Minimalist Approach to Grammaticalization.* Cambridge: Cambridge University Press.

Romaine, Suzanne and Deborah Lange 1991. The use of *like* as a marker of reported speech and thought: A case of grammaticalization in progress. *American Speech* 66, 3: 227–79.

Ross, John Robert 1973. Slifting. In Maurice Gross, Morris Halle, and Marcel-Paul Schützenberger (eds.), *The Formal Analysis of Natural Languages: Proceedings of the First International Conference.* The Hague, Paris: Mouton. Pp. 133–69.

Rossari, Corinne 2006. Grammaticalization and persistence phenomena in two hybrid discourse markers: *la preuve* and *regarde. Acta linguistica hafniensia*, vol 38, SI: 161–79.

Rouchota, Villy 1996. Discourse connectives: What do they link? *UCL Working Papers in Linguistics* 8: 1–15.

1998. Procedural meaning and parenthetical discourse markers. In Andreas H. Jucker and Yael Ziv (eds.), *Discourse Markers: Descriptions and Theory*. Amsterdam: John Benjamins. Pp. 97–126.

Ruhi, Şükriye 2009. The pragmatics of *yani* as a parenthetical marker in Turkish: Evidence from the METU Turkish Corpus. *Working Papers in Corpus-based Linguistics and Language Education* 3: 285–98.

Rysová, Magdaléna 2017. Discourse connectives: From historical origin to presentday development. In Katrin Menzel, Ekaterina Lapshinova-Koltunski, and Kerstin Kunz (eds.), *New Perspectives on Cohesion and Coherence*. Berlin: Language Science Press. Pp. 11–35.

Salmons, Joseph 1990. Bilingual discourse marking: code-switching, borrowing and convergence in some German–American dialects. *Linguistics* 29: 453–80.

Sankoff, David and Shana Poplack 1981. A formal grammar for code-switching. *Papers in Linguistics* 14, 1–4: 3–45.

Saxena, Anju 1988. The case of the verb 'say' in Tibeto-Burman. *Berkeley Linguistics Society* 14: 375–88.

Schiffrin, Deborah 1987. *Discourse Markers* (Studies in Interactional Sociolinguistics, 5). Cambridge: Cambridge University Press.

Schneider, Stefan 2007a. Reduced parenthetical clauses in Romance languages. In Nicole Dehé and Yordanka Kavalova (eds.), *Parentheticals* (Linguistics Today, 106). Amsterdam: John Benjamins. Pp. 237–58.

2007b. *Reduced Parenthetical Clauses as Mitigators: A Corpus Study of Spoken French, Italian and Spanish*. Amsterdam: John Benjamins.

Schourup, Lawrence 1985. *Common Discourse Particles in English Conversation*. New York: Garland.

1999. Discourse markers. *Lingua* 107: 227–65.

2001 Rethinking *well*. *Journal of Pragmatics* 33: 1025–60.

2011. The discourse marker *now*: A relevance-theoretic approach. *Journal of Pragmatics* 43, 8: 2110–29.

Schreiber, Henning 2014. Imports and exports in linguistic markets in the West African Sahel. In Carole de Féral, Maarten Kossmann, and Mauro Tosco (eds.), *In and Out of Africa. Languages in Question: In Honour of Robert Nicolaï*, volume 2: *Language Contact and Language Change in Africa*. Leuven: Peeters. Pp. 251–68.

Schwenter, Scott A. 1996. Some reflections on *o sea*: A discourse marker in Spanish. *Journal of Pragmatics* 25, 6: 855–74.

Schwenter, Scott A. and Elizabeth C. Traugott 1995. The semantic and pragmatic development of substitutive complex prepositions in English. In Andreas H. Jucker (ed.), *Historical Pragmatics*. Amsterdam: John Benjamins. Pp. 244–73.

Shibasaki, Reijirou 2018a. From the inside to the outside of the sentence: Forming a larger discourse unit with *jijitsu* "fact." In Sylvie Hancil, Tine Breban, and José Vicente Lozano (eds.), *New Trends on Grammaticalization and Language Change*. Amsterdam: John Benjamins. Pp. 333–60.

2018b. On the rise of *Douride* "no wonder" as a projector and the reformulation of discourse sequential relations in Japanese. In S. Fukuda, M. S. Kim, and M.-J. Park (eds.), *Japanese/Korean Linguistics*, volume 25. Stanford, CA: CSLI Publications. Pp. 383–95.

2019. From nominal predicates to pragmatic markers. *Paper presented at the conference on Current Trends in Linguistics.* Université de Rouen, March 27–28, 2019.

2020. From a clause-combining conjunction to a sentence-initial adverbial connector in the history of Japanese: With special attention to *totan(-ni)* "at the moment." In S. Fukuda, M. S. Kim, and M.-J. Park (eds.), *Japanese/Korean Linguistics*, volume 26. Stanford, CA: CSLI Publications. Pp. 87–104.

Shinzato, Rumiko 2017. Grammaticalization of PMs/DMs/MMs in Japanese. In Chiara Fedriani and Andrea Sansò (eds.), *Pragmatic Markers, Discourse Markers and Modal Particles* (Studies in Language Companion Series, 186). Amsterdam: John Benjamins. Pp. 305–33.

Simon-Vandenbergen, Anne-Marie 2007. *No doubt* and related expresssions. In Mike Hannay and Gerard J. Steen (eds.), *Structural–Functional Studies in English Grammar: In Honour of Lachlan Mackenzie* (Studies in Language Companion Series, 83). Amsterdam: John Benjamins. Pp. 9–34.

Simon-Vandenbergen, Anne-Marie and Dominique Willems 2011. Crosslinguistic data as evidence in the grammaticalization debate: The case of discourse markers. *Linguistics* 49, 2: 333–64.

Sohn, Sung-Ock S. and Jieun Kim 2008. A corpus-based discourse analysis of Korean *icey*: A synchronic and diachronic analysis. *Korean Linguistics* 14: 177–202.

Specker, Elizabeth 2008.The use of bilingual discourse markers: Identity in mediated learning. *Arizona Working Papers in SLA & Teaching* 15: 97–120.

Stein, Dieter 1985. Discourse Markers in Early Modern English. In Eaton, R. et al. (eds.), *Papers from the 4th International Conference on English Historical Linguistics.* Amsterdam: John Benjamins. Pp. 283-302.

1990. The semantics of syntactic change. Stylistic, natural, and varietal factors in the development of English "do": A case study. *Series Trends in Linguistics.* Berlin: Mouton de Gruyter.

2020. Atomizing linguistic change. Linguistic change: A radical view. In Drinka, Bridget (ed.), *Historical Linguistics* 2017. Amsterdam: John Benjamins. Pp. 321–43.

Stolz, Christel and Thomas Stolz 1996. Funktionswortentlehnung in Mesoamerika: Spanisch-amerindischer Sprachkontakt (Hispanoindiana II). *Sprachtypologie und Universalienforschung* 49, 1: 86–123.

Stolz, Thomas 2007. *Allora*: On the recurrence of function-word borrowing in contact situations with Italian as donor language. In Jochen Rehbein, Christiane Hohenstein, and Lukas Pietsch (eds.), *Connectivity in Grammar and Discourse.* Amsterdam: John Benjamins. Pp. 75–99.

Streeck, Jürgen 2002. Grammars, words, and embodied meanings: On the uses and evolution of *so* and *like. Journal of Communication* 52, 3: 581–96.

Suzuki, Ryoko 1998. From a lexical noun to an utterance-final pragmatic particle: *wake.* In Toshio Ohori (ed.), *Studies in Japanese Grammaticalization: Cognitive and Discourse Perspectives.* Tokyo: Kuroshio. Pp. 67–92.

2006. How does "reason" become less and less reasonable?: Pragmatics of the utterance-final *wake* in conversational discourse. In Satoko Suzuki (ed.), *Emotive Communication in Japanese.* Amsterdam: John Benjamins. Pp. 35–51.

Svartvik, Jan (ed.) 1990. *The London-Lund Corpus of Spoken English: Description and Research* (Lund Studies in English, 82). Lund: Lund University Press.

Swan, Toril 1982. A note on the scope(s) of *sadly*. *Studia Linguistica* 36, 2: 31–40.

Sweetser, Eve Eliot 1987. Metaphorical models of thought and speech: A comparison of historical directions and metaphorical mappings in the two domains. *Berkeley Linguistics Society* 13: 446–59.

____ 1988. Grammaticalization and semantic bleaching. In Shelley Axmaker, Annie Jaisser, and Helen Singmaster (eds.), *Berkeley Linguistics Society 14: General Session and Parasession on Grammaticalization*. Berkeley, CA: Berkeley Linguistics Society. Pp. 389–405.

Tabor, Whitney and Elizabeth C. Traugott 1998. Structural scope expansion and grammaticalization. In Anna Giacalone Ramat and Paul J. Hopper (eds.), *The Limits of Grammaticalization*. Amsterdam: John Benjamins. Pp. 229–72.

Taglicht, Josef 2001. *Actually*, there's more to it than meets the eye. *English Language and Linguistics* 5, 1: 1–16.

Takahashi, Hidemitsu 2012. *A Cognitive Linguistic Analysis of the English Imperative: With Special Reference to Japanese Imperatives* (Human Cognitive Processing, 35). Amsterdam: John Benjamins.

Taylor, John R. 1989. *Linguistic Categorization: Prototypes in Linguistic Theory*. Oxford: Clarendon.

Thompson, Sandra A. and Anthony Mulac 1991. A quantitative perspective on the grammaticization of epistemic parentheticals in English. In Elizabeth Closs Traugott and Bernd Heine (eds.), *Approaches to Grammaticalization*, volume 2 (Typological Studies in Language, 19, 2). Amsterdam: John Benjamins. Pp. 313–29.

Thompson, Sandra A. and Ryoko Suzuki 2011. Grammaticalization of final particles. In Heiko Narrog and Bernd Heine (eds.), *The Oxford Handbook of Grammaticalization*. Oxford: Oxford University Press. Pp. 665–77.

Torres, Lourdes 2002. Bilingual discourse markers in Puerto Rican Spanish. *Language in Society* 31: 61–83.

____ 2006. Bilingual discourse markers in indigenous languages. *International Journal of Bilingual Education and Bilingualism* 9: 615–24.

Torres, Lourdes and Kim Potowski 2008. A comparative study of bilingual discourse markers in Chicago Mexican, Puerto Rican, and MexiRican Spanish. *International Journal of Bilingualism* 12: 263–67.

Tottie, Gunnel 2011. *Uh* and *um* as sociolinguistic markers in British English. *International Journal of Corpus Linguistics* 16: 173–96.

____ 2014. On the use of *uh* and *um* in American English. *Functions of Language* 21: 6–29.

____ 2015. *Uh* and *um* in British and American English: Are they words? Evidence from co-occurrence with pauses. In Rena Torres Cacoullos, Nathalie Dion, and André Lapierre (eds.), *Linguistic Variation: Confronting Fact and Theory*. New York: Routledge. Pp. 38–55.

____ 2016. Planning what to say: *Uh* and *um* among the pragmatic markers. In Gunther Kaltenböck, Evelien Keizer, and Arne Lohmann (eds.), *Outside the Clause* (Studies in Language Companion Series, 178). Amsterdam: John Benjamins. Pp. 97–122.

Traugott, Elizabeth Closs 1982. From propositional to textual and expressive meanings: Some semantic-pragmatic aspects of grammaticalization. In Winfred Lehmann and Yakov Malkiel (eds.), *Directions for Historical Linguistics*. Amsterdam: John Benjamins. Pp. 245–71.

1988. Pragmatic strengthening and grammaticalization. In Shelley Axmaker, Annie Jaisser, and Helen Singmaster (eds.), *Berkeley Linguistics Society 14: General Session and Parasession on Grammaticalization*. Berkeley, CA: Berkeley Linguistics Society. Pp. 406–16.

1989. On the rise of epistemic meanings in English: an example of subjectification in semantic change. *Language* 65, 1: 31–55.

1995. The role of the development of discourse markers in a theory of grammaticalization. *Paper presented at the International Conference of Historical Linguistics XII*, Manchester.

2003. Constructions in grammaticalization. In Brian D. Joseph and Richard D. Janda (eds.), *The Handbook of Historical Linguistics*. Oxford: Blackwell. Pp. 624–47.

2007. Discussion article: Discourse markers, modal particles, and contrastive analysis, synchronic and diachronic. *Catalan Journal of Linguistics* 6: 139–57.

2008. The grammaticalization of NP of NP patterns. In Alexander Bergs and Gabriele Diewald (eds.), *Constructions and Language Change*. Berlin: Mouton de Gruyter. Pp. 23–46.

2014. Intersubjectification and clause periphery. In Lieselotte Brems, Lobke Ghesquère, and Freek Van de Velde (eds.), *Intersubjectivity and Intersubjectification in Grammar and Discourse: Theoretical and Descriptive Advances*. Amsterdam: John Benjamins. Pp. 7–27.

2015. Investigating "periphery" from a functionalist perspective. *Linguistics Vanguard* 1, 1: 119–30.

2016. On the rise of types of clause-final pragmatic markers in English. *Journal of Historical Pragmatics* 17: 26–54.

2018. Modeling language change with constructional networks. In Salvador Pons Bordería and Óscar Loureda Lamas (eds.), *Beyond Grammaticalization and Discourse Markers: New Issues in the Study of Language Change* (Studies in Pragmatics, 18). Leiden: Brill. Pp. 17–50.

in press a. Is *back to my point* a pragmatic marker? An inquiry into the historical development of some metatextual discourse management markers in English. *Journal of Catalan Linguistics*.

in press b. Combinations of metatextual markers: A historical perspective. *Journal of Pragmatics*.

Traugott, Elizabeth Closs and Richard B. Dasher 2002. *Regularity in Semantic Change* (Cambridge Studies in Linguistics, 96). Cambridge: Cambridge University Press.

Traugott, Elizabeth Closs and Graeme Trousdale 2013. *Constructionalization and Constructional Changes*. Oxford: Oxford University Press.

2014. Contentful constructionalization. *Journal of Historical Linguistics* 4, 2: 254–82.

Trousdale, Graeme 2008. Constructions in grammaticalization and lexicalization: Evidence from the history of a composite predicate in English. In Graeme Trousdale and Nikolas Gisborne (eds.), *Constructional Approaches to English Grammar*. Berlin: Mouton de Gruyter. Pp. 33–67.

Underhill, Robert 1988. Like is, like focus. *American Speech* 63: 234–46.

Unger, Christoph 1996. The scope of discourse connectives: Implications for discourse organization. *Journal of Linguistics* 32: 403–39.

Urmson, J. O. 1952. Parenthetical verbs. *Mind, New Series* 61, 244: 480–96.

van Bogaert, Julie 2011. *I think* and other complement-taking mental predicates: A case of and for constructional grammaticalization. *Linguistics* 49, 2: 295–332.

van Dijk, Teun A. 1980. *Macrostructures: An Interdisciplinary Study of Global Structures in Discourse, Interaction, and Cognition*. Hillsdale, NJ: Erlbaum.

van Gelderen, Elly 1993. *The Rise of Functional Categories*. Amsterdam: John Benjamins.

2004. *Grammaticalization as Economy* (Linguistik Aktuell/Linguistics Today, 71). Amsterdam: John Benjamins.

Van Lancker Sidtis, Diana 2009. Formulaic and novel language in a "dual process" model of language competence: Evidence from surveys, speech samples, and schemata. In Roberta Corrigan, Edith A. Moravcsik, Hamid Ouali, and Kathleen M. Wheatley (eds.), *Formulaic Language*. Volume 2: *Acquisition, Loss, Psychological Reality, and Functional Explanations* (Typological Studies in Language, 83). Amsterdam: John Benjamins. Pp. 445–70.

2012. Formulaic language and language disorders. *Annual Review of Applied Linguistics* 32: 62–80.

Van Valin, Robert D. and Randy J. LaPolla 1997. *Syntax: Structure, Meaning and Form*. Cambridge: Cambridge University Press.

Vincent, Diane 2005. The journey of non-standard discourse markers in Quebec French: Networks based on exemplification. *Journal of Historical Pragmatics* 6, 2: 188–210.

Vincent, Diane, Sebastião Votre, and Marty LaForest 1993. Grammaticalisation et post-grammaticalisation. *Langues et Linguistique* 19: 71–103.

Wackernagel, Jacob 1897. Vermischte Beiträge zur griechischen Sprachkunde. In *Programm zur Rektoratsfeier der Universität Basel*. Basel: Universität Basel. Pp. 3–62.

Waltereit, Richard 2001. Modal particles and their functional equivalents: A speech act–theoretic approach. *Journal of Pragmatics* 33: 1391–417.

2002. Imperatives, interruption in conversation and the rise of discourse markers: A study of Italian *guarda*. *Linguistics* 40, 5: 987–1010.

2006. The rise of discourse markers in Italian: A specific type of language change. In Kerstin Fischer (ed.), *Approaches to Discourse Markers* (Studies in Pragmatics, 1). Amsterdam: Elsevier. Pp. 61–76.

Watanabe, Honoré 2010. Fillers and their relevance in describing Sliammon Salish. In Nino Amiridze, Boyd H. Davis, and Margaret Maclagan (eds.), *Fillers, Pauses and Placeholders* (Typological Studies in Language, 93). Amsterdam: John Benjamins. Pp. 173–87.

Weinreich, Uriel [1966] 1989. On the semantic structure of language. In William Labov and Beatrice S. Weinreich (eds.), *Uriel Weinreich: On Semantics*. Philadelphia, University of Pennsylvania Press. Pp. 37–96.

Weydt, Harald 1969. *Abtönungspartikel*. Bad Homburg: Gehlen.

Wichmann, Anne 2011. Grammaticalization and prosody. In Heiko Narrog and Bernd Heine (eds.), *The Oxford Handbook of Grammaticalization*. New York: Oxford University Press. Pp. 331–41.

Wichmann, Anne, Anne-Marie Simon-Vandenbergen, and Karin Aijmer 2010. How prosody reflects semantic change: a synchronic case study of *of course*. In Hubert Cuyckens, Kristin Davidse, and Lieven Vandelanotte (eds.) *Subjectification*,

Intersubjectification and Grammaticalisation. Berlin: Mouton de Gruyter. Pp. 103–53.

Wiemer, Björn 2014. Quo vadis grammaticalization theory?, or: Why complex language change is like words. *Folia Linguistica* 48, 2: 425–67.

Wilkins, David P. 1992. Interjections as deictics. *Journal of Pragmatics* 18: 119–58.

Wilson, Deirdre 2011. The conceptual-procedural distinction: Past, present and future. In V. Escandell-Vidal, M. Leonetti, and A. Ahern (eds.), *Procedural Meaning: Problems and Perspectives.* Bingley: Emerald Group Publishing. Pp. 3–31.

Winford, Donald 2003. *An Introduction to Contact Linguistics. Code Switching: Linguistic Aspects.* Malden, MA: Blackwell. Pp. 126–67.

Wischer, Ilse 2000. Grammaticalization versus lexicalization: "Methinks" there is some confusion. In Olga Fischer, Anette Rosenbach, and Dieter Stein (eds.), *Pathways of Change. Grammaticalization in English.* Amsterdam: John Benjamins. Pp. 355–70.

Witosz, Bożena 2017. Metatext in the discourse of the theory of text, stylistics and pragmalinguistics. *Forum Lingwistyczne* 4: 107–12.

Wolfenden, E. P. 1971. *Hiligaynon Reference Grammar.* Honolulu: University of Hawai'i Press.

Woolford, Ellen. 1983. Bilingual code-switching and syntactic theory. *Linguistic Inquiry* 14: 520–36.

Yliniemi, Juha 2019. *A Descriptive Grammar of Denjongke (Sikkimese Bhutia).* PhD dissertation, University of Helsinki.

Zhang, M. 2016. A multidimensional analysis of metadiscourse markers across written registers. *Discourse Studies* 18, 2: 204–22.

Zwicky, Arnold M. 1985. Clitics and particles. *Language* 61, 2: 283–305.

Language Index

!Xun 247
Akie 243
Albanian 216, 223
Arabic 218, 230, 233

Bulgarian 3

Chukchi 217
Cimbrian 216, 223

Dutch 12, 216, 226, 264

English 3, 7–9, 12, 14–16, 19–20, 23, 25,
  28–29, 43–46, 51, 58, 61, 65–68, 70,
  74–85, 87, 91–143, 155–56, 163, 188,
  212, 214, 216–18, 220–29, 239–40,
  242–43, 247, 249, 253–56, 259, 261, 264
Estonian 38–39

French 12, 79–80, 82, 91–92, 124, 130,
  144–66, 212, 214–15, 217–20, 223, 226,
  228, 235, 243, 247, 255, 258–59, 264

German 3–4, 12, 130, 212, 216, 224–26, 228,
  247, 264
Guaraní 222

Hebrew 5, 216, 220, 222–25, 228–29
Hiligaynon 222
Hungarian 155

Italian 6–7, 31, 216–17, 222–23, 227, 230,
  241, 243, 258, 260

Japanese 5, 21, 28, 71, 81, 84, 87, 92, 156,
  167–95, 241–43, 247, 250, 252–53, 264–66
Jula 217–18, 226

Kalenjin 1
Korean 1, 7, 9–10, 24, 51–52, 68–69, 79,
  81–82, 84, 92, 156, 173, 196–210,
  240–41, 248–52, 264, 266

Ladin 216, 223, 227
Latin 34, 79, 130, 162, 212

Maltese 216, 223
Mandarin Chinese 264
Mayan 217, 221–24
Molise Slavic 216, 223
Moroccan Arabic 226–27

Norwegian 12, 214, 219

Persian 5, 230–34, 247
Portuguese 246, 248, 257

Rapanui 222
Romanian 260

Samo 217–19, 226, 228–29
Shaba Swahili 214–15, 220, 223,
  235
Spanish 3, 212, 216–18, 220–27,
  247
Sranan 227
Swahili 3, 230–33

Totonac 222
Turkish 34, 216, 230–33

Urdu 5

Yucatec 222
Yupik 217

Author Index

Aarts, B. 56
Abraham, W. 6, 12
Ädel, A. 8, 237–38
Ageneau, C. 263
Ahn, M. 84, 196–99, 202, 204–6
Aijmer, K. 6, 10, 12, 19, 21–22, 24, 26, 30, 46,
    51, 81, 89, 97, 132, 155, 247–48
Aikhenvald, A. Y. 256, 270
Ameka, F. 263
Amir, N. 51
Amiridze, N. 261
Amouzadeh, M. 21, 29, 230–32, 234, 247–48
Andersen, G. 6, 213–14, 217–18
Andersen, H. 88
Aoki, H. 168, 170, 172
Arnovick, L. 21, 30
Arroyo, J. L. B. 3–4, 21
Asher, N. 89
Auer, P. 16, 22, 53, 245

Backus, A. 215–16
Baker, O. R. 219
Barth-Weingarten, D. 10, 30–31, 44, 69
Bax, S. 1
Baynes, K. B. 237
Beeching, K. 5–6, 46, 49, 93, 101, 103–4,
    116–19, 132, 135, 153, 155
Beijering, K. 12, 21–22, 30, 50
Bell, D. M. 14–15
Berk-Seligson, S. 215, 217, 222
Biber, D. 45, 72, 85, 261–62
Blakemore, D. 6, 8, 10, 49–50, 72, 89, 93, 230,
    232, 251
Blass, R. 50
Blum-Kulka, S. 215–16
Bolly, C. 17, 29, 82, 144, 259
Börjars, K. 18, 39
Borreguero Zuloaga, M. 243, 248
Boye, K. 20, 39, 62
Breban, T. 79–80
Breu, W. 223

Brinton, L. J. 6, 8, 11, 15–25, 27, 31–32, 42,
    45–47, 50–51, 53, 57–58, 69, 71, 75, 80,
    82–84, 86, 89, 91, 100–11, 124, 133,
    136–39, 155–56, 215, 242, 244–46, 249,
    254, 256–57, 259
Brody, J. 215, 217, 221, 223–24
Bybee, J. L. 39–42, 61

Campbell, L. 38
Cap, P. 237
Carter, R. 6
Choi, J. B. 196
Cinque, G. 5
Claridge, C. 12, 21, 25, 30, 91, 106–8,
    129–31, 212, 242, 245, 249, 254
Clark, H. H. 12, 224, 237, 261–64
Claudi, U. 39–41, 61, 69, 83
Cornillie, B. 12
Coulmas, F. 4
Couper-Kuhlen, E. 10, 30–31, 44, 69
Craig, C. G. 83
Crible, L. 9–10, 89
Croft, W. 27, 75
Cuenca, M. J. 12, 132

D'Arcy, A. 35, 53, 116–21, 246
Dasher, R. B. 7, 16, 18, 31–32, 45, 80, 167,
    188–90, 194, 245, 247
Davidse, K. 82, 112, 121, 123–26, 245, 255
Davies, M. 56
Davis, B. H. 261
de Rooij, V. A. 144, 213–15, 220, 223, 235
De Wolf, S. 82, 112, 121, 123–26, 245, 255
Debaisieux, J. M. 237
Defour, T. 21, 30, 46, 81, 91, 132–36, 144,
    156–61
Degand, L. 12, 15–16, 18, 27, 29–30, 32,
    45–46, 65, 79–80, 144, 151–56, 245, 248
Dehé, N. 19, 66, 72–74, 106
Dér, C. I. 6, 10, 51, 62, 155
Detges, U. 5, 12, 23, 53, 62, 144, 155, 215, 241

Deulofeu, J. 237
Diessel, H. 92
Diewald, G. 6, 16, 18, 31, 45–46
Dik, S. C. 97
Dostie, G. 20–21, 45, 69, 82, 88, 144, 149, 248, 257, 259

Emanatian, M. 69
Emonds, J. 103
Erman, B. 6, 21, 30, 50, 141
Espinal, M. T. 48, 50, 66, 106, 108, 249
Evans, N. 79, 249
Evers-Vermeul, J. 15–16, 18, 27, 30, 32, 46, 65, 79–80, 144, 151–56

Fagard, B. 50, 79–80, 144–48, 151–53, 155, 245, 248, 256–60
Faust, M. E. 237
Fedriani, C. 11–12, 221, 240, 251
Ferrara, K. W. 51, 97
Fforde, J. 75
Fiorentini, I. 215–16, 223, 227
Fischer, O. 11, 19, 24–25, 47
Flores-Ferrán, N. 215, 218
Foolen, A. 10
Fox Tree, J. E. 12, 224, 237, 261–64
Frank-Job, B. 16, 20–23, 30, 49–50
Fraser, B. 6, 9–11, 45–46, 48–50, 89, 97, 100, 244
Fried, M. 92, 123
Furkó, B. P. 3, 6, 8, 10, 36, 47, 50, 67, 132, 247, 253
Fuschi, L. 12, 257

Gaines, P. 6
Garachana, M. 212
Genette, G. 8, 236
Gernsbacher, M. A. 237
Gévaudan, P. 144, 215
Ghezzi, C. 11, 221, 246, 248–49
Giacalone Ramat, A. 18, 31
Givón, T. 39–41, 79–80, 268
Gohl, C. 53
Goldberg, A. E. 27, 75
Gonen, E. 51
González, M. 6
Goria, E. 11, 216, 219, 221, 257
Görlach, M. 217
Goss, E. L. 215, 218, 221
Gould, S. J. 67
Grant, A. P. 215, 217
Grice, H. P. 49
Günthner, S. 16, 21–22, 30, 53, 245, 269

Haegeman, L. 50
Haiman, J. 62
Hakulinen, A. 248
Hancil, S. 51
Hansen, M. B. 10–12, 15, 18, 21–22, 31, 36, 45, 48–53, 79–80, 82, 88–89, 105, 144, 149, 151–52, 154–56, 162–65, 215, 238, 240, 247, 250, 255, 258, 262, 264
Harder, P. 20, 39, 62
Haselow, A. 5, 8–10, 12, 18, 23, 52, 72, 81, 97–100, 141, 154, 237–38, 241, 248
Haspelmath, M. 17, 24, 39, 52, 62, 64, 77
Hayashi, M. 20, 23, 262, 264–66
Heine, B. 6–7, 11, 18, 26, 30, 36–37, 39–43, 45, 49, 51, 53, 56–57, 59, 61–62, 64–70, 72–75, 81–83, 88, 105–6, 108, 110–11, 113, 116, 138, 141, 154, 176, 211–13, 215, 220–21, 237–39, 243, 246–49, 253, 257, 268, 270–72
Hengeveld, K. 33–34
Hilpert, M. 27–28
Himmelmann, N. P. 43
Hirschberg, J. 51
Hirst, D. 51
Hlavac, J. 215
Hooper, J. B. 20, 73
Hopper, P. J. 16–17, 23, 61–64, 77, 83, 148, 164, 180, 207, 268, 271
Huddleston, R. 45, 85, 106, 249
Hünnemeyer, F. 39–41, 61, 69, 83
Hyland, K. 8, 237

Ichihashi-Nakayama, K. 16
Ifantidou-Trouki, E. 251

Johnstone, B. 237
Jucker, A. H. 6–7, 10, 23, 48–51, 58, 81, 83, 87, 89, 132–36, 155, 240, 245

Kac, M. B. 49
Kaltenböck, G. 6–7, 11, 26, 36, 45, 50, 57, 66–67, 72–75, 79, 85, 105–6, 108, 113, 138, 220–21, 237–39, 245, 249, 253, 269, 272
Kanaan, L. 231
Kavalova, Y. 66, 72–75, 106
Kerouac, J. 116
Kibiki, M. J. 3
Kim, J. 196, 201, 241
Kim, M. H. 69, 196, 200–2, 245, 248
Kim, T. Y. 196
Kitahara, Y. 174, 182
Klamer, M. 41
Kleinknecht, F. 246
König, C. 243, 246–48, 257

Koo, H. J. 11, 196–97, 246
Kotsinas, U. B. 6, 21, 30, 50, 141
Kowal, S. 12, 261–63
Kranich, S. 21, 79–80
Kuteva, T. 6–7, 11, 26, 35, 40–42, 45, 49–51,
    57, 61–62, 64, 66–67, 72–75, 82, 105–6,
    108, 110, 113, 121, 138, 153, 176, 207,
    212, 220–21, 237–39, 249, 251, 268, 270,
    272

LaForest, M. 29
Lamiroy, B. 6, 256, 258
Langacker, R. W. 271
Lange, D. 116–18, 121, 246
LaPolla, R. J. 34
Lass, R. 67
Lee, H. 196
Lee, J. 69, 196, 200–2, 245, 248
Legère, K. 243, 246, 248, 257
Lehmann, C. 17, 22–24, 30–32, 34–35, 39, 44,
    51–53, 61–62, 77, 82–83, 173, 184, 271
Lenk, U. 48–49, 136
Lenker, U. 18, 31, 45
Levinson, S. C. 10, 247
Lewis, D. M. 6, 10, 51, 53, 93–96, 112–15,
    153
Li, C. N. 41
Lipsky, J. M. 213, 215
Litman, D. 51
Livescu, M. 246
Livnat, Z. 51
Long, D. L. 237
López-Couso, M. J. 16
Loureda Lamas, O. 45, 240
Lyons, J. 7

Mackenzie, J. L. 33–34
Maclagan, M. 261
Maclay, H. 261
Mann, W. C. 93
Markó, A. 155
Maschler, Y. 49, 155, 213, 215–16, 220,
    222–25, 227, 229, 237, 246
Matasović, R. 33
Matras, Y. 213, 215–16, 219–22, 228, 234
Matsumoto, Y. 167, 177–79, 195, 245, 250
Matthews, P. H. 46
Matzen, L. 51
Mauranen, A. 8, 237
Mauri, A. 18, 31
Mauri, C. 18, 31
McCarthy, M. 6
Meehan, T. 116, 118
Meillet, A. 271
Méndez-Naya, B. 16, 126–29, 141, 247

Méndez-Naya, M. J. 16
Miyashita, H. 16
Mkhatshwa, S. N. L. 69
Molinelli, P. 11, 246, 249
Morita, Y. 188
Moyer, M. G. 215, 227
Mulac, A. 16, 19, 53, 103
Müller, M. 1
Mutz, K. 16, 21, 30
Muysken, P. 219, 226, 228, 235

Nakayama, T. 16
Narrog, H. 33–34, 36, 174, 189, 192
Nelson, G. 56
Nicolle, S. 33
Noora, A. 21, 29, 230–32, 234
Norde, M. 12, 21–22, 30, 35, 38–39, 48, 50,
    53, 63, 88, 180, 208
Norrick, N. R. 262–63
Nzoimbengene, P. 248, 257

O'Connell, D. C. 12, 261–63
Ocampo, F. 21, 29–30, 48
Olshtain, E. 215–16
Onodera, N. O. 21, 30–31, 51, 71, 92, 155,
    167–73, 180, 185–88, 194–95, 199, 243,
    245, 252
Osgood, C. E. 261
Östman, J. O. 92, 123

Pagliuca, W. 39–42, 61
Palander-Collin, M. 16, 19
Park, J. 245
Pawley, A. 237
Perkins, R. D. 39–42, 61
Piccoli, G. 223
Pietrandrea, P. 12
Pinto de Lima, J. 31
Pons Bordería, S. 6, 45, 91, 212, 240
Poplack, S. 69, 213, 215–16, 219, 224, 226,
    235
Potowski, K. 215–16
Prat, C. S. 237
Prévost, S. 18, 23, 31, 45–46, 79, 144–51
Pullum, G. K. 46, 85, 106, 249

Quirk, R. 6, 16, 37, 45, 85, 106, 108, 124

Ramat, P. 88
Redeker, G. 6
Reh, M. 39–41, 61, 83
Reinhart, T. 72
Rhee, S. 1, 7, 10–11, 16, 24, 26, 51–52, 67–68,
    79, 92, 173, 196–99, 202–4, 206–10, 240,
    245, 248–52

Rissanen, M. 19
Roberts, I. G. 33, 35, 271
Romaine, S. 116–18, 121, 246
Ross, J. R. 20
Rossari, C. 149
Rouchota, V. 50
Roussou, A. 33, 271
Ruhi, S. 215, 230–33
Rysová, M. 155

Saavedra, D. C. 27
Salmons, J. 213, 215, 218–19, 221, 224, 226, 228
Sankoff, D. 69, 213
Sansò, A. 11–12, 221, 240, 251
Saxena, A. 41
Schiffrin, D. 9–10, 24, 50–51, 100, 117, 132, 155, 221, 223
Schneider, S. 72, 144, 244
Schourup, L. 2, 6, 8, 10, 23, 48–50, 89, 132, 135–36, 155, 251
Schreiber, H. 213, 215, 217–19, 226, 228–29
Schwenter, S. A. 10, 113
Shibasaki, R. 28, 84, 167, 169, 174–76, 180–85, 195, 241
Shinzato, R. 167, 180
Simon-Vandenbergen, A. M. 6, 10, 12, 18, 29, 32, 45–46, 51, 65, 81, 91, 122, 124, 126, 132–36, 156, 160, 212, 242
Sohn, S. O. 196, 201, 241
Souza, M. 246
Specker, E. 215, 225
Stein, D. 8, 28
Stolz, C. 220, 226
Stolz, T. 215–17, 220, 222, 226, 243, 248
Streeck, J. 116–18, 246
Suzuki, R. 81, 100, 156, 167, 191–94, 246
Svartvik, J. 56
Swan, T. 36–37
Sweetser, E. E. 40, 69
Swiggers, P. 6, 256, 258

Taavitsainen, I. 240
Tabor, W. 33, 37, 50–51, 53, 113, 184
Taglicht, J. 8
Takahashi, H. 256
Taylor, J. R. 30
Thompson, S. A. 16, 19, 41, 53, 93, 100, 103
Torres, L. 215–16
Tottie, G. 12, 261–64
Traugott, E. 4, 6, 8–9, 11, 15–16, 18, 22–25, 27–29, 31–33, 35, 37–45, 47, 49–51, 53,
58–62, 64–65, 80, 83, 92–96, 101, 113, 124, 141, 155, 167, 177–78, 180, 183–84, 188–90, 194, 215, 243, 245, 247, 255–56, 260, 268, 271
Trousdale, G. 18, 27–29, 32, 35, 39–45, 47, 51, 53, 65, 141, 183

Underhill, R. 116
Unger, C. 8, 32, 251
Urmson, J. O. 73

Van Bogaert, J. 16, 18–19, 21, 26, 28, 31, 45, 48, 53, 78, 82, 110–11, 253
Van Dijk, T. A. 237
van Gelderen, E. 33, 271
Van Lancker Sidtis, D. 237
Van Linden, A. 82, 112, 121, 123–26, 245, 255
Van Valin, R. D. 34
Varner, K. R. 237
Vincent, D. 18, 29, 39, 144, 149
Votre, S. 29
Vrba, E. S. 67

Wackernagel, J. 244
Walkden, G. 18, 39
Wallis, S. 56
Waltereit, R. 7, 12, 16, 21, 23, 29–31, 44–45, 48–49, 51, 53, 62, 69, 87, 241, 249–50, 256, 258–60, 269
Watanabe, H. 262
Weinreich, U. 7
Weydt, H. 12
Wichmann, A. 51–52, 72
Wiemer, B. 73
Wilkins, D. P. 7
Willems, D. 29, 91, 156, 160, 242
Wilson, D. 10, 81, 89
Winford, D. 69, 213
Wischer, I. 24–25, 31, 50
Witosz, B. 8, 236
Wolfenden, E. P. 222
Woolford, E. 69, 213

Yap, F. H. 84, 196, 204–6
Yliniemi, J. 248, 262
Yoon, K. E. 20, 23, 262, 264–66

Zhang, M. 8, 237–38
Ziv, Y. 6, 50–51, 155
Zwicky, A. M. 8, 51

Subject Index

adverb
  clause-internal deictic manner 189
  commentary inductive 183
  contrastive epistemic 156, 159
  deictic temporal 200, 247
  largely fossilized sentence-initial 175
  temporal 200, 202, 217, 222, 229, 241, 243,
    247, 255
adverbial
  invariable monomorphemic 147
  syntactically dependent 146
  syntactically integrated 147, 152
  temporal 31, 81, 94, 96
affix 208
agreement 5, 61, 92, 108, 127–28, 135, 199,
    207, 227, 240, 271, 289, 292
ambiguity 59, 102, 131, 141–42, 145
analogy 182
anchoring 37, 74–75
announcement 188
appraisal, positive 132
approximation 117, 119
argument
  patient 191
  verbal 146
assertion 157, 198, 203, 281
attention-getter 128, 201
attrition 52, 63, 105
autonomy 64, 77, 88, 120, 269, 271

backflagging 219, 226–28, 235
bleaching, semantic 131
Bolly and Degand (2013), proceduralization 29
borrowing 87, 124, 211–13, 215, 217–24, 226,
    228, 230, 233, 235, 274, 281, 288, 293–94
boundaries,prosodic 130
boundary, loss of morpheme 116
bracket 9, 117, 169, 222
break,prosodic 114, 176

c-command,scope 33, 50
catcher, attention 127

categories, formulaic 88, 268
censure 205
chain model 141
clarification 105, 117, 119–20, 232
clause
  apodosis 107
  comment 20, 66, 101, 108, 136, 138–39,
    278
  elliptical interrogative 136
  imperative 107
  matrix 16, 19–20, 103, 276
  nominal predicate 180
  protasis 106–7, 110
clitic 177–80, 250
coalescence 25, 31, 63–64, 283
code-mixing 213
code-switching 69–70, 213, 216, 218, 220,
    222, 226, 228, 235, 275, 281, 291, 293,
    298
coherence 112–13, 148, 153, 223
cohesion 63, 187, 223, 247
collocations 159–60
colloquialization 182
comparison,typological 60
complement
  infinitival 102
  verbal 107, 149–50, 291
complementizer x, 19, 65, 102, 122, 270
component 5, 28, 56, 59, 62, 65, 134, 222,
    225, 230
compositionality 82, 140
compression 113
concession 93, 135
condensation 30, 129
conditional 2, 43, 79, 97, 106, 110, 153,
    162–64, 189, 193, 245, 249, 274
conjunct 85, 153–56, 250
connective x, 2, 20, 31, 43, 71, 85, 114,
    152–53, 158, 169–70, 172–73, 176, 178,
    182–84, 189, 201, 207, 241, 251–53,
    288
connector 173–74, 282, 294

copula 71, 168, 170, 174–75, 191–93, 205, 243, 252
confirmation,emphatic 196
confrontation 202
construction
  clause-like 203
  nominal possessive 113
  nominal predicate 181, 192, 241
  possessive 159
  sequenced-sentence 175, 184
constructionalization 28–29, 183, 296
context, concessive discourse 125
contrast
  adversative 170
  temporal 201
convention, new orthographic 100
conversion 58, 69–70, 267
cooptation 13–14, 26–27, 44, 56–57, 59, 65, 67–73, 76–78, 80–81, 84–90, 94, 96, 98–100, 103–5, 107, 109–16, 120–21, 124–25, 128–31, 133–35, 139–41, 143–44, 147, 151, 153–54, 156–61, 164–65, 169, 172–73, 175–76, 179–80, 183–84, 187–88, 190, 192, 194–95, 201, 203–4, 206–9, 211, 214–15, 234, 236, 239–44, 248, 250–51, 253, 256, 258, 265, 267–68, 271–72, 284

debonding 38, 180, 208
decategorialization 17, 38, 51, 53, 63–65, 78–79, 82, 84, 96, 100, 105, 110–11, 127, 131, 139, 147, 158, 161, 165, 169, 173, 176, 178, 202, 204, 206, 259
deixis 7, 47
deictic 10, 117, 188, 189, 200, 247, 248, 265
deletion 19
degrammaticalization 38–39, 88, 180, 208, 283, 291
demonstrative,distal-visible 203
dependency 11, 18, 32, 39, 65
desemantization 110
detachment 37, 50
device
  discourse-structuring 12, 153, 208, 261
  emphatic attention getting 133
  text-structuring 20
digression 148
disagreement 2, 132, 135, 227, 229, 264, 289
disalignment 199
disbelief 205
disconfirmation 196
discontent 7, 199, 205
discontinuity 135
discourse connectives 10

discourse function 54, 67, 73, 89, 106, 110, 129–30, 173, 184, 204, 241–42, 257, 263
discourse grammar 13, 45, 66, 72–73, 154, 183, 220, 236–37, 284
discourse management 235, 243, 268, 272, 296
discourse monitoring 71, 106, 125, 179, 208, 239, 269
discourse processing 8, 26, 38, 58, 67, 69, 71–73, 76, 80, 143, 156, 173, 236–38, 241, 260, 267, 272, 284
discoursivization 21, 29
disjunct, clause-final parenthetical 117
disjunction 18, 32, 37–39, 42, 44
distinctiveness
  morphological 110, 139, 173, 176
  prosodic 52, 58, 77, 83, 89, 96, 179
divergence 23, 131
diversification, functional 135, 234

elaboration 32, 101, 117, 119–20, 135, 157–59, 161, 198–99, 232
elaboration request 198
emotion 84, 205–6
emphasis 7, 47, 152, 198–99, 292
erosion 38, 65, 79, 81–84, 105, 121, 150, 165, 178, 194, 204, 259
  optional 165
evaluation 49, 193, 203, 259, 270
exclamative 68, 88, 216, 218, 268, 272
exemplification 101, 105, 117, 120, 212, 297
exemplifying 116
experiences, recurrent 137
expletives 22, 88, 218, 268, 272
expression
  epistemic 122
  predicative 205
extension, context 41–43, 61–62, 64–65, 81, 89–90, 96, 104, 115, 121, 125–26, 143, 148, 153, 165, 170, 173, 188, 190, 193, 195, 204, 234, 266
extent, temporal 200

factor, socio-cultural 240
filler 224, 260, 263, 274, 283, 297
  pause 261
fixation 17, 22, 31, 50, 53, 78, 110, 129
flexibility, positional 80–81, 125, 147, 153
floor-holding 198
foregrounding 151
formation
  analogical 150
  nonce 59
forms, tag 101
friendliness 206, 209
fumble 1, 100

function
  basic hedging 106, 129
  concessive 96
  context induced 96
  contrastive 168, 171, 243
  counter-expectation marking 206
  dual 181
  emphasizing 205
  expressive 169, 171
  ideational 168
  intensifying 126
  metatextual 29, 48–49, 68, 71, 77, 85, 101,
      104, 107–9, 114, 133, 137, 141, 147, 158,
      171, 178–79, 187, 223, 236, 265
  mitigating 202
  negative emotion marking 84, 206
  procedural 100, 105, 140
  reformulative 162
  replacive 113
  rhetorically concessive 125
  text organizing 189, 222
functionality, discourse-oriented 125
functionalization 17

gradualness 140–42, 275
grammar
  construction 75, 183, 277, 280–81
  discourse see discourse, grammar
  thetical 45, 72, 80, 89, 236, 239, 286
grammaticalization 13, 15–35, 37–54, 56–57,
      59, 61–66, 69–72, 76–79, 81–85, 87–91,
      96, 100, 102–5, 108–10, 112, 115,
      120–21, 124–25, 127, 129, 131, 134–36,
      138–43, 147, 151–52, 154, 157, 161,
      165–66, 169, 172–73, 176–80, 183,
      185–86, 188, 190, 192, 194–95, 204,
      206–11, 218, 234, 247–48, 251, 256,
      258–60, 265–68, 270–72, 274–76,
      279–81, 283–84, 286–92, 294–98
group, intonation 83, 96

hedge
  general 109–10
  mild 188
hedger, pragmatic 206
hedging 106, 116–17, 129–30, 145, 164, 190,
      242
hesitation filler 12, 223–24, 261
hesitator, interjective 12, 223, 261
highlighting 8, 73–74, 117, 130, 222,
      258, 262
honorifics 127

identity, morphosyntactic 110
incredulity 205

independence, functional 269
indeterminacy 102
indexical 247
inferencing, invited 104
inferring, the act of 193
illocution 68
illustration 86, 117, 120, 149, 252
imperative xi, 7, 14, 87, 107, 160, 224,
      227, 229, 236, 241, 247–48,
      256–60
information, retrieval of 137
initialness 194, 199
initiation, topic 198–99
integration
  external 78
  internal 78
  prosodic 52, 86, 97
integrity 193
intensifier, productive 127
intent
  clarification of discourse 119
  communicative 59, 142
interaction, speaker–hearer 219
interjection, non-grammatical 186
interruption, polite 132
intersubjectification/intersubjectivity 8, 194,
      227, 286
intonation, exclamative 165
inquiry, indirect 136
irritation 206, 209

judgment, evaluative 81, 193, 203

layering 17, 23, 207
level
  metatextual 45, 67, 71, 76–77, 105, 215,
      239–40, 242, 267
  speech act 163
Lewis (2011)
  antithesis, the coherence relation of
      112
  idea, backgrounded 113
  idea, informationally salient 113
  relation, contrastive 112
  split, functional 113
linguistics, historical 140, 272
loan translation 124, 130, 212

marker
  conversation-structuring 153
  future tense 23, 34, 61
  hesitation x, 100, 232, 282
  interjectional 164
  invariable 139, 176, 202, 206
  politeness 206

pragmatic 6–7, 11, 16–17, 24, 26, 41, 47, 49, 53, 221, 244, 249, 265, 276, 280, 282, 287, 290, 294–96
predicative 170, 252
referential 223
synthetizing and listing 163, 255
topic xi, 175, 180
topic orientation 97
marks, punctuation 44, 58–59, 66, 95, 126, 128, 130, 146–47, 158, 161, 165, 169, 172, 184, 187
meaning
additive 157
adversative 172, 177
connective 6, 10, 170, 172, 177, 252, 275, 281, 288, 290, 292, 296
contentful 189
contrastive 95
epistemic 42, 123
justificational 96
metacommunicative 108
non-lexical sentence-external 198
propositional 109–10, 136, 138
metadiscourse 8, 237, 285, 298
mirativity 206, 209
mitigator, face-threat 132, 135
mobility, positional 130
modality, epistemic 61
modification 11, 37, 135, 231

network, prototype 162
Noora and Amouzadeh (2015), proceduralization 29

objection 125, 132
obgligatorification 23, 30
Onodera (2007), involvement marker 92, 185
ossification 131
other-correction 132

paradox, decategorialization 76
particle
clause-final adversative 71, 170, 252
connective 170, 178, 252–53
enclitic 177, 250
functionally reduced 193
invariable 96
modal 11, 273, 283
pause-filling 199
persistence 131, 148, 164, 292
placement, constrained 48, 68, 253
pluralizer 207
point, temporal 200
point-making 169, 173
politeness, negative 110

possession, nominal 145
pragmaticalization 13, 18, 20–27, 29–31, 46–47, 67, 80, 88, 141, 155, 186, 188, 194, 265, 267, 272, 274, 278, 282–83
precision 105, 157, 159
predicate, nominal 174–76, 180–82, 192, 241
preposition
complex replacive 112
composite 116
process, pragmaticalization 186
projector 174–76, 181, 183, 293
propagation 70
prosody 54, 59, 68, 73, 77, 95, 99, 104, 108, 114, 120, 125, 128, 130, 135, 139, 147, 151, 153, 158, 161, 165, 169, 172, 176, 178–79, 184, 187, 197–98, 202, 204, 206, 208, 257, 263, 278, 282, 286
protest 199, 208–9
proximal 200, 203, 264

question, rhetorical 248
question tags 72, 74, 88, 213, 218, 226, 248, 268

re-perspectivization 151
reanalysis 21, 29–30, 35, 69, 121, 207, 241, 282
reasoning, the speaker's 192
reassertion, emphatic 198–99
rebracketing 179
reconstruction 5, 16, 56, 58–60, 71–72, 76, 104, 112, 120, 123, 137, 140–42, 145, 152, 156, 167, 172, 190, 211, 234, 255, 264, 269–71
historical 141
reduction, morphological 150
reformulation 225, 231
refutation 171–73
reinforcement 188
relation
additive 189
conceptual–conditional 97
sequential 99
theme–rheme 175, 177
relationship
paradigmatic 100
sequential 223
relevance theory 8, 10, 23, 89, 251
reluctance 199
renewal 23
reorientation 151
repair 11, 101, 103, 225, 232, 254, 262
replication
contact-induced 124, 212
reply
affirmative 138
emphatic 137

response
  affirmative 188
  dispreferred 132
restriction, positional 100
rheme 175, 177

sarcasm 205, 209
schema
  conditional 189
  discourse 114
scope, semantic-pragmatic 44
self-affirmation 198
self-correction 132
self-repair 254
sentence, interrogative 159–60
shift
  abrupt discourse 148, 150
  smooth discourse 148
shifter, topic 154
signal, attention 133
signaling, the function of 119
similarity 119, 121
silence, interactional 132
solidarity 117, 132
specialization 23, 131
status
  emblematic 225
  syntactically unattached 29, 38, 48, 68, 86,
    184, 220, 265
stigmatization, social 132
structures, indeterminate 102
substance, loss of phonetic 121, 204
substance, prosodic 121
subjectivity 8, 227, 286, 290

suitability 240–41
surprise 7, 156, 198–99
  feigned 198

thetical
  conceptual 106
  constituent anchored 75, 111, 253
  constructional 74, 139
  epistemic stance marking 121
  formulaic 66, 122, 139
  invariable 161, 176
  utterance anchored 75, 111, 163
topic, unresolved 97
transfer, metaphorical 69
Traugott (2018),implicating causal reasoning
  96
turn-taking 223, 228, 241, 256

uncertainty 199
unidirectionality 88, 180, 271, 285
unit
  accentual 178
  invariable particle-like 96
univerbation 17, 24, 26, 79, 82, 96, 105, 110,
  139, 147, 159, 161, 169, 173, 204,
  206

variability, positional 54, 67, 90, 122
variation 48, 84–85, 162, 198–99, 279
viewpoint, imaginary third-person's evaluative
  203
vocative 228, 272

word, monomorphemic 169

CPSIA information can be obtained
at www.ICGtesting.com
Printed in the USA
LVHW010932170821
695490LV00003B/460